Up from the Vault

ALSO BY JOHN T. SOISTER AND FROM MCFARLAND

*Conrad Veidt on Screen: A Comprehensive
Illustrated Filmography* (2002; paperback 2009)

*Of Gods and Monsters: A Critical Guide to Universal Studios' Science
Fiction, Horror and Mystery Films, 1929–1939* (1999; paperback 2005)

BY JOHN T. SOISTER WITH JOANNA WIOSKOWSKI

*Claude Rains: A Comprehensive Illustrated Reference to His Work
in Film, Stage, Radio, Television and Recordings* (1999; paperback 2006)

Up from the Vault

Rare Thrillers of the 1920s and 1930s

JOHN T. SOISTER

McFarland & Company, Inc., Publishers
Jefferson, North Carolina, and London

The present work is a reprint of the illustrated case bound edition of Up from the Vault: Rare Thrillers of the 1920s and 1930s, *first published in 2004 by McFarland.*

LIBRARY OF CONGRESS CATALOGUING-IN-PUBLICATION DATA

Soister, John T., 1950–
Up from the vault : rare thrillers of the 1920s and 1930s / John T. Soister.
p.   cm.
Includes index.

ISBN 978-0-7864-4923-1
softcover : 50# alkaline paper ∞

1. Suspense in motion pictures.   2. Motion pictures — Catalogs.   I. Title.
PN1995.9.S87S65   2010   791.43'655 — dc22   2004001531

British Library cataloguing data are available

©2004 John T. Soister. All rights reserved

No part of this book may be reproduced or transmitted in any form or by any means, electronic or mechanical, including photocopying or recording, or by any information storage and retrieval system, without permission in writing from the publisher.

Cover art from the 1934 film *Double Door*

Manufactured in the United States of America

*McFarland & Company, Inc., Publishers
Box 611, Jefferson, North Carolina 28640
www.mcfarlandpub.com*

For Earl and Slick,

who have put up with me all these years …

Os quiero.

Table of Contents

Acknowledgments   xi
Introduction   1

The Mystery of Dr. Fu Manchu (1923)   9
The Unknown Purple (1923)   30
The Sorrows of Satan (1926)   38
While London Sleeps (1926)   50
The Monkey Talks (1927)   57
The Chinese Parrot (1927)   66
Stark Mad (1929)   73
The Unholy Night (1929)   80
High Treason (1929)   94
The Spider (1931)   105
Eran trece (1931)   113
The Monkey's Paw (1933)   127
Trick for Trick (1933)   135
Deluge (1933)   143
The Vanishing Shadow (1934)   151
The Witching Hour (1934)   165
Double Door (1934)   172
Black Moon (1934)   178
Le Golem (1936)   186
The Scarab Murder Case (1937)   199
Sh! The Octopus (1937)   207

Appendix: *The Mystery of Dr. Fu Manchu. Episode 10: The Fiery Hand*   219
Index   227

Acknowledgments

You really get a feel for the inadequacy of your own efforts when you set out to write a book. You've got so many piles of primary and secondary sources all over the place, you don't know where to look first. (Not helping one bit is your wife, who's constantly dusting these piles or moving them to other, less troublesome locations, all the while glaring daggers at you and muttering, "This house is becoming a real pigsty." Let me immediately point out that this didn't actually happen to me — Uh-uh — but this type of spousal assistance has been *known* to occur.) Somehow, though, despite the plethora of arcane data you've managed to accumulate, you find holes in your narrative almost everywhere you look. This is where your friends come in.

The following of my friends (some of whom I've yet to meet face to face) came in at precisely that moment. Nor did they come empty handed (although no one brought cake). No, siree, they provided me — us, really — with illustrations, information, criticism, and opinion, and, more than once, with videos of the pictures under discussion.

I have to start off by thanking Bob Dickson, and not only for his willingness to invade the Academy at a moment's notice and for that exquisitely rare newspaper ad on *The Unknown Purple*. More importantly, I want to cite his being an infallible source of insight and common sense. Most importantly, I want to express my deep appreciation for his friendship. Espero que yo pueda ayudarte así cuandoquiera me necesites, Roberto.

Quite a few of the rare stills to be found throughout this book were provided by the Mandelbaum brothers, owners and CEOs of New York's wonderful Photofest. They (and their dedicated staff) have never failed to come up with photographs from the *damnedest* titles I've tossed their way, and that's quite an accomplishment. Thank you, gentlemen.

I knew him as Eddie Hulse back in the '60s, when we met via fanzines like *Photon*. When we crossed paths again, a couple of years ago, he was Ed Hulse, respected professional writer, and the old boy is now the Big Kahuna behind *Blood 'n' Thunder*, an absolutely marvelous magazine dedicated to adventure, mystery, and melodrama in general, and to pulp fiction and movie serials in particular. Ed generously presented me with a video of *The Spider* some time back, and that led directly to my gassing about it herein. You the man, Ed.

Henry Nicolella has been helping me with my projects for several years now, and *Up from the Vault* sees that proud tradition continue. Henry has never minded my begging, sniveling, or groveling; in fact, his frequent care packages to me (reviews, videos, translations, opinions) have probably brought him close to insolvency more than once. He wrote a grand afterword for *Conrad Veidt on Screen*, and he has promised to bail me out yet again with an upcoming study of Paul Wegener's fantasy films. (Let's see you back out *now*, Nicolella!)

Dennis Payne (Cinema Classics, 171A Rink Street, Suite 222, Peterborough, Ontario, Canada K9J 1R3) was my video source for many of the obscure titles I've commented on, and I can't recommend him highly enough. Den's product is first-rate, and he's as honest as the day is long (on or about June 22) when it comes to describing the quality of his prints. He's friendly and helpful, too, and his prices are reasonable, and he's never been averse to my picking his brain in any of my "emergency" e-mails. What else could you ask for from a video company (or a friend)?

I'm sure that everyone looking at this page will recognize Arthur Lennig's name, as every genre fan my age I know either has Professor Lennig's original book on Bela Lugosi or is kicking himself for not having it. The revised, expanded edition is assuredly out by now, however, so maybe the kicking has ceased. Art freely gave me a copy of his chapter on *The Sorrows of Satan* (taken from his comprehensive biography of D. W. Griffith, in progress as I write these words), along with his permission to quote what I needed. A true film historian, an authoritative (and *readable!*) author, and a generous friend, Arthur Lennig is a gem, and his books ought to be nestled comfortably on everybody's shelves.

Serial superbuff Jim Stringham is a wellspring of factual knowledge and informed opinion on Universal's *The Vanishing Shadow*, so let me pat his back for sharing both (and a thick file of stills) with us. I also want to thank Marty Kelly — another serial maven and a hell of a nice guy — for laser copies of his rare VS lobby cards and the nod to use same in this book.

Steve Joyce has been collecting film-related literature for years, and he's been most kind in pointing me to source novels and plays and the like. Steve is the proud owner of one original copy (out of 25 or so, methinks) of Noel Pemberton-Billing's drama, *High Treason*, and he hesitated not in getting a Xerox copy to me. My hope for Steve is that his library of rare source literature grows like wheat in Kansas and that he continues to take pity on grasping, penurious researchers like me.

Tessa Forbes of the British Film Institute has been a godsend to me since I was scribbling madly about Universal horror films some years back, and I hope she never hits the lottery and quits her job. Wait ... that's not right. I hope she *does* hit the lottery and is thus able to augment her already richly creative side, while opting to continue her work at the BFI. Unlike the men I've sung of above, I've actually met Tessa — several times, in fact — while I was burrowing through the BFI's stacks and files, and I've always come away marveling at her dedication, knowledge, and warmth. Any chance of your crossing the pond and working for the Billy Rose Collections at Lincoln Center, Tessa?

I'd also like Elisabet Helge of the Svenska Filminstitutet to move hither, because I'm equally in her debt. Elisabet has gone w-a-y beyond the call of duty, both to track down stills and then to identify some of the really obscure folks who insisted on standing next to the stars. In addition to her professional savvy, she has often responded to my e-mail caterwauling with the patience and sagacity of a world-class bartender. If and when we finally get together, Elisabet, the Aquavit's on me.

The *Deluge* chapter is in every way more comprehensive due to contributions by Gus Fowler-Wright, grandson of Sidney Fowler-Wright, author of the picture's source novel, and I'm grateful to him. I'm also grateful to John A. B. Wright, a veritable font of information on movie scores and the musicians who wrought them, for taking the time to write about Louis Levy and the songs he helped pen for the sound version of *High Treason*.

Ancestors of the current chapters on *Sh! The Octopus*, *The Unholy Night*, and *Eran Trece* may be found in *Guilty Pleasures of the Horror Film*, *More Guilty Pleasures of the Horror Film*, and *Cult Movies* magazine, respectively. My thanks to the Svehlas, the Svehlas, and Buddy Barnett (respectively) for allowing me to amend what they had originally published.

Thanks, too, to Gary Banks, Harry Long and Eric Stott for chipping in with info when I needed it; to Paul Ydstie for a copy of *The Unknown Purple* theatrical program; to P. J. Angel, Charles P. Mitchell, Sig Menchel, Richard Bojarski (Bojak!), Neil Pettigrew, Richard Dacre, and George Koch for graphics, stills, and/or videotapes; to Zdena Curinová, of the Národní Filmov Archiv, for some great shots from *Le Golem*; to Dr. Lawrence Knapp and Dr. Richard Brinley—who must have despaired of ever seeing any of my promised coverage on the Stoll Fu Manchu series—for background and support (You owe it to yourself to visit their awesome Sax Rohmer website: www.njedge.net/~knapp/FuManchu/htm); to Jerry Schneider for the skinny on long-gone studios; to Jon Mirsalis, for the skinny on long-gone motion pictures; to my colleagues, Jay Evans and Dean Bertsch, for making computers less mysterious and more accessible; and to Wendy Cunningham—now of Post-Net—who allowed me to send first-class lasers (instead of priceless original stills) to my publisher.

If I forgot anyone (and I tried not to, I really did), please forgive me. I'll getcha next time.

The "Earl and Slick" of the dedication are my younger siblings—Cheryl and Bill—who had to endure an inordinate amount of parental fawning on the firstborn when we were all kids and teenagers. I want to close out this "thank you" section by thanking them both for everything they've done for me and all that they've meant to me all those years, even when the breadth of the USA was separating us. So, guys, if I never had the time to tell you formally before now, YOU'RE THE BEST.

Introduction

I was a child in the '50s—born in 1950, in fact—and, like so many other of my colleagues, I had a defining life-moment when I first laid eyes on *Famous Monsters of Filmland*. Actually, my utter dependence upon the magazine began with the second issue—I somehow managed to miss the inaugural number—and lasted well over a year. Editor Forry Ackerman (FJA to insiders) apparently had an infinite supply of mind-blowing photographs from "imagi-movies" that featured some of the most deliriously incredible creatures and riveting personalities I'd ever come in contact with. FJA's prose was hardly deathless (I was being molded literarily by the good sisters of Saint Joseph, who regularly exposed me and my classmates to the classics, albeit in slightly bowdlerized form), but his pictures…. Even the cooler, older guys (like the seventh graders) had to admit that most of those monster movies looked really neat.

Famous Monsters (*FM* to insiders) was a quarterly early in its existence, so I probably replaced issues 3, 4 and 5 a couple of times each (sundry copies being lost to some of those cooler, older guys, or to one or another of the nuns, who were always snatching comic books, *Mad* magazine, and *FM* in their quest to stem communism) before—in my newsstand vigil during the octave of issue number 6—I came upon *Castle of Frankenstein* (*CoF* to insiders). Flushed with astonishment and flush (my allowance), I bought both *FM* #6 and the newcomer and scurried back to my house, preparing to OD on stories, "stills" (a new word, meaning photographs from movies), and puns. I was pleasantly surprised to find that *CoF* head honcho, Calvin Beck, eschewed FJA's habit of writing down to his audience and interspersed in-depth accounts of fantastic literature and artwork among the film articles. It was apparent that Beck's magazine offered the same deliriously incredible creatures and riveting personalities as did Ackerman's, but dished them out with a bit more substance, falling short only in terms of the sheer quantity of illustrations *FM* unveiled on a regular basis.

I was now hooked on both books, and despite my ever-growing awareness of the differences among the sundry Monsters Frankenstein and the various offspring each of the "great" monsters seemed to have—at least, per the titles I was memorizing—I began to despair of ever seeing even a *fraction* of the innumerable "creature features" that were trotted out for my edification and enjoyment every two or three months.

Fast forward, forty years. Technology has grown (as have I), and not only have I seen an impressive number of those pictures, through the miracle of tape recorders, 16mm film, VCRs, and laser- and DVD-players, I have (at one time or another) *owned* many of them. Few, indeed, are the films that have eluded my ambitious and only slightly myopic search throughout those four decades (or eight lustrums, per FJA). Nor am I alone in this achievement. True children of Dr. Acula and Charles Foster Kane (Beck had more mainstream ties than Ackerman did) can count on the fingers of dozens of hands the "imagi-movies" they've sat through time and again.

Still, there are those few, maddeningly succulent titles that have eluded most, if not all, of us. And that's where this book comes in: The common denominators of the pictures examined herein are their celebrity and obscurity. Most of the titles will be familiar, as they've received mention — usually in discussions of other, related, more readily available films — even if their details haven't. Some of the films discussed herein are lost, some are damned near lost, and the balance are to be had if one is willing to look for them.

The Scarab Murder Case, for instance, has all but vanished from God's green earth (and, to an overwhelming extent, that includes the film's publicity materials, too). In a perfect world, movie buffs outfitted with a VCR and a nice Chianti ought to be able to sail right through the Philo Vance canon from alpha to omega, but that pesky little British programmer has — by its absence — been gumming up the game plan for over half a century. Granted, there's always the thought that S. S. Van Dine's novel is still out there to be had, but this is poor consolation. Moving one's eyes along the printed page exercises those organs, hones the imagination, and encourages personal interpretation; nonetheless, having someone else do the interpretive work — which is then paraded *before* one's eyes for purposes of edification and entertainment — is an alternative, enthusiastically coveted conduit to pleasure. In fact, this latter track is the raison d'être of film fans. As the Wilfred Hyde-White impersonation in question has not as yet fallen conveniently from its niche in the cupboard of some Mancurian cold water flat, the backstory of the filming of *The Scarab Murder Case* will have to substitute for cogent observation on the picture itself.

Paul Leni's vision of Earl Derr Biggers's *The Chinese Parrot* has also gone missing these many years; indeed, it may well be the El Dorado of Charlie Chan cinema. (Allow me a moment to duck the invective being hurled by Warner Oland devotees.) It's unclear whether the picture disappeared gradually, as the number of physical prints winnowed away through use and attrition and the negatives decomposed due to neglect, or whether the success of the sound Chans — with their newly crafted screenplays, eagerly anticipated formulas, and popular leading actors — mitigated against the preservation by a rival studio of a mute one-shot, based on what was likely the weakest of all the source novels and headlined by one of the most bizarre silent film personalities imaginable. It is, therefore, the widespread appreciation for the extant Paul Leni expressionistic oeuvre that has made the loss of this particular film an occasion of mourning. The fact that 35mm prints of Leni's work were in demand virtually everywhere following his success with *Das Wachsfigurenkabinett* (1924) may account for *The Chinese Parrot*'s eventual reappearance upon the scene. Until that occurs, however, my comments on the hither and whither of the production may have to serve as the water in the soup.

Coincidentally, another filmic Charlie Chan adventure may be found in these pages: *Eran trece*, the Spanish-language variation on *Charlie Chan Carries On*, the first of those near-mythic (and lost!) Warner Oland sound Chans. Several new books on the Charlie Chan films have been published within the last few years, yet — even among these—critical commentary on this Hispanic hybrid has been sparse. The film may be found with scarcely any effort at all, but without English subtitles. (A recent glance at eBay showed the film available in both VHS *and* DVD!) Sure, there's recourse (once again) to the novel, and copies of the *Charlie Chan Carries On* continuity script are available to researchers, but the picture's presumption to survival—when its glossy, Hollywood "big brother" has seemingly copped it, once and for all—seems to annoy some fans, while frustrating others. Come what may, *Eran trece* ought to be regarded as more than a mere bizarro-world version of *Charlie Chan Carries On*.

Virtually all of Stoll Studios' *The Mystery of Dr. Fu Manchu* shorts of the '20s *do* exist, closeted among other vintage nitrate elements in the vaults of the British Film Institute, but they haven't seen the light of the carbon arc in years. So far as I've been able to determine, the unofficial BFI position on the 35mm elements I was able to screen on a flatbed some years back is eerily similar to the collective opinion of modern German cinema on Conrad Veidt: Why bother, when there are so many other films and personalities more deserving of the study and attention? This is about the point where we start barking about one man's meat and another man's poison and so forth, and I guess there are only so many hours in a day and so many pounds or dollars or euros in a budget. Still, how many genre offerings have slipped away over the years, not because of time or money or lack of opportunity, but because of highly subjective apathy? Other than via a trip to the BFI, I don't know where or how one would get to see any of these A. E. Coleby two-reelers.

Allowing for the substitution of The Museum of Modern Art for The British Film Institute, the same may be said for Fox's *Trick for Trick*.

From roughly the mid-20s till the mid-30s, there was lots of magic in the movies, both on the screen and behind it. Magic, now—not hypnotism, spiritualism or necromancy, although there was certainly no shortage of arm wavers, watch spinners, automatic writers, card readers, voice throwers, shamans, fakirs, charlatans, mystics, and generic raisers of the dead to be had. Nor am I speaking of Georges Méliès–style magic, which had been an unmistakable mélange of rococo imagination, outlandish accoutrements, rudimentary camera tricks, and impish humor. Rather, I'm referring to William Cameron Menzies–style magic, which—while also depending upon rococo imagination and outlandish accoutrements—evinced technically advanced camera tricks, a near-paranormal understanding of light and perspective, and the genius to suffuse reality with wonderment.

This distinction is meant neither to disparage the incredibly innovative M. Méliès nor to trivialize his Ur-influence on the sort of movie special effects that came to be referred to as "trick photography." The man obviously worked like a slave on each of his hundreds of Star films, and a recent DVD compilation of the best and the brightest of these reveals a painstaking attention to background detail that many times holds the modern viewer's attention even as the elementary, if undeniably charming, tricked-up "live" action sequences chug along up front. Le monde du M. Méliès is so totally fabricated, so transparently fraudulent, that it can exist only outside of the boundaries of time and space. Its essence is imagination and bravado: A Star film is like a performance by an old-fashioned conjurer, who—bearded and bedizened and surrounded by mystical boxes and garishly painted cylinders—dares you to deny that you're captivated by his tricks, even if you are privy to all his secrets.

Méliès's particular magic —"essentially conceived for the proscenium," if I may use Paul Rotha's excellent phrase — was considered passé by 1912, roughly the year when the feature-length film began to make inroads in France. His studio—the renowned Théâtre Robert-Houdin — was demolished in 1923, and by the mid-20s there wasn't a magic theater in all of France. Come 1930, the grand old man himself could be found selling sweets and toys in a small street kiosk in the Gare Montparnasse.

By "Menzies-style" magic, I mean the visual opulence that has come to be associated with the name William Cameron Menzies. As director or — more frequently — art director, the man fabricated worlds that somehow touched the viewer's inner child; anyone familiar with either the dream-like Arabia of Douglas Fairbanks's sumptuous *Thief of Bagdad* (1924) or the nightmarish stretches of the backyard sandpit in *Invaders from Mars* (1953) doubtless knows what I mean. Striking lighting, angles and composition were the underpinnings of his trademark visual design, and he'd typically go the extra mile to manipulate a perspective, achieve an effect, or shave a superfluous inch from a set. In speaking of Menzies, James Wong Howe's biographer Todd Rainsberger wrote, "His sets were so precisely designed that they even dictated the lenses to be used in each shot."

Menzies grew into his reputation slowly, however. Comparisons to the Stuttgart-born Paul Leni, whose own take on spatial and temporal exotica —*Das Wachsfigurenkabinett*— hit Berlin screens a month or two before *The Thief of Bagdad* premiered in New York City, were inevitable. When finally imported to the United States as *Waxworks* in 1926, Leni's macabre masterpiece won him international renown and an invitation to Tinsel Town. Roland West's *The Bat* was released that same year, though, and audiences and critics alike were quick to realize that in Menzies they had a homegrown Leni, for the picture's design reflected the look of the decade's classic German horror films without betraying its American origins. West's next picture, *The Dove* (1928), was his last silent, and Menzies— whose sets therein helped him cop the first ever Academy Award for Art Direction — retained the Germanic accents he had earlier assumed, although the screenplay dealt with Latin passion and betrayal. Regrettably, Menzies did not participate in the Roland West melodrama discussed at length elsewhere in this tome: *The Unknown Purple* (1923).

He did, of course, work on a trio of early '30s thrillers whose dramatic pivot was magic and the occult, and a discussion of two of those follows herewith. Together with Kenneth McKenna, Menzies codirected *The Spider*, and modern sources indicate he labored alongside Gordon Wiles as well. He went on to provide the sundry special effects for the studio's third exercise in prestidigitation, *Trick for Trick* (1933), and many of those same sources hold that same opinion about the art direction in that third magical mystery tour as well. Menzies codirected the second entry in Fox's triad—1932's *Chandu the Magician*— with Marcel Vernal and lent yet another hand (albeit again sans screen credit) with the design.

Because *Chandu* has already enjoyed its fair share of drizzled ink—and since that feature emerged from the mist some while back—I've elected to marshal my resources and opine solely on its two, more obscure siblings. *The Spider* is out and about, but *Trick for Trick* has— so far as I am aware — but one home.

Which is one more than *The Unknown Purple* can claim. This 1923 science-fiction feature has been lost for decades, and there's not a whole lot of information on it in print. Film historian Scott McQueen has been about the only authority to comment at length on the picture to date, but enough editorializing is done in the pertinent entry in Phil Hardy's popular *Encyclopedia of Horror Movies* to make the latter observation suspect. For many fans to date, *The Unknown Purple* has been an unknown commodity. Hopefully, the rudimentary notes in this volume will serve as a springboard for someone else's research into what appears—from most contemporary critiques and background information—to be a most fascinating contribution to the genre.

Another early (but post–*Invisible Man*) treatment of transparent humanity is Universal's 1934 chapterplay *The Vanishing Shadow*. *Shadow* has more in common with *The Unknown Purple* than with the James Whale and Claude Rains masterpiece, as both films relegate their dramatis personae unseen while leaving vestiges—a purple miasma in the earlier film, that damned shadow in the later—to hang about and muck things up. For all that, the invisibility angle wasn't the biggest hook the picture had to offer. There was one hell of an Art Deco mechanical man that figured into things somehow, although not too many folks were certain of the details. The same few stills appeared and reappeared to tantalize interested parties, but for quite a while there, the serial itself wasn't forthcoming. Nowadays, however, there *is* joy in Mudville: *The Vanishing Shadow* has been retrieved and restored and is widely available in wonderfully crafted VHS and DVD versions.

Probably not too many people (other than Rin-Tin-Tin fans) are actively missing *While London Sleeps*, the wonder dog's only venture into horror. Actually, other than those same Rinty fans, there may not be too many people anywhere who are actively *aware* of *While London Sleeps* and for whom its being lost is no great hardship. According to most of the contemporary critiques of the film, in fact, the hardship lay in the viewing of it. Still, when the stock of vintage thrillers begins to grow thin—and not because you're being persnickety, either—you wish that the films that had been panned way back when were still around, if only to give you the chance to say "Yea!" or "Nay!" yourself.

Warners' *Stark Mad* is in the same boat, said boat having slipped beneath the waves years ago. Shot on an admitted shoestring, but possessed of a wonderful cast, a bizarre and illogical script, and a brace of monsters (including—Yowzah!—a gorilla), the picture would definitely have a strong following nowadays, even if folks who perpetually cleaved to the cinematic high road wouldn't be caught dead at a screening. The eponymous simian in William Fox's *The Monkey Talks* was neither a gorilla—although the number of gorillas to be found hither and yon on the silent screen was legion—nor a monster, but, rather, a lovesick little man with the weirdest occupation in Paris. You'll have to make for the George Eastman House if you want to see this fascinating Raoul Walsh effort for yourself, but the dramatic pivot on which it turns may be found in almost any of Lon Chaney's genre offerings.

I wish the earlier versions of *The Witching Hour* were out there on video, as the 1934 Paramount production is, but at least we can be grateful for a projectable print of the 1921 version. Over the last decade or so, the number of black-and-white films shown on television has plummeted drastically, with the result that virtually only American Movie Classics and Turner Classic Movies haven't turned their corporate backs on them. (It's disturbing to note, however, that AMC has begun a transformation for the worse, not only by adding commercial breaks, but also by shifting to a policy whereby most of their "classic" films seem to have released in relatively recent years.) As 16mm prints have also been drying up (due to the switch to video and now DVD on the part of TV stations, airplanes, the armed forces, etc.), the future of many of these old(er), less-celebrated pictures may lie with film collectors, rather than with the studios that produced them, or the conglomerates that have acquired the rights to them.

In the chapter on *The Monkey's Paw*, I opine that the Simpsons' *Treehouse of Horror* variation is the best-known screen adaptation out there, and nothing has transpired since I put that essay to bed to make me change my mind. Dennis Payne has informed me that British TV back in the '70s presented a take on the tale and that he recalled the production as being excellent. While I'm happy to be able to noodle at the keyboard and add some credits to the essay, the fact that I was clueless about this one until very recently keeps Homer and the family in the forefront of *Paw* aficionados. Fama est that there are clips from the 1933 RKO production in the hands of private collectors and archives, but reliable information about the clips seems to be as scarce as the clips themselves.

Ted Turner has done a great deal of good with his Turner Classic Movies. Titles like *Black Moon*, *Sh! The Octopus*, and *The Unholy Night* have popped up from time to time on TCM, and I'm sure that these beautiful prints have served as upgrades for many of the "gray market" companies that have made their living drop-shipping tapes to hardcore, obscurity lovers such as me. I've read lots of comments on how rediscovered thrillers are never as exciting as stills and adjective-heavy, printed remembrances of them indicate, but I'm just grateful to have the pictures where I can see them and come to my own conclusions. Sure, I've been disappointed — Who hasn't?—but I've yet to find a newly uncovered "lost" film that didn't have *something* tucked in it that made the time spent with it worthwhile. If only once. I'll admit right now that *Black Moon* is not my favorite of the films covered herein and that *The Unholy Night* has kept me amused again and again. (And at the risk of being hooted down and run out of town on a rail, I'll admit — here, in the comparative safety of parentheses— a fondness for *Sh! The Octopus*. The picture is sui generis and seems either to attract or repel viewers; apparently, no one can leave the lighthouse without having been profoundly affected by the experience.)

Julien Duvivier's *Le Golem* and D. W. Griffith's *The Sorrows of Satan* are both present and accounted for, and you'll probably note that my tone is a tad more serious and respectful in dealing with these pictures than it may appear to be in the essays on *Trick for Trick* or — all right — *Sh! The Octopus*. This must have been done unconsciously (that may not be the right word), as I had hoped to keep the tenor of the book consistent throughout. In going over the text just prior to finishing the whole enchilada, though, I discovered that I hadn't thrown any pies at the two filmic heavyweights, nor did I crack wise (much) about their films. Decades after the release of these pictures, the men and their handiwork still merit a gravitas that others have lost due to the passage of time. What can I say? *The Sorrows of Satan* is easier to track down than *Le Golem*, but decent enough copies of the former and a splendid prerecord of the latter exist.

Grazie a Dio for the Italians and the Rome Film Archive. Over the past few years, prints of *Deluge* (covered herein) and *Seven Footprints to Satan* (maybe next time) turned up in Roma, and they (and their Italian intertitles) have made their way to American televisions courtesy of some enterprising video companies. Discoveries like these suffuse us all with hope that other "lost" pictures (my number one quest is Laurel and Hardy in *Hats Off*) may have been filed under foreign-language names that differed from their American release titles. Whenever I have a spare moment, I translate a few of the *Seven Footprints* intertitles into idiomatic English, so someone's going to have had that work already done for them if they're preparing to tackle the Benjamin Christensen comedy-thriller.

For all I know, the BFI's silent print of Maurice Elvey's *High Treason* may be the only print extant on this interesting pacifist drama. Students of British cinema and researchers can always arrange for a screening at the Stephen Street facilities, but to date there hasn't been any discussion about issuing any kind of video copy for home use. In this case, the BFI is the repository of the original elements of the picture, with Carlton International the concern that holds the rights.

When all is said and done, the market for obscurities is quite specialized, and one is forever confronted with the argument that nothing is deservedly obscure. I won't deny that a couple of these films are probably of interest to those in the know *because* they're unfamiliar; who can say with authority that, were they as ubiquitous as *Casablanca* or *Frankenstein*, our gabbing about them wouldn't prove to be more innately enjoyable than our viewing them. From the subsequent discussion online and in print, it appears that the recent stills-only "restoration" of Tod Browning and Lon Chaney's *London after Midnight* did little more than refuel the fire of the "Was it or wasn't it any damn good to begin with?" debate that had been smoldering for decades.

Some genre buffs have become a tad wearied by lifelong analysis of the classics and are more open to new experiences, even if said experiences may remain secondhand at present or may disappoint when circumstances change. Differences of opinion are what make the world go 'round, of course, and I think it's safe to say that there are very few lifelong horror and science fiction and thriller fans who don't positively *thrive* on good-natured arguments over movies such as these.

The greatest pitfall for the commentator on lost films is the temptation to take a stand on a film based solely on the availability (or lack thereof) of contemporary criticism. One can't merely side with the yellowed majority opinion (originally foisted upon open-minded folk who had a quarter in their pockets and a couple of hours on their hands) and then stand back, waiting for applause. Every one of those professional moviegoers approached their responsibility with his (there were very few women critics in the prewar days) own little cavils, and no one finger-pointer ever ought to have been regarded as the last word on anything.

My last words are a wish that this book be an enjoyable read for everyone, an introduction to the joys and thrills of lesser-known genre pictures for many, and a jumping-off point for further research for those few who refuse to let the discussion of these films—or the films themselves—die right here.

John T. Soister
Orwigsburg, Pennsylvania

THE MYSTERY OF DR. FU MANCHU

This series, unequivocally the most arcane entry in the canon of filmed adventures of the world's infamous Yellow Peril, is as poorly documented as is the history of its parent studio: Stoll Picture Productions, at once home to the dullest features and the most exciting short subjects to be found in '20s Britain. The sundry overviews of Fu Manchu on celluloid that have been published intermittently over the years unfailingly begin with a nod to this collection of shorts and just as inevitably move on with scarcely any additional comment.

This is an observation, however, and not a criticism: Stills are devilishly difficult to track down, promotional paper seems to have gone the way of the dodo, and the films themselves—those at the British Film Institute and other archives—have until only recently appeared to be doomed to extinction through lack of funds and attendant benign neglect. In the fall of 2003, however, Britain's National Film Theatre screened all fourteen surviving episodes of the fifteen-part *Mystery of Dr. Fu Manchu*, as part of its program "Silent British Adventure Series," and these short films received an appreciative reception that was long overdue.

Author Sax Rohmer—born Arthur Henry Ward in February of 1883 and subsequently given to changing his nom de plume frequently before settling on that one—had introduced the Chinese evil genius to Western civilization in October 1912. British readers encountered the not-so-good doctor via *The Mystery of Fu Manchu*, while Yanks nosing about that same corner pored over *The Insidious Dr. Fu Manchu*, the novel's American release title. Further adventures followed in fairly short order, but before those hit the bookstores, the character made an unbilled guest appearance in Rohmer's *Yellow Claw* (1915), surely a sign that the Mandarin had attained both enviable notoriety *and* renown, even at that early date.

While Rohmer was an exciting and prolific author, he proved to be no great shakes as a businessman, and—per Rohmer authority and webmaster, Dr. Lawrence Knapp—early on had employed Robert Somerville, a literary agent who was, in his own way, as Machiavellian as Fu Manchu would ever be. Until late in 1927, Rohmer had failed to demand a meticulous accounting of his income, usually inquiring about royalties only when he was in immediate need of cash. While he was certainly aware that rights to the evil doctor had been assigned to Stoll Picture Productions for the purpose of fabricating a series of short films, he was most likely ignorant of the exact terms of the contract, and this personal naiveté and lack of business savvy may have been the straw that ultimately broke this first film franchise's back. When, several years down the road, Pioneer Studios released some two-reel melodramas centering on an Oriental genius, Rohmer's Fu Manchu would be bypassed in favor of a Yellow Peril sired by the studio's scenario department: Dr. Sin Fang, whose modus operandi, accoutrements and impersonator all bore the ash marks of their more illustrious predecessor. In the interim, though — when, for all Rohmer knew, everything was just hunky-dory — Stoll did his famed creation proud. The first series of two-reelers fell heir to (per an atmospheric puff piece in the *Kinematograph Weekly*) "the greatest publicity campaign ever attempted in film history," and its fifteen episodes picked up the slack left by the Eille Norwood's *Sherlock Holmes* shorts (also at Stoll), the last of which had been released a month earlier.

Stoll Picture Productions was the brainchild of Sir Oswald Stoll, a prosperous theater owner who by 1919 had begun looking into supplying his own product. His fledgling company hit big almost right away with *Mr. Wu*, a reworked stage play from 1913. Along with a few profitable (if maudlin) women's pictures, the feature — remade definitively by MGM in 1927, with Lon Chaney playing a brace of the eponymous characters — proved so successful that Sir Oswald forswore exhibition for production, where (he was now convinced) the real money lay. The titled entrepreneur quickly took on partners. His company went public, and a cavernous old airplane factory was bought, effectively giving the new concern the most spacious indoor stages in the country. Registered in mid-1920, Stoll (as the studio was immediately called) retained screen veteran Maurice Elvey to oversee production, purchased some of the finest photographic technology available anywhere, announced a slate of uplifting films based on contemporary British literature, and immediately began to bore the socks off a population that wanted its regular dose of national pride at the very least *colored* with excitement. It wasn't long before Sir Oswald was reduced to rummaging through his old exhibitor's baggage, as he searched desperately for the key to filling the island nation's movie houses.

As Rachael Low relates in her epic *History of the British Film, 1918–1929*, contemporary criticism soon became depressingly antiphonal: "Stoll films are dull films."

> Good equipment could not overcome unsuitable stories mechanically adapted, poorly mounted in standard sets, edited and sometimes re-edited by cutters whose task was all too often to make the best of a bad job. It was a film factory without creative leadership [p. 125].

The company thus pandered to exhibitors with costly trade shows, wherein the latest adaptation of a recent national bestseller was unreeled in all its sumptuously overcast, yet dramatically undernourished, glory, while invariably being touted as the next cinematic sensation. From 1920 to 1923 — with Elvey at the helm of the more palatable efforts — the roster of contributing authors grew to include such heavyweights as Edgar Wallace, E. Phillips Oppenheim, H. G. Wells, Arthur Conan Doyle and Sax Rohmer. American expatriate René Plaisetty, whose directorial efforts for the studio were second only to those of Elvey himself, had managed to make Rohmer's *Yellow Claw* one of Stoll's few bright spots in its first year of production.

While the quality of the company's feature films was alarmingly uneven, Elvey's fifteen two-reel adaptations of Conan Doyle's *Adventures of Sherlock Holmes* (in 1921) set high standards for popular entertainment that few other studios even tried to match and which — until later in the decade — none did. (A particularly notable—

and canny—attempt was Master Films' string of *Tense Moments with Great Authors*, which featured such anxiety producers as George du Maurier's *Trilby*, Charles Dickens's *Fagin*, and Alphonse Daudet's *Sappho*.) Per Robert W. Pohle Jr. and Douglas C. Hart's *Sherlock Holmes on the Screen*, Elvey deserved the credit for casting the aging (sixty years old) Norwood as the timeless detective; per the consensus of extant contemporary reviews, it was Norwood's talent and charisma that were credited with carrying the series. Eager to capitalize on the success of the two-reel package, Stoll followed up with a five-reel version of *The Hound of the Baskervilles*. Alas! While the feature attracted greater attention than had the shorts, it also received a greater number of slings and arrows. It would take two subsequent parcels of Holmes's short escapades—*The Further Adventures* in 1922 and *The Last Adventures* in 1923—before Elvey dared the fates once again, and the company's second (and last) Sherlockian feature, *The Sign of Four*, would serve to remind everyone why they had gone to the two-reel format in the first place.

With Sir Denis Nayland-Smith and Dr. Petrie as spiritual clones of the Great Consulting Detective and his amanuensis, it likewise made sense to go the short-subject route in presenting the assorted schemes of Fu Manchu to the masses. Rohmer's source novels were fairly lengthy, but they were also rather episodic, much along the lines of the silent serials that had captivated movie audiences on both sides of the Atlantic. Keeping the films' running times to around twenty minutes would thus allow average moviegoers to become involved in the mechanics of the melodrama without the danger of their becoming bored with any one particular story or bewildered by too many plot wrinkles. In fact, Rohmer's characters were by that time nearly as familiar to the great unwashed as were Conan Doyle's, so lengthy segments of exposition or character development might only hinder the unreeling of otherwise ripping good yarns. What's more, when taken regularly in small doses, the exotic lilt to the rather basic scenarios provided a much-needed break from the bland and achingly predictable nationalistic fodder that usually occupied the rest of the program.

There is no record that, as Elvey had done with Norwood, director A. E. Coleby personally tapped Harry Agar Lyons for the formidable doctor, but the Irish actor had essayed any number of costume roles—including Robin Hood and the Devil himself—since his motion picture debut in 1905, and the Chinese supercriminal was right up his alley. Nor is there any claim that (again, like Norwood) the character man was a master of disguise. In his mid-40s when *The Mystery of Dr. Fu Manchu* was in production, Lyons had no hint of Oriental caste about him (as did the Swedish Warner Oland), nor did he undergo any extensive makeup treatment (as would Boris Karloff). Extant photographs of him in costume, however, indicate that he played the part with his eyebrows shaved. Perhaps coincidentally, but more probably due to his becoming associated with the part (thanks to Stoll's pervasive distribution of the series in the United Kingdom), Lyons soon found his movie career stalling, and, by middecade, it appears that he had been released from his Stoll contract. Data show his post-Fu Manchu appearances to be sporadic and of varying quality. He began to gravitate almost naturally (and perhaps inevitably) to oriental roles; not only was the Dr. Sin Fang saga in his future, but, come sound, he would enact a *singing* Mandarin in the Fred Paul musical, *In a Lotus Garden*.

Paul played opposite Lyons in both Fu Manchu series and directed *The Further Mysteries* as well. (Paul also directed a couple of the *Thrilling Stories from the Strand Magazine*, another collection of Stoll shorts that proved popular and profitable enough to warrant a second helping.) This cinematic "dual citizenship"—acting and directing—was as commonplace as fog in London where shorts were concerned, and there were very few technicians who didn't leap into the frame-line from their director's chairs when necessity dictated. Late in life, Claude Rains would speak of how his father, Fred, had performed both duties when British cinema was in its infancy and an entree into the industry was almost to be had for the asking.

Fred Rains had been cranking 'em out for years before Fred Paul made his debut, but *Mystery* director A. E. Coleby had been Johnny-on-the-spot as early as 1907, when he wrote, directed, and starred in *Serving a Summons*, a one-reeler for short-subject specialist studio Crick and Sharp (later, Crick and Martin). His work became increasingly impressive as the years rolled along, and in 1922—following Stoll's picking up his *Froggy's Little Brother* (a full-blown five-reeler)—he stayed on with the company. Several years later, after the release of a couple of relatively significant features starring Hollywood's only Japanese matinee idol, Sessue Hayakawa (*The Great Prince Shan* in 1924 and *Sen Yan's Devotion* [featuring Harry Agar Lyons in yet *another* Oriental role] in 1925), Coleby left Stoll. Even as his former studio sought to expand, Coleby was lured away by the prospect of setting up shop for himself, and this he did (along with his ex-boss, R. H. Cricks) with his F(aith) H(ope) C(harity) Company. FHC's gain was Stoll's loss, and when Maurice Elvey also defected for the stability of (British) Gaumont, it was the beginning of the end for Sir Oswald's conglomerate.

> Owing to Sir Oswald's reluctance to install an American sound system and his efforts to promote an unsuccessful British invention, the studios were late in converting to sound, and [Herbert] Wilcox [an independent producer], who had been filming there, decided to build his own studio at Twickenham [Low, p. 162].

Stoll thus went from being an industry leader in terms of volume to (briefly) the distribution arm for companies that hired out its facilities, before virtually fading away by the end of 1928. (The company name was hailed onscreen for one last time when its corporate remnant distributed Butcher Productions' *Great Gay Road* in 1931.) Rachel Low reports that despite Sir Oswald's sundry schemes, the company was some £200,000 in the hole after seven years.

The Mystery of Dr. Fu Manchu (erroneously referred to as "*The Mysteries*" by some of the contemporary British trade magazines) was a collection of fifteen semi-autonomous two-reelers, adapted by director A. E. Coleby and Frank Wilson from Sax Rohmer's ever growing literary output. The studio admitted that the scenarios had been pretty much lifted from the author's original short stories (published as far back as October 1912 in the *Story Teller* magazine, the *New Magazine, Collier's*, et al.), and Kinematograph Weekly (April 26, 1923) advised interested exhibitors that the studio heads

> are spending many thousands of pounds upon what they consider to be the greatest publicity scheme yet devised. Hundreds of the finest bill-

posting sites in the United Kingdom have been secured to herald the series; Tube lifts and Tube stations will be utilized; advertisements will appear in newspapers all over the country, and Methuen and Co., Ltd., is publishing special editions of *The Mystery of Dr. Fu Manchu*, *The Devil Doctor*, and *The Si-Fan Mysteries*, from which the series has been adapted [p. 121].

In addition to Stoll's attempts at having Harry Lyons's gaunt visage staring down at tube patrons and pedestrians everywhere, other industry publications recommended that theater displays be jazzed up via purple lighting, Chinese lettering on upright narrow panels, and attendants attired in Chinese costumes. The Methuen and Co. volumes were likewise touted as lobby decoration, as were the sundry pertinent copies of *Story Teller* magazine, replete with lurid cover art. (The exhibitors were also rather shamelessly exhorted to tie in with *The Eye of Siva*, a Fu Manchu play that was making some noise on the West End at that time.) The scope (and cheek) of such an aggressive publicity campaign is best appreciated when one recalls that *The Mystery of Fu Manchu* was a series of *short subjects*, normally meant to augment—not overshadow—the current feature film.

Sir Oswald previewed the first four shorts via the trade show circuit. (All fifteen short subjects were released throughout the United Kingdom on the same day—September 10, 1923—with the understanding that the two-reelers would meticulously crisscross the island kingdom within two months of their first showings.) Location shooting in and around London made the episodes rather more fun for ticket buyers who could readily identify the locales, and no one minded that when the evil genius's name made it to the title cards, it was only at times hyphenated. *Bioscope* magazine (August 30, 1923) advised its readership that each short originally began with a brief "prologue," in which Lyons's Mandarin was "dimly observed at a table poring over books and presenting a picture of concentrated malevolence." The May 17, 1923, issue of *Kinematograph Weekly* offered a rather reserved reaction to the trade show samples:

> Based on the well-known stories by Sax Rohmer, these two-reelers afford average entertainment, judging from the four episodes screened. Produced in serial form—although each episode is more or less complete in itself—they lack the "punch" of the ordinary serial, and are rather on the slow side. The mixture of the Oriental atmosphere with ordinary Western life gives them a certain glamour, and if they are handled properly, they ought to go well.

The featured cast remained the same throughout Coleby's series, with Lyons as the doctor; Joan Clarkson as the slave girl, Karamenah; Fred Paul as Sir Denis Nayland-Smith; the venerable H. Humberston Wright as Dr. Petrie; and Frank Wilson—who had helped Coleby massage the Rohmer tales into filmable format—as Inspector James Weymouth. The cinematography honors were shared by D. P. Cooper and Phil Ross, H. Leslie Brittain did the editing, and the art direction fell to Walter H. Murton, who

> was undoubtedly hampered by the parsimony of the company, which usually involved him in the use and re-use of stock sets.... He was responsible for the appearance of countless Stoll films, heavily conventional, unimaginative, dark and unrealistic [Low, p. 124].

A few secondary cast members (Julie Suedo as Zarmi, and Pat Royale as Aziz) also popped up now and again.

The Scented Envelopes was numerically the first of the two-reelers, and it was trade-shown (along with *The West Case*, *The Clue of the Pigtail*, and *The Call of Siva*) at the Alhambra Theatre almost four months prior to general release. The May 17, 1923, number of *Kinematograph Weekly* briefly recounted the episodes' plotlines, and several additional entries are outlined in later issues of *KW* and other trade publications. These, however, are never identified by their individual titles, but rather are listed as "another in the series of detective tales concerning a Chinese doctor, by Sax Rohmer."

Critics were quick to compare Coleby's set of episodes devoted to Fu Manchu with Elvey's *Sherlock Holmes* series, and the Chinese evil genius always came up short. As early as May 31, the *Bioscope* reviewer opined that

> the new series is very much cruder, both in subject-matter and in treatment, than the Doyle stories. Whereas the latter had a skillfully worked out logical interest, the former are merely stereotyped melodramas, which make no attempt to be plausible, but depend entirely upon the appeal of lurid sensationalism [p. 56].

The same reviewer complained that the mad mandarin "appears to have no motive in his numerous murder plots," which are carried out "by the most roundabout and laborious methods conceivable." The reviewer's lack of familiarity with (and appreciation for) the movie serial format must have been evident to even the densest of exhibitors.

The surviving commentaries are virtually as one in finding the photography to be at least "good," and faint praise is occasionally thrown director A. E. Coleby's way. The edge was apparently taken off those overly familiar Stoll sets by having the exteriors of most episodes shot in and around London. (Per the established custom, night scenes and some exteriors were tinted green, while many of the interiors were printed with an amber hue. In addition, the titles take on an ersatz-Oriental character—and are printed in yellow—when they reflect Fu Manchu's speeches; his sundry Occidental foes are given more mundane, white-on-black typeface.) And while some of the commentators may have been found wanting in their regard for movie serials, they were singularly aware of the series' creative deficiencies, especially when stacked up against the exotica of the Rohmer source material. The *Kinematograph Weekly* reviewer noted rightly in the May 17 issue how "In *The Scented Envelopes*, a common or garden lizard has been substituted for a giant centipede, and the thrill of the story is completely lost."

Amid all this grousing about implausibility and inadequacy, though, there was praise for the assorted scenarios' fidelity to the source literature and some fairly decent notices for the members of the Fu Manchu troupe. It was felt that "H. Agar Lyons makes a sufficiently striking figure of this curious malefactor," although "He is not in the least Oriental-looking, but most successfully simulates an American." Nonetheless, despite his blatantly non-Chinese demeanor, Lyons's portrayal cleaved more closely in spirit to his literary counterpart than did Oland's mandarin, and Stoll's attention to detail provided Lyons's archfiend his beloved marmoset. Lyons is garbed in oriental splendor when nestled in his lair but affects a suit and cravat, cape, and slouch hat when venturing forth into the streets.

Fred Paul was thought to be "duly strong and silent" as Nayland Smith, even though it was observed that his "success as a sleuth is not very marked in the opening episodes." Joan Clarkson was deemed "attractive" as the luckless Karamenah, and the same reviewers felt "H. Humberston Wright does what he can with the unfruitful role of Dr. Petrie — a rather colorless substitute for Holmes' faithful Watson." No extant critique comments on how the lithe and lovely Karamenah ended up wed to the undeniably geriatric Petrie.

The program was successful enough to merit a sequel. Reports in the trades blurted that "a new record is likely to be established with *The Mystery of Dr. Fu Manchu* series," said record presumably being financial, and the following year found Fred Paul taking over for Coleby, who had moved up to work on features exclusively. Whereas the huge sum spent to publicize *The Mystery* had been disproportionate to the monies actually budgeted for shooting, available evidence suggests that *Further Mysteries* received a pro rata increase in production funds. Able to address that negative criticism about dreary or patently phony sets, then, Paul wasted little time in heading for London's Chinatown section, and the July 24, 1924, *Bioscope* related how

> Harry Agar-Lyons, in the guise of a Chinaman, created great excitement among the genuine Chinese, who cheered whenever he triumphed in the story [p. 33].

Paul's eight two-reelers were released en masse as the *Further Mysteries of Dr. Fu Manchu* on August 7, 1924; existing records don't reveal whether the abbreviated number of shorts this second time around reflected a sudden flurry of budgetary problems, critical indifference, or Rohmer's ongoing difficulty with his agent.

Save for Joan Clarkson, most of the original cast reprised their roles. Why Dorinea Shirley was tapped as the replacement Karamenah and whither went Miss Clarkson cannot be answered from surviving news items. There is quite a bit less trade coverage of Paul's follow-up series than there had been for the original program, and this may indicate that the bloom was off the rose by July of '24. Only three of the new episodes (numbers one, two and four) were shown to potential exhibitors, and it is only because of the limited press they received that we are aware of their nature. Plot information (below) on episodes three and six is courtesy of the BFI collection. At this time, I can find nothing on episodes five, seven and eight.

The August 24, 1924, issue of *Bioscope* admitted that the series contains "plenty of action and variety" and that members of the company "play the parts for all they are worth." The nameless reviewer nevertheless felt constrained to mention that

> The chief mystery about Fu Manchu is any possible motive for his career of crime, and the impunity with which this homicidal maniac goes about his deadly work without attracting the attention either of the police or the commissioners in lunacy [p. 41].

Apparently, ceding free rein to an Oriental master criminal in London was one thing; having his unimpeded actions hint at shortcomings in the Metropolitan Police Force was quite another.

Now the truth can be told: Before Chuck Barris, there was ... Fu Manchu! Harry Agar Lyons in *The Call of Siva*.

For whatever reason, the Stoll Fu Manchu shorts ended with the release of *Further Mysteries*. While the company would continue producing profitable strings of short subjects (two sets of those *Thrilling Stories from the Strand Magazine* flanked the Rohmer films), the infamous evil doctor would have to wait for Paramount, Warner Oland, and the coming of sound to get his villainous machinery back in motion.

However, in August 1928, Fred Paul and Harry Agar Lyons unveiled a half dozen two-reelers for Paul and A. M. Brooks's Pioneer Films. Borrowing everything from Sax Rohmer's brainchild except for the nomenclature, and mindful of the sundry pitfalls of their earlier Stoll experiences, the men created the *Dr. Sin Fang Dramas* to pick up where Fu Manchu had left off. Lyons, of course, was Sin Fang, while Paul, once again, was his nemesis (herein called Lt. John Byrne) as well as his director. Patrick K. Heale tailored the disjointed scenarios—which pitted Byrne against the evil criminal schemes of Dr. Sin Fang, the head of a Chinese gang in London—from this derivative piece of whole cloth. Pioneer Films did not have Stoll's depth of resources, though, so Fang's nefarious schemes were concentrated in blatantly lower-rent neighborhoods and confined to threadbare, claustrophobic interiors. It appears that only episode five—*The Adventure of the Torture Cage*—is known to exist. No matter whether due to penury, mediocre writing, or slapdash production values, Sin didn't raise half the hackles that Fu did, and the series faded away after episode six, *Under the Tide*, was contractually screened.

Surprisingly, however, almost a decade later, Sin Fang (and Harry Agar Lyons) made something of a triumphant return in an hour-long feature shot by Victory Pictures and released in the United Kingdom by MGM. Fred Paul was not involved with *Dr. Sin Fang*, so Robert Hobbs assumed the guise of John Byrne here and in the sequel, *Chinatown Nights*, a 70-minute-long Victory production distributed throughout Britain by Columbia in 1938. Anthony Frenguelli was the director for the pair. Joining Hobbs in both films were Anne Gray (as heroine Sonia Graham) and Nell Emerald (as a Mrs. Higgins); according to BFI records, Emerald had also produced the first feature.

In the initial feature, Sin Fang, having been sentenced to death, escapes from the police and murders the judge who condemned him; a handsome young man and a fearless young lady eventually track him to his lair. Per the *BFI Monthly Film Bulletin*, "The story needs no comment. The settings are poverty-stricken, but the photography is adequate. Some of the acting is very bad, but Anne Gray acts well, within the limitations of the plot." The second time around, science fiction reared its intriguing head, as film historian Denis Giford reports that the doctor "kidnaps a girl for her brother's 'Silver Ray.'"

Both *Kinematograph Weekly* and the *BFI Monthly Bulletin* cast a critical eye on *Dr. Sin Fang*, and neither cared much for the character, the cast, or the story. I've been unable to find any written trace of trade or popular opinion on *Chinatown Nights*—the *Monthly Bulletin* notes the film's existence without pausing to comment further—nor is there any indication that either picture was ever released in the United States.*

The sheer volume of villainy perpetrated by Harry Agar Lyons while in skull cap and chung-sam should have at least resulted in the actor's being tagged "Britain's most enduring Yellow Peril": The twenty-nine two-reelers and brace of features in which he plotted and schemed as either Fu Manchu or Sin Fang spanned some fifteen years. Born in Ireland in 1878 and educated there as well, Lyons made his stage debut in 1898 in *The Derby Winner* at the Theatre Royale in Drury Lane. He went on to play leading roles onstage in London and the provinces, while making the occasional foray (from 1905 on) into the cinema. Lyons's first films of note were a back-to-back pair of dramas for Brightonia Pictures in 1913: He was Captain Levison in *East Lynne* (Fred Paul costarred in a rival production of the same film released a month earlier)

---

*There is some evidence that *Chinatown Nights* may have been a re-issue title of *Dr. Sin Fang*, but the extended running time of the 1938 release plus the plot-line discrepancies seem to argue against this.

and Captain Jack in *Mercia the Flower Girl*. (Future *Sin Fang* alumna Nell Emerald was the female lead in both productions.) Lyons alternated stage and screen appearances for the remainder of his life, although, as was stated earlier, his identification by the public with Rohmer's evil doctor severely limited the scope of his future movie roles; his poor judgment in reassuming the mantle of Oriental evil a few years later apparently only cemented his cinematic doom. Research has failed to disclose when the screen's first Fu Manchu entered that great Limehouse District in the sky.

It would remain for Hollywood to pick up the gauntlet hurled down by Harry Agar Lyons and Stoll Pictures, and there was no shortage of production companies to do so. Paramount and MGM would furnish Fu Manchu with top-shelf casts and accoutrements, while the independent studios on Poverty Row gave the occasional Chinatown denizen a moment of glory under a lonely streetlamp. (And everyone's absolute last choice for a ravening Chinese mastermind — Bela Lugosi — would be tapped for Republic's deliriously riveting *Mysterious Mr. Wong* in 1935.) Tales of Oriental beauties and implacable hatchet men shared screen time with sagas of Tong wars and secret societies, as cinematic displays of Oriental perfidy were in abundance throughout the '30s. In fact, it was only the onset of World War II that saw the near-Kabuki image of the Chinese master criminal supplanted by the all-too-real (albeit soon stereotyped) depiction of the cunning and merciless Japanese villain.

Still, the movies' fascination with Sax Rohmer's Fu Manchu would see the Mad Mandarin rise again and again and again. And while it's a given that "The world has not seen the last" of "the cunning yellow devil," even in this age of political correctness, it's a shame that these short films — his cinematic roots — have until recently been allowed to lie fallow.

The Mystery of Dr. Fu Manchu

Stoll, September 10, 1923 (Stoll reissue, 1926)

Recurrent Cast: Harry Agar Lyons as Dr. Fu Manchu; Fred Paul as Nayland Smith; Joan Clarkson as Karamenah; H. Humberston Wright as Dr. Petrie; Frank Wilson as Inspector James Weymouth

Credits: *Director:* A. E. Coleby; *screenplays:* A. E. Coleby and Frank Wilson; based on the stories by Sax Rohmer; photographed by D. P. Cooper and Phil Ross; photographed at Cricklewood Studios, London; *editor:* H. Leslie Brittain; *art director:* Walter H. Murton; all episodes two reels

A note on footage lengths: In cases where there are two footage lengths given, the first was taken from Denis Gifford's *British Film Catalogue 1895–1985* and the second from the prints at the British Film Institute; running times reflect the BFI footage at silent speed, although their information doesn't indicate any hard and fast correlation between footage length and running speed. With some exceptions, the lengths derived from the BFI are shorter and correspond to footage measurements taken from BFI archival prints. This may reflect in some instances the absence of that "standard prologue." Opening expository chapter titles are printed in boldface type.

Episode 1 — *The Scented Envelopes* — 2,400 feet

Cast: Charles Vane as Sir Crichton Davey; Booth Conway as Mordain; Robert English as Sir John Astley

(As *The Scented Envelopes* is the only episode missing from the BFI's holdings, we must turn to the May 17, 1923, issue of *Kinematograph Weekly* for the kernel of its plotline.)

Nayland Smith, entrusted by the British and Chinese authorities in Peking with the task of bringing Dr. Fu Manchu, a master criminal, to justice, comes to London and enlists the help of his friend, Dr. Petrie. Knowing Sir Crichton Davey to be in danger, they go to warn him, only to find that he has been mysteriously murdered. The same night an attempt is made on Smith by means of a poisonous insect [which is attracted by the scent in those envelopes]. He kills it and realizes how Davey met his death.

Episode 2 — *The West Case* — 1,800/1,709 feet; 22 min.
 Cast: Wyngold Lawrence as Frank Norris West

"Frank Norris West, American inventor of the West Aero-Torpedo, in which the War Office is keenly interested, is staying in a flat in King's Mansion when early one morning..."

West phones Scotland Yard to report that his apartment has been invaded by a Chinaman. Inspector Weymouth arrives to find West has collapsed, and Smith and Petrie — whom Weymouth alerts immediately — determine that the American has been heavily drugged. Smith knows of the Aero-Torpedo and examines the inventor's bedroom safe, which is still locked. Petrie sends for an antidote to the chloral hydrate pills West has taken and, upon recovering, the American — after wildly shouting "Chinamen! Chinamen!" — opens the safe to find it empty. West admits having gone to the Oriental Club off Piccadilly Circus, so Smith and Petrie head there.

From a private booth in the club, they notice the woman, Karamenah, pass a message to a black man nearby. Smith and Petrie give chase but lose the man, and they are equally unsuccessful in following Karamenah, although they overhear her instructions to the cabbie: "Lady Wimbourne... Second." Back at the apartment, Petrie discovers that West's pills had been laced with hashish, doubtless put there by the mysterious woman who accompanied the American home from the club the previous evening. (It is never explicitly stated that this woman was Karamenah, however.) West explains that Lady Wimbourne is an ocean liner, due to leave Tilbury that very day.

As they race to the docks, Smith explains his theory regarding the theft: Fu Manchu's marmoset climbed the outside of the building holding a fishing line, attached to a rope. Using the secured rope, Fu Manchu and a dacoit entered West's rooms, where the American — his mind clouded by hashish — became susceptible to Fu Manchu's command that he open the safe. Boarding the ship, Smith questions a Burmese man who tries to escape, having thrown his walking stick over the side. He is quickly captured, but one of Fu Manchu's dacoits has recovered the stick, and it is not long after that the Chinese master criminal pulls the stick's handle to reveal the plans.

Episode 3 — *The Clue of the Pigtail* — 1,700/1,688 feet; 22 min.
 Cast: Ernest Spalding as Shen Yan

At a river police station, Nayland Smith and Dr. Petrie view the dead body of

Detective Cadby. On the body is a pigtail attached to a bald wig. Petrie is sent to Cadby's lodgings and there finds Karamenah. She asks him to save her from Fu Manchu. Disguised, Smith and Petrie go to Shen Yan's opium den. Being suspected, they have to fight their way out and, in opening a door, come face to face with Fu Manchu. They fire their revolvers, but Petrie disappears down a trap into the river. Fu Manchu escapes, and Smith and Petrie are saved by Karamenah.

Episode 4 — *The Call of Siva* — 1,700/1,630 feet; 21 min.
    Cast: Harry J. Worth as Graham Guthrie

"With all the forces arrayed against him, Dr. Fu-Manchu still pursues his devilish inscrutable way."

Karamenah overhears Fu Manchu ordering one of his dacoits to capture Nayland Smith. Smith and Petrie, meanwhile, decide to visit Graham Guthrie, a British resident of North Bhutan currently staying at the Hotel Cecil in London, as they fear Fu Manchu will try to prevent Guthrie's safe return to Bhutan. En route to the hotel, the men are captured by dacoits, bundled into a truck, and subsequently chained up in Fu Manchu's dungeon. The mad mandarin threatens them with pythons, wire jackets, spiders and scorpions before revealing that Guthrie will die from the "call of Siva" at 12:30 that very night; Smith shudders, remembering his own time in Rangoon. Fu Manchu leaves and Karamenah arrives to free the men, who don blind-folds and are led to a riverbank. They swear to remain blindfolded until the clock strikes.

Big Ben strikes 10:30, and the men discover they are on the River Thames by Windsor Castle. As they race for the last train to Waterloo, Smith explains that the victims of the "call of Siva" would commit suicide by throwing themselves off buildings. Rushing to the Hotel Cecil, the men warn Guthrie that if he wants to leave England alive, he must follow their every instruction. Meanwhile, as Fu Manchu watches from Cleopatra's Needle, one of his dacoits scampers along the hotel roof. The dacoit hangs over the edge of the roof and makes a noise at Guthrie's window. Smith, armed with a revolver, leans far out the window, anchored by Guthrie and Petrie. The dacoit lassoes him with a rope and begins to strangle him, but Smith shoots the would-be killer, who falls to the street below.

Angered at the failed attempt, Fu Manchu returns to his lair, where he berates Karamenah and injects her with a drug. Later, in Petrie's study, an image of Fu Manchu walks between the doctor and the adventurer, and they both shudder.

Episode 5 — *The Miracle* — 1,712/2,032 feet; 27 min.
    Cast: Stacey Gaunt as Lord Southery; Napier Barry as Henderson; Austin Leigh as the valet; Pat Royale as Aziz

Smith has compiled a list of prominent men whom he feels are in danger due to Fu Manchu and, when Lord Southery is found dead, goes to investigate. Both Henderson (Southery's legal advisor) and the dead man's valet inform Smith that the nobleman died following a seizure after drinking port. As Fu Manchu advises members of the Si-Fan that Southery will be sent on to China, where he will begin to work for their organization, Karamenah visits Smith and Petrie to ask for their help in attending to her younger brother, Aziz, who is deathly ill.

Concealed in a corner of an opulent room in Fu Manchu's lair, the men watch as the evil genius injects the boy—who appears as if dead—with the contents of a certain bottle. Aziz is immediately restored to consciousness. Karamenah passes the bottle to Petrie, who escapes and—together with Smith—uses the mysterious liquid to restore "life" to Southery. Fu Manchu and his dacoits are too late to prevent the nobleman's recovery, and they flee, along with Karamenah. Smith discovers that Southery's valet—a minion of Fu Manchu—had poisoned the port, but the man takes poison and eludes the hangman.

Episode 6—*The Fungi Cellars*—1,630/1,607 feet; 21 min.
   Cast: Pat Royale as Aziz

   Karamenah, the slave girl, promises to deliver Fu Manchu to Nayland Smith and Dr. Petrie if only they will save her brother, Aziz. She leads the two men in company with Weymouth to the Chinaman's haunt, forces them to carry out her brother and then shows them Fu Manchu, asleep, at the same time begging them not to enter his room. The three adventurers promptly disobey, with the result that they fall through a trap in the floor.
   Together with Karamenah, the men are bound hand and foot by dacoits, while Fu Manchu gloats. As the police enter one end of the lair, Fu Manchu lowers a glass wall that traps them in a room where large fungi are growing on the walls. The fungi throw off large spores, which poison the trapped police in full view of their three bound comrades.
   Reinforcements arrive, and Fu Manchu bundles his bound prisoners onto a boat, preparing to make his way down the Thames to freedom. The boat is outfitted with a bomb on a time fuse. The evil doctor is about to kill Karamenah when Weymouth breaks loose and begins to struggle with Fu Manchu; both men fall into the water. The captives are rescued by a police boat before Fu Manchu's bomb can explode. Weymouth, leaving the mandarin to drown, is picked up, but the Chinaman is safely washed ashore.

Episode 7—*The Knocking on the Door*—2,228/2,179 feet; 29 min.
   Cast: W. G. Saunders as James Weymouth, Pat Royale as Aziz

   "In a struggle on a motorboat, Fu-Manchu and Inspector Weymouth fell overboard. So far no trace of them has been found."
   At Maple Cottage—Inspector Weymouth's home—Nayland Smith, Dr. Petrie and Karamenah console James Weymouth, the inspector's brother. In his struggles with Fu Manchu, it appears that the inspector was poisoned by a needle intended for Karamenah and is now behaving as though insane. What's more, James relates how the inspector's wife wakes up every morning at 2:00 A.M. to the sound of a knocking at the door. Instructing James to keep them informed, the three—plus Karamenah's brother, Aziz—make for Madame Tussaud's waxworks. Aziz comes across a wax figure that frightens him, and he tells the others he has just seen Fu Manchu! The figure—that of a bearded gentleman—leaves the building and Smith et al. follow him; the man is Professor Jenner Monde. Petrie escorts Karamenah and Aziz to their hotel room—which is under police guard—and returns to Smith's digs, where they are visited by James Weymouth. He, too, has heard the knocking on the door, followed by fiendish laughter! Petrie and Smith accompany the inspector's brother back to Maple Cottage.

Karamenah (Joan Clarkson) and Dr. Petrie (H. Humberston Wright) look on as Fu Manchu (Harry Agar Lyons) raises the blood pressure of young Aziz (Pat Royale).

Meanwhile, Karamenah, Aziz, and the police guard leave for Petrie's house, as the young woman has received a message supposedly from Petrie advising her that she is in danger. Karamenah's taxi is attacked by dacoits, and she is once again in Fu Manchu's power. At Maple Cottage, Petrie is upset by a vision of Fu Manchu in both a clock and his cigarette case. The knocking at the door reveals Inspector Weymouth, now completely insane. As Weymouth is restrained, word comes to Smith that Jenner Monde has been apprehended. Racing to London, Smith unmasks Monde as Fu Manchu. The men work out a deal whereby Fu Manchu agrees to restore Weymouth's sanity, but in a spot where his methods may not be observed. Bringing everyone together in a deserted cottage on a desolate heath, the evil genius does as he has promised. Weymouth emerges from the cottage, sane and with a note in hand. Before the police can storm the cottage, however, there is a tremendous explosion. Later, Smith reads the note: "I am called by one who may not be deceived. Out of fire I came — into fire I go. Search not my ashes as I am lord of the fire! Fu-Manchu!"

Episode 8 — *The Cry of the Nighthawk* — 1,773/1,767 feet; 25 min.
    Cast: Harold Cundell as Forsyth

Nayland Smith believes that Fu Manchu is behind the mysterious death of a man from the Forest Hill area, whose face is covered with scratches. Intending to kill Smith that very night, Fu Manchu checks on the sleeping Karamenah (who, following a beating, is back in his power) and readies a black cat, whose claws have been coated with a fast-acting poison. Back at his surgery, Petrie readies himself to attend to Forsyth, a late-arriving patient. Everyone — Forsyth, Petrie and the just-arrived Smith and Inspector Weymouth — is drawn to a tree bathed in light, outside the surgery. Forsyth runs to investigate, but a dacoit in the tree, uttering a cry like a nighthawk, drops the cat onto Forsyth's raised face. As the dacoit escapes, Forsyth stumbles across the street and dies at Petrie's feet, the unfortunate victim of an assassination attempt on Nayland Smith.

The next morning Smith — armed with milk, fish and a trowel heads off to find Fu Manchu. While boarding a tram, Petrie notes a suspicious old woman, whom he follows into a field, where she is setting a trap. The old woman is Karamenah, whose bruised and bloody back explains her temporary allegiance to Fu Manchu. Dropping her sack and belongings, the scarred woman makes her escape. Not long thereafter, Petrie comes upon Smith on an island in a lake. Smith wades onto the shore, explaining that he has buried something with deadly claws, and then chastises Petrie for allowing Karamenah to go free.

That evening the tree is again covered with light. Smith and Petrie carefully make their way over to it, and Smith shoots the dacoit he sees in its branches. Smith explains that the nighthawk cry made the victim look up, and the poisoned claws of the cat did the rest. They leave the scene. Fu Manchu, angered that he has again been foiled, appears — and then disappears — in front of the tree.

Episode 9 — *Aaron's Rod* — 1,862 feet (BFI holds only reel 1 — 689 feet; 12 min.)
  Cast: Percy Standing as Abel Slattin; Bob Vallis as Busker (Reel 1 of *Aaron's Rod* is missing from the BFI holdings; at present, I have been unable to discover its contents anywhere. The following is the plot summary of reel 2.)

Smith, Petrie and Weymouth are at the house of Abel Slattin, who has been killed in a mysterious manner. Fu Manchu, with an unwilling Karamenah at his feet, has a servant beaten when he fails to bring the mad mandarin the authentic "Aaron's rod," a walking stick with a serpent's head for a handle. The servant is sent to retrieve the genuine article. Weymouth phones Smith — who is at his apartment, pondering Slattin's death — to inform him that someone broke into the victim's house and then escaped. Smith returns to the house, determined to catch the burglar if and when he returns to the scene.

Fu Manchu's servant does indeed return — through a skylight — but he is overpowered by Smith and rendered unconscious by Petrie, who is wielding Aaron's rod, which he has taken from a nearby rack. Smith examines the rod and has Petrie look at the other stick, still in the rack. Petrie does so and exclaims that the rod is alive: The serpent's head is *moving*! As Smith explains how Slattin was killed, a flashback shows the unfortunate man being bitten by the snake.

Episode 10 — *The Fiery Hand* — 2,174/2,223 feet; 29 min.
  Cast: Pat Royale as Aziz

Smith and Petrie are asked by Inspector Weymouth to investigate the mysterious deaths of two previous tenants at "The Gables"; both have apparently been frightened to death! Disguised as two professors of the occult, the men plan on spending the night in the reportedly haunted house. Left alone, Petrie is nearly scared out of his wits by the tinkling of invisible bells, the opening and shutting of doors without human agency, and the appearance of a naked arm whose fiery hand clutches a dagger. Explaining away the phenomena, Smith reveals that he believes the house to be another den of Fu Manchu! The men decide to investigate a studio on the grounds also.

Back in London, Aziz, a young boy, asks the pair to rescue his sister, Karamenah, from Fu Manchu and in a flashback describes how she was captured by Fu Manchu in the desert. Leaving the boy with a police sergeant, the men disguise themselves, enter the studio, and find Karamenah. She warns them to leave; they ignore the warning and fall into a trap in the studio cellars. Fu Manchu prepares to torture Smith with ravenous Cantonese rats, while Petrie, who has been bound hand and foot by dacoits, has the means to spare his friend a horrible death by using "the friend's sword." Petrie is about to kill Smith when Karamenah creeps onto the scene and shoots Fu Manchu. The three escape; it is later reported that the Mandarin's body could not be recovered because the cellars had collapsed.

Episode 11—*The Man with the Limp*—2,000/1,988 feet; 26 min.
Cast: Julie Suedo as Zarmi; Roy Raymond as Sgt. Fletcher

"Dr. Petrie has taken a suite of rooms in the New Louvre Hotel for Nayland Smith, who has been sent for Sir John Trevor, former British ambassador at Pekin."

Waiting for Smith, Petrie hears a noise in the hall and investigates but fails to see the man with the limp who has made the noise. Although Fu Manchu is presumed dead, Smith fears for Sir John's life, and the nobleman's valet, Beeton, leads Smith to his master, who is delirious and unable to speak. Sir John writes a note — "Guard box! Beware man with limp. Beware Si Fan!" — and the men rush into the other room in time to prevent Zarmi from making off with a box. She escapes, but Petrie discovers flowers in Sir John's bedding. Smith has his friend wash his hands at once, explaining that those were "flowers of silence" that first cause a loss of speech and then death. The men take turns standing watch over Sir John. Petrie hears the limping man and then rescues the slumbering Smith from a light fixture — outfitted with a flower of silence — that has been lowered near his face.

The next day, Inspector Weymouth and Sergeant Fletcher inform Smith that the Joy-Shop Club is run by a man with a limp, and Smith decides to visit. He first intends to take Sir John's box via taxi to a bank vault for safe storage; he never makes it to the bank, as Zarmi had been driving the taxi. Petrie alerts Weymouth and then the doctor — now in disguise — and Fletcher head to the Joy-Shop Club. While police reinforcements wait outside the club, the men enter, where they are greeted by Zarmi. After a man with a limp passes through the club, Zarmi has the two men move a large crate, which — they are convinced — holds the body of Nayland Smith. Moving the crate outside, the men signal for the police, while Zarmi, the man with the limp and a dacoit make their escape on a boat. The club is raided, Nayland Smith is rescued and the crate is found to contain both the treasure of the Si-Fan and Sir John Trevor's box. Smith reveals that the man with the limp was Fu Manchu.

Episode 12—*The Queen of Hearts*—1,750/1,918 feet; 25 min.
Cast: D. Bland as Logan; Julie Suedo as Zarmi; Fred Raynham as Sir Baldwin Frazer; Madge Royce as the Negress

Petrie is awakened by Smith and informed that renowned surgeon Sir Baldwin

Frazer has disappeared. With Inspector Weymouth, the men interview Logan, Frazer's secretary. Logan recounts how a mysterious woman has implored the surgeon to go off with her to examine her sick mother. Suspicious, Logan contacted Scotland Yard. Smith and Weymouth scout the London streets, while Petrie is instructed to wait at the hotel. Tired of waiting, Petrie goes out and sees Zarmi, a female member of the Si-Fan. Following her into the countryside via taxicab, Petrie is set upon by thugs in the employ of Fu Manchu and hidden in a cart full of laundry in charge of a Negress.

Smith and Weymouth worry about Petrie, who shortly thereafter returns in a dazed condition. In a flashback, he tells them how he was taken to a house where Sir Baldwin was being held prisoner. Fu Manchu, limping and with a contorted face, explains that due to a bullet wound he suffers from partial paralysis; he wants Baldwin Frazer to operate and Petrie to act as anesthetist. Both doctors refuse initially but then agree when Karamenah is threatened. After the operation, both men are released: Frazer with a sizable fee, but Petrie has had to draw the high card to determine his fate, and the queen of hearts was the reward for him.

The screen's first portrayer of Sax Rohmer's Mad Mandarin: Harry Agar Lyons as Stoll's Fu Manchu.

Episode 13—*The Silver Buddha*—1,570/1,583 feet; 21 min.
   Cast: E. Lewis Waller as Salaman

On the lookout for Dr. Fu Manchu, Smith and Petrie wander about near the British Museum. Smith enters the museum, and Petrie heads toward an antique shop on Museum Street, where he browses among the artifacts. About to leave, Petrie spots Karamenah; he reenters the shop and, in an effort to avoid suspicion, inquires about a silver Buddha. The salesman prevaricates, so Petrie knocks him out cold. Pressing a panel behind the Buddha, he is confronted by Fu Manchu.

The evil Mandarin reveals that he plans to make Petrie one of his experimental chemists. Left alone by Fu Manchu, Petrie is released by Karamenah. In order to safeguard the girl, Petrie ties her up and escapes by swinging on the hook of a crane that is positioned near the window. Fu Manchu shoots at the fleeing man—but misses—and orders that the antique shop be abandoned on the spot. Petrie heads by taxi to Scotland Yard, where Smith and Inspector Neymouth order a raid on the Museum Street premises. They arrive too late, though; Fu Manchu has escaped again.

Episode 14 — ***The Sacred Order*** — 1,700/1,843 feet; 24 min.
   Cast: Percy Clarbour as Inspector Wills; Laurie Leslie as a dacoit; H. Manning as Mandarin

   A servant of Fu Manchu arrives at Smith and Petrie's residence and offers to hand over Fu Manchu, but only one of the pair of adventurers may accompany him. As proof of his intentions, the servant shows Smith the "Sacred Order," a document promising that all doors will be opened for Sir Denis. Smith agrees to go, but he slips the order out of its box and gives it to Petrie, returning the box to the servant. They go, and nothing is heard of Nayland Smith from that point on. Inspector Weymouth raids one of Fu Manchu's lairs, but Smith is not being held there.

   Anxious about his friend, Petrie takes a taxi to the docks; leaving the Sacred Order in the care of the driver, Petrie explores the docks. While walking through some tunnels, he is grabbed by dacoits and imprisoned alongside Smith. Meanwhile, a furious Fu Manchu, having discovered the Sacred Order missing, attacks his servant. Back in the cell, Petrie awakens and releases Smith, although he puts the chains back on Smith and feigns unconsciousness when he hears someone approaching. Karamenah enters with a servant, who ties Petrie up. When they leave, Smith frees himself from the unlocked chains and unties his friend.

   In making their escape, the men overhear Fu Manchu being threatened for having lost the Sacred Order, a circumstance regarded as sacrilegious. As they consider fleeing via a trap door used by a dacoit, the men are warned by Karamenah not to do so, but to follow her. Hesitating, the adventurers are captured once again. Taken to Fu Manchu, Smith strikes a bargain: They will return the Sacred Order to Fu Manchu in exchange for their freedom and safe passage. Fu Manchu agrees, Petrie retrieves the document from the taxi driver, and he and Nayland Smith are set free.

Episode 15 — ***The Shrine of the Seven Lamps*** — 1,672/1,689 feet; 22 min.
   Cast: Roy Raymond as Sgt. Fletcher

   En route to London, Petrie shares a compartment with a mysterious woman who causes him to dream of Fu Manchu. On the way to meet Smith, the doctor sees the Mandarin's pet marmoset; he follows the animal into a house and, from a veiled doorway, witnesses a Si-Fan ceremony. Among the gang is a disguised Nayland Smith; outside, Weymouth and the police prepare to raid the Si-Fan headquarters. The lady from the train enters, and Smith gives the signal for the raid. Fu Manchu tries to escape but is cornered by Petrie. The villain offers to trade Karamenah for his own safety. Petrie agrees but is instead locked up with Karamenah as the Mandarin prepares to escape anew. He is shot by Smith.

   A reception is held in Peking in honor of the gallant detective and his colleagues. After Smith is decorated, Petrie asks for the hand of Karamenah, who has so often helped the men in their struggles against Fu Manchu.

The Further Mysteries of Dr. Fu Manchu — Stoll — August 7, 1924

   Recurrent Cast: Harry Agar Lyons as Dr. Fu Manchu; Fred Paul as Nayland Smith; H. Humberston Wright as Dr. Petrie; Frank Wilson as Inspector James Weymouth; Dorinea Shirley as Karamenah

Credits: *Director:* Fred Paul; *screenplays:* Fred Paul; based on the stories by Sax Rohmer; photographed by Frank Canham; *art director:* Walter H. Murton; all episodes two reels

Episode 1—*The Midnight Summons*—1,791 feet

The dead body of Fu Manchu is stolen from a mortuary by his followers, and in a short time, Nayland Smith learns in Burmah [sic] that the notorious doctor is still alive. He recognizes Karamenah, Fu Manchu's unwilling slave, who, having married Dr. Petrie, has been rekidnapped by the Chinaman and is now wandering through Burmah during a lapse of memory.

Episode 2—*The Coughing Horror*—1,775/1,871 feet

Cast: Fred Morgan as Antonio Strozza; Johnny Butt as Farmer; Harry Rignold as Coughing Horror; Henry Wilson as Dacoit

Smith and Petrie are captured by Fu Manchu, but Smith saves one of Fu Manchu's victims, Antonio Strozza, and before long all are rescued by the police.

Strozza hides out at his cousin's farm, but he is awakened nightly by the "Coughing Horror," an apelike creature that tries to strangle him. Strozza's cousin goes to Smith and Petrie for help, and the men return to the farm, concealed in a wagonload of baskets. As the Horror attacks Strozza that very night, Smith and Petrie battle it with such determination that the creature's arm is torn off at the socket. Wounded, the Horror rejoins Fu Manchu; tragically, Strozza is found dead, with the Coughing Horror's hand still at his throat.

Episode 3—*Cragmire Tower*—2,040/1,714 feet

Cast: George Foley as Hagar; Rolfe Leslie as Kegan Van Roon and Ki Ming

Smith and Petrie are decoyed to Cragmire Tower by the mysterious Kegan Van Roon. As it becomes evident that Van Roon is really Fu Manchu's associate, Ki Ming, the two men narrowly escape with their lives.

Episode 4—*The Green Mist*—1,734 feet

Hurrying back to England, Nayland Smith assists in the rescue of a clergyman who is being tortured by Fu Manchu. He is nearly suffocated by a poison gas with which Fu Manchu endeavors to destroy Sir Lionel Barton, an Egyptologist.

Episode 5—*The Café L'Egypte*—2,270 feet

Episode 6—*The Golden Pomegranates*—2,100/2,094 feet

Cast: Julie Suedo as Zarmi; Fred Hearn as Waiter

Smith and Petrie get their hands on Fu Manchu's Tulum Nur Chest. Together with Karamenah, they take the chest to their hotel, where, during the night, a would-be thief tries to force it open; he collapses and dies, screaming: "Golden pomegranates!" Running out for help, Karamenah is nearly captured by Zarmi, but she is rescued by Inspector Weymouth. The men force open the chest and find that the pomegranates within conceal the poisoned lance that killed the thief. Karamenah agrees to bring them to Fu Manchu's haunts. While she, Petrie and the police wait outside, Smith—disguised as a drunken seaman—enters, but he's quickly spotted by Fu Manchu, himself in disguise.

Shortly thereafter, as a funeral procession passes by, Petrie and the police raid the place. Outside, Karamenah is spotted by dacoits, who make off with her. Nothing of Smith can be found, except for his pipe, but Petrie remembers the funeral procession and deduces that it was his partner who was in the casket. Meanwhile, in the cellar, Fu Manchu gloats over Smith, who's stretched out on the floor, and Karamenah, who is imprisoned in a mummy case. The Mad Mandarin releases snakes and rats into the cellar, but Smith and the girl are rescued by Petrie and the police, who have forced one of Fu Manchu's accomplices to reveal their whereabouts. Fu Manchu, however, makes his getaway.

Episode 7 — *Karamenah* — 2,366 feet

Episode 8 — *Greywater Park* — 2,390 feet

Dr. Sin Fang Dramas — Pioneer — April 1928

Recurrent Cast: Harry Agar Lyons as Dr. Sin Fang; Fred Paul as Lieut. John Byrne; Evelyn Arden as Betty Harberry; Wally Patch as Bill Riggers
Credits: Producers: Fred Paul and A. M. Brooks; director: Fred Paul; screenplay: Patrick K. Heale

Episode 1 — *The Scarred Face* — 1,908 feet

Episode 2 — *The Zone of Death* — 1,970 feet

Episode 3 — *The Light on the Wall* — 1,930 feet

Episode 4 — *The Living Death* — 1,908 feet

Episode 5 — *The Adventure of the Torture Cage* — 1,992 feet

In a pub, Bill Riggers overhears a Chinaman, Ya Ling, and a bowler-hatted man discuss how Sin Fang "will pay 1000 pounds for the seal," and he follows the two when they leave. Moments before they all arrive at a back-alley door, another man is admitted there and taken to Sin Fang: The man imparts some news to the doctor, who becomes visibly excited. Soon after, Ya Ling and the man in the bowler are let into the building, and the man is seated in the room where Sin Fang had just been. Outside, Riggers finds the door locked and is unable to get in.

In another part of London, Lieut. John Byrne is talking with Evelyn Anders, holding her hand all the while. The phone rings: It is Riggers, reporting in. He is told to do nothing until Byrne arrives on the scene. Evelyn is agitated upon hearing this, but Byrne kisses her and leaves. Back at Fang's, the bowler-hatted man suddenly finds himself in darkness. Curtains at one end of the room are spot-lit and part to reveal a skeleton. The curtains quickly close, and the beam of light moves and then rests on a mummy case, which opens to reveal Dr. Sin Fang, eyes closed with his arms across his chest. Fang walks slowly out of the case and toward the terror-stricken man; he claps his hands and the lights in the room come on. Meanwhile, in the back alley, Riggers is attacked and overpowered by a number of Chinese, who take the unconscious man into the basement.

Inside, the bowler-hatted man is trussed up and searched. "Deliver up the Sacred Seal and you shall go unharmed!" promises Fang. When informed of Riggers's capture, Fang leaves the room, and the hapless man — who does not have the seal on his person — is strangled by the evil doctor's henchmen. Entering the basement, Fang sees that Riggers has been placed in a large wooden cage: His head is sticking out of the top end, and he is standing on a board some two feet off the floor. While this is happening, Evelyn Anders has alighted from a taxi right outside. In the basement, Riggers, now hanging by his neck in the cage, is released and falls unconscious to the floor, while Fang stands over the prone body of Byrne. Upstairs, when a Chinese henchman dashes out the back door to buy a newspaper, Evelyn slips through the door and makes her way into the room where the body of the strangled man sits. She touches him and he falls to the floor. She gives out a small cry and slips an object she finds on the now vacant chair (obviously the Sacred Seal) into her pocket. As she leaves the room, Fang enters, having been alerted by the woman's cry, but his attention is drawn to the man's body—which is now on the floor—and he fails to see her. As he turns and leaves the room, he is followed by Evelyn.

Following Fang to the basement, Evelyn sees Riggers being placed in a mummy case while Byrne is carried away. Heading outside, she watches Fang oversee the loading of a wooden crate and the mummy case into the back of a van. She follows the van in the taxi in which she had arrived. The vehicles travel through London and out into the countryside. When the van arrives at the side of a lake, Fang and his five henchmen are surprised to find that Byrne is no longer in the crate. Riggers, who has come to in the meantime, leaps from the mummy case and attacks Fang. As the henchmen join in the fight, Byrne, who has been watching from some nearby hedges, rushes in to join the fray. Evelyn's taxi pulls up while the mêlée is taking place, and from the cab's back door alight three policemen, who likewise take part. Fang makes his escape via a motor boat which has been idling nearby, but he's shot by Evelyn, who has produced a revolver.

As Fang's henchmen are marched off into custody, Evelyn hands over to Byrne both the pistol and the Sacred Seal. "Darling," coos Byrne, "you have saved not only my life, but also the world from the curse of Sin Fang."

Episode 6—*Under the Tide*—1,900 feet

Dr. Sin Fang (feature)— Victory — September 1937 — 60/63 minutes

Cast: Harry Agar Lyons as Dr. Sin Fang; Anne Grey as Sonia Graham; Robert Hobbes as John Byrne; George Mozart as Bill; Nell Emerald as Mrs. Higgins; Arty Ash as Professor Graham; with Louis Darnley, Ernest Sefton
Credits: *Producer*: Nell Emerald; *director*: Anthony Frenguelli; *screenplay*: Nigel Byass and Frederick Reynolds; based on the story by Kaye Mason

Chinatown Nights (feature)— Victory— March 1938 — 70 minutes

Cast: Harry Agar Lyons as Dr. Sin Fang; Anne Grey as Sonia Graham; Robert Hobbs as John Byrne; Nell Emerald as Mrs. Higgins
Credits: *Director*: Tony Frenguelli; *screenplay*: Nigel Byass

THE UNKNOWN PURPLE

Carlos Productions— October 1923 — 7 reels/6,950–7,800 feet; 92 min.
Distributed by Truart Film Corporation — States Rights
Cast: Henry B. Walthall as Peter Marchmont and Victor Cromport; Alice Lake as Jewel Marchmont; Stuart Holmes as James Dawson; Helen Ferguson as Ruth Marsh; Frankie Lee as Bobbie; Ethel Grey Terry as Mrs. Freddie Goodlittle; James Morrison as Leslie Bradbury; Johnny Arthur as Freddie Goodlittle; Richard Wayne as George Allison; Brinsley Shaw as Hawkins; Mike Donlin as Burton
Credits: *Director*: Roland West; *titles*: Alfred A. Cohn; *adaptation*: Roland West, Paul Schofield; based on the play *The Unknown Purple*, by Roland West and Carlyle Moore; *cinematography*: Oliver T. Marsh; *set design*: Horace Jackson; *film editor*: Alfred A. Cohn

Synopsis: Scientist Peter Marchmont (Henry Walthall) has succeeded in discovering a purple ray that renders the person using it invisible. Unfortunately, his experiments have taken up so much of his time that his frustrated wife, Jewel (Alice Lake), has found comfort in the arms of James Dawson (Stuart Holmes). Not satisfied with stealing his wife, Dawson frames Marchmont for robbery, and Marchmont is convicted and sent to prison. Jewel divorces her husband and marries Dawson.

Eight years pass and Marchmont is released from prison. Now calling himself Victor Cromport, the vengeful scientist gradually insinuates himself into the Dawsons' social circle, a move that also allows him to spend some time with Bobbie (Frankie Lee), the young son who does not remember his real father. Bobbie's nanny, Ruth Marsh (Helen Ferguson), finds herself attracted to Victor—and he to her—but he cannot allow himself to become distracted from his goal: revenge on his faithless wife and her husband.

Victor arranges a posh soirée, which is attended by the crème of society, and it is here that Mrs. Dawson is handed a note—signed "Unknown Purple"—which warns that at midnight, she will lose the valuable pearl necklace she is even then wearing. Victor sends immediately for protection, and two detectives arrive at the party. As the evening wears on, the Dawsons grow apprehensive, and—as midnight strikes—the room is bathed in a purple light. Out of the light reaches a hand, which snatches the necklace from Mrs. Dawson's neck. The light disappears—as does the necklace—and the detectives are flummoxed, as none of the assembled guests has budged from the dining room table.

A short while later, the Unknown Purple invades the Dawsons' home. From the cone of purple light emerges that hand, which pens a note advising that the safe will be robbed that very night. The detectives are engaged again, but their efforts, which include strewing sand on the floor around the safe, lead to naught. The Unknown Purple ignores the safe and makes instead for the basement laboratory, where Peter Marchmont had long toiled. Retrieving notes and records from their secret cache, the light heads back to the home of Victor Cromport.

All that remains to be done is to frame the Dawsons for theft, much as the couple had framed Peter Marchmont, and this is accomplished in short order. His revenge complete, Victor reveals himself to be that very same Marchmont, and, joined by Bobbie and Ruth Marsh, he appears to be quite satisfied with what he has accomplished and with the future that faces him.

Notorious for his involvement in the events leading up to the mysterious death of gorgeous film comedienne Thelma Todd — indeed, he was thought to be the actual killer by more than one Hollywood star — Roland West would have doubtless preferred to be remembered solely for his work as actor, playwright, and director.

Roland Van Zimmer was born into a show business family in Cleveland, Ohio, in 1887 and had made a name for himself — said name being "West" — by 1904. His early days were spent acting in vaudeville scenes that he himself had authored, and these talents led to his forming a troupe that traveled throughout America, performing such popular West pieces as "The Underworld." His ability and chutzpah enabled him to enter the growing motion picture industry, and *A Woman's Honor* (1916) — an unremarkable five-reeler for Fox Films— marked his first director's credit. He would direct two more pictures in as many years—*Deluxe Annie* (1918), a popular Norma Talmadge vehicle, followed a second, unremarkable Fox five-reeler — and then he headed back East, armed with "The Unknown Purple," a science-fiction drama he had developed with Carlyle Moore. Film historian Scott MacQueen cites "The Vanishing Men," a treatment West had targeted for the movies back in 1912, as the inspiration for "Purple." He also reveals (in his splendid biographical essay in *Between Action and Cut*[1]) that shortsightedness on the part of the Broadway establishment led to West's funding the production himself.

The play opened to good notices at New York's Lyric Theatre on September 14, 1918, and played to full houses for the better part of a year, buoyed by the strength of word of mouth. The part of Marchmont had been entrusted to Richard Bennett — the biggest marquee "name" in the cast — and while the veteran actor had been treading the New York boards since the end of the nineteenth century, he may be best known for his daughters: Barbara, Constance, and Joan Bennett. In one of the entertainment world's many neat coincidences, actor Frank McCormack appeared not only in "The Unknown Purple"— West's only full-length work — but also in the Broadway staging of Crane Wilbur's "The Monster," which West would later film as a collaborative effort of Tec-Art and his own production company. McCormack appeared in neither film.

Also conspicuously absent from the celluloid "The Unknown Purple" was San Franciscan Edward Van Sloan, who had made his New York debut in the Broadway production and who would make a more far-reaching impression in "Dracula" at the Fulton Theatre in late 1927. (It seems that Van Sloan's onstage character — Richard Bradbury — didn't make the picture, either; picking up the slack on film was actor James Morrison as *Leslie* Bradbury.) Van Sloan would gain his greatest genre renown for his involvement with most of Universal's classic, early 30s' grotesques: Frankenstein's Monster, Dracula, and the Mummy. Ironically, the only charter member of the Big Four that the actor didn't confront was the Invisible Man.

Insofar as there was a 1909 British trick film titled *Invisibility*— in which some 650 feet of film were exposed to show a man buying a magic powder that makes him

James Morrison shows Alice Lake *The Unknown Purple*, the play-at-home version (Photofest).

invisible—and as I'm not completely familiar with the collected works of Georges Méliès, I'll venture to suggest only that *The Unknown Purple* was the first *feature-length* motion picture to deal with human beings being rendered unseen. Depicting a focused purple light at the Lyric Theatre was a cinch, and carefully executed wire work, mirrors, and the ever-popular, table-top trap aided the audience's imagination regarding the invisible Marchmont's antics.

Unfortunately, as the film *itself* cannot be seen, we have only a handful of contemporary critiques with which to gauge the efficacy of those effects onscreen. These are not quite as informative as one might hope, though, as the reviews concentrated on the cast's collective credibility and the entertainment value of the story, rather than on the technical wizardry necessary to pull off the more fantastic plot elements with panache. This critical positioning stands in contrast to the press that greeted Universal's *Invisible Man*, produced almost exactly a decade after West's thriller. Prior to that picture's release, the fans' curiosity was repeatedly piqued; after the New York premiere, readers pored over a raft of coverage on the film's special effects. (The February 1933 issue of *Everyday Science and Mechanics* made the picture's optical marvels its cover story.) *The Invisible Man* enjoyed a couple of advantages that *The Unknown Purple* didn't: The Universal film was the result of years of research, writing and personnel moves; both its "source" novel and that novel's author were well known and well respected; it was released in the midst of the early '30s' horror "boom," while audience anticipation was still high and before critical reaction became dulled by thematic repetition.

By way of contrast, only New York theatergoers would have had more than a passing familiarity with West and Carlyle Moore's source play and, with some five years separating the Broadway and Hollywood treatments, even that awareness would have faded somewhat. (*The Unknown Purple* did tour the Midwest after closing at the Lyric, but '10s' and '20s' road companies commonly shared venues with more broadly popular Vaudeville slates, and theatrical engagements that lasted typically a week or less didn't go very far in encouraging name recognition.) And even though it could boast of Lon Chaney in both *The Hunchback of Notre Dame* and *While Paris Sleeps*, Frank Tuttle's *Puritan Passions*, *Schatten* (*Warning Shadows*) from Germany, and two moody thrillers from First National—*Black Oxen* and *Trilby*—1923 was hardly as genre friendly as was 1933.

Existing critiques and synopses indicate that the titular Purple's first exercise in deviltry was depicted via the use of tinted footage, something that was neither terribly novel nor terribly thrilling, even in 1923. Whatever excitement it caused lay in the sight of Henry Walthall's hand emerging from all that colored nothingness, but with no discoverable credit for a special effects technician, we've not even a clue as to how that hand set about snatching the pearls from Alice Lake's neck. The March 25 issue of *The New York Sun* is the least useful (invisibility-wise) of the critiques I've located, as the most pertinent note sounded was when the reviewer noted that "The purple [in the ray] has too much red in it, which gives it a very cheap theatrical look."

A reel or so later, though, when Marchmont invaded the Dawson mansion, he did so as a purple cone that contrasted greatly with the black-and-white background. The practice of hand-coloring individual frames had been around since Méliès' day, and this explains the *purple* cone. The purple *cone*, however, is another story altogether. *The New York Times* (March 24, 1924) didn't elaborate on the "cone," but at least the reviewer appreciated the difference between Marchmont's two appearances, as he wrote, "[This sequence] is much more effective than those where the whole screen is tinted purple." And it's nigh impossible to understand where *Moving Picture World* stood: "The story is entertaining and mysterious but it is without the superabundance of tricks that make such attractions too baffling for general enjoyment." This appears to be a critical formula positing that the cinematic enjoyment of the great unwashed is inversely proportional to the quantity of thought-provoking effects. *Harrison's Reports* (December 1, 1923) was more enthusiastic:

> The most fascinating feature of the picture… is that which shows the hero enabled, by use of a purple light, an invention of his, mysteriously to disappear from view, without leaving one's presence. The skillful way in which the scenes where this happens are handled impress one deeply; one is made to feel as if such a thing is possible to happen in life.

Regardless of whether they were thankful for a minimum of camera trickery or railed against the producers for forging an unknown purple that was rather more on the maroon side, the critics were as one in patting Henry Brazeale Walthall's transparent back. (*The New York Times* stated, "Mr. Walthall, one of the screen's veterans, is thoroughly at home as Mr. Cromport.") In 1923, Walthall was just about midway through a lengthy and prolific career, one that would end only in death, when the diminutive actor collapsed during the shooting of First National's *China*

The motion picture is gone, and I don't know of anyone who has ever seen a poster, so an ultra-rare newspaper ad remains the best we can do (courtesy of Robert G. Dickson).

Clipper in 1936. Although he had worked closely with D. W. Griffith since 1909 — his portrayal of the "Little Colonel" in 1916's *Birth of a Nation* had assured him of screen immortality — the Alabama gentleman left Griffith following that epic's release and sought to take control of his own destiny. None of the pictures he was involved with during the next ten years attained much importance, including *The Unknown Purple*.[2] What remains impressive, however, is the direct correlation between the varied types of roles Walthall played during that time span and the consistent critical superlatives he received for those performances.

Scattered among Walthall's more than 240 film titles are more than a few of interest to us. He did *The Avenging Conscience*— an atmospheric blend of three Edgar Allan Poe stories—for Griffith in 1914 and then went on to *play* Poe in Essenay's *The Raven* the following year. He thrice crossed paths with Lon Chaney: As Michael "The Lone Wolf," Lanyard, he tracked the villainous Chaney in *The False Faces* (1919); his Father James ministered to Lon's Singapore Joe in *The Road to Mandalay* (1926); and in 1927's *London after Midnight*, Walthall was the murderer, and only hypnotism and a brace of Chaneys could bring him to justice. He shared the screen with Bela Lugosi's heavies (*Chandu the Magician*, 1932) and herrings (Mascot's 1933 serial, *The Whispering Shadow*), and did a marvelous job the year he died as Lionel Barrymore's tragic partner in MGM's macabre *The Devil Doll*. He also performed in *Stark Mad*.

Alice Lake and Stuart Holmes—those dastardly Dawsons—made almost 450 films between them, with Holmes accounting for about eighty percent of those. Having debuted in Brooklyn in September of 1885, Miss Lake was just this side of 40 when *The Unknown Purple* was released, so her trysts with Holmes (born in March, the prior year) and trials with Walthall (around since March of 1878) must have struck the younger ticket-buying crowd as rather funny. If nowhere else, the slightly mature ingénue had left her mark some years earlier in a dozen or so classic two-reel comedies that Roscoe Arbuckle and Buster Keaton had crafted for the Comique Film Corporation from 1916 to 1919. Graduating to feature films, Lake spent the 1920s in the same sort of also-ran pictures as Walthall. Walthall worked often and well following the dawn of sound; however, Alice Lake became a casualty.

Stuart Holmes's career also took a distinct downward turn with the coming of the talkies, although the Chicago-born actor plied his craft into the 1960s. His particular dismay lay in seeing the feature roles to which he had become accustomed shrink to (frequently unbilled) bits; his last "uncredit" was 1964's *Seven Days in May*.

Comedian Johnny Arthur made his feature-length debut in *The Unknown Purple*, and he answered Roland West's call yet again to assume the juvenile lead in *The Monster* (1925). Arthur made a career out of playing whiny milquetoasts, and for some his defining moment was his portrayal of Darla Hood's father in the exuberant Our Gang short *Feed 'Em and Weep* (1938). It's unclear from available information just how Arthur's character fit into *The Unknown Purple* scenario. *Variety* notes only that "Johnny Arthur [relieves] the tension through comedy." He's Freddie Goodlittle in *Purple* and *Johnny* Goodlittle in *The Monster*.

West hired Oliver Marsh to photograph the production, and the veteran cinematographer—who counted actress Mae among his siblings—never had much of a genre record, although he shot over 125 shorts and features in the course of almost twenty-five years behind the lens. His only project that approached the sort of full-throttle melodrama that is covered in this book was *Phantom of Paris* (1931), and I've yet to come across anybody who has seen *that* one. Marsh's canny eye was under contract to MGM during the '30s, and the Missouri-born artisan—who died suddenly in May 1941—photographed some of the studio's most notable pictures, among them *Arsene Lupin* (1932), *Night Flight* (1933), *David Copperfield*, *A Tale of Two Cities* (both 1935), and *San Francisco* (1936). Combining the cinematographer's ability with the talent of the Roland West of *The Monster* (released a scant year and a half after *Purple*) may suggest that (a) in terms of composition, *The Unknown Purple* didn't stray far from its stage origins; (b) tints and hand-coloring supplanted starkly lit long shots and close-ups lit from below; (c) most of the action would take place at night, thus ensuring a surfeit of menacing shadow-play. *Variety*'s reviewer "Skig" was impressed:

> More than the usual credit should go to Oliver Marsh, who has handled the intricate lightings most aptly and given them excellent presentation through his photography. The tinting is an important ingredient to the story, and at this house [theater] the purple glow was carried outside the screen itself by the raising of that color through border lights. The instance aided, but slightly draws attention away from the picture [March 26, 1924].

I've not been able to ascertain whether the film's press book suggested the creative theater lighting or whether the theater was under the management of one of William Castle's forebears.

Harriette Underhill (for the *New York Herald Tribune*) preferred the play to the film, and she did not hesitate in informing her readers why:

> On the stage one naturally receives a shock of pleasurable fright when Richard Bennett suddenly before your eyes becomes invisible or turns into a violet ray — when tables walk across the stage all alone and doors open of their own volition. But on the screen one has been seeing these things for years. Why, when the surface was first scratched in the new art it was to produce pictures where furniture moved around by itself and tables were laid out for supper without the aid of human hands. So that part of the original thrill has to be discounted on the screen [March 24, 1924].

Underhill went on to discount the story as well but tried to console any Truart investors who might be reading her column: "It may be, however, that those who did not see the play will be well pleased with the picture." It's intriguing to think that in 1918 Broadway stage mechanics were such that an actor could (apparently) become invisible or turn into a violet ray while mere yards from an attentive audience — and do so credibly, as well. Unfortunately, no theatrical reviews or puff pieces surfaced to corroborate Underhill's recollections of the legerdemain worked at the Lyric Theatre, but I assume that Underhill was hearkening back to Georges Méliès for her magical movie memories.

The Unknown Purple was released throughout major venues by Truart Pictures but was distributed throughout most of the South via the States Rights system. While the "official" (Truart) running time for this lost film is listed at nearly 92 minutes, the prints that made the rounds below the Mason-Dixon line clocked in at anywhere from 82 to 101 minutes.

Notes

1. Edited by Frank Thompson, pp. 105–162. Scarecrow Press, Metuchen, NJ, 1985.
2. This is not to imply that contemporary critics (or audiences) regarded the films as unimportant, merely that the passage of time has shown that they range from being pleasant diversions

to being eminently forgettable. *Harrison's Reports*, for example, concluded that *The Unknown Purple* was "a first-rate screen mystery drama. The production end of it is high class, direction, acting, settings, photography — all being of high order." For all this, there is no inkling that the film was ever rereleased, and time has relegated it — a "charter member" of one of the most popular of film genres— to an obscure corner.

THE SORROWS OF SATAN

Famous Players–Lasky — October 12, 1926 (New York premiere) — nine reels/8,691 feet; c. 111 minutes — general release — February 5, 1927

Distributed by Paramount Pictures

Cast: Adolphe Menjou as Prince Lucio de Rimanez; Ricardo Cortez as Geoffrey Tempest; Carol Dempster as Mavis Claire; Lya De Putti as Princess Olga Godovsky; Marcia Harris as the Landlady; Ivan Lebedeff Amiel as the prince's secretary; Lawrence D'Orsay as Lord Elton; Nellie Savage as the dancing girl; Dorothy Hughes as Mavis's new friend; Eddie Dunn as the marriage clerk (uncredited); Wilfred Lucas as the clergyman (uncredited); with Claude Brooke, Josephine Dunn, Jeanne Morgan, Dorothy Nourse, Barbara Barondess, Owen Nares

Credits: Presented by Adolph Zukor and Jesse L. Lasky; *director*: D. W. Griffith; *screenplay*: Forrest Halsey; based on the novel *The Sorrows of Satan, or, The Strange Experience of One Geoffrey Tempest, Millionaire* (London: Methuen, 1893) by Marie Corelli; titles by Julian Johnson; *adaptation*: John Russell, George C. Hull; photographed by Harry Fischbeck, Arthur De Titta; *art director*: Charles Kirk; *film editor*: Julian Johnson; *assistant director*: Frank Walsh; *orchestral arrangements*: Hugo Riesenfeld; *miniatures*: Fred Waller Jr.; filmed at Paramount's Long Island studio

Synopsis:

Prologue: Lucifer and his supporters, furious that God has created man in His own image, revolt at the foot of the heavenly throne. As he and his followers are transformed from angels into bat-winged demons, Lucifer is renamed Satan and relegated to the position of tempter. The curse continues in no uncertain terms: "Only when all men turn from thee, canst thou resume thy glorious place at God's right hand. Yet for every soul that resists thee, thou shalt have one hour at the gates of Paradise!"

Geoffrey Tempest (Ricardo Cortez), a book reviewer who is barely able to pay the rent, and Mavis Claire (Carol Dempster), a writer of short stories enjoying an equal lack of success, discover their love for one another over a dinner of coffee and rolls one cold, windswept night. The next morning, having enjoyed each other's intimate company (in as much an effort to keep warm as an unbridled act of passion), the two decide to marry. When Geoffrey is told that his services as critic will no longer be required ("You condemn books that everyone likes and praise books no one likes"), however, he returns to his boardinghouse room angry and embittered. Railing against what he perceives to be divine injustice, the unemployed book reviewer snarls, "Money is the only *real* God! I'd sell my soul for money — if there were a Devil to buy it!" A sudden lighting bolt heralds a rainstorm, and, while Geoffrey is closing his windows, the door to his room opens, and a dapper, mustachioed gentleman saunters in.

The gentleman (Adolphe Menjou) introduces himself as Prince Lucio de Rimanez, an old friend of a fabulously wealthy — and hitherto unknown — uncle of

Geoffrey's. Announcing that said uncle has died and named his nephew heir to all his riches, the prince hustles Geoffrey out the door and into the path of the politest of society. Meanwhile, Mavis has returned home from a shopping spree, occasioned by her receiving a "tiny check" in the mail: She has finally sold one of her stories. She busies herself in preparing a little dinner for herself and Geoffrey, whom she expects at any minute. Unbeknownst to her, Geoffrey has already left with the prince, who insisted that "later" would still leave plenty of time to bring the young woman up to date on the news of the inheritance.

Prince Lucio and his charge make their way to an elegant restaurant, where the two dine and the newly minted millionaire is introduced to the Princess Olga Godovsky (Lya De Putti). The princess treats the shabbily dressed young man with indifference until Lucio reveals that large sums of money have just come his way. Waving away as "untimely" Geoffrey's protestations that he should speak with Mavis, Lucio takes the young man out on the town. The night passes and, as dawn breaks, Mavis awakes from her vigil by the dinner table.

Geoffrey has returned to the boardinghouse, but he is again prevented from speaking with Mavis, as much by his own weakness as by the force of Prince Lucio's personality. Thus, Mavis is handed a "goodbye" note—written in Geoffrey's hand although dictated by Lucio—by one of the prince's retainers. Running to the window, she watches as Geoffrey and a dapper gentleman climb into a touring car. Desperately wanting to speak with her ex-fiancé, Mavis chases the car for blocks, but to no avail. Geoffrey has left her for Princess Olga, and the newspapers soon carry notice of their coming nuptials.

The wedding comes and goes, but it isn't long before Geoffrey and his bride both regret their marriage. As the two bicker, new boarders back at the rooming house succeed in having Mavis go out to a party. There, however, she runs into Prince Lucio, who tempts her with riches of her own if only she'll "look after" an elderly man. Despite her impecunious situation, Mavis declines, stating that she'll do things her own way. Surprisingly, Lucio seems relieved at her refusal, and he calls after the departing young woman, "Mavis Claire, though I cannot help you—*you have helped me!*" Almost penniless—she has been told that her editor does not like her recent stories and that "no staff positions of any kind" are available—Mavis grows ill. She collapses into her landlady's arms.

In the interim, Olga has begun to flirt with Lucio. One night, as her husband awakens to find her missing from her bed, she throws herself at Lucio, declaring that *he* is the only man for her. Creeping downstairs, Geoffrey overhears the prince berate the faithless woman, although he cannot fathom the words that are spoken: "Only a little while ago a love that you would never understand raised me a step higher—and now you and your desires drag me back again." Spurned by Lucio, Olga takes poison and dies.

Although he has been blameless in her suicide and has pined aloud for Mavis, Geoffrey once more reviles God: "God's love! God's justice! *I* could run things better than *He* does!" Lucio responds in anger, "I heard you say that once before, Geoffrey Tempest." Deciding to claim what is, in effect, now his—Geoffrey's soul—Lucio reveals himself to the horrified young man in his true form. Confronted by the bat-winged horror, Geoffrey runs out of the mansion and heads for the boardinghouse.

He is pursued every step of the way by the shadow of the demon. Clinging frantically to the bedridden Mavis, Geoffrey begs her to lead him back to God. As Mavis begins to recite the Lord's Prayer, echoed by Geoffrey, the demonic shadow withdraws from her room. At the door, the prince — a faint smile upon his lips— turns and vanishes as mysteriously as he had appeared weeks earlier.

Tales of bargaining with the devil have formed a potent subgenre in the literature of almost every culture, and there is little doubt that the oral traditions that preceded the adoption of pictographs and the invention of alphabets were likewise steeped in such mythic encounters. Traditionally, such tales hinged on the belief that the devil, albeit the quintessential rogue, is at heart a gentleman and is thus compelled to honor the meticulous legalese of contracts. In one variation on the theme, the devil ultimately loses the soul he seeks when his prey — through canniness or contrition — outwits the terms of the deal. In another, just as the human seems to have victory in hand, the dark angel proffers an eccentric — albeit technically flawless— interpretation of a term or condition, and flies off with his prize. If by no means the earliest, Johann Wolfgang von Goethe's *Faust* is certainly the most renowned of these sagas of tempter and temptee, and the flow of films, operas, dramas, ballets, novels, pastiches, parodies and such inspired by the epic work hasn't ebbed yet. (Christopher Marlowe's play, "Doctor Faustus," had anticipated the Germanic drama by some 200 years, but never proved to be as pervasive an influence on the arts. The extrabiblical source of all such verbiage — John Milton's *Paradise Lost*— seems forever to be relegated to required reading lists for grad school survey courses, rather than to the proscenium arch or beaded screen.)

The devil was a frequent leading man in the films of Georges Méliès, where he made his screen debut in 1896's *Le Manoir de Diable*. It took only two years from that point for Englishman George Albert Smith — like Méliès, an enterprising filmmaker and a magician — to expend 75 feet of film stock to record Goethe's masterpiece, which he retitled *Faust and Mephistopheles* for public consumption. Two years after *that*, Edwin S. Porter (who would achieve cinematic immortality with his more mundane *Great Train Robbery* in 1903) directed a stop-motion animation version of the tale for the Edison Studios, which advertised the short film as *Faust and Marguerite*. (In 1909, the studio would shoot a live-action variation on the theme and release that effort as simply *Faust*.) Dozens of one- and two-reel treatments made their way into French, British and American nickelodeons during the early days of cinema, and *The Temptations of Satan*, the first full-length (five reels) feature based on the subject, was thrust upon an unwary America at the end of 1914. In 1917, Fox Films unveiled a "Fox Special Feature," *Conscience*, wherein a prologue depicting John Milton dictating *Paradise Lost* to his daughters gave the viewers a glimpse of those terrible moments when Lucifer and his minions were banned from the heavens forevermore.

Famous Players–Lasky's production of *The Sorrows of Satan* was meant to capitalize on the ongoing popularity of the devil's business, of course, but the back story of the production may prove to be of greater interest to the savvy movie buff than the photoplay itself.

The eponymous source novel, subtitled *The Strange Experience of One Geoffrey Tempest, Millionaire*, had been penned by one of England's most prolific (and eccentric) authors in 1895, the year before Méliès had first empowered the Dark Angel with rudimentary camera tricks. London-born Mary Mackay had won tremendous adulation — to say nothing of having made enormous sums of money — by writing a series of melodramatic romantic novels (usually tinged with psychic overtones and sentimental religious fervor and marked by marginally competent prose) under the nom de plume Marie Corelli. Her first book, *A Romance of Two Worlds* (1886), introduced her to the literary world, but it took *Barabbas: A Dream of the World's Tragedy* (1893) to make her a sensation.

It wasn't long before the author's life was deemed to be as fascinating as her fiction. The Victorian era was a model of eclecticism. Theosophy and psychic religion (Sir Arthur Conan Doyle's preferred terminology) vied with the sundry, established churches for the hearts, minds and souls of believers, yet Corelli's agenda vitae was formed more from her own peculiar takes on life than from any of these. Friends and enemies alike regarded her as a creature of contrasts: While traditional Christianity occupied a very important place in her writings, she remained virulently anti-Catholic in practice. Although she was a lesbian who lived openly with her lover in a restored Tudor mansion bought with royalty money, she nevertheless offered little public support for recognizing the rights of homosexuals in polite society.

Corelli wrote twenty-eight novels before her death in April 1924, but her career had peaked with *The Murder of Delicia* (1896). The works that followed *Delicia* drew ever more hostile reviews, as many literary critics and the more discriminating of the public began to assail the author for her obvious sentimentality and her perceived poor taste. Despite this, Corelli had the satisfaction of seeing some of her novels made into motion pictures during her lifetime. Oddly enough, it was the Fox Film Corporation, an American studio, which first brought a Corelli novel to the screen. *Wormwood: A Drama of Paris* had been published in London in 1890; the subsequent movie version (1915) was adjudged to be reasonably faithful to the printed account of the tragedy of absinthe addiction.

Encouraged by decent box-office returns, Fox then bought the rights to Corelli's earlier work, *Thelma* (published in 1887), a tale of seduction and mountain climbing. Retitled *A Modern Thelma*, the film was released in April 1916; middling receipts dampened Fox's enthusiasm for Corelli, and the whole business put Corelli off America. (As tepid as the movie audience's response had become, it was still much warmer than the reception the novels themselves were accorded in bookstores throughout the United States; apparently, American readers were willing to put up with the lavender prose in question only in small — say, title-card-length — doses.)

In August 1917, then, A. E. Coleby both codirected and starred in a British feature-length adaptation of the author's *Holy Orders* (published in 1908), and two years later, the prolific Maurice Elvey directed the film version of *God's Good Man* (published in 1904) for Stoll Pictures. In March 1921, Elvey gave the Stoll treatment to the author's *Innocent* (from 1911), and that epic remains worthy of note solely for its allowing the twenty-nine-year-old Basil Rathbone to breathe life into the character of Amadis de Jocelyn. Other entries in the Corelli canon were also adapted for the screen, including at least two more *Thelma*s.

Eventually G. B. Samuelson's production of *The Sorrows of Satan* premiered in movie theaters throughout the United Kingdom; the young and very beautiful Gladys Cooper appeared as Lady Sybil Elton, a character that would be missing from the Paramount 1927 remake. There is evidence that scenarist Harry Engholm juggled the source elements a bit for this 1917 production, as Denis Gifford (*The British Film Catalogue: 1895–1985*) summarizes the 5,000-foot silent feature thus: "Girl loves prince who is really Satan but sells herself to the highest bidder." Available information indicates the film had both a prologue set in the heavens and an epilogue grounded in the nether regions. Film historian Arthur Lennig avers that Samuelson's *Sorrows* came about only because of a lack of interest on the part of D. W. Griffith, to whom Corelli had first offered the property.

In her Internet monograph, "Marie Corelli and the Cinema," Jessica Amanda Salmonsen[1] writes that *The Sorrows of Satan* had been filmed in 1911, when Dreadnought Films—an American company—pirated the novel without paying Corelli her royalties. As there is no record of this film having been released, presumably the company was enjoined from doing so. In 1916, continues Salmonsen, the picture was dusted off—new intertitles were fabricated and a bit of editing was done—and the renovated project was presented to the author for her approbation. Payment for the source material was supposedly forthcoming, yet this version also came to a dead end. As I cannot find any information on this production, either (indeed, I can't locate mention of Dreadnought Films *anywhere*), I can offer no explanation for any of this. Perhaps the fact that G. B. Samuelson was standing in the wings, money in hand, diverted the occult novelist's attention.

Apropos of this, Nordisk's *Blade am Satans Bog* (*Leaves from Satan's Book*, 1921) acknowledged that its scenario was adapted from "a novel" by Corelli, without identifying which novel that might have been. Salmonsen theorizes that the source material was *Satans Sorger*, a "mystic-Christian trilogy" that included Corelli's *Barabbas, The Master Christian,* and *Sorrows*. Upon viewing a videotape of the Danish feature, however, I can't detect any direct steals from *The Sorrows of Satan*. I have not, as yet, read either *Barabbas* or *The Master Christian*.

No matter what the ultimate findings on the Dreadnought Films *Sorrows*, Marie Corelli's reputation for being contrary, fanciful and a little off the beaten path has been well documented, and it was her contrariness that prevented *The Sorrows of Satan* from being the first picture shot in Famous Players–Lasky's new London studios in 1920. By 1924, Corelli had passed on to a higher plane, and the late author's estate and the newly named Paramount Pictures came to terms on the rights for the novel. (Famous Players–Lasky and several other enterprises that had merged to form the new company continued to produce features for distribution by Paramount for some time.) Studio infighting (Adolph Zukor excelled at playing Griffith against Cecil B. De Mille) took precedence over bringing the property to the screen, however, so it wasn't until the end of 1925 that the discussion turned again to *Sorrows*.

At that point, with De Mille having left Paramount, the project landed back in the lap of D. W. Griffith, who had passed on it nearly a decade earlier. Half-heartedly (he was no fan of Corelli's prodigious output), Griffith cast about for his leads. His longtime lady friend, Carol Dempster, was a given, but Ricardo Cortez (an Austrian émigré, born Jacob Kranz and subsequently kneaded into a Valentino clone) was penciled in only after the now independent De Mille nixed a loan-out of Rod La Rocque. Longtime Lasky mainstay Adolphe Menjou was a natural for the meticulously attired, urbane Prince of Darkness, and Budapest-born Lya De Putti (whose renown stemmed from her appearances in German cinematic classics by Joe May, Richard Oswald, F. W. Murnau, and E. A. Dupont) made the seductive Princess Olga her debut role in Hollywood.

While Griffith encountered little grief from his actors, he was appalled to discover that a healthy chunk of the budget he was given for *Sorrows* consisted of monies already paid to him in the form of back salary. According to Professor Lennig, the director appealed to Jesse Lasky, and the budget was adjusted upward. Nonetheless, due to costly experimentation with special effects (almost none of which made it into the final cut), only a fraction of the available cash would be seen on the screen. Fortunately, the first few reels of the picture took place in squalid surroundings; the saving graces of clapboard boarding, house sets—as well as several back-lot exteriors—allowed Griffith's minuscule funds to be marshaled for an opulent club scene and a mansion foyer the size of Grand Central Station. And, given Griffith's propensity for extensive rehearsals and numerous retakes, the early-silent-days' practice of hiring "dress extras," who wore their own finery in the scenes for which they were hired, was dusted off to save a dollar.

The Sorrows of Satan opens with a brief, stagey tableau of the angelic rebellion, shot on a Busby Berkeley-esque set of stairs and obfuscated a tad by some undulating optical effects, courtesy of cinematographer Harry Fishbeck. The prologue was thought to be somewhat old fashioned on the day the picture opened, so the sequence was clipped at some point between the film's incarceration in the studio vaults and its resurfacing as an object of study and curiosity in the early '50s. Some years later, the footage was recovered. *Naturally*, it hadn't been stored along with the body of the feature, and the extant prints pretty much reflect what was premiered in 1927. Even without being aware that Griffith was on a monetary short leash, the viewer can't help but feel that, prologue-wise, he is in the presence of a decidedly low-budget spectacle. (Not helping matters is the fact that the camera recorded some of the good angels *hovering* a bit unsteadily on their wires; thus, posturing supplants movement for a noticeable stretch in the short footage.)

The original plan called for Adolphe Menjou to be outfitted in a more or less "traditional" devil's costume, replete with forked tail and mechanical bat's wings. This outfit would be worn twice: following the battle in the heavens, where it would serve as proof positive that Satan was no longer one of the "good" angels (all of whom had blond hair and wore feathers), and at a point in the story where a catalyst of cosmic proportion is required. In his collaborative autobiography, *It Took Nine Tailors*, Menjou related how *that* scene was to have worked:

> I was to make my first appearance during a big garden party. Thunder and lightening were to frighten the guests, and then the heavens were to part and I was to come zooming down from the sky with wings flapping and tail swishing. But I was supposed to be visible only to the audience. The actors couldn't see me until, in the twinkling of an eye and a blinding lightning flash, my devil's trappings had vanished and been replaced by white tie and tails. What a scene! There he stands, the suave and distinguished Menjou, and only the audience knows he is old Satan himself! That sort of hocus-pocus makes great selling talk at a story conference but plenty of grief when it comes time to shoot it [p. 177].

Any moment now, and every one of those blondes is going to be blackened, bat winged, and on his way to perdition.

In all, Menjou spent four days attached to piano wire and suspended in the air. The footage ultimately was scrapped, and Menjou complained that all he had to show for his suffering was "saddle sores" on his ribs. Some quick adjustments were made to the scenario, and, as it stands now, Satan's first appearance — he walks up to a door as his shadow seemingly walks back *from* the door to merge with him; a fascinating example of double exposure and fade — marks one of the very few surviving special effects employed within the story's contemporary framework.

It's doubtful whether the actor is present *at all* in the heavenly prologue. The sequence in the existing print consists solely of long shots, peppered with an assortment of camera angles, and it's virtually impossible to tell one golden-tressed spear carrier from another. At battle's end, following the mass transformation of the losing side into darkly accoutered demons, one is left equally clueless. With his bat-winged apparatus having proved to be a total fiasco, Griffith most likely opted to film the celestial action scene with nothing but extras and stuntmen.

The first twenty minutes or so of earthbound footage unreels slowly, as Griffith takes plenty of time in laying the foundation for his juveniles and making sure that no one misses the discrepancies that exist between the two in matters of faith and morals. The scenario is the basic "boy meets/loses/gets girl" chestnut, tossed lightly with essence of supernatural. For all the interesting camera optics that highlight his entrance and the rather rudimentary shadow work that accompanies his climactic revelation, Menjou's Prince Lucio is more akin to the socially arrogant forces at work in *Brewster's Millions* than to any diabolic entity adept at wreaking cosmic havoc.

Geoffrey Tempest (Ricardo Cortez) comes face to face with the *real* Prince Lucio.

Whereas only the person who *resists* temptation can nudge Satan a notch higher in his quest for personal salvation, man's weak-willed nature condemns the Tempter to almost inevitable success. In the instance at hand, then, there is no need to resort to blatant supernatural folderol in order to set Geoffrey firmly on the road to perdition. Once the machinery has been set in motion, Menjou's demon is thus relegated to the sidelines, where he chugs along, a formulaic element in an overfamiliar story.

The climactic confrontation scene, wherein Prince Lucio sheds his human raiment and reveals himself to Tempest as the bat-winged horror first seen in the prologue, remains the most visually interesting scene in the picture, although it is not terribly cinematic. At first, Lucio seemingly begins to grow larger, but this effect appears to have been accomplished by Menjou's climbing a step or standing on his toes. Tempest then raises his unbelieving eyes to the ceiling — as if taking in the totality of the ever-expanding demon — yet spends most of the subsequent footage gaping at eye level at the creature that casts what is essentially a man-sized shadow. (Given that he is now aware that he's being confronted by the Devil himself, Tempest is rather less than appalled, and some of Ricardo Cortez's gestures and facial expressions are those of a man who is fed up or angry, rather than of someone terrified at this revelation of evil incarnate.)

The January 1927 edition of *Motion Picture Magazine* dismissed Griffith's demon in all of his guises. "Mr. Menjou's performance," stated the anonymous reviewer, "is a little too restrained. Now and then a theatrical gesture or gleam of an eye might have let his audience in on his delight when he achieved his particular end. After all, some things are just theatric… despite the modern school of acting… and Satan abroad in evening dress is one of them." For what it was worth, no one agreed more heartily with the criticism than the man who had worn the tux.

Following the tepidly received *Ace of Cads*, Adolphe Menjou was resignedly gearing himself up for yet another dress comedy. He was, then, pleasantly surprised to find that Paramount wanted him as the lead in *The Sorrows of Satan*, although ultimately he disparaged the picture as "a piece of smorgasbord." While quite pleased at the chance of working with D. W. Griffith, the Pittsburgh-born actor (Adolphe Jean Menjou was his real name) had only Corelli's book to fall back on, as he had been forewarned that Griffith never shot from a script. Menjou got a copy of the novel but didn't like it, and things went downhill from there. "We met every morning in a hall above Keen's Chop House," wrote the actor in his autobiography,

> where Mr. Griffith would explain what we were to do, and then we would rehearse. Interminable hours were spent rehearsing and changing very dull and uninteresting scenes. In the afternoons we went to the studio and shot and reshot… [The] months I spent making *The Sorrows of Satan* were the unhappiest I have ever experienced in this business I love.

Part of the problem may have been that Menjou wanted to play against type, said type being the elegant, slightly world-weary mannequin that won the actor the distinction of being the best-dressed man in Hollywood. The scores of pictures that separated 1916's *Price of Happiness* (his first definite screen credit) from *The Sorrows of Satan* had allowed him a wide variety of roles, but the first few years of the Roaring Twenties saw him cast time and again as a Dapper Dan, so he initially jumped at the chance to play the Prince of Darkness. When most of the planned effects—as overly ambitious and marginally ludicrous as they may have been—were relegated to the waste basket, however, the wind died in the actor's sails. It soon became apparent that, even as the Father of Lies, Adolphe Menjou was doomed to another session in the soup and fish.

Guy Price of the *Los Angeles Herald* admitted that, at first glance, it appeared to be more of the same, with Menjou "wearing evening clothes and his usual blasé manner." As the film unreeled, though, the critic grew more impressed, finding the Griffith-led Menjou "more of the actor and less of the poseur, more of a character and less of a roué." Menjou refused to attend the Broadway premiere and, per his autobiography, never did see *The Sorrows of Satan*.

Ricardo Cortez had portrayed an amorous Hispanic in at least half of the nearly two dozen pictures he had done by the time he pinch-hit for Rod La Rocque, and he must have been grateful that the scenario never once implied that Geoffrey Tempest was the bastard son of Spanish royalty. (Then again, the scenario made no particular effort to underscore the fact that the story took place in England, either.) Early on, his Tempest behaves as any mid-twenties, cinematic Latin might, nearly deflowering Carol Dempster's Mavis Claire mere moments after realizing that the young woman has her eye on him. Mavis reins in her stallion—they later do become intimate, away from prying eyes—and the remainder of the picture details how money is the root of all evil.

Cortez may not have been a great actor, but his pantomime in the several scenes

Dames, devils and daises. An interesting shot that didn't make the final cut.

where Menjou's dapper devil convinces him *not* to make contact with Mavis wonderfully depicts the struggles and the frustrations that signal Geoffrey Tempest's all-too-human weakness. (Reviewer "Skig" of *Variety* observed, "Cortez doesn't impress as being susceptible to Griffith's method of direction.") The climactic metamorphosis sequence — its minor perspective difficulties aside — provides the necessary drama at precisely the right moment, and the prayerful salvation denouement, if perhaps a trifle too pious or pat for us hardened, millennium viewers, buoyed the faith of 1927 audiences, for whom religious warm fuzzies played an anticipated role in pictures such as this. (In 1997's clever *Devil's Advocate*, Al Pacino's Satan-cum-CEO is thwarted, not by prayer and contrition, but via Keanu Reeves's outrage and a handgun.)

The Sorrows of Satan was Carol Dempster's last motion picture, and the lovely young actress went out on a critical high note. Reviewer "Skig," for example, informed his readers that Dempster "leads the cast for plaudits," and the aforementioned Mr. Price gushed that her "winsomeness was never brought more to the fore than in this role. She has woven a thread of sympathy through the part that grips and holds." Mordaunt Hall, critic of *The New York Times*, went on at length:

> Carol Dempster's acting is something exceptional. She imbues the part with pathos and eagerness. She presents the portrait of undying hope, and not even in *Isn't Life Wonderful?* did she give an idea of the talent she displays in this new film.

The nameless commentator at *Motion Picture World* likewise admitted, "It is for Carol Dempster that we save our best adjectives," while using only one: splendid.

By 1926, Carol Dempster had been Griffith's protégé for years, having met the fabled director while a member of the Denishawn Dancers (Ruth St. Denis and Ted Shawn's modern dance troupe), which was then working on *Intolerance* (1916). Following Paramount's *Hope Chest* (1918), wherein she made her debut as a featured player, Dempster moved to a comfy spot under Griffith's wing—Griffith was estranged from his actress wife, Linda Arvidson—whence she would emerge with increasing regularity in consistently more important roles until, with Artcraft's *Girl Who Stayed at Home* (1919), she was a bona fide leading lady.

A good number of the extant screeds on Dempster agree that she was dismissed as being untalented and exploitative by other Griffith regulars. Still the young woman was not spared Griffith's endless preoccupation with minutiae: For *Satan*, she was reportedly photographed 125 times in the act of removing an ironing board from a cupboard. Regardless of whether she had initially enjoyed advantages due to her intimacies with Griffith, she grew into a capable and talented actress. Her performance as the slow-starving Inga in United Artists' *Isn't Life Wonderful?* (1924)—an entry on *The New York Times* "top ten" film list for that year—won over audiences and critics alike. However, despite the fact that her work in *The Sorrows of Satan* had resulted in some of the best notices she had received in her short professional life, after the wrap she walked out on Griffith, Tinseltown, and the whole movie industry. She never regretted doing so. As quoted by Hans J. Wollstein, in a brief biographical essay on the Internet's "All Movie Guide," Dempster revealed, "Maybe my fans would like to know that in real life Carol Dempster had a happy ending."

Given that so much has been written on David Wark Griffith, I would be foolish to attempt a long critique or summation. As I write this, Arthur Lennig (*The Immortal Count: The Life and Films of Bela Lugosi; Stroheim*) is putting the finishing touches on what promises to be the most comprehensive appraisal yet of the man's life and work. For our purposes, it should be enough to know that, even before it was obvious that *The Sorrows of Satan* could not cut it as a road-show attraction, the handwriting was on the wall. Tales of cost overruns (many of which were the result of studio accounting anomalies and not Griffith-induced profligacy), endless rehearsal sessions, and scheduling headaches—plus a seeming dearth of material suitable to the man's particular genius—had shoehorned the erstwhile master filmmaker into a particularly close and uncomfortable niche.

(In *Variety*'s original review of the film, reviewer "Skig" noted that one of the names listed in the movie premiere program—Dorothy Douglas—was nowhere to be found on the screen, a sign that the feature [which opened at New York City's George M. Cohan Theater at 117 minutes] may have been pared prior to its Big Apple debut. A few paragraphs later, Skig observes how, had *Satan* not been a D. W. Griffith picture, it would probably have been whittled down even further, to 80 or 90 minutes. Interestingly, when the film was next discussed in print, its length was listed at 111 minutes. At this stage of the game, Griffith's trademark leisurely pacing was very much subject to criticism.)

Thus, besides being Carol Dempster's swansong, *The Sorrows of Satan* was Griffith's last major silent feature. Happy with neither the source novel nor the subsequent scenario; upset at the studio's duplicitous handling of the project's finances; aghast that the film was extensively recut, without his knowledge and contrary to his wishes; and finally depressed by his conviction that the company's passive reaction to mixed reviews and tepid revenues was purposeful, Griffith parted ways with Famous Players–Lasky shortly thereafter. Of the handful of pictures that lay in his future, only *Abraham Lincoln*— an early (1930) episodic talkie —could be considered a major project.

By the time film writer Edward Wagenknecht[2] put his thoughts on the picture into print, *The Sorrows of Satan* had had a decade's worth of limited exposure as a rediscovered curiosity, more worthy of technical dissection than artistic appreciation. Whether due to his personal disinterest in the relevant Lasky-Griffith negotiations (which saw the latter man to the door before his time) or to the fact that time — nearly four decades had passed by then — had cleared the air, I don't know; however, Wagenknecht hit the nail on the head:

> The supernatural scenes at the beginning of *Sorrows of Satan* showed imagination, and the love story of the first part, where the director was working mainly from his own imagination, had a good deal of his old power and lyricism; but once Maria Corelli's trashy story had taken over, there was nothing much that D.W. Griffith or anybody else could do.

To this day, Griffith's *Sorrows of Satan* has never enjoyed a "proper" release, and fans of any of the principals, the director, or the theme will have to venture again into the gray market to strike a bargain with the devil.

The Sorrows of Satan—G. B. Samuelson — February 1917 — 5,000 feet

Cast: Cecil Humphreys as Prince Ramirez; Gladys Cooper as Lady Sybil Elton; Owen Nares as Geoffrey Tempest; Lionel d'Aragon as Earl Elton; Winifred Delevanti as Diana Chesney; with Alice de Winton as Minna Grey

Credits: *Director*: Alexander Butler; *screenplay*: Harry Engholm; distributed by Walker Film Distributing Company Ltd.

Notes

1. http://www.violetbooks.com/corelli-cinema.html
2. *The Movies in the Age of Innocence*. Norman: University of Oklahoma Press, 1963, pp. 131–132.

WHILE LONDON SLEEPS

Warner Bros.—November 27, 1926—six reels/5,810 feet; 66/52 minutes

Cast: Rin Tin Tin as Rinty; Helene Costello as Dale Burke; Walter Merrill as Thomas Hallard; John Patrick as Foster; Otto Mathieson as London Letter; George Kotsonaros as the Monk; De Witt Jennings as Inspector Burke; Carl Stockdale as Stokes; Les Bates as Long Tom

Credits: *Director*: H.P. (Howard) Bretherton; *story and scenario*: Walter Morosco; *photographed by* Frank Kesson; *asst. cameraman*: Fred West; *asst. director*: William Cannon

Synopsis: Inspector Burke of Scotland Yard (DeWitt Jennings) is concentrating all his forces on the capture of London Letter (Otto Mathieson), a notorious criminal leader in the Limehouse district. The two things that make London Letter doubly dangerous are his possession of Rinty, a splendid dog, and the Monk (George Kotsonaros), a vile creature, half man and half beast, that steals, ravages and kills at the command of the master gangster.

Through the double-crossing of Foster (John Patrick), one of London Letter's gangsters, Burke almost apprehends the gang in the midst of an attempted theft of the Royal Steamship Company's funds, but Rinty's uncanny perceptions foil Burke's coup, and when the dog sounds the alarm, the marauders escape. Without scruple or mercy, London Letter orders his man-beast to kill Foster for his treachery, all of which makes Burke more determined than ever to capture him.

Proud of his dog's prowess, London Letter pits Rinty against another and better trained dog. Rinty loses the fight and is being brutally kicked around by London Letter for his pains when Dale (Helene Costello), Burke's daughter, drives up with her sweetheart, Thomas Hallard (Walter Merrill), who is also a Scotland Yard detective. Dale, furious at London Letter's cruelty to the dog, takes Rinty home with her, and there the almost-human canine becomes devoted to his new mistress and her fiancé.

When Burke learns that Rinty was London Letter's dog, he vows once more to get the master criminal, and he takes Rinty with him on the hunt. In the meantime, London Letter, intent upon a malicious scheme to kidnap the inspector's daughter and hold her for ransom, orders the Monk to make off with Dale. The loathsome creature drags the girl out through her bedroom window without the knowledge of Thomas, who stands guard in front of the house. Half strangled by the man-beast, Dale is carried to London Letter's hideout and there imprisoned, with the Monk chained to the wall nearby.

Meanwhile, Burke and his men, following hard on London Letter's trail, force the criminal to jump and swim for it. Wounded in his efforts to escape, the gangster crawls back to his hideout to die. Returning home, Burke is stunned—as is Thomas—at Dale's disappearance, and the men send Rinty out in search of London Letter. The dog reaches the gangster just as he is about to die. The reunion of Rinty with his former master is touching, but, in the midst of his sorrow, Rinty is aroused to action when a piercing scream from Dale shatters the silence. With a growl, Rinty jumps at the Monk's throat and kills him after a ferocious battle.

London Letter dies as Burke and Thomas batter down the door. They find both criminals dead and Rinty devotedly guarding his mistress from further danger. The alert dog does, however, permit Thomas to take Dale into his arms. As Burke gives the young couple his blessing, Rinty barks his approval.

I recall reading that this picture's title was a not-so-subtle attempt to cash in on an earlier Lon Chaney film, Maurice Tourneur's *While Paris Sleeps*, but I have my doubts. There's no argument over the similarity in titles, of course, but *Paris*—which had been shot as *The Glory of Love* in 1920, only to be withheld from release until 1923, following Chaney's growing renown as the "Man of a Thousand Faces"—was (per existing reviews) nothing especially worthy of association. Still, who could be blamed for arranging even an "inadvertent" link to Chaney? If anything, today's casual student of silent melodrama runs a greater risk of confusing Rinty's adventure with two *other* Chaney films: *London after Midnight* (1927) and *While the City Sleeps* (1928, both from MGM), and the presence of two disparate characters named Inspector Burke (coincidentally, in the "*London*" features) does little to ameliorate the situation.

To that same casual student, the biggest name in *While London Sleeps* is doubtless Rin Tin Tin, the starving pup-cum-wonder dog that had been one of two rescued from the battlefields of France during the Great War by U.S. Air Corps Corporal Lee Duncan. Imported to the states, Rinty went on to make his cinematic debut by playing himself in a low-budget, independent feature, *The Man from Hell's River* (1922), which he effortlessly stole from a cast that included Wallace Beery. Soon enough, the personable German shepherd would play himself for no one save the Warner Brothers, with whom he held an exclusive contract (at $1,000 a week). The upshot of that cushy deal was a string of popular and profitable, silent Rin Tin Tin features released throughout the decade. Following his second and last full-sound film, *Rough Waters* (1930), he retired from Warners and ventured over to Mascot, where he appeared in two serials, *The Lone Defender* (1930) and *Lightning Warrior* (1931). Records show that Rinty—whom Jack Warner had repeatedly called "the mortgage lifter"—died suddenly in April 1932; he was a frolicsome fourteen-year-old (ninety-eight in dog years) at the time of his death. *While London Sleeps* was the only one of the wonder dog's pictures to have horrific elements, and it cannot be argued with certainty whether lovers of the horror film genre (such as it was in 1927) added to the revenues being tallied by Rinty's accountants, or vice versa. What *is* certain is that most of the movie-going public busied themselves elsewhere.

At least it's doubtful that many tickets were sold specifically because Helene Costello was the ingénue. Helene was perhaps best known for being the sister of Dolores and the daughter of Maurice—more renowned Costellos, both—but she did play leads in any number of unremarkable-to-decent movies (mostly for Warners) during the twenties. Like Dolores, Helene had enjoyed the fruits of being a Western Association of Motion Picture Advertisers (WAMPAS) "baby star." This title was awarded yearly (from 1922 to 1929) to the thirteen actresses that that august body regarded as showing the most cinematic promise, and while it cannot be denied that the association was on the mark more times than not, doling out the honorarium to over 100 actresses in an eight-year span meant that the odds of being right were heavily on the house's side. When the talkies arrived, both the WAMPAS honors and Costello vanished from the scene. (Actually, she did have a couple of bits in the mid-thirties' MGM features *Public Hero #1* and *Riffraff* before retiring for good.)

Costello might very well have preferred being remembered more for her playing smaller parts in big movies (she was Mary Astor's maid in the John Barrymore blockbuster *Don Juan*) than for playing damsels in distress in works like *The Fatal Warning* (1929; Mascot's last silent serial, featuring an upcoming Boris Karloff) or *While London Sleeps*. She didn't make enough of an impact as the much-put-upon Miss Burke to warrant her own paean or put-down in the contemporary reviews of *London*—nobody did—but she and just about everyone else (save for the dog) were covered by Variety's blanket assessment: "Technique pretty terrible... Acting also terrible."

For genre buffs, of course, the most interesting character in *While London Sleeps* is the Monk, the "man-beast" played by George Kotsonaros. Kotsonaros was born in Nauplie, Greece, sometime in 1888, and immigrated to the United States soon after the turn of the century. What he did during most of his formative years is unknown, but from the mid-1920s nearly until the time of his death, he spent the odd month or two every year in Hollywood, adding his own particular brand of brutish, ugly menace to over a dozen silent motion pictures. The rest of the time, he toured the country as a professional wrestler.

On May 11, 1931, in what may have been the high point of his mat career, Kotsonaros beat—after a series of unsuccessful earlier matches—and unmasked the dreaded "Masked Marvel" in a grueling match at Madison Square Garden. "George Kotsonaros used to be a fairly well-known wrestler," admitted the Washington Post in its December 9 edition that same year. "Then the movie producers began to glorify the great American gangster, and George's mug was too precious to leave in the ring. He was hauled to Hollywood and did some mighty nice dirty work for the cameras before the tide of moviedom switched to more legitimate fields."

If overcoming the Marvel was arguably Kotsonaros's finest hour in the wrestling ring, it's not so easy to pick a clear winner on the Hollywood scene. Horror fans may find his Monk in *While London Sleeps* a clearly inferior creation when compared with his human-headed ape in Fox's legendary *The Wizard* (also 1927), but such comparisons can be based only on movie stills—in which the most quintessentially banal of predicaments may be manipulated to cause palpitations of the heart—as both features are lost. He also enlivened in his usual fashion Laurel and Hardy's splendid, silent two-reeler, *We Faw Down* (1928); the Hal Roach classic short thankfully survives, and it is here that most folks make Kotsonaros's acquaintance. I, for one, don't find *any* comic undertone at all to Kotsonaros's knife-wielding menace in *We Faw Down*, à la the glint in Noah Young's eye (as the "Tipton Slasher" in *Do Detectives Think?*) or in *any* of Walter Long's or Rychard Cramer's squinty-eyed, gloriously excessive Laurel and Hardy portrayals.

George Kotsonaros was killed in an auto accident in mid-July of 1933, while on a wrestling tour in Alabama. His mantle, if you will, came to rest on the impossibly

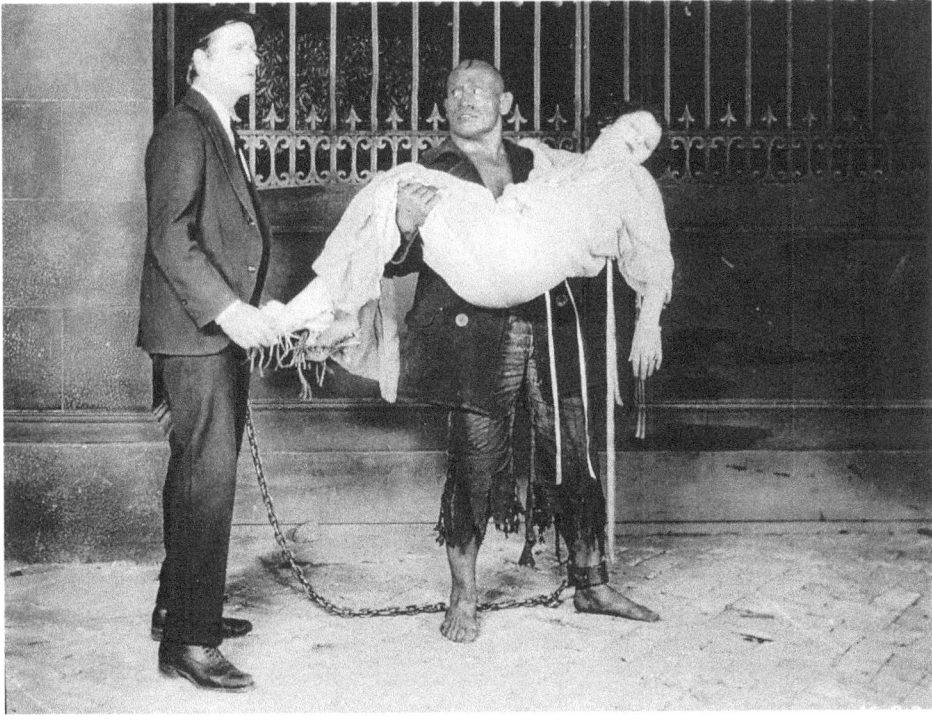

Left to right: Otto Matieson as London Letter (and you thought *Ziggy Stardust* was a stretch!), George Kotsonaros as "The Monk," and Helene Costello as "The Dead Weight."

broad shoulders of Tor Johnson, the Super Swedish Angel, who would make the subspecies "monster-cum-wrestler" into a veritable low-rent art form.

A few readers may recognize the name Otto Matieson, for the Danish character man appeared in some heady silents, including *Scaramouche* (1923), *Captain Blood* (1924), and *The Beloved Rogue* (1927, as Otto Mattiesen). Matieson played the villain of the piece here, and London Letter may well have been the most important part of his career, albeit—with the picture being lost—his presaging Peter Lorre as Joel Cairo in the 1931 Ricardo Cortez version of *The Maltese Falcon* is probably his most notable extant performance. Tragically, barely six months after the release of *Falcon*, Matieson was also killed in an auto accident.

DeWitt Jennings's name may garner a few more nods of the head than Matieson's, what with his turning up in such classic fare as *Seven Footprints to Satan* (1929), *The Bat Whispers* (1930), and *Mystery of the Wax Museum* (1933), but as the Cameron, Missouri, native specialized in police chiefs, judges, and the like, the heads that are nodding doubtless belong to serious genre aficionados. This is to say that, even in one of his biggest genre roles (that of bookseller Louis Bardou in Universal's *Secret of the Chateau* [1934]), he ends up dead very quickly. Whether readers remember him or not, Jennings was—next to Kotsonaros—the biggest genre name in the production.

While London Sleeps marked the first time Howard Bretherton sat in the director's chair without being chased off, and while he did make the occasional incursion into the genre—he directed 1934's *Return of the Terror*, Columbia's loopy serial, *The Monster and the Ape* (1945), and also guided Sidney Toler through his last Charlie Chan adventure, *The Trap* (1947)—most of his hundred-odd subsequent features were Westerns, and whatever name he made for himself was drawn in the dust raised by galloping horses and bow-legged varmints. He wasn't carrying any saddle bags this first time out, though, so the tepid notices his horror picture received can't be chalked up to his not playing to his strengths. Apparently Bretherton capped his career in 1957, when he directed "The Gentle Monster," a last-season episode of TV's *Adventures of Superman*; thus, despite decades of ten-gallon hats and horse manure, the man's professional alpha and omega appear to have been excursions into horror and science fiction.

It was Walter Morosco's idea to move Rinty to Old Blighty, and while that of itself didn't spell doom for the all-American superdog, the drearily predictable horror elements probably did. *While London Sleeps* was one of only four screenplays Morosco penned in 1926. Actually, Morosco's contributions to the industry were some twenty years worth of unimportant feature films (cranked out from 1929 to 1949), wherein he served as producer. Among the efforts where he was *associate* producer were *Charlie Chan at the Wax Museum* (1940), which I like, and *Dead Men Tell* (1941), which I like more; I doubt whether Morosco's impact on these productions is responsible for my liking them as I do. Giving London Letter a bestial henchman rather than the usual armful of nondescript, cap-wearing blokes may have been regarded as a strike for innovation. So, too, may have been the scenario's assigning Rinty (and not the juvenile) the task of felling the Monk moments before his master expires, and the more alert among the audience make for the exits to avoid the rush. Whatever the intent, the execution must have been unremarkable.

The critics were not kind to *While London Sleeps*. Having disposed of the collective thespic endeavor, *Variety*'s "Rush" went on to moan about the camera work:

> It is seldom that a picture comes to light these days where the technical details are not plausibly handled, and no case comes to mind of a product by a going producer that has not at least clear, flickerless photography. There is one bit in *While London Sleeps* where the camera shifted along a line of sitting characters. So inexpert was the management of photographic method that the different figures passed by a series of starts and jerks that almost blur the faces.

Nor did the plot escape the astute reviewer's attention: "The melodrama is laid on so thick it gets into unintended comedy." Paul Thompson, covering the film for *Motion Picture News*, agreed: "I have not seen any picture in months that so vividly recalls the old melodramas of the ten-twenty-thirty-cent days." This was *not* meant to be a compliment on Thompson's part:

> It is not such awfully good melodrama at best and your credulity is stretched to the breaking point by the employment of an ape-like character as the right bower of "The Hawk" [*sic*], the underworld mastermind that was continually thwarting and baffling that great asset of so much English fiction, Scotland Yard—in capital letters. Morosco made a deter-

An original glass slide.

mined effort to send chills up and down the spine by the imminence of this monster's ravishing the heroine, Helene Costello, but somehow it didn't seem to click.

Thompson and Rush had plenty of company when it came to deploring the picture's lurid grounding; nor were they alone in bemoaning what they saw as a waste of the movies' premier wonder dog. It was almost universally held — considering the fact that the picture was written, shot and marketed as a Rin Tin Tin vehicle — that the demands made on the dog's "uncanny cleverness" were very slight. With the above-the-title canine star given little to do that he had not done, variously and perhaps better, in other films, the only special attention afforded him was "more close-ups in an hour than Gloria Swanson ever enjoyed."

Without the actual revenue figures, I'm unable to determine whether *While London Sleeps* ever slipped over to the black-ink side of the ledger. Clearly, the film did not make any of the usual "top ten" lists that year, and it was neither remade nor (apparently) reissued. With the advent of sound, even the best of the Rin Tin Tin silents came to be regarded as amusing curiosities, and it remained for Rin Tin Tin, Junior, to put in his oar for Reliable Pictures' 1935 programmer, *The Test*. (Appearing alongside Junior — as his mate — was a second German shepherd, named Nanette. As Corporal Duncan had named the *other* pup he rescued from death in 1918 "Nanette," we can only conjecture that Rinty's mate in the 55-minute film was enacted by Nanette, Jr.)

As was the case industry-wide, foreign-language titles were shot for overseas markets, and prints were shipped abroad. The fact that no news survives of the picture's financial impact in other countries is not necessarily bad news; however, as the film's commentator in Phil Hardy's Encyclopedia of Horror Movies notes, "The British release version was heavily cut and cleaned up to turn it into a standard Rin-Tin-Tin adventure." The fact that such radical editing was performed in the spring of 1927 isn't terribly surprising, though, even if it did anticipate England's mid-thirties' horror ban by almost a decade. The British Board of Film Censors had been scissoring cinematic imports since 1917, and the London City Council finessed the censors' parameters at the beginning of the '20s. In 1924, the city council had imposed an age restriction, whereby kids under the age of sixteen needed an adult companion in order to get to see a film that was deemed appropriate for adults only. It may have been deemed less trouble to physically snip George Kotsonaros out of the circulating prints than to monitor attendance on this most peculiar Rin-Tin-Tin movie.

It's interesting to note that, while there is a pair of widely disparate running times attributed to *While London Sleeps*, only one citation of footage length is available, regardless of the sources one consults. I can't see any possibility of the fourteen-minute difference being attributed to the idiosyncrasies of hand-cranked projection, so the shorter figure may reflect an edited version (perhaps the British print, mentioned earlier) that I have thus far been unable to track down.

THE MONKEY TALKS

William Fox Productions— February 20, 1927 — 5,500 feet
Cast: Don Alvarado as Armand Durand; Jacques Lerner as François Faho and Jocko; Raymond Hitchcock as Lorenzo; Jane Winton as Musette; Olive Borden as Olivette; Malcolm Waite as Bergerin; August Tollaire as Jules Ostermoore; Ted McNamara as Firmin
Credits: Presented by William Fox; *director*: Raoul Walsh; *scenario*: L. G. Rigby; based on the play Le Singe Qui Parle, by René Fauchois; photographed by William O'Connell; *assistant director*: R. Lee Hough; *makeup*: Jack P. Pierce

Synopsis: Armand Durand (Don Alvarado) — an ex-member of the French Flying Corps who is due to inherit a fortune and a title — is in love with Musette (Jane Winton), a member of a traveling circus. Musette, however, is attracted only to Armand's wealth and position, and when she learns that his father has disinherited Armand because of his feeling for her, she drops him in favor of Bergerin the Magnificent (Malcolm Waite), the circus's husky lion tamer.

As Armand sit mournfully in a café, he's recognized by François Faho (Jacques Lerner), an old chum of his from the Flying Corps. Faho persuades his ex-captain to join the circus and then convinces Lorenzo (Raymond Hitchcock) to hire him. It's not long before the three men, along with Jules Ostermoore (August Tollaire), the circus owner, have banded together to create an act. Unfortunately, the gendarmes catch up with the circus, and it and the act are dissolved, due to nonpayment of outstanding bills. Dubbing themselves the "Four Musketeers," the men decide to dress up Faho and pass him off to curious ticket buyers as a talking monkey.

Some months later, "The Monkey Who Talks" is the hottest act in Paris, and it also appears that Papa Jules has taken over management of the theater where the hirsute Faho appears. Sharing the bill is Olivette (Olive Borden), an attractive young tightrope walker; she finds herself attracted to Armand, and he to her. Faho, now known as Jocko, is also in love with Olivette, and he confesses as much to Armand. In an effort to be fair, Armand promises to give Faho a level playing field regarding the young wire walker: "I will not speak while she cannot see you as a man!"

Complicating matters is the presence of Musette and Bergerin, whose act has been signed on unknowingly by Jules. Armand informs Lorenzo of Musette's treachery, though, and Lorenzo has Jules cancel the lion-tamer's contract. Musette first tries to change Armand's mind by throwing herself at him, but the steadfast young man will have none of it. Seeking revenge, she and Bergerin then plot to steal Jocko and replace him with another, wild monkey, a move that would assuredly ruin the now-famous act. Bergerin quickly puts his plan into operation.

In the rooming house where the "musketeers" share living space, Lorenzo is called away to answer the phone, and two ruffians enter through the window and carry Jocko off. A real monkey is then brought in and left in his place, but Lorenzo soon discovers the switch and alerts Armand. The men, hoping that Faho will escape his captors and return on time, head for the theater, with the real monkey in tow. Meanwhile, the two thugs bring Jocko to Bergerin's circus wagon, where they lock him in a cage built into the wagon's wall.

At the theater, Lorenzo and Armand lock the monkey in Jocko's cage; Olivette frees him moments later and brings him up to her dressing room. Back in the circus wagon, Jocko manages to force the cage door open. He frees one of Bergerin's lions and lures the beast into the cage inside the wagon. Jocko locks the lion up and heads for the theater. At that very moment, Olivette is being

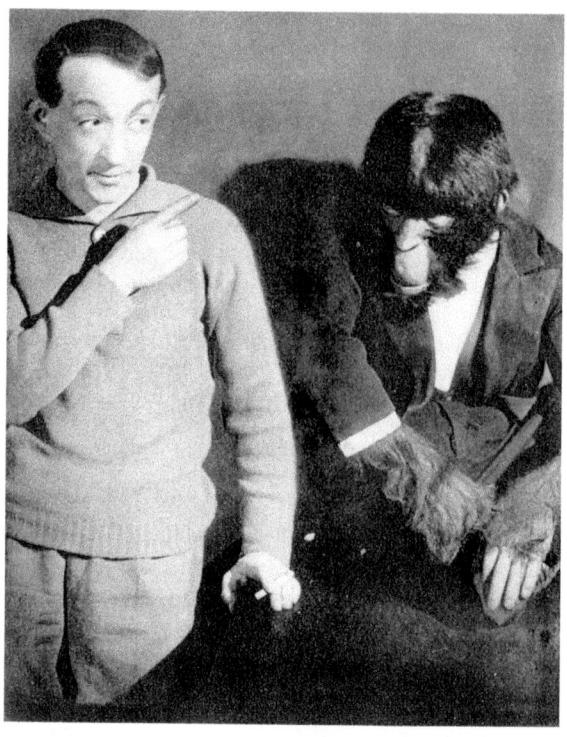

Trick photography allows Jacques Lerner to confront his Baser self in this publicity photograph, released when *The Monkey Talks* was a Broadway stage play.

attacked by the monkey, who chases the frightened woman throughout her dressing room. Olivette faints and thus does not see Jocko climb through the door transom to rescue her. Real and fake monkey battle, and the real monkey stabs Jocko with a knife taken from the dressing room table. Before the monkey can carry Olivette out over the rooftops of Paris, Armand and Lorenzo break down the door. They watch as the monkey, having scampered across to the roof opposite, is shot down by gendarmes.

Jocko has been mortally wounded, but he insists on going through his act onstage one last time. He dies in Olivette's arms, and the curtain falls.

Soon after, Olivette and Armand board a train and speed away to build a life together.

The Monkey Talks is an odd a little picture as the titular ersatz-chimp is an odd little beastie. You can very easily do some mental stretching to imagine this as a Tod Browning or Lon Chaney vehicle, what with the circus background that Browning loved so much and the "grotesque-in-hopeless-love-with-naïve-young-beauty" element that provided the sexual tension in just about every makeup film Chaney made. The segue from circus to vaudeville is a necessary move indoors so as to utilize standing or jury-rigged sets which are neither as extensive nor as interesting as those used in (insert your favorite Browning or Chaney picture here). Brief, long shots of the theater interior *may* have been photographed on Universal's "Phantom" set, an observation that's reinforced somewhat by a couple of vertical tracking shots that follow the dramatis personae up several levels of backstage stairs that look awfully familiar.

If you've read what's been published to date on *The Monkey Talks* and then view the picture, the first thing that hits you is the difference between the characters' names as written in the film's title cards and as reported in just about every critique and article (and the AFI Catalog). The synopsis uses the nomenclature from the picture. The sundry reviews and publicity pieces that saw print following the picture's release insisted that Don Alvarado played "Sam Wick," that Jane Winton and August Tollaire were "Maisie" and "Mata," respectively, and that Jacques Lerner impersonated "Jocko Lerner." The disparity is most likely due to the fact that this second set of names was used in René Fauchois's acclaimed source play, which preceded the Fox film by months and which had successful companies running simultaneously in New York, London, and Paris. It is said that New York had problems with "Faho," and thence came "Jocko Lerner." Could be. It remains unclear why M. Tolliare's name was switched onscreen from "Mata" to "Jules Ostermoore," especially when backdrops and posters hanging from the circus wagons still trumpet "Mata" to the customers. However, as Mordaunt Hall refers to Jane Winton as Maisie in the body of his review of the film for *The New York Times*, facile explanations may not be the order of the day.

The Monkey Talks opened at Broadway's Sam H. Harris Theatre on December 28, 1925, and closed about 100 performances later, making the New York production less successful than either the London or Paris presentations. Philip Merivale was the Big Apple's "Sam Wick," Luther Adler played "Lorenzo," and Lerner, of course, was the monkey. The plot of Fauchois's play differed somewhat from that of the subsequent motion picture, chiefly in the fact that, onstage, the villains came to recognize the fact that Jocko was not a real monkey. In the Fox production, neither Musette nor Bergerin is ever in the know, and Jocko expires in Olivette's arms without that tearful young woman becoming aware that she's cradling a gnarly, balding *man* who loves her.

When Fox bought the rights to the play, the studio wasted no time in planting advance notices in the trade press. Some changes made between the advances and the premiere included the substitution of Don Alvarado for Edmund Lowe (who was then running breathlessly from *One Increasing Purpose* to *Is Zat So?*) and Raymond Hitchcock for J. Farrell MacDonald (busy on *Ankles Preferred*), L. G. Rigby's being tapped for the scenario rather than J. T. O'Donohue, and the disappearance altogether of writer Gladys Unger. Don Alvarado had been discovered (c. 1917) and renamed (from José Paige) by Jack Warner, who was always—like everybody else—searching for another Valentino. Alvarado looked sufficiently Latin to impersonate a lovesick Frenchman, and he came cheaply enough to allow *The Monkey Talks* to remain on a rather austere budget. Raymond Hitchcock had been a familiar face to theatergoers since the beginning of time, and there's little doubt that his affable demeanor softened Lorenzo's rather rough edges, in essence making the character a *lovable*, larcenous libertine.

Virtually all of the movie's early establishing scenes are exteriors, shot in fields or on back-lot sets, and the screenplay neither wastes much time in positing a circus background, nor makes much effort in supporting that position. Granted that the six-reeler clocks in under an hour, but it can't be three minutes from the time Armand dangles a bejeweled bracelet in front of Musette's eyes to her giving him the gate and heading back to the burly Bergerin. Shortly after that Armand, Lorenzo, Jules, and Jocko show up clad in some *very* peculiar tights, and the audience is thus meant to infer that the quartet has scrabbled together an act. A blink of an eye later, and the circus has been shut down due to financial woes, the four men—dressed in what may pass for mufti in some alternate universe—wander off into the woods, and the kernel of the talking monkey scheme has been introduced.

No footage is expended on developing the scam. The jump from those few pithy phrases on title cards to the understanding that "Le singe qui parle" is now the toast of Paris is instantaneous. If some seat holders were a bit slow in understanding that the frequently repeated montage shot of applauding hands is reacting to Jocko, Olive Borden's Olivette says as much in her introductory titles. (She can't possibly being expecting thunderous ovations for her own "act," which seems to consist entirely of her walking rather unsteadily for about ten feet on a straight wire suspended eight feet above the stage floor. Still, her turn receives more screen time than Bergerin and Musette's lion-taming bit, which—as photographed—consists of their bowing to the audience and then *exiting* the cage.)

Olive Borden's ingénue is largely gorgeous, although there are moments when—her eyes widened in horror or her lips pursed in disapproval—she's the spitting image of Shelly Duval's Olive Oyl. The script requires that Olivette be a trifle arrogant and shallow—odd for a stock romantic lead at that time—while simultaneously undercutting the notion that she has any professional right to be haughty. This is both a departure from convention and something of a dramatic redundancy, as the plot has already has floated a capricious, snooty, pointedly untalented female—in the person of Musette.

Olivette also tends to caprice. At one juncture, having invited Jules and Jocko into her dressing room, she bids the impresario "good day," as she is intent on being left alone to play with Jocko; however, she grows weary of monkeyshines not ten seconds later and shows Jocko the door as well. Borden does get to display her figure and quite-lovely legs via a selection of skimpy, form-fitting costumes and such, worn throughout the film. With her physical assets thus overshadowing her being slightly personality challenged, it's little wonder that the "real" monkey who attacks her late in the proceedings very obviously has romance on his mind.

In an hour-long picture, there's not a great deal of time to waste on frivolities like character development, so all of the principals are sketched rather than drawn. Lorenzo and Jules, for example, being cinematic Frenchmen, have only larceny and les femmes jolies on their minds, and the sight of Hitchcock and Tollaire—one on the wrong side of sixty and the other, visually his ancestor—hitting on a couple of lovelies by the riverbank makes you shake your head in amusement and admiration. Musette is a gold digger, and Bergerin—of necessity, the heavy—is the vein she's currently mining. The moment the notion of revenge scampers through the ranges of Musette's mind, actress Jane Winton screws her face into a scowl that has *Mae Busch* written all over it.

Even Jacques Lerner, the celebrated monkey impersonator, has little time to build a person out of François Faho (or a monkey out of Jocko). Apparently, the sight

It must have been tough for Jocko to keep his eye on the oranges and not on Olivette's gorgeous legs. Jacques Lerner, Olive Borden.

of Faho hanging on a rope or doing one-armed cartwheels is all it takes for Armand to prognosticate about monkey suits and suitcases filled with francs. The little man agrees immediately — no thoughts were given to liability insurance in those simpler days — and, as mentioned earlier, within six meters of 35mm footage, Paris is at his furry feet.

The monkey makeup was an early effort by Jack P. Pierce, a man who surely needs no career précis here. Pierce seems to have provided three different treatments. There is a detailed makeup, which is quite simian in appearance, and this is used whenever Jocko is afforded a medium close-up. (There are no extreme close-ups in the picture, and only the "human" characters are ever photographed in bust shots.) This makeup doesn't always match whatever Lerner is wearing for long shots (such as when he's performing his "act," wherein he has to move his mouth to speak), and it's miles above the mask that the actor doffs for a breather whenever he's safely behind locked doors with his fellow musketeers.

That second monkey — the "real" one — is another small actor wearing a twin of Lerner's long-shot treatment. (In an online commentary on the film, the writer reports that this second monkey is a *genuine* monkey and that "The contrast between Lerner and a real ape is so obvious, we lose all possible belief in his disguise." Balderdash.) There *is* a priceless moment when Bergerin has his two thugs drag this second monkey in on a leash: "I found a monkey that looks exactly like Jocko; it means our fortune," he crows. "My monkey in these clothes, Jocko in our cage, all in an hour, and then we leave the country!" With the budget not allowing for a full-body fur piece, the fact that this "substitute" monkey *is dressed in a sweatsuit* passes without onscreen mention.

Like Olivette, Jocko's turn at the Follies Bergères is a tad elementary. Brought onstage by Armand, Jocko grabs his placard from the vaudeville easel and then points to himself. Clad in a top hat and overcoat and wearing a suit, he rides a bike in a tight circle before being seated at a table. He lights a cigarette, has a cocktail, and then moves downstage, where he gabs, briefly.

> ARMAND: "What is your name?"
> JOCKO: "My... name... Jocko."
> ARMAND: "And tell them whom you love."
> JOCKO: "Jocko... love... Master."

And there you have it. After toiling through that epic-length performance, Jocko leaves for the dressing room, where he removes his mask, gasps for air, and immediately has another cigarette.

That's the pattern—such as it is—and that's why the scene in which the hoodlums kidnap Jocko and substitute the "real" monkey is awkward and predictable. On that fateful day, Faho is fully costumed and masked when he joins Lorenzo at the table. He sits down to eat while *wearing the mask* and is still fully accoutered when Lorenzo is called to the phone. The patron saint of coincidences must have smiled to note that the "real" monkey, schlepped in through the window by the bad guys, is wearing an exact twin of the suit Jocko has chosen to wear that day!

There's also a scene—a lengthy throwaway, although it reinforces Lerner's attraction to Olivette—where the musketeers are having a birthday bash for the enchanting young wire walker. Lolling about on the grass—albeit dressed in cravat and finery—each man produces a wrapped present for the ingénue, *as does the monkey!* What's more, as the men are fawning and Olivette is gushing, Jocko is reclining, cigarette holder between his teeth, legs crossed, clearly lost in deep thought. It's a good thing that Olivette is denser than concrete, or she might notice that this is not just a monkey that talks; it is, rather, a full-fledged, world-weary member of the bourgeoisie!

This sort of uncertain characterization would most certainly not have been present had Lon Chaney impersonated Jocko. Chaney's renowned ability to focus on the personality and motivation that drove his characters would have precluded any "slips" such as this one. What's more, Faho's ongoing prayer—"I sometimes wish she could see through this hideous mask; could see me as I am; know that I think and love as other men"—not only mirrors the recurring theme of many of the Chaney canon entries, it also foreshadows the underlying sentiments of Conrad Veidt's Gwynplaine in *The Man Who Laughs*. (If I may be permitted to leap ahead a few years, the picture's *near climax*—where Olivette is *almost* lugged across the Parisian garret tops by the "real" monkey—brings to mind the more successful scene that closes out the action in Universal's *Murders in the Rue Morgue* [1932]).

The climactic struggle between monkeys is done largely in silhouette and shadow play, and this is not only stylistically pleasing, but also dramatically necessary: The unbilled actor who fills out the second monkey suit is positively dreadful in his impersonation. Once in Olivette's dressing room, he expresses lust and menace by crouching low and holding his arms straight out at his sides. Suspense is maintained as Olivette apparently forgets how to slide the bolt that will open her dressing room door, and the tension is palpable as she runs into her closet, *he* runs into her closet, and then she runs *out* of her closet, whereupon she promptly collapses and transforms into a mannequin. More than slightly incredible is the wrap-up to the simian battle, which ends only when the "real" monkey pulls a knife on Jocko and stabs him into submission.

There are a couple of other scenes that are equally stupefying. Jocko manages to escape from the circus wagon cell by (apparently) snapping the chains that augmented the door lock and thereafter breaking the lock. He then looses a lion and finagles the beast into this same cage! Now you have to ask yourself how big this particular circus wagon is, what with its having a cell large enough to accommodate a fully grown lion built into one of its walls. Well might you ask. Later on, Bergerin uses his key to unlock that same, broken door (no chain can be seen anywhere) — expositing villainously to Musette without once glancing into the cell — and the lion rushes forth to do in the wicked couple. This raises the question of the size of the cell once again — a lion obviously can hide in its voluminous shadows — to say nothing of the cat's propensity to be as quiet as a mouse and as odor free as freshly laundered socks.

Another stunner is Jocko's deathbed scene, which really isn't a deathbed scene, but more of a "the show must go on, so let me bid everyone a fond adieu and then head onto the stage, where I will do everything I did earlier, only with increasingly poor coordination and less vigor, before expiring in the arms of the damsel whom I love from afar" scene. Setting the scene for the slower members of the audience, Lorenzo bellows, "Something terrible has happened! Faho has been mortally injured!" in front of everyone (*including* Faho). Dragging himself to his feet, the monkey man works the room, shaking hands and saying goodbye to the crowd, before heading for the stage. There he does pretty much what he had done earlier, but, when cued by Armand ("And tell them whom you love"), he responds, "Olivette! Olivette!" Had this been a Lon Chaney vehicle, the Man of a Thousand Faces would have shed the mask and done some last-minute soul baring, sending the ingénue (and the audience) into heart-rending sobs. Here, the monkey dies without either exposing his lovesick face or giving Olivette a chance to shift her tear ducts into high gear.

The picture got some good press, with Jacques Lerner winning most of the kudos. The *New York Herald-Tribune*'s Harriet Underhill was alone in her lack of appreciation for Olive Borden, but I agree with most of what she says:

> Jacques Lerner, the clever little man who played the monkey in the stage production, has the same role in the screen version. We can see no reason why he should not be the star of the piece, for he gives a remarkably fine performance. But the producers have chosen Olive Borden for this honor. Miss Borden is a self-conscious young woman, who purses her lips, arches her insteps and is thoroughly irritating all the time. If this be acting, make the most of it!
>
> [April 2, 1927]

Fred, over at *Variety*, found the picture to be "full of atmosphere and replete with suspense," and while I'll go along with the atmosphere, I'm not buying the suspense. The *Kinescope Weekly* critic complained that "Circus and sawdust form the settings, which are never on a big scale," and, once again, that's right on target. I haven't been able to discover the final costs for *The Monkey Talks*, but there's no way anyone can say that all the money's on the screen. The several inserts of the theater audience may very well be footage taken from *The Phantom of the Opera*, and, other than that, Olivette's dressing room may well be the largest interior in the picture.

The prolific Raoul Walsh's previous forays into the genre had pretty much been limited to his producing *The Thief of Bagdad* (1924), and *The Monkey Talks* proved to be his last incursion. Going from a megabucks, high-prestige production to an assumedly moderately priced feature with rather limited appeal may have had something to do with this, but (thankfully) there was no shortage of directors ready, willing, and able to pick up the genre slack. Surprisingly, given the decent notices the film received on the whole, Walsh's hand in things was occasionally slapped. *The New York Times*'s Mordaunt Hall complained,

> Unconvincing as some of the episodes are, they are nonetheless interesting. Mr. Walsh knows how to tell a shadow story, but the idea of having to cope with a human being that is foisted on audiences as a monkey is possibly a task beyond the ken of any director. Still, there are some episodes that might have benefited by pondering over the amount of common sense the heroine of this story was to possess. She hears the supposed monkey tell her that he loves her, and while she is aghast at the animal impersonator's remark it never dawns on her that Jocko is not a monkey. The screen demands more decided realism than the stage, and therefore one not only reflects on the incidents that are projected but also upon those that are not depicted. Hence one wonders why Olivette, the heroine of this adventure, continued to be blind to the disguise of the small man.
>
> [April 5, 1927]

I'd have been a lot happier if the screenplay hadn't stuck a halo on the "small man." He saved Armand's life during the Great War, he saves Olivette's honor by fending off the monkey in the Great Dressing Room Brawl, and he even saves those last-performance ticket buyers from disappointment and the uncertain travails of refund seeking by running through his act although impaired by a lethal stab wound. The guy is so good that you just know he's the tragic hero pictured on page 12 of "Dr. Drama's Illustrated Guide to Theatrical Types." He'd probably go on forever, riding his bike, barking a few phrases and then pouring himself a stiff one, except that — for a grotesque — a noble death is the inevitable end to epic, unrequited love; just ask Don Quixote, Cyrano de Bergerac, or Quasimodo, none of whom ever seriously expected to get the girl. Chaney's sundry offbeat characters never got the girl, either, although they usually made it to the last reel with great expectations. When the smoke clears in *The Monkey Talks*, one finds the entire hirsute charade less fantastic than the notion that the vapid Olivette would *ever* choose Faho over the mustachioed mannequin, Armand.

What appears to be the only surviving print of the picture is held at the George

Her Mom had warned Olivette never to allow herself to be pawed by strange... men. Olivette Borden in the clutches of the unbilled "Second Monkey" (Photofest).

Eastman House in Rochester, New York. The preprint material shows extensive image deterioration, with fully half of the footage barely visible, even when run on a flatbed viewer. Even under these less-than-optimum conditions, *The Monkey Talks* displays an oddball charm, and — although it may never come to be available via home video technology — when screened before an enthusiastic audience (and accompanied by a suitable musical score), it may very well still pack the kind of punch that won it good notices so many years ago.

THE CHINESE PARROT

Universal (Jewel) — October 23, 1927 — seven reels/7,304 feet — c. 65 minutes

Cast: Marian Nixon as Sally Phillimore; Florence Turner as Sally Phillimore (older); Hobart Bosworth as Philip Madden and Jerry Delaney; Edward Burns as Robert Eden; Albert Conti as Martin Thorne; Kamiyama Sojin as Charlie Chan; Fred Esmelton as Alexander Eden; Edgar Kennedy as Maydorf; George Kuwa as Louie Wong; Slim Summerville, Dan Mason as Prospectors; Anna May Wong as Nautch Dancer; Etta Lee as Gambling Den Habitué; Jack Trent as Jordan

Credits: *Director:* Paul Leni; *producer:* Carl Laemmle; *adaptation and scenario:* J. Grubb Alexander; based on the eponymous novel by Earl Derr Biggers; *titles:* Walter Anthony; *photography:* Ben Kline

Synopsis: Sally Randall (Marian Nixon), daughter of a wealthy Hawaiian planter, marries Phillimore, the man of her father's choice, though she has sworn her love to Philip Madden (Hobart Bosworth). Tearing from her throat the priceless pearls given her by her father, Madden declares that someday he will buy her at the same price. Twenty years later, now a widow in financial straits, Mrs. Phillimore (Florence Turner) returns to San Francisco and offers for sale through her jeweler the last of her possessions, the pearls. Accompanied by her daughter, Sally (Marian Nixon), she goes from the ship to the offices of the jeweler to meet the unknown purchaser, who turns out to be Madden.

She is astonished and then humiliated, as Madden does not bother to conceal the desire he has for the young Sally. Mrs. Phillimore is unable to deliver the pearls at once, having entrusted them to Charlie Chan (Kamiyama Sojin), a Chinese detective who has come over as a steerage passenger in the guise of a coolie. Madden warns that the sale is contingent on her delivering the pearls to his desert home the following day; Sally's presence is also part of the demand.

Arriving home, Madden is blackjacked by thugs, who keep him a prisoner in his own hacienda. Jerry Delaney (Hobart Bosworth), one of the thugs (who bears a striking resemblance to Madden), impersonates the millionaire while Madden's secretary, a notorious crook, helps carry out the pretense when Sally arrives in the company of young Robert Eden (Edmund Burns), the jeweler's son.

Sally and Robert, conscious of a very strained atmosphere, are astounded when they learn that Charlie Chan (Kamiyama Sojin), who still carries the pearls, has arrived ahead of them disguised as a tramp and has been hired on as cook to the Madden household. They agree to keep silent while he makes his investigation. While at dinner, a weird voice shouts "Help! I'm being murdered!" The voice is traced to a parrot, the property of a Chinese servant who has disappeared. Apart from these words, the parrot speaks only Chinese, and Chan immediately steals the bird away, trying to find out what he knows.

Another day passes. Robert, believing Sally to be in love with Madden, is anxious to get the whole thing over with and return to San Francisco. He demands the pearls from Chan and is about to hand them over to Delaney when another member of the gang, fearing a double cross, knocks at the door and Robert's suspicions are again aroused. He hides the pearls under a newspaper in the living room.

Later, his suspicions allayed, Robert goes to retrieve the pearls but finds them missing. He accuses Delaney of taking them; Delaney, in turn, accuses other members of the gang. Everything is in a state of turmoil when Mrs. Phillimore and the elder Mr. Eden (Fred Esmelton) arrive. While explanations as to what has happened are circling the room, the door opens and in walks the real Madden, who has been released by Charlie Chan. Chan explains that the Chinese parrot had witnessed the kidnapping and had told him all about it. The crooks are taken away, Mrs. Phillimore falls into Madden's arms, and Robert and Sally realize how they feel about each other.

Chan hands the pearls to Madden, who throws them out into the desert. They have caused nothing but trouble, he declares, adding that everyone is better off without them.

There was very little risk involved when, in 1929, Paramount decided to film Warner Oland's Fu Manchu misguidedly plotting the downfall of certain English military officers present in China during the Boxer Rebellion. There was no downside to having Oland enact a villainous Mandarin; indeed, the Swedish actor had enjoyed industry-wide demand since 1915 by doing just that. Nor was there any reason to doubt that this latest take on the evil, "heathen Chinee" would do well at the box office. As I've noted elsewhere, cinematically, the Yellow Peril *always* ensured good returns. Fine Arts Films' *Sable Lorcha* (1915) may have been the first, American feature-length film to deal with vengeful Orientals; records are somewhat vague. What cannot be denied is that the "exotica factor" it and subsequent pictures offered went a long way to overcome otherwise banal, predictable plotlines.

When Earl Derr Biggers's Charlie Chan novels began appearing in the late 1920s, they were unique in that they offered an alternative to the stereotypical Chinaman (slavering, would-be rapist of white women, or laundryman) with whom the American public had grown accustomed. Biggers offered his readership a heroic Oriental detective, sufficiently accommodating in personality (all that "Please" and "Thank you" business), unthreatening in demeanor (the nonhardboiled Charlie relied upon wit and ratiocination, rather than his fists), and removed from his Asian homeland (he worked for the Honolulu police department) to quell any underlying xenophobia. The novels quickly garnered a sizable following, and the year after it was first published, *The House without a Key*—Biggers's first Chan offering—went before the Pathé cameras. The result—a ten-chapter, silent serial—is generally mentioned in print en passant, as it disappeared into the night decades ago.

So, too, did *The Chinese Parrot* vanish without a trace. In addition, this 1927 Universal "jewel" is usually afforded the slightest of comments before it is shunted aside in order to concentrate on the classic Chan features produced by Fox. Absent the film itself, of course, few new critical points can be scored. Nevertheless, it is possible to jury-rig a few observations by playing with the information we *do* have, and most of the fun of dealing with "lost" films lies therein.

Originally, Carl Laemmle bought the rights to Biggers's newly crafted *Chinese*

Martin Thorne (Albert Conti) is wondering how intelligent Charlie Chan can be, standing *under* the Chinese parrot.

Parrot intending the property as a vehicle for Conrad Veidt, who was then under contract to Universal Pictures. John Barrymore had lured the lanky German to Hollywood the previous year when he telegraphed that he could not make *The Beloved Rogue* if Veidt did not come west to play France's King Louis XI. Following *Rogue*'s release, First National quickly approached Veidt with a one-picture deal for the lead in *The Easiest Way*, a screen adaptation of an old play that had been then kicking around for nearly twenty years. When the project ran afoul of the censors, however, Connie (as Veidt affably insisted on being called) turned his attention to Universal, where Uncle Carl traded both on his own German origins and a multipicture contract to reel him in.

Both $1,500 a week and the southern California sun put Conrad Veidt in a mellow frame of mind, and the fact that his old colleague, Paul Leni, was to direct *The Chinese Parrot* may have made the role of Charlie Chan more palatable than it might have been otherwise. It was Leni's *Das Wachsfigurenkabinett* (Waxworks, 1924) that had first brought Veidt to John Barrymore's attention, so playing the Oriental detective would have been an enjoyable — and painless — way of repaying the favor. The March 12, 1927 issue of the *Universal Weekly* crowed that, in preparation for the part, Connie had been photographed as Chan by the Freulich studio "with enough clever portraiture to fill all the art magazines in the United States."

Unfortunately, during a conference held in Universal City the week *before*, Carl Laemmle had taken Veidt off the project, as many of the studio executives, other actors, directors, and critics had thought it almost wasteful to cast Connie in a "Chinese" role. Uncle Carl rationalized the reversal by explaining that Conrad Veidt was "the one man in the world to play the role of the Rabbi in *Lea Lyon*," Universal's production of one of the classic plays of the Viennese stage. Before the publicity machinery could start puffing at full steam, though, Connie was yanked from *Lea Lyon* and injected into George Melford's ersatz Devil's Island melodrama, *A Man's Past*. (Just for the record, Nigel de Brulier was cast as Rabbi Mendel in Universal's *Surrender* [originally titled *Lea Lyon*], which was released in November 1927.)

A thoughtful Sojin as Charlie Chan, years before Warner Oland and his distinctive fedora.

The role of Chan went to Sojin, of course, and the Japanese actor copped the best notices of everyone in the production. Born Sojin Kamayama in Sendai on January 30, 1884, the emaciated character specialist appeared in almost fifty Hollywood features (billed variously as Sojin, So-jin, Sojin Kamiyama, Kamiyama Sojin, and — as in *The Chinese Parrot*— K. Sojin) before returning to Japan in 1930. The actor had made his Hollywood debut as the Mongol prince in Douglas Fairbanks's awesome *Thief of Bagdad* (1924), and the next few years saw him appearing in featured roles opposite such Hollywood stalwarts as Lon Chaney (*The Road to Mandalay*) and John Barrymore (*The Sea Beast*, both 1926). By 1929, he had "arrived" to such a degree that in *Seven Footprints to Satan*, he played *himself*. Sojin remained active in the film industry after his return to Japan, but it's not known whether he enjoyed the almost cult following he had in the States. The wizened actor — a unique presence in every sense of the word — died in Tokyo in 1954.

Next to Sojin, Paul Leni got the best notices. The director had completed *The Cat and the Canary*— another "jewel" on which the normally parsimonious Universal spent a great deal — scarcely a month before shooting started on *Parrot*. In that brief time, however, America found itself stunned by the ease with which Leni's bag of expressionist tricks had weathered the Atlantic crossing. Universal's *Cat and the Canary* was as profitable at the box office as the John Willard stage play had been on Broadway, and the movie critics easily outdid their theatrical counterparts when it came to superlatives. The fact that he had also designed the sets (which were fabricated by Charles D. Hall, who would make a name for himself with Castle Dracula and that infamous watchtower wherein the Frankenstein monster was jolted into life) gave Leni and his star an added luster in the weeks that followed *Cat's* release.

According to the run of contemporary reviews, it wasn't so much *The Chinese Parrot*'s more mundane settings that came back to haunt Leni, but the weakness of Biggers's source story. Even after veteran screenwriter J. Grubb Alexander adapted it for the screen, the novel's melodramatic excesses and preposterous denouement — the solution to the mystery hinges on the eyewitness "testimony" of a parrot that speaks Chinese — undermined the director's efforts to craft a blockbuster twice running. For all that, a judicious reading "between the lines" of the contemporary critiques shows that Leni hadn't lost his touch, despite the weakness of his material. *Harrison's Reports* (January 7, 1928), for example, found the acting to be "out of date," the continuity "bad," and the logic, at times, "ridiculous." "Yet," concluded the review, "[*The Chinese Parrot*] is able to sustain the interest pretty well from the beginning to the end." The picture's visuals must have been quite striking to offset a litany of weaknesses like that one.

The New York Times's reviewer seconds that theory, as he states:

> In his present offering Mr. Leni once more proves that with individual treatment an only fair-to-middling story can be made into a film that is at once original and imaginative.... The production progresses in a straightforward and natural manner. By an ingenious use of shadows, lights and photographic angles, Mr. Leni has created the eerie atmosphere necessary in a house where sudden death and sinister happenings occur.
>
> [January 2, 1928]

When Leni the designer was brought short by the ordinariness of manor houses and haciendas, Leni the director reached deeper into his bag. "The atmospheric mood is further heightened," revealed the *Times* critic, "by having a figure of death hover over the house in the desert and also by the insertion of a skeleton's hand in some of the scenes when the pearls are shown."

Leni's early death resulted in his achieving almost cult status as one of the quirkiest — and most creative — cinematic directors ever. The Stuttgart-born technician was a professional colleague of Conrad Veidt, both in their native Germany as well as in Hollywood. Veidt had appeared in one of Leni's earliest efforts, *Das Rätsel von Bangalor* (*The Mystery of Bangalore*), back in 1917. By the time the men had tucked *Prinz Kuckuck* (*Prince Cuckoo*, 1919) and *Patience* (1920) under their collective belt, *Das Wachsfigurenkabinett* — hailed as one of the greatest "episodenfilm" even made — was their only remaining collaborative project before they immigrated, separately, to Tinseltown in 1927.

Acknowledged as a master of expressionist filmmaking, Leni had worked as stage designer for Max Reinhardt's renowned Berlin theater company before breaking into the movies. The young man's talent for graphic art led to his designing the company's posters; later, this visual flair translated into the brooding pictorial compositions of *The Cat and the Canary*, *The Man Who Laughs* (with Veidt, one last time; 1928), and *The Last Warning* (1929). It's obvious from this lineup (and the lost *Parrot*) that Carl Laemmle had imported Leni to specialize in offbeat thrillers for Universal. The notion that he (and Conrad Veidt) would have headed Uncle Carl's "dream team" for the studio's upcoming production of *Dracula* is thus much more than idle speculation.

Sadly, *The Last Warning* was the director's last feature film for Universal — indeed, his last feature anywhere. Paul Leni died suddenly of blood poisoning on September 2, 1929.

Parrot went on to make money, although the excitement at the till was doubtless due to the picture's being the second Paul Leni offering, rather than the second Charlie Chan opus. *Variety* opined that the picture was "A very good Universal program of the thrilling mystery stuff," even though the story was "applesauce." The oriental angle, however, was *not* a plus according to the show business bible. Reflecting the casual racism of the time, the nameless reviewer admitted that "E. Sojin [sic] played the Chink, and from the name he is." Apart from disparaging the Japanese actor (and Sojin had registered his bona fides in *The Thief of Bagdad*, back in 1924), the commentator goes on to downplay the role of Charlie Chan:

> [Sojin plays] the Chink sleuth as a Lon Chaney cook-waiter, and if he weren't doing a Chaney it was because Chaney can't stoop that low. Another two inches lower and the Chink would have been doing Bugs Baer's lizard gag on Lon.
> [January 18, 1928]

The same critic did admit "Bosworth is always the good actor," and the venerable Herbert was the only member of the *Parrot* cast to escape the *Variety* dissection with all his limbs intact. Even the Brits, who spilled the beans to the exhibitors (via the *Bioscope*) *months* before the average bloke saw the picture (*Parrot* wasn't released in the United Kingdom until March 19), singled out the veteran thespian: "Hobart Bosworth plays a dual role with his usual power and sense of character, and contrives to present two totally distinct personalities with little aid from make-up." Or, apparently, from Herr Leni, who went unnamed in the write-up and who scarcely merited comment save for the remark that his direction "seems to verge on eccentricity."

Even in 1927, Hobart Bosworth (born in Marietta, Ohio, two years after Lee surrendered at Appomattox) had been around pretty much forever; his first recorded credit was *The Sultan's Power*, a Selig short released in 1907. Bosworth alternated between acting and directing during the teens (he founded his own film company in 1913) before settling into a prolific career — well over 150 films! — as a blustery character type who almost never got the girl. (Kevin Brownlow[1] relates how Bosworth — who had lost both his voice and his stage acting career following a bout with consumption — had been enticed into *Sultan* by director Francis Boggs, who rather sensibly pointed out how having no voice presented no obstacle to success in silent pictures.)

The hardy actor was two months on the wrong side of sixty years old when *Parrot* was released. This meant he was not only nearly two decades older than Florence Turner, whose Mrs. Phillimore collapsed gratefully into his arms at the picture's climax, but almost forty years older than Marian Nixon, who played the younger Sally (Randall) Phillimore at the picture's outset. As none of the extant reviews mention either the employment of a younger thespian or Mr. Bosworth's apparent unsuitability in this early sequence, apparently Paul Leni and Ben Kline's camera magic was working overtime. For the record, Bosworth worked steadily in films up to Warners' *Bullet Scars* (1942), a year before his death.

Closing out the cast were Edmund Burns as the typical, basically useless juvenile, Florence Turner as the old(er) version of one of Marian Nixon's two roles, and Nixon. None of these were either canonized or castigated in the extant reviews, so we can proceed without hesitation. Gorgeous Anna May Wong was a year away from England and *Piccadilly* (1929), her first "big" picture, and a couple of years removed from the popularity that would be hers in the early '30s. The part of Maydorf was played by one Ed Kennedy, soon to be known far and wide and fondly as *Edgar* Kennedy, who would join the Hal Roach Studios in 1928. The rest, as somebody said, is history. (No paid scribe saw fit to say anything whatsoever about Edgar's contribution to *The Chinese Parrot*.)

To cap things off, let me return to that lowdown from the *Bioscope* (from September 1, 1927): "The most theatrically effective part is that of the Chinese detective, played by Sojin, the Japanese actor, who specializes in cold blood villainy, and it must be admitted that he is well played up to by a very handsome macaw."

As with the box-office returns, the frustrated sigh that arises whenever *The Chinese Parrot* is discussed among film buffs is more likely due more to its being a lost Leni rather than a lost Charlie. The Charlie Chanatics out there — more frequently purely fans of the character rather than aficionados of the medium — have traditionally coasted down the pre-Fox avenues, preferring to start their engines with Warner Oland's first appearance. (Oland's first appearance was in *Charlie Chan Carries On* [1931], like *The Chinese Parrot*, a lost film; please see *Eran trece* in this volume. The gushing thus starts with *The Black Camel* [also 1931].) When pressed, the average Chan fan will cheerfully admit to missing any of the lost Olands (*Charlie Chan's Chance* [1932] and *Charlie Chan's Greatest Case* [1933] are also nowhere to be found) much more than the Leni silent.

Nonetheless, if the team of Leni and Veidt might well have raised Universal's *Dracula* to "pantheon" status, the team of Leni and Sojin ought at least to pique the interest of anyone who claims to love movies and mysteries.

Notes

1. *The Parade's Gone By*. New York: Alfred A. Knopf, 1968, p. 30.

Stark Mad

Warner Bros.—February 2, 1929—seven reels/6,681 feet—70/74 minutes (Vitaphone sound) also: March 2, 1929—4,917 feet (silent)

Cast: H. B. Warner as Prof. Dangerfield; Louise Fazenda as Mrs. Fleming; Jacqueline Logan as Irene; Henry B. Walthall as Captain Rhodes; Claude Gillingwater as James Rutherford; John Miljan as Dr. Milo; André Beranger as Simpson, the guide; Warner Richmond as First Mate; Floyd Shackelford as Sam, the cook; Lionel Belmore as Amos Sewald

Credits: *Director*: Lloyd Bacon; *scenario and dialogue*: Harvey Gates; *titles*: Francis Powers; *original story*: Jerome Kingston; *cameraman*: Barney McGill; *assistant director*: Frank Shaw

Synopsis: Bob Rutherford and Simpson, his guide, have disappeared while on a hunting trip to a dangerous part of the Central American jungle. Bob's father (Claude Gillingwater) organizes a search party and hires a yacht that subsequently anchors at the point on the coast where the young man was last seen. The group includes Mrs. Fleming (Louise Fazenda), Mr. Rutherford's secretary; Irene Hawley (Jacqueline Logan), Bob's fiancée; Captain Rhodes (Henry B. Walthall), commander of the yacht; Amos Sewald (Lionel Belmore), an explorer who has been engaged to lead the expedition; Dr. Milo (John Miljan), a naturalist; the first mate (Warner Richmond), and, of course, Mr. Rutherford.

When one of the sailors meets a mysterious end, the crew threatens to mutiny. Meanwhile, Professor Dangerfield (H. B. Warner), an authority on Central America, has canoed some four hundred miles to intercept the search party. He has with him Simpson (André Beranger), who had managed to escape from the jungle at the cost of his wits. Dangerfield attempts to dissuade the group from going ashore, as he views Simpson's condition as a virtual guarantee that Bob has not survived.

Mr. Rutherford insists, however, on continuing the search for his son, and everyone disembarks. Although he is treated in an insulting fashion by Sewald, Dangerfield insists on accompanying the group. Irene finds herself strangely attracted to the man, despite herself. The raving mad Simpson is left behind, chained to the deck of the yacht, but the bloodhounds are taken along with the party. The group comes upon the ruins of an ancient Mayan temple and decides to spend the night within its spacious confines. Weird noises cause the bloodhounds to run off after some unseen prey, and, as Rutherford, Irene and Dangerfield pursue the dogs, the single lantern left with the remainder of the party is mysteriously extinguished.

The three come upon a huge door that is just in the act of closing. Throwing themselves against it, they force it open just enough to admit Irene who, with a piercing scream, disappears! Managing to pry the door open again, the men discover a gigantic ape, chained to the middle of the floor. As the other members of the search party catch up with them, they maneuver around the ape and make their way through other chambers in the great stone temple. Suddenly, Captain Rhodes is whisked away by a strange monster with great hairy talons. The night is filled with hair-raising adventures, as messages are found, warning the intruders to leave the jungle at once, at the peril of their lives.

Rutherford hears a familiar whistle and is sure it is that of his missing son. Despite the fact that the whistling continues at intervals throughout the night, no one is able to locate Bob. An arrow narrowly misses Dangerfield. Later, when another flies into Sewald's side in the darkness, killing him, Dangerfield is blamed in view of the animosity that had existed between the two men. When all the lanterns go out, it is discovered that the oil containers have been punctured! The party decides that the ape is able to fasten and unfasten his chain and that he does so instinctively when he returns from a foray.

Despite the madness of the moment, Dangerfield and Irene begin to gravitate toward each other. The members of the expedition are relieved when Captain Rhodes stumbles back into their midst but quickly grow suspicious when they discover that his supposedly paralyzed arm is not disabled in any way. Rhodes quickly runs from the room and bolts the door from the outside. He activates a mechanism that causes the floor of the room to disintegrate gradually — starting at the center — with the flagstones dropping into the morass far below. As the yawning hole increases in size, the would-be rescuers are forced closer and closer to the walls, the only opening being a small window, high on one of the walls. As Dangerfield lifts Irene toward this aperture, the ape appears and pulls her through.

Irene faints. Simpson, the mad guide, appears at the window, giving the whistle that he had learned from Bob Rutherford. With gradually returning reason, Simpson unbolts the door just in time to release everyone before the floor gives way completely. He explains that the deranged hermit who formerly occupied the temple ruins had killed Bob several months earlier and that Simpson had then killed the hermit, only to fall victim himself to the horrors of the jungle.

Available information indicates that *Stark Mad* is one of those "cusp of sound" films that remain more intriguing for their being lost than for their reportedly being any good. Premiering first as an all-talking effort — courtesy of the Vitaphone sound-on-disc technology — the picture spawned a silent sibling, intended for theaters that hadn't as yet rewired to confront the inevitable. Neither version has survived the intervening years. Nor has anyone been able to locate a set of the sound discs, so — unlike the case of Universal's *Cat Creeps* or of MGM's *Rogue Song*, both of which were released scarcely a year after *Stark Mad* — there are no means of assessing the film as a motion picture.

The existing plot recap — courtesy of the Library of Congress — offers little in the way of cohesive information, failing as it does to indicate what happened to either Captain Rhodes or the ape or just who this "hermit" was in the first place. We're also left in the dark about are why Rhodes was such a cad, what his motivation was in taking on this particular job, and what that "hairy monster with the great talons" had to do with anything, as it is obviously a different — and more enigmatic — menacing beast than the gorilla. We're unsure what caused the sailor's death aboard the yacht; how Rhodes managed ultimately to escape from that impressively taloned critter; and why Dangerfield and Simson have journeyed some *four hundred miles* by boat, when it apparently takes but a day's hike to get to the temple where all the hubbub originally took place. As the synopsis was taken from Warners' own press materials, the state of the scenario as filmed can only be imagined.

But understanding the picture's dramatic thrust is less troublesome. Despite its Central or South American location, *Stark Mad* was a spiritual clone of *Seven Footprints to Satan*, *The Monster*, *The House of Horror*, and any number of other entries that may be found in a rundown of Hollywood's genre offerings of the late 1920s. Transparent plot devices (the aforementioned search for missing relatives or girlfriends and the reading of the will being the most venerable) conspired to get the dramatis personae onto the scene, whence a series of wooly adventures—spuriously established, incredulously executed, and simplistically explained at the end — would propel the plot until the footage ran out. As in the case of *Satan*, superior source material was occasionally left begging, and genre lovers of our generation bemoan the loss of opportunity, but no one can argue definitively now that audiences then would have reacted more favorably had these pictures rung "truer" or been less formulaic.

Thus, we're puzzling over a hybrid that consisted of virtually every then-known horror element in the movies. The film was rooted in an old dark house vein that had, by 1929, already been overmined; still, the scripted variation on the theme — the requisite gorillas, trapdoors, and nefarious mechanisms were to be found in an abandoned Mayan temple — was not altogether unamusing. The proscribed madcap dash through the sundry walls and doors was thus set within the larger framework of a "jungle quest," a subgenre that had become wildly popular through the writings of Edgar Rice Burroughs and Arthur Conan Doyle (and the subsequent filmed exploits of Tarzan and George Edward Challenger), and that would see its apotheosis in RKO's incomparable *King Kong*. Lunatics, mysterious messages, and achingly obvious comic relief went with the territory, if not with the geographical location.

The source of Harvey Gates's action-filled if derivative screenplay was an "original" piece by Jerome Kingston, an unremarkable member of the studio's story department. Kingston's trackable contributions to the history of cinema may be limited to four or five bland Warners' films, but Gates was nothing if not prolific. The Hawaiian-born storyteller had been cranking them out since 1914, and while few of the 180-odd pictures with which he was involved made either the critics or the ticket buyers sit up and take notice, his penning the screenplays for a brace of delirious Bela Lugosi cheapies—*Black Dragons* (for which he also provided the wildly improbable original story) and *The Corpse Vanishes* (both Monogram, 1942)—ensures him a secure little spot in the horror-lover's heart. *Stark Mad*, of course, was much closer in pitch and melody to Warners' earlier *The Terror* (1928) than to either of these, or even to Universal's *WereWolf of London* (1935), wherein Gates helped Robert Harris move Harris's original story a step or two closer to the screen.

Coincidentally, cinematographer Barney McGill had also worked on *The Terror* and *Stark Mad*, but the pictures' status as lost denies us the opportunity to view the veteran camera op's technique. McGill photographed John Barrymore in both of his 1931 Warners' thrillers, *Svengali* and *The Mad Genius*, however, and a perusal of the fluid camera work of those two gems allows us a wistful sigh as to what might have been with the earlier films.

Original herald of *Stark Mad*.

Stark Mad was directed by Lloyd Bacon, who had to have been well aware that his stable of canny actors was galloping along a well-worn track. Born in San Jose, California, in 1889, Bacon drifted south when he was in his mid-twenties and entered the bastard art form as a member of Charlie Chaplin's stock company at Essanay. When Chaplin signed on at Mutual shortly thereafter for a munificent pile of cash, Bacon, Bud Jamison and Edna Purviance went right along with him, and one of the most consistently outstanding series of comic shorts in motion picture history was the result. By the mid-'20s, Bacon moved to the rear of the camera and began a directorial career that would span three decades and number over one hundred feature films.

In one of his many volumes, Leslie Halliwell tagged the director "competent, rather than brilliant," and this may well have been the case. Bacon directed Warners' classic 1933 musical, *Forty-Second Street*, but only after Mervyn Leroy dropped out due to illness, and his work on the studio's subsequent musical blockbuster, *Footlight Parade*, has always been overshadowed by Busby Berkeley's choreography (and the controversy over dance credits shared by Berkeley with choreographer Larry Ceballos). As his strengths obviously lay outside the parameters of the horror film, Bacon was most likely assigned to direct *Stark Mad* either via the luck of the draw or because he might have had some professional affinity for the work of Louise Fazenda.

Fazenda, of course, had also been around since the early teens, creating and honing to perfection a country bumpkin persona, first for Universal's Joker Comedy unit, then for Mack Sennett's Keystone Comedies. Sennett thought highly enough of her to quell his girlfriend Mabel Normand's frequent demands for classier assignments by threatening to "send for Fazenda." Moving up from one- and two-reelers to feature films, the comedienne was the frequent first choice for distaff comic relief roles in the increasingly popular run of comedy thrillers. She appeared in Roland West's *The Bat* (1926) and Roy Del Ruth's *The Terror* (1928) prior to *Stark Mad* (maybe this is why *Variety* groused: "Some of the comedy, notably the stock in trades of Miss Fazenda, doesn't register because of familiarity") and headlined (as "Louise") in Benjamin Christensen's *House of Horror* just after it. It is interesting to note that, until relatively recently, all of Fazenda's comedy thrillers were considered lost. In light of the earlier comment from *Variety*, and with *The Bat* again available via the home video market, one may safely assume that Fazenda's Lizzie Allen is the soul sister of her Mrs. Fleming in the picture currently under discussion.

Even admitting to the predictability of Louise Fazenda's antics, the *Stark Mad* cast is a good one, and the few reviewers the picture seems to have encountered all paused in their head shaking to give a nod to the actors.

Ingénue Jacqueline Logan had started her brief career in the 1920 Broadway revival of *Floradora* and soon (and briefly) was one of Flo Ziegfeld's girls. Making her way back out west, the beauteous Texan was snapped up by the burgeoning film industry and soon became one busy woman; she appeared in some sixty Hollywood features before sound tolled her professional doom. She flirted with the talkies via a trio of pictures made in Britain in 1930 and 1931, but John Barrymore's *General Crack* marked her last appearance of note. Of interest are Logan's well-crafted performances in *The Faker* (1929, opposite Warner Oland) and *King of the Kongo* (again '29, and featuring the not-quite-ready-for-prime-time Boris Karloff). We must rely upon published reports and pictorial reconstructions to acknowledge the actress's playing opposite a brace of Lon Chaneys in Goldwyn's *Blind Bargain* (1922), as that film is lost. Arguably Logan's best-received role was that of Mary Magdalene in Cecil B. DeMille's New Testament epic, *The King of Kings* (1927). The Christus in that one was H. B. Warner, who, coincidentally, would end up with the actress affixed to his arm at the denouement of *Stark Mad*.

That's H. B. Warner behind the gun, about to plug one of the two on your left. And that's Jacqueline Logan on the left, aghast that the guy in the gorilla suit is grabbing one of the two on his right.

Henry Byron Warner was old world and old school, born in London in 1875 and treading the boards at the age of eight. Warner found himself playing featured roles in Hollywood flickers as early as 1914, and by the time of his death, a few days before Christmas 1958, he had chalked up more than 130 films to his credit. For many savvy film lovers, his portrayal of Christ in the aforementioned silent classic was the high point of his lengthy career. For many more "just plain folks," Warner is best remembered as Mr. Gower, the near-tragic druggist redeemed every holiday season by Jimmy Stewart's George Bailey in Frank Capra's *It's a Wonderful Life* (1946). For a handful of us, he shines as Col. J. A. Nielsen in a quartet of late '30s Bulldog Drummond pictures; as the eminently blackmailable Priam Andes in 1932's radio-derived melodrama *The Phantom of Crestwood*; as Dr. Carl Houston, the well-intentioned scientist who melds Vivienne Osborne's murderous bent with Carole Lombard's shapeliness in Paramount's 1933 *Supernatural*; as presiding Judge Hawthorne, in William Dieterle's delightful *Devil and Daniel Webster* (1941); or even as himself — one quarter of the bridge foursome Joe Gillis calls Norma Desmond's "waxworks" — in *Sunset Boulevard* (1950). It's a shame his arrogant, obnoxious Dangerfield — ultimately, *Stark Mad*'s love interest — is going missing at present.

Villainy of the oily kind was John Miljan's usual métier, but extant *Stark Mad* synopses fail to indicate whether the actor's Dr. Milo was another study in type or whither the doctor went once the fur started flying. Like so many of his colleagues,

Miljan brought his stage savvy to the screen, and his experience allowed him to move right into featured parts and the occasional lead. His genre debut was as *Faust*'s Valentin in Chaney's *Phantom of the Opera*, although he went unbilled onscreen and misspelled (John Miljuan) in the press book. The heavy from Lead City, South Dakota, could also be found in *The Terror* (1928), *The Unholy Night* and the talkie remake of *The Unholy Three* (1930), as well as in nearly a hundred other features produced from the mid-'20s until the late '50s. Miljan died, a victim of cancer, in January 1960.

Stark Mad also represented another foray into the fantastic for Henry B. Walthall, who receives a bit more coverage in the chapter on *The Unknown Purple*.

Nobody cared much for *Stark Mad*, and *Variety*'s thoughts on the film — "Elevated eyebrow gentry will sneer at this sort of entertainment, but the masses may find it diverting" — were pretty much typical of the aggregative criticism. Director Lloyd Bacon doubtless encouraged his cast to overplay for all they were worth, and the studio-bound jungle scenes — replete with whatever pertinent sound effects could be captured by strategically positioned microphones — must have been a hoot, albeit not for the highbrows. The extant stills suggest a production low in budget but high on imagination, and it is a pity that *Stark Mad*— which may well have lived up to its name in sheer unlikely comic melodrama — has slipped through the cracks.

THE UNHOLY NIGHT

MGM — September 14, 1929 — 95 minutes
Cast: (In Lord Montague's home) Ernest Torrence as Dr. Ballou; Roland Young as Lord Montague; Dorothy Sebastian as Efra Cavender; Natalie Moorhead as Lady Violet; Sydney Jarvis as Jordan, the butler; Polly Moran as Polly, the maid; George Cooper as Frye, the orderly; Sojin as Li Hung, the mystic; Boris Karloff as Abdoul Mohammed Bey [unbilled]
(In Scotland Yard) Claude Fleming as Sir James Rumsey; Clarence Geldart as Inspector Lewis
(The Doomed Regiment) John Miljan as Maj. Mallory; Richard Tucker as Col. Davidson; John Loder as Capt. Dorchester; Philip Strange as Lieut. Williams; John Roche as Lieut. Savor; Lionel Belmore as Maj. Endicott; Gerald Barry as Capt. Bradley; Richard Travers as Maj. MacDougal
Credits: *Director*: Lionel Barrymore; *screenplay*: Edwin Justus Mayer; based on the story "The Doomed Regiment/The Green Ghost" by Ben Hecht; *adaptation*: Dorothy Farnum; *titles*: Joe Farnum; *recording engineers*: Paul Neal, Douglas Shearer; *art director*: Cedric Gibbons; photographed by Ira Morgan; *film editor*: Grant Whytock; *gowns*: Adrian
The Unholy Night was released in both sound and silent formats.

Synopsis: Like so many of its contemporaries, *The Unholy Night* begins with a prologue:

> The amazing revelations pictured here are compiled from one of the most sensational murder cases on police record. The rare psychosis [*sic*] of the crime and the method of its exposure are stranger than fiction... because they are true!

The "greatest fog London has ever known" is in its twelfth day, and the local villains are taking every advantage of it to wreak havoc on the citizenry. Attacked and nearly throttled while navigating the pea soup is Lord Montague (Roland Young); only the scream of a passerby saves his neck. Recovering (with a brandy and soda) at Scotland Yard, "Monty" is informed by Sir James Rumsey (Claude Fleming) that nearly a third of the fourteen survivors at Gallipoli (where Monty had served with valor) have been throttled (more successfully) over the past few days. To keep the ranks from shrinking further, Sir James and Inspector Lewis (Clarence Geldart) arrange (with Monty's help) for the remaining officers to don their regimental uniforms and assemble that very night at Montague mansion.

That very night also finds a séance being held in the parlor of the manor house. When the lights are raised, several more cast members (Natalie Moorhead as Lady Vi, Monty's sister; Ernest Torrence as her beau, Dr. Ballou; and wonderful old Sojin as Li Hung, medium par excellence) are thrust into the narrative. Sir James moves in to confer with Dr. Ballou, but the arrival of some of the regimental survivors draws the audience away. Lieutenant Savor (John Roche), Major Endicott (Lionel Belmore), and Colonel Davidson (Richard Tucker) — the senior man — are the first to enter, and all are concerned about the still-absent Major Mallory (John Miljan). "Poor old Mallory," moans Endicott. "I saw him three weeks ago, with his shrapnel-scarred face. He looked as if he'd been shell-shocked only the day before." Ben Hecht was known for packing maximum exposition into minimum verbiage, and Lionel Belmore had just uncorked a beaut of an example.

Other officers join them, and the whole kit-and-caboodle breaks into a chorus of "Auld Lang Syne." Back in the drawing room, the butler greets a new arrival, who is conspicuous for *not* being in uniform: "The gentlemen are in the kitchen, sir. Will you join them, Major Mallory?" The scarred officer declines and warms his hands by the fire. From the kitchen, singing merrily (if not terribly well) all the way, comes the body of officers bearing a huge silver bowl brimming with a whiskey punch concocted from a traditional recipe. Monty spots Mallory sitting on the sofa, and he and the others surround their comrade, slapping him jovially on the back. He falls. "Great heavens," Monty mutters. "Mallory, too!"

Dr. Ballou examines the fallen man and confirms his having been murdered. The soldiers are astounded; the police, annoyed. Things get worse when a veiled and shrieking woman cascades into the room and then collapses. The lady is Efra Cavender (Dorothy Sebastian), daughter of the late Marquis of Cavender, who had dishonored his regiment by switching sides and fighting against his own men after being captured at Gallipoli. Before all this can be digested, in walks Abdoul Mohammed Bey (Karloff), who announces that he has just arrived in England with both the Lady Efra and her late father's will. Pointing to the first, he proceeds to read the second:

> Having for many years nourishing [sic] a deep and undying hatred for the officers of my regiment who forced me to leave England unjustly and who subsequently at Gallipoli sentenced me to be shot, I leave, to be divided equally among them, the sum of one million pounds. I do this in the firm conviction that nothing so soon cause discord among friends and destroy character as the sudden inheritance of wealth which I leave them, with my curse and the hope for their utter ruin. Furthermore, I leave to my daughter, Efra, an equal amount — the residue of my estate and name as her guardians the officers of the regiment. I do this in the sure knowledge that where money fails, nothing so quickly cause discord among men as a beautiful woman.

(It's unclear whether the grammatical shortfalls of the will are due to the marquis's own struggles with English syntax or to Abdoul Mohammed Bey's lugubrious delivery, but the logical monkey wrench — Cavender is claiming that the boys ganged up on him before he switched ranks at Gallipoli — has to be discounted if everything is to remain nicely black and white.)

Anyhow, harrumphing heroically, the officers swear that nothing can drive a wedge into their communal friendship or dissolve their spirit of camaraderie. Sir James, however, proceeds to put a damper on things: "Well, gentlemen, I suppose you know what this will means. We now have a motive for the murders." As the officers had scattered throughout Monty's house in search of the requisite ingredients for that high-voltage punch, no one has an airtight alibi for Mallory's murder. Still, in an effort to confound the deadly plot, Monty renounces his share of the claim to the marquis's testament and calls upon his fellow officers to do the same. To a man, his comrades—none of whom is as well off as his lordship—refuse to follow suit. Despite this dispiriting turn of events, the men launch into another round of "Auld Lang Syne."

Dr. Ballou gives Efra a quick once-over—the poor dear has taken to bed—and the officers head upstairs to turn in. At the stroke of midnight (Big Ben appears to be situated somewhere on the mansion's grounds), the camera pans around the darkened drawing room, past the fireplace, and to the curtains of the alcove where Mallory lay. The curtains flutter, a pair of hands draws them apart, and the major himself creeps through! Bearing a strangler's rope, Mallory makes for Colonel Davidson's room; a moment later, noises of a struggle are heard in the hallway.

Morning. Monty is aghast to discover the colonel's body, and the police converge on the room. Sir James and his men move to an adjacent, larger bedroom, where—as the camera pans once again, this time at floor level—six bodies are seen! And more bad news from below: Mallory has flown the coop, leaving only a note, which—thankfully—is read aloud by Sir James:

> Pray for me. When you read this, I will be with my comrades whom I loved and killed. They suffered, but not as I have. Shell-shocked, cataleptic; drove me mad. This morning, something snapped in my brain. I know now what horrible things I have done. There is no other way out. You will find me at the gate, under the tree.—Arthur Mallory

This sort of thing, of course, makes Dr. Ballou look rather inept professionally, and when Mallory *is* found—stabbed through the heart—the physician blusters that the note had been forged, the body had been moved, and the stabbing had been done post mortem. Sir James turns up the heat: Monty is now the last of the regiment, and the million pounds is his. If something were to happen to him, however, Lady Vi—whom Dr. Ballou fervently wishes to make his own—would inherit the tainted fortune. Is there no end to suspicion and accusation?

SIR JAMES: "Mallory had a hand in this, but he was not alone. We have still to find his secret."
DR. BALLOU: "I'm afraid he has taken his secret where the living will never trace it."
SIR JAMES: "Then if the living fail us, we must call upon the dead to help us."

Big Ben once again chimes midnight. Li Hung is quietly admitted to the manor house, whereupon he begins to ready his séance gear and to make certain of the dagger he has secreted in his sleeve.

With Monty, Efra, Vi and Ballou on the divan, Sir James orders the séance to begin; the lights are extinguished. Li Hung removes a veil from over his head and peers into his crystal, which now provides the only illumination in the room. (The shot of Sojin's angular face, lit from below, is the most striking image in the picture.) Faintly, the strains of "Auld Lang Syne" drift through the air. In a long shot, the chairs that flank either side of the rectangular séance table are at once filled with the transparent forms of the murdered officers of the regiment. Efra screams, and the lights are turned up instantly. "They were here!" the terrified woman shrieks.

Calm is restored, but the lights are no sooner doused than the officers are back in formation, pointing accusing fingers at the divan. Efra rises and moves toward the table: "Go away! What have I done to you?" She is further horrified to see the ghost of Mallory, standing off to one side. Reaching out, she puts her hand *through* the scarred specter. "Get back to your graves!" she screeches at them all. To Mallory: "As long as you live, you do as I tell you.... You kill for me! You kill them all for me!"

In the confusion, covered by the pervasive blackness, someone grabs the knife from Li Hung's hand. The figure stabs Efra and then runs into the hall. Through the door, a man is seen to collapse onto the floor. Efra is pronounced dead, Inspector Lewis informs everyone that Mallory has killed himself outside the séance room, the officers of the regiment pile out from behind a huge ornamental screen, and Sir James turns to Monty: "Lord Montague, we owe you an explanation."

Abdoul Mohammed Bey lopes into the room and explains—again, via flashback—how Efra was furious that her father had left half of *her* money to the regiment and how, by using her knowledge of the "hypnotic secrets" on the weak-willed, smitten Mallory, she had sought to wreak a terrible revenge. Ballou reveals that his midnight reexamination of Mallory had shown him to be alive, but in a cataleptic state: "Before your very eyes, Mallory became an apparent victim, you were all held here under suspicion, and the ghost left free to strike you all down that very night." The doctor had signaled the police through an open window, and they were awaiting Mallory's murderous attack in Davidson's room. The rest of the night was spent trying to snap Mallory out of the trance he was in. No luck; the veteran had sunk too deeply. "At dawn, he wrote the confession and then tried to do away with himself."

Dr. Ballou continues: "When we read Mallory's note in the library, [Efra] felt her plan had succeeded." Ironically, it was Efra's scream in the séance room that finally awakened the major. "In that desperate moment of realization, he grabbed Li Hung's dagger, stabbed the girl and himself, and put a tragic end to our séance." As to how Monty et al. saw the "ghosts," Li Hung demonstrates how his complex series of lights and mirrors produced the transparent figures.

The drama winding down, Monty is off for an assignation with a Miss Gabby LaVerne, but not before the regiment launches into another rendition of "Auld Lang Syne."

Many pictures made on the cusp of the sound era showcased silent stars who were a heartbeat—or a nasal whine—away from assuming a new role in the studio's next production: ticket buyer. It wasn't just uncertain vocal timbre or a Joisey accent that separated some actors from their livelihood, of course. There were also those who could not shake their reliance on what became known as "silent film technique," the decades-old set of standardized actions and reactions in which highly concentrated pantomime sought to compensate for the missing aural dimension. Still others were shown their way out the door for reasons totally unrelated to talent or suitability to the new medium: As more than one biography of John Gilbert has argued, the moguls used the coming of the talkies as the perfect means of unloading annoying or embarrassing personnel without running the risk of lawsuits over breach of contract. An actor who might win a legal battle would find no relief in the law from the inevitable blacklisting that followed. Besides, lancing the boil could be done with greater precision and less mess via studio publicity campaigns; in most cases, a shift in emphasis was all that was needed to effect a shift in interest. Naturally, the same films that shuttled some players off into forced retirement also introduced an array of "new faces," a good number of which had actually been working in the industry for years.

MGM's *The Unholy Night*, which featured an array of the silent screen's bigger names, was an interesting wrinkle in this pattern. Saying hello to talkie patrons was Roland Young, the unflappable Londoner who would achieve (arguably) his greatest cinematic celebrity as Thorne Smith's befuddled hero, Cosmo Topper. *Night* was Young's first sound film, and the top-billed actor hadn't had much of a track record in silents, either. He had appeared as Dr. Watson to John Barrymore's Sherlock Holmes in Goldwyn Pictures' 1922 eponymous offering, and that—plus a turn as "Houdini Hart" in Film Guild's forgettable *Grit* (in 1924)—was all she wrote. Young had made his name on Broadway, where he had debuted in *Hindle Wakes* in 1912, and from which (following a slew of successes) he emigrated in 1929, when the call came out from Hollywood for stage-trained thespians to strut their stuff in talking pictures. Thus it was that the forty-one-year-old Young signed with MGM and soon thereafter found himself taking direction from Lionel Barrymore—himself no slouch when it came to histrionics under the proscenium arch—in *The Unholy Night*. Some five-dozen feature films followed over the course of the next three decades, and, when he died in New York on June 5, 1953, Young bowed out with a sterling reputation as a character actor and light comedian.

If Roland Young's cabin on the *S.S. Unholy Night* was undeniably first class, Boris Karloff's berth was little better than steerage. Karloff had also been born in London in 1887, but on November 23, twelve days after Young. While Young had made his dramatic debut in that city following his training at the Royal Academy of Dramatic Arts, Karloff first graced the stage in Nelson, British Columbia, following the series of boldfaced lies he offered a theatrical agent in Seattle. Young made his way into the talkies via the route outlined earlier; Karloff swapped his ragtag, meandering stage experience for the luxury of staying in one place, when he signed on as an extra in United Artists' *His Majesty, the American*, in 1919. Nevertheless, at the time of *The Unholy Night*, Karloff had already shown his face—or his arm, or his back—in roughly fifty silent films and a brace of hybrids: Fox's feature *Behind that Curtain* and Mascot's ten-chapter serial *King of the Kongo* (1929, the pair) had both silent and part-talkie versions playing on neighborhood screens. Why then was he—a veritable veteran of the bastard art of cinema—forced to lope repeatedly across the screen here and mouth his exposition *unbilled*?

Of course, unlike Roland Young, Boris Karloff had no extended contract with MGM or any other company. He had no extended contract anywhere. His participation in *Night* was due, rather, to Lady Luck: He just happened to be in the right place at the right time. What was rather luckier for him, however, was the presence of Lionel Barrymore.

Back in 1925, Barrymore had fled a string of Broadway flops to migrate to Hollywood, where the climate and Paramount's promise of $10,000 augured well for his future. Arriving a scant six weeks after his brother John had hit town, Lionel set out to work. In the ensuing year, he appeared in no fewer than ten pictures, which, he admitted, were done solely for the money. The most notable of these may have been *The Bells*, a filmic version of a play in which his sister, Ethel, had appeared nearly thirty years earlier. *The Bells*, a low-budget production filmed in southern California by a company licensed out of New York, didn't pretend to aspire to greatness although it has weathered the years since with a patina of accomplishment and respect. More germane to this discussion than the picture's merits, however, is the fact that the pivotal role of the mesmerist was played by that free-spirited (and always available) actor, Boris Karloff.

The *Bells* mesmerist is generally considered to be Karloff's first important role, and to no small degree the thirty-eight-year-old actor's success with the part was due to Barrymore. Lionel took an interest in Karloff and spent some time "sketching an intricate makeup idea to accentuate the Englishman's unusual bone structure and heighten his characterization" (James Kotsilibas-Davis, *The Barrymores*: Crown Publishers, New York, 1981, p. 59). Folks who knew them had always said that a talent for drawing ran in the Barrymore brothers' veins. It didn't take too many drinks to get the "Great Profile" to admit that he would have been much happier had everyone just left him alone, free to doodle with his pencils, and Lionel's various sketches became highly prized acquisitions as quickly as he could dash them off. Whether one shrugs off Lionel's study of Karloff's facial planes (as a blatant steal from Werner Krauss in *Das Cabinet des Dr. Caligari*) or marvels at its foreshadowing of a subsequent, more momentous, study (by James Whale, prior to his casting the monster in *Frankenstein*), one can't ignore the fact that the established star took pains to help his struggling journeyman colleague. Nor was this lost on Karloff. As his long-time friend Cynthia Lindsay noted, Karloff "frequently mentioned" that appearing in *The Bells* with Barrymore was "one of the greatest experiences of his young life" (*Dear Boris*: Alfred A. Knopf, New York, 1975, p. 33.)

Following *The Bells* (and fifth billing), Karloff appeared in a string of features for a variety of studios in which he moved from bit parts to recognizable extra work to featured roles to unbilled cameos and back again. From late 1926 through the release of *The Unholy Night*, the only company that consistently gave featured billing to the meandering Briton was Mascot, for whom *King of the Kongo* was their penultimate mutual project. Still, with Karloff's name onscreen in the Mascot chapterplay and with his having been listed among the cast for Fox's *Behind That Curtain* ("a Soudanese servant"; not much, maybe, but higher billing than E. L. Park received as Charlie Chan), his ending up with a paycheck but no onscreen mention in *The Unholy Night* might well be seen as a step backward. Regardless of the direction of that particular step, however, Karloff welcomed another opportunity to work with Lionel Barrymore.

This time around, though, thanks to Irving Thalberg, the elder Barrymore brother was in the driver's seat. Thalberg, who had pulled up anchor at Universal and set sail for MGM in February 1923, when confronted once too often with Uncle Carl's perennial cry of poverty, saw Barrymore's stage-enhanced gift for language as a viable tool for guiding less well-equipped actors through the labyrinth that was the talkies. (More candidly, Thalberg's passing on the chance to woo and win Rosabelle

Laemmle mitigated against his circumventing her father's policy of hiring and promoting relatives over the merely talented or deserving.)

The Unholy Night was based on a short story by Ben Hecht, for whom the picture was more notorious in the planning than in the execution. Hecht was a pal of the Barrymore brothers, having been introduced to them by Gene Fowler some years earlier. Penned as *The Green Ghost*[1] (the name by which Boris Karloff would refer to the picture until the end of his life), the story was stolen from Hecht's desk—claimed its author—by Leyland Heyward, who was desperate for material with which to embark on a career as a literary agent. The scandal, such as it was, was really nothing but a minor brouhaha; Hecht was far more concerned with the success of (and the receipts from) *The Front Page* and *Underworld*, stage and screen triumphs, respectively, that would enable the hitherto budget-conscious newspaperman to purchase a glorious, centuries-old, colonial house that fronted on the Hudson River.

On the cinematic end of things, Lionel maneuvered the cast through the various twists and turns of his friend's thriller as if they were all Barrymores. Thus, more than one movie critic noted disapprovingly the rather deliberate choreography in which the players indulged, an observation that Lionel had effected more than once when delivering his own sides onstage. In an effort to justify Thalberg's faith in his supposed vocal expertise, the neophyte director had given the screenplay's many dialogue exchanges the same dramatic weight as its (relatively few) true action sequences. While the resultant stasis might have irked several of the reviewers, Karloff and others were grateful that Barrymore took the tack that he did. "When I played my big scene, finding my dead wife," Boris later recalled, "I realized Lionel had analyzed the scene inside and out and given me hints that enhanced my own interpretation."[2]

Even granting the worth of the analysis, there's no denying the picture's ninety-two-minute length works against everybody's best interests. Whatever novelty the presence of dialogue may have had back in 1929, even then the banality of much of *this* dialogue worked against the novel intrigue of the narrative. Hand in hand with this cavil went another, which was almost unanimously cited by contemporary critics: Edwin Justus Mayer's adaptation of the Hecht original tended to make more points than were dramatically necessary, which is the reason for the picture's inordinate length. The numerous, protracted reaction shots could be no one's fault save Barrymore's, but Hecht and Mayer had to take the heat when it came to entire sequences that added nothing but running time. When the film opens, we're *plop!* in the middle of a days-long rash of random, violent crimes, all of which are blamed on the dehumanizing effects of the London fog. Moments later, following that fog-obscured assault on Monty, Scotland Yard hands his lordship a brandy-and-soda and the disturbing news that His Majesty's Fourth Rutland is being systematically decimated. No one—not Monty, not Sir James, not Inspector Lewis—posits a connection between the madness in the city streets and the fate of the doomed regiment, even for an instant. Why, then, does the audience have to sit through a series of unrelated attacks following the opening credits? For atmosphere? "It is very difficult to make out what the director is driving at during some of the sequences," noted Mordaunt Hall of *The New York Times*, thus giving both author and scenarist a bye.

Aside from a couple of these superfluous stretches, however, the picture does move at a decent enough clip; it also occasionally grinds to a halt, as Barrymore has the aging comrades at arms warble "Auld Lang Syne" several times. Time is likewise squandered injecting minuscule bits of personality into each of the officers, to no apparent end. True, the rotund Lionel Belmore apart, the survivors *do* appear to be little more than a cadre of brunette, mustachioed clones, so any half-hearted stab at individuality ought to win Barrymore and Mayer points for effort. Still, unless one were taking notes, who could possibly keep straight which trussed and buttoned dragoon snarled what at one or another of his apoplectic colleagues? There's really nothing more on the plate here other than some of the earliest — and flimsiest — efforts at creating red herrings that could talk.

Barrymore's direction, while meticulous, is more theatrical than cinematic: Some sequences of appreciable length are devoid of camera movement, while others are ill served by lengthy pans — somewhat akin to a stage-length sweep of a ticket-holder's head — where a succession of quick cuts could have enlivened the pace. This unfortunate tendency is nowhere more evident than in what ought to have been the most gruesome scene of all: the discovery that all of the regimental veterans have been murdered. As Ira Morgan's camera pans low along the bedroom floor, one after another the bodies come into view in what surely was intended to be a breathtaking vista. As the camera keeps rolling, though, and corpse after corpse gets his own close-up, you can't help but wonder just how battle-worthy this particular regiment was, when (apparently) one crippled psychopath with a piece of rope can throttle the lot of 'em.

Dialogue-wise, Roland Young is as amusing as all get-out, mouthing Ben Hecht's snappy rejoinders and inquiring after a brandy-and-soda as often as drawing a breath, but the problem is in that Monty is the only witty character in the picture. By comparison, virtually everyone else is such a stick in the mud that Monty appears to be on loan from some other project. This lopsided apportionment of brilliance may allow Monty to shine brightly, but it doesn't do a thing for the rest of the cast, and *The New York Times* was moved to question whether the undeniable bons mots were apropos in the first place. Nevertheless, *The Unholy Night* was Young's first sound film, and — even some seventy-odd years after the fact — it remains apparent that the actor benefited greatly from his stage experience: Even the cleverest of lines may suffer when delivered as if from the depths of a well or the length of a churchyard.

Although Barrymore had managed to make Roland Young's *Night* more glorious vocally than he had John Gilbert's that same year, he fell short of the mark when it came to introducing his actors to the fine art of reacting realistically. Once the full complement of characters has sauntered, paraded or swooped by the lens, not a one of them will settle for a casual glance or an understated gesture when a rococo flourish, replete with flared nostrils and furrowed brow, can be had for little extra effort. At times perplexing, often ludicrous and always Barrymore-ish is the propensity everyone has to shoot glances sideways, to fume and glower, and to overreact, and the existence of these excesses in the release print is a virtual guarantee of their directorial imprimatur. John Barrymore stated for the record that he regarded his older brother as being "frequently sublime," but, as was true of most of John's carefully crafted assessments, the half that was left unspoken was usually the more telling.

As was the custom, the pendulum had swung from the tastes and techniques of the previous medium to those of the newer technology. The early talkies were wont

The battle-scarred Major Mallory (John Miljan) is up to no good.

to eschew background music (save for themes trumpeted under main and end titles and such), as if to distinguish themselves further from their silent forebears, from whom sound was continuous melody, flowing endlessly forth from orchestra or pipe organ. There's little music in *The Unholy Night*, but by the time the aging swashbucklers break into their third dispirited rendition of "Auld Lang Syne," you're wishing there were less. Nor are there many creative sound effects to pick up the slack: Some miscellaneous screams, Sojin's caterwauling, and the bewildering accents affected by Karloff and Dorothy Sebastian are the only departures from the routine.

And, as for plot holes, the lady Efra's approaching rigor mortis in Abdoul's bony arms means there's a million in cash stuck in limbo. What happens to the other million? You know, the million for which the officers of the Fourth Rutland had briefly soiled their collective honor? Once the heavy's been dispatched, there's no point in renouncing any of that promised gelt, but the picture ends without so much as a nod to the presumed cause of so much murder and mayhem.

From the atmospheric credits (a shrouded skeleton waves its arms under the scrolls, yet over an effective chiller-diller theme), through the fog-drenched London appurtenances, to the solidly British expanses of the Montague mansion, the film unreels enjoyably. Those look-alike Gallipoli survivors may have feet of clay in their well-shined riding boots, but you're glad to discover they're all still kicking at the climax. Yes, there's a lot of talk (this was Ben Hecht's first talkie and only his second screen credit) and, yes, lots of that lots of talk ultimately leads nowhere, but there's action enough to keep the ship on an even keel. As the nameless reviewer from the *New York Post* revealed, "All in all, *The Unholy Night*, at one time or another, shows more corpses than *Hamlet*, *Macbeth* and *Othello* all in one evening."

In his talkie debut, Young a standout, not only due to his receiving the lion's share of the scripted wit, but also because the affable actor — who speaks volumes with a scratch of his head or a tug at his ear — attracts one's eye almost instinctively. Most of his fellow officers wear faces that were familiar to moviegoers of the twenties but which have dropped from memory with the passage of time. Contemporary audiences would have suspected that something was not quite kosher when Major Mallory was apparently murdered early on, as the major was played by John Miljan, too big a name then to waste in so profligate a fashion.

For someone unfamiliar with the picture's twist and turns, the sudden appearance of the quirkily accented Boris Karloff is a hoot. Although the Briton's Abdoul Mohammed Bey has a couple of fairly substantial scenes and provides some key exposition, even with Barrymore's vocal coaching and scene analysis, Karloff has to be heard to be believed, trying valiantly to sound as close to a lovesick lawyer named Abdoul as his stilted dialogue and trademark lisp would allow. For all that, Barrymore biographer Kotsilibas-Davis reveals how Lionel was thrilled with Karloff's marked improvement (in the scene where Abdoul comes upon the newly defunct Efra) following their having put their heads together: "After the scene was shot, the director approached his victorious actor, loathe to take any credit for the improvements. 'By God, you cunning old devil, you,' Lionel exclaimed. 'I knew you could do it! That performance was as different as chalk and cheese.'"[3] It's not completely clear which of the two men was loath to take credit, but, given the final result, their *both* balking at doing so is completely understandable.

Dorothy Sebastian does her best at approximating Karloff's vocal bravado, but her accent comes and goes once she unveils for the houseguests. Efra is really more of a noisy, pantomimic role, though, than one dependent upon the parsing of nuanced dialogue, so the lovely actress needn't have paid her accent any more mind than she did. To further the story, it's enough that Sebastian gives her sundry gasps and screams, striving all the while to stay erect long enough to bat eyelashes or glare daggers at that herd of punch-swilling songsters. Some interested folk couldn't make it much past her entrance, however, as that's when the plot began hemorrhaging convolutions. That *Post* critic wasn't speaking in a vacuum when he groused:

> At [one] point, Dorothy Sebastian, swathed in veils, walks into the room and faints. After this enough things happen to fill up the rest of this

page. I regret to say that the story does not hold up, becoming extremely involved and containing several anticlimaxes.

[September 6, 1929]

Aside from Karloff, the appearance of the gap-toothed and emaciated Sojin is another cause for rejoicing. Sojin—like Karloff—also has two scenes in *The Unholy Night*. His floating noggin in the first of these is appropriately macabre, but this is merely a warm-up for the climax. Following Efra's coming loose at the seams and Mallory's sticking knives in her and himself, Sojin's Li Hung takes center stage. He proudly points Monty to a wall-length mirror, and—in an absolutely incomprehensible rush of fractured syllables (*Night* marked the actor's debut in talkies)— "explains" how the regimental shades were made to appear at the séance. If this unfathomable recitation weren't enough of a joy, a clarinet-toting George Kuwa materializes as well. The screen's first two Charlie Chans had both graced Paul Leni's *Chinese Parrot* in 1928. With *Parrot* a lost film, though, it falls to *The Unholy Night* to preserve this happy, conspiratorial moment for posterity.

Ernest Torrence is allowed to span the extremities of the picture with his character's integrity and professional competence intact. Mugging shamelessly throughout, Torrence justifies the overuse of his rubber face via his rather loquacious explanations at the wrap. The actor makes an acceptable (if highly unlikely) hero, and roles like that of Moriarty in Fox's 1932 production of *Sherlock Holmes* were usually much more to his (and to his fans') tastes. Probably most familiar to nongenre moviegoers as Buster Keaton's bewildered dad in *Steamboat Bill, Jr.*, the Scottish Torrence died in 1933, cutting short his career in sound films.

With few exceptions, critics withheld their beneficence from *The Unholy Night*. *Variety* (October 16, 1929) stated that:

> It takes nearly two hours for the Hecht version to cover a lot of aimless conversation, running around, and performances like a bunch of college amateurs, before the whirligig of complications and drivel are all contradicted in a few long-winded speeches by Dr. Ballou and Sir Rumsey of Scotland Yard... It's an all-talker and a 100% lemon.

The New York Times (October 12, 1929) was much nicer:

> An incoherent and tantalizing talking picture, called *The Unholy Night*, is sojourning at The Capitol.... It is hardly a story suited to the screen, for what seems real in one chapter is discovered to be a staged fake later on.

Film Daily—a trade paper aimed at exhibitors and showmen—was a trifle more enthusiastic:

> Ben Hecht wrote the story, and with his masterly story telling style made it appear better than the theme and plot really are. Then again you have a superior cast, and their performances are uniformly fine. It will give fans a thrill anywhere.

[October 20, 1929]

So was *Bioscope*:

> The power and fascination of this picture is undeniable. The cast is a strong one.... Every character speaks with remarkable distinctness.
> [November 20, 1929]

For what it's worth, *The Unholy Night* is just too much of a good thing. Lionel Barrymore never takes a few seconds to underscore anything when a minute can be had; skeletons are closeted everywhere; everyone has their own studied eccentricities; glares, grimaces and groans are a dime a dozen; and demonstrably innocent people draw visible sighs of relief when informed that they couldn't have been guilty of something they hadn't done anyhow. Subtlety is nowhere to be found despite the protracted running time, and we have far too many superficially similar characters to allow for effective comparisons or contrasts.

However, there's that doozy of a séance scene, Roland Young's infectious personality, Boris Karloff *and* Kamiyama Sojin. One may quibble that the scales don't quite balance, but for lovers of guilty pleasures, any measurable gold at all is as good as the mother lode.

Postscript: The picture was advertised as *The Green Ghost* nearly until the very moment of its national release, when *The Unholy Night* was substituted. The field is divided with regard to this eleventh-hour switch. One school of thought attributes the decision to the rumor that the working title centered on an element in the picture that was so little emphasized that virtually none of the members of the preview audiences could remember its even being mentioned. Another theory is that there may have been some question of copyright raised by Stuart Martin, the author of a then-in-print novel titled *The Green Ghost*. Evidence indicates that Martin, whose *Ghost Parade* and *The Secret of Lourdes* continue to gather dust in the Library of Congress archives, penned a good handful of books on paranormal and supernatural themes that were published in the late '20s.

The film also enjoyed the distinction of having a foreign-language version shot in its wake. Photographed on the MGM soundstages shortly after *Night* went into postproduction, *Le Spectre Vert* (*The Green Ghost*) was (per Morris Gilbert, the Paris correspondent for *The New York Times*) the first film made in Hollywood exclusively for export to France. Utilizing most of the same technical personnel as did its American sibling, *Spectre* proffered a French translation of Edwin Justus Mayer's screenplay, rather than a Gallic adaptation in which elements which didn't "travel" well would be replaced for the convenience of the target audience.

Contemporary reviews of *Spectre* were, on the whole, more favorable than those of *The Unholy Night*. "No mistake about this one," crowed "Maxi" for the international edition of *The New York Times*:

> It has the Hollywood stamp from start to finish. No detail is left out, as is usually the case with local product. A hit here, due for a long run and sure to please locally owing to the native love for detective stories.

Clocking in at ninety minutes, the film opened in Paris on May 7, 1930, and was still going strong at year's end. None of the records I've been able to track down mentions Boris Karloff in conjunction with this Gallic version (the *Bibliothèque du Film*

The shades of two of the doomed regiment may be seen on the left and that of Major Mallory on the right. The others (*left to right*) are Ernest Torrence, Natalie Moorhead, Dorothy Sebastian, Sojin, Roland Young, and Claude Fleming.

does note "So-jin" in its cast listing), so presumably the Briton worked his magic only for American audiences. Of the French cast, Georges Renavent (Dr. Ballou) turned up in dozens of English-language pictures shot in Tinseltown, and he, fellow Parisian Jules Raucourt, and André Luguet, a Belgian, were commended by the critics on their ability to speak their native language well. Lovely Jetta Goudal — whom the French considered a product of Hollywood although she had been born in Amsterdam — was thought to speak French "with an accent partly English, partly German." No one thought to comment on Canadian Pauline Garon's pronunciation.

"The picture is well cast and acted," concluded Maxi. "Its one drawback, if that, is that those more sensitive in the audience get the creeps."

Le Spectre Vert—MGM — May 7, 1930 — 90 minutes

Cast: André Luguet as Lord Montague; Jetta Goudal as Lady Efra; Pauline Garon as Lady Vi; Georges Renavent as Dr. Ballou; Jules Raucourt as Sir James Ramsay [*sic*]; with Marcelle Corday, Pierre de Ramey, Albert Petit, Arthur Hurni, André Berley, Barrier, Youca Troubetzkof, Jacques Vanaire, Arnold Korff, So-jin [*sic*], Eugène Stuber, Georgette Rhodes

Credits: *Director:* Jacques Feyder [Lionel Barrymore, uncredited]; *screenplay:* Edwin Justus Mayer; based on *The Doomed Regiment* by Ben Hecht; *adaptation:* Dorothy Farnum; French version of scenario and additional dialogue: Yves Mirande, Frédéric Mauzens; photographed by William Daniels; *art director:* Cedric Gibbons; *sound:* Douglas Shearer

Notes

1. Several contemporary commentaries insist that Hecht's short story was *The Doomed Regiment*.
2. Kotsilibas-Davis, p. 85.
3. Ibid.

HIGH TREASON

Gaumont-British — silent version: 90 minutes — Trade show August 9, 1929; general release September 9, 1929 — sound version 100/95 minutes (nine reels; 8,350 feet) — March 13, 1930

Cast: Jameson Thomas as Major Michael Deane; Benita Hume as Evelyn Seymour; Basil Gill as Stephen Deane, president of Europe; Humberston Wright as Vicar-General Stephen Seymour; Henry Vibart as Lord Sycamore, the presiding judge; James Carew as Lord Rawleigh; Hayford Hobbs as Charles Falloway; Milton Rosmer as Ernest Stratton; Judd Green as James Groves; Alf Goddard as Badger; Irene Rooke as senator; Clifford Heatherley as delegate; Raymond Massey as peace league delegate; Wally Patch as commissionaire; Kiyoshi Takase as tunnel bomber; with René Ray

Credits: *Director*: Maurice Elvey; *producer*: L'Estrange Fawcett; *scenario*: L'Estrange Fawcett; based on the play by Noel Pemberton-Billing; *cinematographer*: Percy Strong; *second assistant camera operator*: Alan Lawson; *art director*: Andrew Mazzei; *assistant directors*: David Lean, Fred V. Merrick; theme song "March on to Peace" by Patrick K. Heale and Walter Collins; dance number "There's Nothing New in Love" and incidental music by Louis Levy, Quentin Maclean, and Desmond Carter; a British Acoustic Film (sound version)

Synopsis: The year is 1940. When a passenger car attempts to smuggle liquor through a frontier station on the border, a grenade is thrown by guards on one side of the fence. This leads to an exchange of gunfire, and the incident itself threatens to incite war between the Atlantic States and the Federated States of Europe. "Secret forces," blares a radio broadcast from New York, "are driving the great continents into war as surely as they did in 1914. We look to London, the headquarters of the World League of Peace, to prevent a conflict."

The London of 1940 is an extensive metropolis, quite removed from the vista a citizen of the late '20s would have recognized. The air is speckled with airplanes and dirigibles, and the Thames seems also to have grown wider and more heavily traveled. Dr. Stephen Seymour (Humberston Wright) heads the World League of Peace, ably assisted by his daughter Evelyn (Benita Hume). Evelyn, it devolves, is in love with Major Michael Deane (Jameson Thomas), officer-in-charge of the Mobile Air Staff of the European Ministry of Air. Everyone seems bellicose at the ministry, as is witnessed when one of Deane's staff harrumphs about declaring war when footage of the altercation at the border is aired on the major's teleradiograph, a combination phone/television screen.

Concerned as Dr. Seymour is about Evelyn's dining out with Michael that night, he has far weightier things on his mind. The Atlantic States Council is debating whether to send an ultimatum to the European government, and Seymour must make sure to communicate with the New York Peace League headquarters to defuse the situation. Seymour's message arrives in time to be read at the meeting, but frightened council members conjure up visions of destruction by air ("And that," thunders the doomsayer, "is modern war!").

As the debate continues, the camera tracks back to reveal that a group of black-clad, heavily smoking privateers has been eavesdropping on the proceedings via another teleradiograph. The group stands to make quite a bit of money if it can prod the politicos into organized hostility. "Fortunately," chuckles one of the munitions men, "politicians never realize the part played by professional agitators in provoking war."

War is on Evelyn's mind as she and Michael head out for an evening of dining and dancing. Even as the couple is tripping the light fantastic at a trendy club, a group of agitators has rigged a bomb to explode in the midst of the Channel Tunnel. The detonation collapses the tunnel, killing everyone aboard the London-Paris dining-car express, and the revelers at the nightclub are informed of the incident via an announcement board hanging on the wall. "The government has decided on immediate mobilization," they are advised; "All men under fifty and all women subject to the Conscription Act of 1938 will report immediately to their depots." Evelyn and Mark part company, seemingly doomed to be on opposite sides in the impending war. "You've no moral courage," she tells him, when he moves to join his men. "You're really ... a coward!"

At Mobilisation Centre number 3, a line of dispirited women in civvies channels through a door at the far end of the hall, from which emerges a line of trim, white-uniformed, ersatz-military women. As this transformation takes place, the munitions group is initiating an assault on the Peace League headquarters. A biplane, flying scarcely yards above the building's roof, drops its bomb, and the ensuing conflagration seems almost apocalyptic in scope. Miraculously, Dr. Seymour escapes unhurt; he informs Evelyn that he's off for a last-ditch meeting with the president. "I am a man of peace, but I go prepared!"

The president of Europe is, at that very moment, polling his counselors: peace or war? When the vote comes back a draw, President Deane (Basil Gill) casts the tie-breaker for war. He intends to announce the declaration of war to the world at midnight. Evelyn, meanwhile, has headed over to the mobilization center, where she attempts to rally the white-clad women, the vast majority of whom are members of the Peace League. Clad from head to foot in black, Michael and his aviators confront the women. "I warn you," Michael snarls at his erstwhile dance partner, "don't interfere!" "And I warn you," Evelyn answers, "your planes shall never start."

The soldiers cock their weapons and seem ready to fire on the women, when the teleradiograph on the wall interrupts: "Stand by! At midnight the president of Europe will make an announcement of worldwide significance." Pacifists and warriors stand around, awaiting word of their fate; Evelyn leads the women in the "Peace Song." In the presidential rooms, Dr. Seymour and the president square off, ideologically. The president admits he could call off his forces if he so desired, and that's all the Peace League vicar-general needs to hear. Allowed to address the world via radiotelegraph, Dr. Seymour announces that Europe will submit to arbitration in an effort to avoid war. Furious at his having been fooled, President Deane fires a weapon at Dr. Seymour, who pulls a pistol of his own and shoots the black-clad politician dead. Turning to the broken screen of the teleradiograph, Dr. Seymour advises the waiting world, "There will be no war."

Spurred on by these words, Evelyn exhorts her female companions to run out into the aerodrome, which they do; within moments each plane is surrounded by the women in white. Despite having heard the words over the teleradiograph, Michael orders his soldiers to "clear the women from the aerodrome!" The men, however, refuse to open fire. Presently, Michael is handed written orders to go off duty, and the deadly impasse is at an end.

A presidential aide and some soldiers breach the locked doors of Deane's office, and Dr. Seymour is led away. "I killed him to prevent war. It was the only way to peace," the stunned pacifist confesses. Seymour is brought to trial and found guilty of murder. A reconciled Evelyn and Michael listen in disbelief as the vicar-general of the World League of Peace accepts his sentence: "I am... content."

We're in a pickle right off the bat. Virtually all of the press materials consulted in preparation for this piece (including the original press book, obtained through the microfiche collections at the BFI) have *High Treason*'s high drama taking place in 1940, eleven years after the picture's release date. It's obvious that folks back then were much more optimistic about the geometric progression of scientific knowledge than they've been ever since. For instance, when Stanley Kubrick unveiled *2001: A Space Odyssey* in 1968, I remember thinking then how incredible the world was going to be, some thirty-one years thence. (Astronauts had just walked on the moon, you know? Anything was now possible.) Come 2001, not only was I not primed to cavort on the ceiling of a spotlessly white spaceship, I was still dealing with dirty subways, lost luggage, and airline food.

The aforementioned pickle isn't the scenarist's overactive imagination, but the fact that the introductory titles of the silent version of *High Treason* maintain that we'll be gawking at Britain in 1950! I don't know whether the talkie prints were set an additional decade in the future (as if to posit some bizarre symbiosis with the picture's sound technology), or whether no one involved in the actual filming bothered to check with the studio's publicity mills until after truckloads of erratum-bearing press information were dumped on an unsuspecting world. (The press book I mentioned earlier was from the *sound* version.) In the course of doing research, I was informed that the British Film Institute's print of the talkie version consists of the visuals only: "The film material that we hold is mute; the original sound material was destroyed when it began to deteriorate by the laboratory that held the film previous to its deposit with the BFI." Thus, we'll have to wait for one of those rogue collectors who (thankfully) lurk in filmdom's shadows to tell us about the temporal grounding of the talkie *High Treason*. British film-music writer John A. B. Wright has advised me that the (sound) trailer to the film has survived.

Noel Pemberton-Billing's three-act *High Treason*—first performed at London's Strand Theatre on November 7, 1928—was facilely set "some time in the future," thus sparing any worrisome anticipation on the part of ticket holders. The play enjoyed an indeterminate—but brief—run, and the first-night cast included Ursula Jeans, H. A. Saintsbury—renowned to aficionados of obscure thrillers for his portrayal of Sherlock Holmes in Samuelson Film's *Valley of Fear* (UK, 1916)[1]—and up-and-coming stage and screen director James Whale. Acting in *High Treason* did not deter Whale from involving himself with the design and direction of Anthony Mervyn's *Dreamers*, a spiritual saga about the transmigration of souls. Nor, following that pro-

High Treason

duction's rather rapid demise, did it enjoin him from falling heir (via a current dispassion with tales of pacifism and the Great War) to R. C. Sherriff's *Journey's End*, dropped into his lap by the Stage Society, which had nowhere else to turn.

History, unfortunately, has not been so kind to Mr. Pemberton-Billing. Concise biographical data have thus far eluded my efforts to track them down, and but some sketchy, unsupported and rather adulatory remarks may be found in C. G. Grey's preface to the printed text of *High Treason*.[2] Per Grey, the playwright was a pacifist, an inventor (reportedly responsible for, among other things, the sports car, the long-playing record, and the British national insurance plan), a seafarer, an aviator, a squadron commander of the Royal Naval Air Service, and a member of Parliament. After the war, the newly idle juggernaut "busied himself with the housing problem" and went on to invent new types of houses before taking off for Australia.

Grey concedes that this shopping list of the man's many interests "gives no impression of [Pemberton-Billing's] character, other than that he is constitutionally combative and quite undefeatable." As *High Treason*—both onstage and onscreen—has dropped off the face of the earth in the intervening decades, it may be argued that his putting pacifist pen to paper resulted in the man's only poor inning. If, as the preface maintains, "Professional critics and convinced pacifists alike condemn[ed] the play," one is left to wonder just why the property was thought worthy of a blatantly expensive adaptation to film.

Perhaps the reason is that Fritz Lang's *Metropolis* had landed in Britain in March of the previous year, and the edited epic (it was trade shown at 10,000 feet) had impressed everyone. *The Bioscope* summed up its exhibitor-oriented critique by crowing how the picture was "the most remarkable and unique spectacle ever shown on the screen" (March 24, 1927). Even *The Times*, London's most venerable organ of measured understatement, admitted (on March 22 of that same year) that *Metropolis* "proves how wide are the boundaries of [cinematographic technique] and how little they have hitherto been explored." Those must have been fighting words to the national collective cinematic consciousness, for the search was soon on for grist for a similar, albeit more imposing, mill. (Highlighted by a selection of scene stills from Lang's masterpiece, the March 15, 1927 edition of *The Morning Post* asked its readership, "Are British Films menaced by a German 'Hollywood'?"—two days *before* the Ufa import had its UK premiere.) *High Treason* was to be Britain's defiant response to *Metropolis*.

Now, with the exception of several examples of Michael Balcon's ineffable good taste and Alfred Hitchcock's burgeoning genius, "the English silent cinema" and "the full-length motion picture" did not enjoy a happy marriage. While the industry could crank out notable short subjects with regularity, it proved unable to infuse the lion's share of its output of feature films with anything remotely resembling fascinating qualities. Perhaps because they were (in the words of Claude Rains) "so *very* British," the island empire's cinematic movers and shakers set out to record for posterity seemingly every nuance of daily British life. Paeans to the folk who made England great—if only by their doggedly providing the most mundane of services to their communities—were produced in impressive numbers (and latter-day commentary on these has maintained that the sheer number of such pictures remains their *only* impressive attribute), as were studies of the sundry lords and ladies who had breathed British air since the dawn of mankind. Undeniably valuable filmic records of Shakespearean goodies as enacted by world-renowned interpreters were offset by adaptations of drearily banal literature that were foisted on the public solely because the originals had been authored by Britons. An argument could easily be made that England's silent cinematic arm succeeded in taking one of the most remarkable peoples on earth and making them as bland and colorless as the London fog.

In addition to its being a countermeasure to *Metropolis*, *High Treason* may also have been regarded as a consciously administered antidote to British cinematic stultification. The following text (taken directly from the picture's press book) assured potential audiences that they were going to be treated to sights they'd never seen before:

> HITHERTO, most of the sound and dialogue films shown in this country have either presented stories of the stage or crime and in consequence, an insistent demand for "something different" has arisen. *High Treason* breaks the spell of stereotyped "talkies"; more than that, it is sufficiently unusual to be distinctive in film entertainment either sound or silent.
>
> Based on a play by Pemberton Billing, it presents a picture of the world in 1940 [*sic*] when the Peace Movement has grown [to] large enough proportions to take militant action to prevent war. No greater theme could be found for dramatization at this day when the whole world is seeking a way to permanent peace; but it may be remarked that since the primary purpose of this film is entertainment and not propaganda, the producers have wisely interwoven the world's greatest theme, the omnipotence of love in all ages and the triumph of humanity.
>
> In 1940, we shall live in a mechanized world, civilization may be tottering, but the human heart and women's assertion of their power will save the situation. This is what is pictured in the story of two great federations of states, those of Europe and those of America, on the verge of a war which is prevented by the action of the founder of the peace League in shooting the President of the federated European States as he is about to broadcast a declaration of war to the world. The trial of the man who killed another man to save the world is a martyrdom that provides the dramatic climax of the film.
>
> Such a story affords opportunities for unique visual and sound effects, and the film shows us London in 1940, with the new Charing Cross Bridge, double-decker streets, aeroplanes, airships and helicopters which rise from and land on the roofs of buildings in the heart of the City; television in everyday use, news simultaneously broadcast in sound and picture, the Channel Tunnel in operation, the nightclub of the future with its mechanical instruments for jazz music and lady fencers as cabaret turns; fashions of 1940, with plus fours for the women and soft silk shirts and knee breeches for the men; in short, an age of scientific marvels and sartorial surprises.

Tickets to *High Treason* just flew out the door, although it was apparent to almost everyone that the picture's spectacle (and not its pacifist theme) was the drawing card. *Kinematograph Weekly*, a trade journal aimed at giving the skinny to the thousands of UK exhibitors, moaned that "The story is too vague and illogical to create any great interest or point any particular moral. There is a moral, but it remains obscure unless one takes the trouble to delve beneath the surface. The dialogue, too, is utterly undistinguished."

Viewing the silent version — which is still extant and available, through the BFI — one notes that, apart from some really minor gaffs it shares with *Metropolis* (like fixed-wing aircraft negotiating turns without dipping a wing), *High Treason* succeeds in bearing a British soul. As knowing one's mind and persevering in the face of contrary opinion is the basic stuff of "stiff upper lip," it would not do to have the aviators and the pacifists enact their conflict in shades of gray. Soldiers, therefore, are uniformed in black, while the myriad forces of pacifism (mostly women, it seems) are attired in white. (In one of *High Treason*'s most obvious borrowings from *Metropolis*, an endless row of conscripted female Londoners in stylish mufti enters a changing room via one door, only to emerge through another as an endless line of dispirited, seemingly mesmerized, white-clad clones.)

Rather than depicting a central London as a supercity that defies logic and mocks reality, art director Andrew Mazzei contented himself (and his budget) with miniatures that represent an admittedly more impressive — yet still plausible — Thames embankment skyline and glass paintings that moderately exaggerate the New York skyscrapers with which most Brits were familiar only via newsreels. Likewise, the decadent Yoshiwara Club — where Metropolis's moneyed set is driven in paroxysms of lust by the false Maria — has its English counterpart in the more subdued (but no less bizarre: The "hesitation one-step" has to be seen to be believed) anonymous cabaret[3] in which Evelyn Seymour tells Michael Deane to take a hike. A take on the Channel Tunnel (which was even then an on again-off again project that wouldn't see completion and an official opening for nearly *seven decades*) provides some much-needed action, besides being another indulgence in British optimism for the future. If anything, it appears as if the British technicians were determined not to indulge in the architectural excesses of the earlier German epic, and *The Bioscope* did not offer the only commentary that took pride in the fact that "The forecast of London and New York in the future shows imagination of design within the bounds of possibility and steers clear of the exaggerated fantasy of *Metropolis*."

Inside those less awesome edifices, however, the English imagination was left unfettered. The audiences of 1929 may have had no inkling that technology would one day present them with ballpoint pens, but they were left gaping at "teleradiographs." Those and other sorts of video screens are pretty much omnipresent, in fact, hanging as they do from just about every wall in every building in the screenplay. The silent print I viewed makes a valiant effort to show that each screen has its own loudspeaker and that there's never a pneumatic tube or two far off. (Apart from the pneumatic tubes — which, if memory serves, hit their apex in the late 1950s as department store accouterments — the vision of ubiquitous audiovisual apparatus was pretty much dead on.) Presaging later days when overuse would render the effect unexciting, there's a pip of a shot where the camera tracks backward to reveal that the meeting of the Atlantic States bigwigs has been on a video screen all the while and that the warmongers have been eavesdropping!

No onscreen credit was afforded to Gaumont's special effects people, and neither the press book nor any of the documentation I've been able to track down from myriad sources over the last couple of years lends any help whatsoever. Those anonymous technicians had every reason to be proud of their miniature work — the various settings and mobile pieces are excellently constructed and reasonably well lit — even if jaded millennium viewers would never regard them as anything other than miniatures. (Still, they are *miles* ahead of the nondescript New York skyscrapers destroyed in *Deluge*.) The bombing that collapses the Channel Tunnel is more adroitly handled than the isolated bombing mission of a low-flying biplane, although the resultant damage in both cases leads one to believe that the London of the future is constructed of little else than wooden beams and loosely packed dirt.

Effects and costuming apart, the production is quite uneven. Prolific he may have been, but Maurice Elvey was never one to meld profound narrative vision with technical brilliance. One of his best efforts was undoubtedly Gaumont's *Hindle Wakes* (1927), a remake of his earlier (1918) take on Stanley Houghton's amiable play. Still, as film historian Henry Nicolella points out, the latter picture's successes may have been due to the fact that "Victor Saville co-directed and that film had the advantage of Jack Cox's superb cinematography." When assigned a feature and then left to his own devices, Elvey usually resorted to recording the scenario in the straightforward manner that so typified early British cinema.

In fairness to Elvey, Gaumont assigned L'Estrange Fawcett as line producer and scenarist. Fawcett and Elvey had worked together the previous year on *Smashing Through*, a comedy adventure tale in which Elvey had produced Fawcett's screenplay. Chronologically, *High Treason* was only Fawcett's second shot at a screenplay, and he went on to write only three more, all comedies. If the adaptation of what was intended to be a prestige production had been handed to a screenwriter with a proven track record or (at least) a measurable presence in the industry, the relative banality of the film's first unit work would lie squarely on the shoulders of Elvey (and cinematographer Percy Strong). Given that the weaknesses of the story *as filmed* were almost universally singled out for criticism by otherwise salivating British movie writers, one is left to wonder why the decision was made to entrust this expensive project to (essentially) a cinematic novice.

The six-month span between silent and sound releases points to problems that may have arisen at Gaumont-British about the filming of the talkie version. Brief mention of the talkie jump-start came from *Variety*:

> What every British producer has done to date is to follow the American lead—years later. Not so, Maurice Elvey. When he saw the talker wave coming he stopped production for eight months and then with no sound studio and a lousy untried recording system, set out to make a glorious clean-up or a terrible flop.

Musical arranger Louis Levy also made some en passant remarks in his book, *Music from the Movies* (London: Marston and Company, Ltd., 1948): "Although technical difficulties compelled us to hold up *High Treason* for several weeks while some of the dialogue was redone, the musical side was 'in the bag.'" It's impossible to compare the two versions, scene by scene, in order to determine whether some of the silent footage was reprinted and utilized with voice-over, or whether—except for long shots and scenes like the airport confrontation (which were too dark to spot which lips were moving)—all new footage was shot for the new release. Gaumont's press book omitted any word of those technical difficulties and crowed as only a press book can:

> The sound recording is the world's best, for voices, music and effects alike, and is particularly good in the graphic realism of the aeroplane raids, the explosion in the Channel Tunnel and the women's triumphal

Benita Hume is using the teleradiograph to flirt with Jameson Thomas; behind her back, Dad Humberston Wright (in the frame) is double-checking her phone bill (Photofest).

> singing of the Peace Song — to mention but a few of the "high spots" in the film.

Would that the tradeshow invitees had read the press book and then passed on the film: There was virtual unanimity that the picture's dialogue track was in need of a quick fix. Mindful that those were *British* theater managers who sank or swam according to audience levels, *The Bioscope* admitted:

> [Sound], unfortunately, was the weak point at the trade show on Thursday last. The synchronization was far from perfect, many of the voices were blurred and inaudible from a volume of sound [*sic*], and a mechanical orchestra emitted such music as to stamp it as the most diabolical invention of the age. The fact that many of the speeches, notably that of the Judge, improved as the scene went on suggests that these are defects that will be eliminated in future presentations.

Sound or no, the acting in *High Treason* is quite decent all the way around, yet there was obviously a disparity between British *film critics*, who regarded artistic competence as a starting point, and *British* film critics, who gushed over the profusion of English actors jabbering away in a homespun, high-budget talkie. *Kinematograph Weekly* typified the first school of thought when it stated:

> Benita Hume makes an attractive Evelyn, but is not equal to the limited emotional demands. Humberston Wright looks the part of the president of the Peace League, but the role does not allow him very much scope. Jameson Thomas is adequate as Michael, while Basil Gill is effective as the president of Europe. [August 15, 1929]

The more blatantly nationalistic *Bioscope*—which had earlier complained about the picture's sound—now pandered to the Union Jack and swore that, although they may have had trouble *hearing* the actors' tones,

> Jameson Thomas as the airman hero; Basil Gill, a very commanding figure as the president of the European States; Humberston Wright, impressive and affecting as the fanatical Peace advocate; Benita Hume, looking very lovely as the heroine, and Henry Vibart, the epitome of dignity as a judge of the High Court, all played with such distinction and dramatic effect as to prove that British players are unrivalled when called upon to use their voices and their own intelligence.
> [August 14, 1929]

Exhibiting the sort of no-nonsense, cut-to-the chase observations for which the American trade press had become noted, *Variety* was anything but prolix:

> A pip of a cast and Elvey's old stage producing days show in the directing of this all-talker, all-screecher. Chief among the eye-fillers is Benita Hume, humdinger. She's the first femme they've flashed on a British screen who didn't look like a powdered frump.
> [October 2, 1929]

I don't how the contemporary seat holders felt. Again, *High Treason* was released long enough after the Great War and sufficiently before World War II not to have a built-in audience base for a pacifist theme, but several of the commentators had some questions about the kind of pacifism being presented. What with the vicar general of the World League of Peace gunning down the president of Europe in an act of cold-blooded murder—and then lying like a rug on a worldwide radio broadcast—the picture wasn't portraying the sort of ethical behavior that every British Mum and Dad were supposed to be hoping for where their children were concerned. The idea that Mr. Pemberton-Billing might have benefited from a brief coming to grips with the concept before committing his thoughts to paper was penned by at least one country vicar to at least one local English newspaper. Unfortunately, the philosophy that the end justifies the means didn't originate with Pemberton-Billing, and members of some of today's sundry extremist groups have shown themselves perfectly willing to commit murder to achieve their own goals or frustrate those of their opponents. I seriously doubt whether Ralph Spence, George Bricker, or any of the production staff on Warner Brothers' *Sh! The Octopus* screened *High Treason* for ideas on how to depict the violent underbelly of peace leagues.

Without the soundtrack of the talkie version available, one can only guess at the musical value of the peace song into which Evelyn (and anyone standing in her shadow) launches at moments in which inspiration is required. The recurrent anthem is titled "The Peace Song" in the silent print but was composed (music by Walter Collins, lyrics by Patrick K. Heale) as "The March to Peace" originally. (In the sound version, the march was presumably sung by Benita Hume or mouthed by her and sung by Marni Nixon's great-grandmother.) The march and a dance piece titled "There's Nothing New in Love" (most likely played for the "hesitation one-step" mentioned earlier) were the only two original numbers in the picture. As for any other music that may have appeared in the sound release, John A. B. Wright mentions that

"Louis Levy had been a music 'fitter' for Gaumont British for some years and we assume that the 'score' for *High Treason* is mostly stock material from music publishers' libraries (probably Campbell Connelly)."

High Treason holds one's attention without being particularly striking either as pacifist propaganda or science fiction. The idea that a mere eleven (or even twenty-one) years would see such incredible advances in communications, architecture, aerodynamics, and the comfort-oriented domestic sciences smacks of fantasy, rather than sci-fi. This is despite the fact that most of the flashier devices shown would end up as mundane labor savers by the end of the twentieth century and were, in fact, present in embryonic form in 1929. There is no denying either the scientific legitimacy of many of the ideas presented, or the inherent charms of future fashions; what is ludicrous is the conceit that everything has been designed, implemented and grown mundane within the brief span of eleven years. The underlying story had been done before and has been done since; in almost all cases, it has been done better. Nonetheless, *High Treason* has a fascination about it that is hard to explain but easy to appreciate. Here is a sampling of British opinion:

> "One of the most arresting of film productions." (*Daily Mail*)
>
> "Nothing that one can say of this great and greatly successful effort can exaggerate its significance…. In having contrived a great entertainment, Maurice Elvey has achieved a masterpiece." (*Sunday Pictorial*)
>
> "Not only the best talking film yet made, but the screen's greatest achievement in imaginative construction." (*Daily Express*)
>
> "The wealth of spectacle and the accuracy of detail make this picture a most impressive production… great entertainment." (*Daily Chronicle*)
>
> "A remarkable British talkie, perhaps the best yet." (*Sunday Times*)
>
> "*High Treason* is a masterpiece. Whereas, in most talking pictures, sound has been timorous and blatant in turn, it is here eloquent and triumphant." (*Referee*)
>
> "*High Treason* is very realistically staged, and, indeed, the mise-en-scène altogether is on the grand scale." (*Daily Telegraph*)
>
> "With some healthy editing, shearing the last reel or more completely, *High Treason* can be made into acceptable entertainment for any house anywhere. They'll like it or they'll hate it, but they'll all go." (*Variety*)

Notes

1. In fact, Saintsbury had essayed the role of the Great Consulting Detective upon the British stage more than one thousand times before the 108-minute feature film was shot. In the England of the day, the classically trained actor was the Sherlock Holmes of his generation.

2. The playwright financed a very small vanity edition (twenty-five copies), and photocopies of copy number seven (presented to Ursula Jeans) came into my possession due to the kindness and generosity of silent film buffs Steve Joyce and Henry Nicolella. Book searches and author queries addressed to any number of libraries, archives and literary periodicals have not uncovered any other editions of *High Treason*.

3. I can't possibly improve on the press book's helpful verbal tour of the cabaret, so I won't try: "Before the development of the dramatic crisis in the café scene, womenfolk will enjoy a rare feast of future fashions. And not only in clothes; cabaret dancers are replaced with feminine exhibitions of fencing, a phantom orchestra plays with a full complement of jazz instruments but no instrumentalists, while the guests dance a new kind of hesitation one-step. Note too that the guests dine reclining on divans and that the men have gone back to knee breeches, soft silk open-neck shirts and opera cloaks for evening wear."

THE SPIDER

Fox Film Corp.—September 27, 1931—65/59 minutes

Cast: Edmund Lowe as Chatrand; Lois Moran as Beverly Lane; El Brendel as Ole; John Arledge as Tommy; George E. Stone as Dr. Blackstone; Earle Foxe as John Carrington; Manya Roberti as Estelle; Howard Phillips as Alexander and Paul; Purnell Pratt as Inspector Riley; Jesse De Vorska as Goldberg; Kendall McComas as Ole's son; Ruth Donnelly as Mrs. Wimbleton; William Pawley as Butch; Warren Hymer as Officer Schmidt; Ward Bond, C. A. Bachman, Anders Von Haden as Policemen; Raymonda Brown, Marguerite Caverley, Doris Morton, Lee Kinney as Usherettes; Pat Haley as Electrician; John Lester Johnson as Nubian Slave; Robert Kerr as Stagehand; with Violet Bird, Margaret Mayo, George Milo, Frank Henry, Charles Hammond, Helen Long, Helen Lambert, Jimmy Gray, Peggy Graham, James McPherson

Credits: *Directors:* William Cameron Menzies, Kenneth McKenna; *associate producer:* William Sistrom; *assistant director:* R. L. (Leslie) Selander; *continuity and dialogue:* Barry Conners, Philip Klein; *contract writers:* Albert Lewis, Leon Gordon; photographed by James Wong Howe; *art director:* Gordon Wiles; *film editor:* Al de Gaetano; *music score:* Carli Elinor; *sound recording:* Alfred Bruzlin; based on the play *The Spider* by Fulton Oursler and Howell Brentano

Synopsis: Chatrand the Great (Edmund Lowe) is the featured attraction at the Tivoli, one of New York City's numerous vaudeville houses. The master magician is quite renowned—his stage show is even now being broadcast over the airwaves—and his mystical talents are well displayed via a series of breathtaking illusions. In the second half of his show, which is to be devoted to feats of mental magic, Chatrand introduces his assistant, Alexander (Howard Phillips). When it is revealed that Alexander—an amnesiac—had been found wandering about Washington, one of the radio audience, Beverly Lane (Lois Moran), wonders aloud whether the mysterious assistant might really be her lost brother, Paul. Uncle John Carrington (Earle Foxe) shrugs off the idea.

Beverly and Uncle John head over to the theater and arrive between shows. The picture of Paul in Lois's locket doesn't bear much resemblance to the poster of Alexander at the Tivoli entrance; still, to be fair, Chatrand's assistant is wearing a mask in the display. Inside, through a peephole in the curtain Chatrand espies Beverly, whom he recognizes because of a picture in the locket Alexander has. The magician runs to his assistant and hypnotizes him on the spot: "You will hear a voice you've heard before. You will see a face you know. When this happens, you will remember everything clearly, without effort."

The show starts. Chatrand works the audience, holding up objects he's taken from audience members, while Alexander—masked and hooded—identifies them from the stage. When the magician reaches Beverly, the girl hands him her locket, much to Uncle John's displeasure. "I remember! I've seen it before!" thunders Alexander, as a shot rings out. A hand wearing a spider ring drops a gun to the floor as chaos ensues. Onstage, Alexander collapses; in the audience, Uncle John does likewise. The police are called, and Chatrand has Dr. Blackstone (George E. Stone) assist the wounded man.

The police arrive, and Officer Schmidt (Warren Hymer) loudly takes over. Alexander is discovered in a heap onstage, and next to him lies a pistol that has been fired once. At first Chatrand says the gun is a prop in the act; upon closer inspection, however, he says that he's never seen that pistol before. Alexander comes to in a chair onstage; he and Beverly recognize each other. Alexander (Paul) then blurts out, "He tried to kill me and I had to do it!" Needing time to think, Chatrand tosses his cloak over the cop's head and disappears through a stage trap. As the police comb the theater for him, Paul tells his sister that he fled after hitting Uncle John, who was suspected of embezzling the siblings' funds. Thinking his uncle had died, Paul left for parts unknown.

Beverly tells Chatrand that Paul has been relating events that had happened two years earlier. Uncle John had had many enemies, and one man — who had lost a great deal of money because of John — has of late been calling him regularly. The police enter moments later, and not only don't they believe the exposé of Uncle John, Inspector Riley (Purnell Pratt) arrests Paul for murder: Carrington has expired.

Against his better judgment, Riley agrees to let Chatrand stage a "séance," as the murderer must still be in the theater. The house lights are dropped, Paul is placed in a trance, and within moments, wispy, white-shrouded figures cross over the medium's head. The central figure metamorphoses into a large hand, which begins to write as Paul fades from sight. The hand blurs and becomes a featureless face. "Who are you?" Chatrand asks. The apparition intones:

> "I am John Carrington. There is a man present who swore he'd kill me.
> He is now sitting in the audience. My eyes are boring into his guilty soul.
> His hands are trembling.... His conscience is yelling like a thousand
> fiends, and yet I shall name him."

A shot rings out, shattering the glass pane on which "John Carrington" had appeared. Paul is unhurt, and Riley discovers a handcuff-less Chatrand sporting a small, Carrington-like beard. What's more, the murder weapon has disappeared from under the inspector's nose. Chatrand wants another crack at working on the murderer's nerves; Riley, in desperation, agrees.

The lights fade as the music rises. The curtain opens, and Chatrand once again places Paul in a trance. Paul stands and recounts his vision:

"I see an elderly woman ... [and] a man beside her. I see ... poverty. The man wishes to kill himself, but first, something else ... vengeance!" As the police watch carefully, the audience members begin to react. Paul "sees" darkness ... something white, white in darkness... masked men and women, knives, blood, an operating table... the man is there. "I see a hand.... On the hand is a spider ring!" In the audience, frantic hands pry the ring loose; it is kicked away from its owner.

Chatrand has Paul zero in on the murderer. "What row is that man sitting in?" "Row three... row four... row five." "What is the number of his seat?" "The number of the seat is...." Again a shot rings out; in silhouette, Chatrand falls. The lights are brought up instantly, and Paul rushes to help the wounded magician.

In the aisle stands Dr. Blackstone. "I killed him," he confesses. "I'm glad I did it. He deserved it. Robbed me of thousands of dollars!" Blackstone is led away, while Bev is relieved that Chatrand has only been scratched by the shot. As the audience begins to file out of the theater, Chatrand and Bev get to know each other a little better.

The Spider is all style and very little substance, having — essentially — about a two-reeler's worth of story in a programmer's package: Girl brings cranky uncle to theater to see whether amnesiac is her brother; he is. Someone in theater shoots cranky uncle. Police think magus or amnesiac did it; they didn't. Who did? Magician finds out. Finis. There is virtually no character development, no love interest (Beverly and Chatrand getting chummy at the fade is too precious for words), and no denouement: Dr. Blackstone — who has thrice discharged his revolver without raising the eyebrows of the persons in the adjoining seats — just sort of gives himself up. With the film running a taut (but somewhat repetitious) 65 minutes, one is hard pressed to understand how the eponymous 1927 Broadway play could have held the audience's attention (with intermissions) for well over two hours. Perhaps it was just the season for capes and claptrap: Bela Lugosi opened in *Dracula* at the Fulton Theatre on October 5 of that same year.

The picture marked the directorial debut of the aforementioned Mr. Menzies (1896–1957), whose strength was in imaginative set design and appointments, rather than in the choreography of his line speakers. No matter, there is little doubt that he — together with genius cinematographer James Wong Howe — made the most of his actors' movements. The men's interaction results in an opulently striking climactic scene — in which Chatrand exhorts Alexander (Paul) to look further into his soul to name the murderer — that lesser technicians might have rendered as a mundane display of talking heads. Using spartan lighting to enormous effect, Menzies and Howe never photograph magician and seer twice from the same spot. As Lowe and Phillips modulate their voices to suit the histrionics of the moment, director and photographer likewise continually shift camera angles and adjust perspectives, thus giving power and impact to what could have been a study in stasis and monotony. Screened some years back at the Museum of Modern Art, *The Spider* was thought to be "striking, with mysteriously silhouetted figures moving against stark, austere backgrounds, and strongly jagged diagonals used as an accentuating compositional device."

Menzies was born in New Haven, Connecticut (coincidentally, later the home of Petrie and Lewis, one of the most prestigious manufacturers of magician's apparatus in the world), in 1896 and followed Horace Greeley's advice not long after attaining his majority. Refreshingly, the young man did not enter the industry through the more usual route (cattle calls for extras), but rather as an art director (albeit uncredited) on *The Naulahka* (1918), a rather strange Antonio Moreno vehicle for which Menzies concocted sets that credibly suggested the Indian subcontinent. (Menzies's equally uncredited co-art director was Polish-born Anton Grot, who brought his own distinctive visual palette to such thrillers as *The Mad Genius*, *Svengali* [both 1931], *Doctor X* [1932], and *Mystery of the Wax Museum* (1933].) He then joined the art department of Famous Players–Lasky, where he received his first onscreen credit for his sketches of the offices at the New York police headquarters, which drawings

Edmund Lowe may be waving his arms, but he and his magical milieu are in the hands of William Cameron Menzies.

were reproduced as sets for *The Teeth of the Tiger* in 1919. The following year he was promoted to *credited* art director (for Raoul Walsh's *Deep Purple*), and away he went.

Like several other pictures covered in this book, *The Spider* originated under the proscenium arch. Fulton Oursler and Lowell Brentano's melodrama had opened at Chanin's Forty-Sixth Street Theatre on March 22, 1927, moving to the Music Box the middle of June. Based in part on "The Man with the Miracle Mind," a short story Oursler had penned under the nom de plume Samri Finkel, *The Spider* was damned with faint praise but nevertheless lasted some 319 performances before closing. There couldn't have been time for more than a couple of deep breaths before the play was revived (for a whopping sixteen performances) in February 1928. (Both times around, the Broadway Chatrand the Great was John Halliday, a dapper thespian whose stage mien and cultured voice would facilitate his entry into the talkies. The man who wore the cape for the play's national tour was William Courtenay, a tall, dark New Yorker who was—however briefly—being considered for the title role in Universal's 1931 photoplay *Dracula*.)

In the source play, Chatrand had been only one performer on a vaudeville slate. In the film, he's not just the only act on the bill, but also (if his named stitched on the front curtains is any indication) the theater's life's blood. Not having to share stage or storage space with other folks gives Chatrand the run of the building, and this, in turn, gives Menzies the chance for a little creative self-indulgence: The magician's trapdoors lead to a warren filled with colorful cabinets, props and trappings that would do the Phantom of the Opera proud. Moments after the almost luminescent main titles, Menzies has Lowe performing a brace of colorful illusions, straight out of Howard Thurston's repertoire. (Magical cognoscenti chuckled at *The Spider*'s indulging in a couple of magical in-jokes: Paul, the amnesiac, has been given the stage name "Alexander," after one of the premier conjurers conjuring away at the end of the 19th century, while George E. Stone is called "Blackstone," after one of Thurston's greatest rivals.

The titular "spider" is, in fact, a MacGuffin. Worn rather unobtrusively on the murderer's gun hand throughout the picture, the arachnid-shaped ring is given the slight attention it deserves only when Alexander mentions it. Let's face it; inasmuch as the folks sitting in the seats adjacent to and before and behind Dr. Blackstone can't pinpoint where that slew of GUNSHOTS is coming from, the idea that an idiosyncratic piece of jewelry is going to help identify the killer is risible. (The cinematic ring merits the briefest of close-ups only as the killer frantically rips it from his finger. I can't imagine how they focused the Music Box audience on the ring while the onstage "audience members" were having conniptions.)

Oursler and Brentano's original text has been out of print for eons, but I did manage to track down a ragged old copy some time back. Apart from the magician's being only one act of many — and the always interesting premise of having a drama set in a theater within a theater — there isn't any significant difference between the stageplay and the Conners and Klein screen adaptation. In the play (and in Grace [Mrs. Fulton] Oursler's subsequent novelization of same), Carrington is involved with "the largest dope ring in New York," and Blackstone's outrage is moral. In the movie, however, Carrington's an embezzler or a con artist or something, and Blackstone's finances have caused his trigger finger to grow itchy. Also, the film's shallow lovey-dovey stuff — true love at first sight runs neck and neck with eleventh hour conversion experiences as the most exasperating of all cinematic conventions — is handled more adroitly in the play. Still, even there one has to suspend disbelief so that the perceived need for supernatural aid in discovering the whereabouts of a pistol-firing lunatic in a crowded theater is seen as carrying more dramatic portent than a May-October romance that's been tossed in the hopper as a sop to distaff ticket-buyers.

A logical sticky point that's shared by both play and film is the (perhaps inadvertent) compression of time. Chatrand's magical feats and Alexander's mental demonstrations are held in what is essentially real time. Their tricks and displays are subject to very little editing prior to that first shot's ringing out in the silence. After Carrington is sent shuffling off to Buffalo, *reel* time takes over, and events are elided, hurried and otherwise massaged to jibe with the narrative thrust and not the clock. Nonetheless, the entire story unfolds within the course of a standard, if slightly protracted, turn at the Tivoli Theater. Traps are sprung, cops are called, chases are undertaken, and so on, but everything wraps up within a couple of hours of the outset of the performance.

However, with the seat holders at the Tivoli still a captive audience, and with Inspector Riley having only moments before announced both a murder and an incipient arrest, outside the theater a newsboy is peddling copies of the extra edition that trumpets "Man Murdered in Theater!" What's more, the front page bears a photo of Carrington! Someone might want to have a look-see over at the newspaper offices, as it's pretty obvious they have a psychic of their own on the payroll.

The magical effects, the costumes, the lighting, the off-kilter séance sequences

The front cover of the herald would have you think there's something going on between Edmund Lowe and Lois Moran. So would the last forty seconds of the picture.

(directed by Menzies, with input from Wong Howe; McKenna moved the actors around during the more mundane scenes), and Edmund Lowe are the picture's joys. Lowe was *not* one of the highlights of Fox's later *Chandu the Magician*, a rather juvenile rendition of the successful radio series of the same name. Despite the team of Menzies and Wong Howe once again sharing the driving, the tale of Frank Chandler — an American who surrounds himself with yogis until he wins the colorful sobriquet by which all other mystics shall know him — and his princess and a death ray and a wild-eyed villain didn't wow them in the boonies or anyplace else. Every viewer worth his salt realized that Chandu bested Roxor (the wide-eyed villain) only because the script had it so; all the atmospheric lighting in the world couldn't keep Lowe from fading to near-transparency beside Bela Lugosi's operatic heavy. Lowe cut quite a figure in a top hat and cloak — in his salad days, at any rate — and the role of Chatrand easily accommodated the actor's waxed mustache. In fact, from the top of his brilliantine hair to the tips of his patent leather pumps, Lowe's Chatrand seems every inch the model for Lee Falk's Mandrake the Magician. (Falk had tinkered with his Mandrake prototype back in 1924, but the comic strip didn't appear until ten years later, after the young man had sold his concept to King Features Syndicate. Falk entrusted commercial illustrator Phil Davis with the artwork, and Menzies's *Spider* might well have offered the inspiration for Mandrake's final, "classic" look.)

The dearth of dramatic detail lets *The Spider* down, though; that, and the overabundance of so-called comic relief. Chief among the perpetrators of this last is El Brendel, an ex-vaudevillian from Philadelphia whose lifelong comic persona was a mild-mannered Swedish bumpkin. Distressingly, Brendel showed up in quite a few feature films during the '30s, playing dreadful variations on a theme that was dreary enough to begin with. In the seventy-odd films in which he appeared from 1926 until just before his death in 1964, El(mer) impersonated Swedes named Oley, Ole, Olson, Olsen, Ollie, Ole Olson, Olley Olsen, Oley Olesen, Ollie Swenson, and Olaf Hanson. In the 1930's sci-fi musical *Just Imagine*, he was "Single O." He's Ole once again in *The Spider*, and he's just ol-ful.

After admitting that the picture was better than average in keeping audiences from dozing off in the heat of the afternoon, *The New York Times* complained about the sound: "The fault is not with the magic," noted reviewer A.D.S., "but with the everlasting crowd noises, which cackle and buzz and howl until the tender-eared pray for surcease from the dynamic microphones." Apparently more disposed to reviewing talkies that took place in church, Mr. S also found some fault with the comic relief, although he neglected to mention Brendel by name. *Variety*'s anonymous critic *did* use the "B" word, but felt that Brendel "was treated badly in the material dishing."

On the whole, the contemporary reviews lauded Menzies and Wong's pictorial storytelling, while hedging their enthusiasm over the thin material with which they had to work. "That this didn't result in a sock mystery talk is the fault of too much attention to the central idea and not enough to side issues that might have contributed plenty." (This is *Variety* again.) "In the ghostly stunt the camera shows its superiority over the limited legit stage in creating such strong dramatic illusions. Picture is handsomely mounted." Years later, after a screening held for museum members and guests, the Museum of Modern Art decided that "*The Spider* is... striking, with mysteriously silhouetted figures moving against stark, austere backgrounds, and strongly jagged diagonals used as an accentuating compositional device." Neither the original film notes (distributed at the screening) nor their online kin remarked about the dearth of a plot line or the plethora of comic relief.

I don't have any idea how anyone could have come up with *The Midnight Cruise* as a working title for this picture, but that's what it says in the *AFI Catalog* and elsewhere. You'd need to be psychic yourself to spot any of the surviving elements of the Oursler/Brentano play in Twentieth Century Fox's 1945 reworking of *The Spider*. Magic and mystery were metamorphosed into a mundane tale of murder and private eyes, liberally doused with '40s slickness and tailored to the charms of Richard Conte. Not a bad outing when considered on its own merits, but I can't see the ties to the Broadway original for the life of me.

The Spider is out there, but you'll have to search the nooks and crannies for it.

ERAN TRECE

Fox Film Corporation — 79 minutes — December 4, 1931 (New York); February 9, 1932 (Barcelona)

Cast: Juan Torena as Dick Kennaway; Ana María Custodio as Elen Potter; Rafael Calvo as Inspector Duff; Raúl Roulien as Max Minchin; Blanca de Castejón as Peggy Minchin; Miguel Ligero as Frank Benbow; Amalia Santee as Señora Benbow; Carmen Rodriguez as Señora Rockwell; Julio Villarreal as Doctor Lofton; José Nieto as Capitán Kin; Carlos Díaz de Mendoza as Walter Decker; Lia Torá as Sybil Conway; Martín Garralaga as John Ross and Jim Maynard; Antonio Vidal as Paul Nielson; Ralph Navarro as Inspector Gardner; Raymond López as Martín; Manuel Arbó as Charlie Chan

Credits: *Director*: David Howard; *screenplay*: Philip Klein and Barry Conners; based on the novel *Charlie Chan Carries On*, by Earl Derr Biggers; photographed by Sidney Wagner, ASC; *assistant photographer*: L. B. Abbott; *sets*: Joseph Wright; *Spanish translation*: José López Rubio

Synopsis: At the outset of a guided tour around the world, elderly American millionaire Luís Potter is found strangled in a London hotel. Considering the sundry clues found at the scene of the crime (including a hearing aid, a luggage strap, and a small bag of pebbles), Inspector Duff (Rafael Calvo) concludes that Potter had been murdered in another room and his body brought to this one afterward. He grills Dr. Lofton (Julio Villarreal), the tour leader, about his movements and those of his other group members but makes little headway. One such member, Walter Decker (Carlos Díaz de Mendoza), claims to have heard no suspicious noises in the night despite occupying the adjoining room. As he squints, trembles, and glares menacingly during the questioning, we realize that Decker is lying and that we have just arrived at the outskirts of Red Herring City.

Duff's investigation is aided somewhat by the hotel's night watchman, who reveals that, at 2:00 a.m., he had come upon a man lurking outside the Potter door, and that he can identify that man. At 4:00 a.m., however, the watchman had been whacked over the head by someone whom he *cannot* identify, but he did manage to tear his assailant's jacket pocket while on his way to the floor. More good news: A bona fide member of the group is Max Minchin (Sr. Roulien), an ex-gangster from Chicago. As Duff and Inspector Gardner (Ralph Navarro) reckon the murder to be an inside job, having an established villain on hand makes the finger pointing a whole lot easier.

The lobby is crowded with group members and potential suspects waiting to be grilled, when in walks Paul Nielson (Antonio Vidal), noted New York criminologist and fellow passenger. The old gent has barely made it through the anteroom before he keels over. In a flash, Dick Kennaway (Juan Torena), Nielson's traveling companion and personal attendant, administers smelling salts while explaining that the criminologist's tendency to faint dead away at the drop of a hat has made his revival a relatively unexceptional part of Kennaway's daily routine.

Nielson takes to the couch, so Duff heads for the lobby where, in quick succession, he meets and sizes up the following: Capitán Roland Kin (José Nieto), a young opportunist whose title is a self-imposed honorific and whose being up to no good is apparent; Señora Rockwell (Carmen Rodriguez), an insightful dowager with a keen eye and a good heart; and John Ross (Martín Garralaga), a laid-back lumber exporter from the far-off regions of Tacoma, Washington. It goes without saying that no one has seen, heard, or tasted anything even remotely dubious.

But there's more good news! The night clerk has identified the errant young man in the hall as Capitán Kin. Kin admits his folly but claims that he had merely lost his way while looking to borrow a book from Nielson. Duff's not crazy about the explanation but lets it pass. Interrupting more of the same are the Benbows, Frank (Miguel Ligero), and his wife (Amalia Santee), group members who are never without a camera or an unwilling subject. Getting nowhere fast, Duff orders that no one leave London without the permission of the authorities, then takes a moment to console Potter's granddaughter, Elen (Ana María Custodio), and to reassure her about the canniness of a certain Chinese friend of his: "*un hombre muy astuto.*"

Back at Scotland Yard, the inspectors compare notes and take to shaking their heads: That very night, the tour group is leaving on a lengthy cruise, stopping everywhere from France to Italy to Greece to Singapore, and — official threats or no -there's not enough evidence to hold them in London. As the group heads off to circumnavigate the globe, Duff discovers that Walter Decker had bribed a hotel employee not to reveal that he had switched rooms with Potter the night of the murder! Nonetheless, the deceitful Decker soon gets his; during a hotel stopover in Nice that evening, a gloved hand, poking out from behind some shrubbery, fires a fatal shot and then plants the gun in Decker's stiffening fingers in order to give the impression of suicide.

Duff shows up in the morning, takes in the situation at a glance, and calls Sybil Conway (Lia Torá), knockout actress and Decker's estranged wife. Sybil meets with Duff at the hotel, where she admits that, years earlier, she had been married to a certain Jim Maynard — a jewel thief of no mean reputation — and that she had run away from Maynard with Decker and a couple of bags of diamonds. Maynard swore a ghastly revenge, so there's little doubt that either the bag of pebbles was meant to be a harbinger of death or that Jim Maynard is traveling as one of the group. Sybil agrees to unmask Maynard for Duff, but she is shot dead (the gloved hand again) as the elevator slowly carries her and the inspector down to the hotel lobby.

Again, with no evidence hard or fast enough to hold anyone (or everyone), the group is off once again, with Elen instructed to notify Duff of any nefarious goings-on via telegram. All is quiet from San Remo to Hong Kong; Dick Kennaway and Elen take a shine to one another, but no one else shuffles off to Buffalo en route to the Orient. In Hong Kong, though, Elen overhears a merchant calling out Jim Maynard's name; she promptly alerts the group, a move that puts her in danger. Despite an attempt on her life at the Pacific Cable Company office, she gets a wire off to Duff. The tenacious Scotland Yard man arranges to fly to the group's next landfall — Honolulu — also, providently, the home of his old friend and colleague, Charlie Chan.

Chan (Manuel Arbó) and Duff enjoy a friendly reunion, sharing memories and impressions as they're driven to police headquarters. There, in an unguarded moment, Duff is shot in the back by that mysterious gloved hand. Threatening to resign from the force if denied permission to take over the investigation, Chan packs to accompany the ship to San Francisco, the final stop on Dr. Lofton's tour. He asks his superiors to inform Duff that *"Charlie Chan sigue adelante!"* ("Charlie Chan carries on.")

With only a few days (six, per the novel) to wrap things up before the Golden Gate Bridge comes into view, Chan introduces himself to the group, which he advises of Duff's critical condition. Naturally, a few of the passengers object to being interrogated by a policeman without credentials, but everyone more or less agrees to go along for the sake of the fallen inspector. Nothing of apparent import is unearthed over the next several days, but from the number of times he intones *"Gracias muchísimas,"* it's clear that the Honolulu sleuth is making progress.

Back in his stateroom, Chan is nearly shot by the gloved hand at the porthole, but the little detective manages to tear off the glove and confiscate the gun, if not the gunman. Elen shows up with an unusual little monkey-shaped figurine; it's an omen of silence, maintains Chan, who had found its twin beside the wounded Duff. Courtesy of Dick Kennaway, Chan comes upon quantities of omens of silence, carefully packed away in Paul Nielson's stateroom. Before he tumbles onto these, however, he also discovers the partner to the murderer's glove hidden in Dr. Lofton's cabin and a torn pocket in the jacket that Capitán Kin is about to toss over the side.

The night before they are all to disembark, Max and his wife throw a little farewell party, and Chan is invited. Prior to making his grand entrance, however, the crafty policeman sits at his writing desk and pens a rather interesting note:

> *Dr. Lofton: Para evitarle una situación desagradable, no diré nada ni efectuaré su detención hasta que lleguemos a San Francisco.*
> *Gracias muchísimas. Charlie Chan*

> (Dr. Lofton: In order to avoid an unpleasant scene, I will not say anything nor will I arrest you until we arrive at San Francisco.
> Thank you so much. Charlie Chan)

Four envelopes—addressed by name to Nielson, Ross, Kin, and Lofton—lie on Chan's desk. On the fantail, Chan interrupts Dick and Elen (who have finally gotten up the nerve to experiment with a kiss) and asks Dick for his support at the Minchin soirée.

The party is in full swing with music, streamers, funny hats, and acres of champagne bottles. Max and his wife sing a song to great applause, and then another, and then a third, before turning over the floor by asking for some lies from Capitán Kin. Chan joins the fête after shoving his notes under the appropriate stateroom doors and is in time to hear Ross giving a rundown of his impressions of the investigation. In response, Chan will reveal only that Potter had been killed mistakenly back in London. Watching the partygoers carefully for their reactions, the detective announces that he's not saying anything else until he takes the guilty person into custody upon their arrival in San Francisco. With this cheery news, the party breaks up, and the tour members return to their cabins.

In a series of matching sequences, Lofton, Kin, Ross, and Nielson muddle through their notes, reacting variously. In his own stateroom, Chan (with Dick Kennaway's help) is fabricating a mannequin to resemble his humble and unworthy self; this is positioned just so, giving the impression (with the stateroom lights just so) that Chan is meditating in his easy chair. The men hit pay dirt within moments, as a shadowy figure pumps a shot at the inky silhouette. Charlie and Dick wrestle the assailant into the cabin, where, with the aid of a couple of ship's officers, they subdue him: Ross is Maynard! Setting the tone for scores of unmasked bounders yet to come, Maynard is aghast to discover that he had been tricked into revealing his identity by a note which Charlie Chan had sent to virtually everyone!

The following day, San Francisco! As the music swells, Chan dictates a cheerful telegram to the recovering Duff, and Elen and Dick get in one last embrace before clearing customs.

Technically speaking, Twentieth Century–Fox's Charlie Chan series is a prime example of "crossoveritis." The adventures of the quick-witted (albeit slow-moving) Oriental policeman are as comfortable as old slippers, not only to fans of the great movie detectives, but also to aficionados of the horror and science-fiction genres as well. There are very few well-seasoned buffs who don't rejoice when their hero casts pearls of Chinese wisdom before corralling some murderous swine—from the United States, throughout Europe and the Orient, and back again—all the while drawing a paycheck from the staggeringly permissive Honolulu Police Department.

Impersonated by Warner Oland and winningly assisted in many instances by Keye Luke, Fox's Charlie Chan almost immediately developed an enthusiastic following, as ethnicity (derived from Earl Derr Biggers) and eccentricity (courtesy of Oland) melded into a classic formula. It wouldn't be long before ticket buyers looked forward to such predictable treasures as the death of the second victim (Charlie always lost one or two secondary cast members before the truth came out), the nearly successful attempt on the Chinese detective's life, and the grand confrontation scene, in which the flimsiest of evidence would be masterfully manipulated in order to bluff the villain into coming clean. Chan's (and Fox's) standard operating procedure would continue—with the blessing of picture-goers everywhere—for a good half-dozen years and sixteen features. Sidney Toler would step into the box as the "designated Chan" upon Oland's death, and Fox (and then Monogram) would continue with Toler (and then Roland Winters) for years (twelve) and features (twenty-eight) to come.

The plot elements and personality traits which would be as eagerly awaited as flowers in the spring, however, were nowhere to be found in any of the pre-'30s Chan tales. Oland took his first at bat with Hamilton McFadden's *Charlie Chan Carries On* (1931), but the crafty policeman had earlier struck out on three pitches: *The House Without a Key* (1926), *The Chinese Parrot* (1927), and *Behind That Curtain* (1929). *Key* was a ten-chapter serial which, despite its fidelity to Biggers's source novel, garnered tepid reviews and indifference at the box office; unheralded during its first run, it continued to shrink from sight until it achieved its greatest fame—as a lost film. *Parrot*, although also lost, deserves more intensive mourning: It was the handiwork of that macabre German genius Paul Leni and featured the always compelling Kamiyama Sojin as Chan. Fox's own early talkie *Behind That Curtain* emerged not long ago from the shadows, but even the presence of an up-and-coming Boris Karloff does little to enhance one of Biggers's lesser mysteries or to enliven E. L. Park's rendition of everyone's favorite Chinese sleuth.

Like two of its three predecessors, *Charlie Chan Carries On* has disappeared, so it's impossible to witness how the seeds of the Oland icon were planted. And while photos of the actor smiling ingratiatingly or glaring inscrutably are readily available, these are a poor substitute for the motion picture itself. Per the continuity script found in the UCLA Arts and Special Collections Library, the film was a slightly bowdlerized version of Biggers's eponymous novel, but here, too, we are forced to rely on an artifact rather than on the movie itself. Oland and director Hamilton McFadden's second Chan epic—*The Black Camel*—is out and about, thankfully, so a perusal of background and performance there may provide one with enough clues to make some informed deductions about *Carries On*.

Not only helpful in terms of reconstructing the English-language picture, but also with a good deal of social and cinematic significance of its own is *Eran trece*, Fox's Spanish-language production of *Charlie Chan Carries On*. The fact that this "export edition" has survived while *Carries On* has slipped into a black hole is nothing short of miraculous. While the studios carefully monitored their domestic releases—the distribution of prints, the scheduling of play dates, deliveries, returns, flat rates and percentages—all were duly noted with a meticulous attention to detail worthy of Scrooge and Marley—their foreign product was usually geared more toward making a quick killing and then moving on.

Prints of an export film enjoying its first run would be sent to the studio's pertinent "foreign office"—occasionally run by a native-born middleman working for a piece of the action—which would oversee distribution, circulation, and collection of revenues. From theaters in the larger cities, the prints would be shipped to outlying districts, where they would travel the circuit, always subject to local censorship (the Catholic church could usually be counted on to intrude), deterioration, and less-than-ideal storage conditions. Far from the all-seeing eyes of the accountants back in Hollywood, prints would sooner or later be written off as too worn for further commercial use or simply vanish altogether. And while their camera negatives and other first-generation elements were warehoused at the studio facilities, early-'30s, foreign-language materials weren't given top priority in the later switch from nitrate to safety film; many titles which escaped destruction due to less-than-optimum conditions abroad were done in by apathy here at home. Were it not for the pack-rat propensities of private collectors over the years, there would be fewer titles still.

Sound compounded the felony, as it had signaled the death not only of the silent era, but also the age of virtually effort-free product aimed at overseas markets. As long as there were title cards, everyone—from slinky Austrian femmes fatales to skulking Hungarian heavies—spoke English (and Spanish and French and Italian and German) with nary a grammatical glitch or hint of an accent. When technology forced people to speak for themselves, however, careers were frequently sent into tailspins (when not destroyed outright), screenwriting became less an application of romantic balderdash and more an exercise in dramatic realism, and each new technological breakthrough had to make room for its successor. Stopping to take a breath or count costs would leave one far behind the rest of the pack.

Despite the impression created in MGM's classic *Singing in the Rain*, dubbing was not the first step in salvaging reputations or retaining foreign markets. The earliest sound technicians were hard pressed just to keep volume and intonation consistent while anxious actors more or less hurled their best vocal efforts at the potted plant strategically placed midframe. In a frantic stab at muffling their characteristic whir, cameras were muted with blankets or installed within airtight cubicles, from which cameraops had to be regularly rescued and revived. The almost insufferable heat of the lights—necessary for the exposure of slow, panchromatic film within the confines of newly outfitted sound stages—wreaked havoc with sound equipment and left cast members parched and nearly speechless.

While moguls and artisans from New York to Hollywood worked feverishly to overcome the attendant curses that accompanied the blessing of sound, overseas markets—highly lucrative and by no means expendable—had special demands of their own. For foreign moviegoers, sighing over John Gilbert or lusting after Pola Negri was far less important than being able to follow the nuances (such as they were) of the story; there was no shortage anywhere of homegrown actors and actresses over whom one could later sigh and lust. Hence, there were few francs, lire, or pesos to be squandered over Hollywood has-beens mangling English prose in front of ill-concealed, primitive microphones. Then again, apart from folks who were desperate for entertainment, no one would shell out local coin of the realm for *silent* features anymore, either.

From late 1927, Hollywood began to withhold from domestic release movies already in the can, preferring to doctor them as well as they could to suit sound-hungry audiences. So as not to risk breaking the bank with every picture, part-talkie hybrids were concocted when potential returns were adjudged less than optimum. New films were scheduled for both formats—sound and silent—as the studios felt the financial pinch of rewiring their movie palaces and the independent theater owners were playing both ends against the middle. Moreover, the availability of product with sound on disc gave the more frugal entrepreneur breathing room before having to inevitably cough up for the more expensive (but all-pervasive) system of sound on film.

When Fox decided to shoot a second version of *Charlie Chan Carries On* for their Hispanic markets, they were going along with a well-established and profitable custom. Per Juan B. Heinink and Robert G. Dickson's *Cita en Hollywood*, there had been some hundred-odd other features and shorts—made in Hollywood and farmed out to Spain and to Spanish America—which had preceded the Biggers's mystery. Hal Roach Studios, for example, had made it a regular practice to have Stan Laurel and Oliver Hardy (among others) augment their physical comedy with phonetic readings of dialogue translated idiomatically into the Spanish language (among others). This practice was perceived by Roach as a charming means of dealing with a necessary evil, and foreign Laurel and Hardy buffs came to hold the two comedians in higher regard than ever for their efforts to relate to international audiences.

Most of the films that were reworked with Hispanic casts were selected on the basis of their suitability to the Hispanic temperament, which favored a mixture of the adventurous, the romantic, the humorous, and the bizarre. Because a great part of the early '30s film-slate fit this catchall description rather neatly, the variety of

The names are Spanish and Hispanic, but that's Warner Oland's kisser on this ad art.

material exported from Hollywood to Latin climes was quite extensive. Still, while the mysterious and sensual *Drácula* transcended his Transylvanian bent to earn mucho dinero south of the border (and elsewhere), the Germanic mindset of Universal's *Frankenstein* wasn't given much chance of surviving the translation, and Hispanic aficionados initially had to muddle through the English-language print when and where they could find it.

It wasn't long, of course, before the dubbing process was perfected, and the production of separate but equal versions of the same film for domestic and foreign release became a luxury rather than a necessity. Some bilingual actors continued on in Hollywood, a handful (like Martín Garralaga, Antonio Moreno, and Lupe Vélez) enjoying reasonable success in careers that depended upon proficiency in their second language. Others stayed on but alternated between character roles in American-release pictures and leads down Mexico-way. Still others returned whence they came, preferring the comforts of home to the inbred inequities of Movieland.

There was little point (and less money) in exposing white-bread America to any of these foreign-release pictures. Between the language barrier and the fact that very few of the actors meant anything at all to non-Hispanics, even the most prestigious of these "sister productions" would have been little more than an idle curiosity. As the flip side to the instant fame associated with the movies was the probability of an equally instant descent into obscurity — the phrase "out of sight, out of mind" was honed to perfection in Hollywood — a great part of the '30s Spanish-language cinema legacy was allowed to slip from the public's consciousness without a second thought.

Hence, while many film buffs are aware of the "Spanish" version of the 1931 *Drácula* (due, in the main, to MCA's much ballyhooed video release), and some remain cognizant of numerous other foreign-language editions of early '30s features and shorts, the existence of a Hispanic take on the first of Warner Oland's Charlie Chan films may be a bit of a shock to a good number of movie fans. What's more, with the film itself extant but not widely available, opportunities for criticism or appreciation have been few.

Due to the complete disappearance of the American original, it's impossible to compare *Eran trece* with *Charlie Chan Carries On*. Thankfully, save for the names of many of the characters and a medley of Raúl Roulien favorites, *trece* cleaves remarkably closely to the narrative found in Barry Conners and Philip Klein's continuity. In both script and extant Hispanic film — as in Biggers's novel — Charlie and Inspector Duff share the honors when it comes to losing a few of the featured cast and nearly become statistics themselves. Missing in both, though, is what would become perhaps the most cherished institution of all: the scene in which the murderer would be adroitly plucked from the crowd by some sidearm snookery on the part of the hereto underestimated Charlie Chan.

Also (thankfully) left behind by both treatments is Kashimo, Charlie's Japanese, low-comic assistant. It's tough to determine just what was running through Earl Derr Biggers's mind when he decided to saddle the sagacious sleuth with an inept lieutenant. It's tougher though to puzzle out why the Fox scenarists would oust the assistant from *Charlie Chan Carries On* (when a bit of "humor" might have relieved Inspector Duff's relentless frustrations) and then include him in *The Black Camel*, where one need have looked no further than Bela Lugosi's priceless performance for comic relief.

Altogether, Warner Oland wended his formulaic way through six Chan pictures before introducing his Number One Son, Lee (Keye Luke), to the public in the seventh—*Charlie Chan in Paris* (1935). For the remainder of the Oland canon, Lee would serve as a sort of Kashimo-come-of-age, proffering affectionate comic interplay with his father and frequently (but not always) coming upon a much-needed clue in the nick of time. *Carries On (Eran trece)* sets the tone for all this with a photograph of the Chan clan on Punchbowl Hill. Bearing an indisputably Chan-ish inscription (*Nunca el zorro ve el final de su cola*—"The fox never sees the tip of its own tail"), the photo depicts the sleuth (Oland's image in both films), his wife, and their eleven children, arranged in descending order of size and age. It may only be coincidental, but the picture's Spanish title (which translates as *They Were Thirteen*) might just as well refer to the detective-inspector's family as to the dwindling number of tour members on their ill-fated trip around the world. (A most pleasant vignette in *trece* has Chan seen off at the Honolulu docks by his wife and his eldest son, John. True to Lee Chan's spirit, if not to his name, John's chief concern is his being allowed to use the family car in his father's absence. A bit confusing, however, is the script's having Mrs. Chan bid her husband a heartfelt sayonara.)

Photographed some seven months after its American cousin had wrapped, *Eran trece* employed José Lopéz Rubio's adaptation of the Conners-Klein screenplay. Comparing the existing Spanish materials with both Biggers's work and the extant continuity script shows the major departure from the original to be the footage devoted to the vocal talents of Raúl Roulien, a South American cabaret singer and song writer who graced a handful of (mostly Spanish-language) features in the early '30s and whose greatest fame "north of the border" was his role as Julio Rubeiro in RKO's groundbreaking *Flying Down to Rio* (1933). Roulien's Max Minchin helps pad the running time by singing not one but three inconsequential little songs, aided only by his wife, Peggy (Blanca de Castejón), and a series of funny hats. As there is virtually no chance that Hamilton McFadden would have allowed *his* Max Minchin — sour-faced Warren Hymer—to even open his mouth to music, *Eran trece* must have been targeted (to some degree) at the Brazilian's nightclub groupies. This being 2003, most of these have doubtless shuffled off this mortal coil, thus leaving the picture saddled with an inherent weakness rather than buoyed up by an obvious strength. Nevertheless, since nostalgia in itself has always encouraged crossoveritis, Roulien (who died in September 2000 at the venerable age of 95) may be winning over whole generations of new fans as we speak.

Some buffs familiar with *Eran trece* complain about the lack of action in the film, but if blame must be apportioned, it resides with the screenplay itself, which, while boasting an impressive body count, is rather short on physical thrills. With the first murder a fait accompli, the audience starts out feeling a bit shortchanged. Things are not helped when the next couple of assassinations prove to be fairly discreet, and as none of the subsequent attempts is successful (albeit Duff's nearly being killed is unexpected and quite disturbing), the adrenaline doesn't flow as rapidly as today's viewers—conditioned by nonstop evisceration — might wish. Still, that gloved hand is kept quite busy throughout the picture. (At times, it seems to have a life of its own. When Duff is shot in Charlie's office, the hand snakes through the open window and, without the slightest sign of an errant eye or two with which to sight the gun, fires with near-deadly accuracy.)

Sharing a screenplay doesn't mean that *Eran trece*'s director shadowed *Carries On*'s Hamilton McFadden's every camera set-up, so the film — the last of David Howard's Hispanic exports— must be considered on its own merits. Howard (1896–1941), who had assisted King Vidor on various of that gentleman's pictures, made his directorial debut — and his name — in Fox's foreign-language division. Under Howard's direction here, Sidney Wagner's camera moves enough to merit mention, if not a great deal of discussion. The men do manage to limit the number of talking-head sequences (which overpopulated early '30s mysteries such as this) and, by altering the camera angles and depth of field, to keep the early scenes from appearing more stage bound than they are. The lighting is uniformly adequate, except during the climactic set-up in and around Chan's stateroom, when things are a shade too dark for comfort. Some effects (like the rear projection traffic screened behind Duff and Charlie's jaunt to police headquarters) are cheesy and inept, and certain shortcuts taken (like saving a few bucks by using Oland's photo at the opening) are to be deplored. As Howard and his crew undoubtedly drew upon the same technical resources available to Hamilton McFadden, there is no need to theorize that the studios stinted on effects work for the less critical and more forgiving Latin audiences.

About the best that may be said of the stock-footage clips of the Sphinx, the Blue Mosque, English bobbies on the move, and a brace of Indian elephants which supplant location shooting is that they were doubtless used in *Charlie Chan Carries On*, too. (Egged on by a flock of good notices from the critics— including Mordaunt Hall of *The New York Times*— Fox sprang for steamship tickets, and Hamilton McFadden sent Oland, Bela Lugosi, et al. to Honolulu for *The Black Camel*. The extravagance marked the first — and last — time that Charlie Chan ever got closer to Punchbowl Hill than was possible via standing sets and rear projection.)

Whereas Warner Oland had only to exaggerate his natural demeanor a tad in order to emerge as a credible Chinese, Manuel Arbó would have had to wallow in full-blown ethnic acrobatics to achieve the same end. Refusing to indulge in obvious gestures, the Spaniard from Madrid may well have felt that underplaying the racial elements of the role was less dangerous than skirting caricature with flamboyance. (The years spent under the tutelage of Ernesto Vilches [an intense and chameleon-like thespian, whom many regarded as the "Spanish Lon Chaney"] doubtless instilled in the young actor both a sense of dramatic balance and the capacity for good judgment.) This is not to say that Arbó was not equal to the task; it's just that — to longtime Chanatics and fans of Warner Oland in any of his guises— Arbó's interpretation doesn't strike any familiar chords.

In 1931, of course, this made no difference whatsoever. *Charlie Chan Carries On* unveiled a new, heroic Warner Oland to legions of moviegoers who had been weaned on the Swedish actor's many scoundrels. Oland had traded upon the visible evidence of his part-Mongol heritage throughout the silent era and had spent a hefty part of his already lengthy career impersonating Oriental villains (a noteworthy exception to both instances was his role as Al Jolson's dad in *The Jazz Singer*). His Charlie Chan was a new wrinkle on an old bolt of cloth, and the public eagerly embraced both persona and impersonator. The bilingual ticket holder looking to make comparisons when *Eran trece* was released (some nine months after *Carries On* and six after *The Black Camel*) had only to deal with an interpretation of rather recent vintage and not with an icon sculpted in marble. Patrons conversant in both English and Spanish, therefore, had a choice of Chans, each fresh and more than competent; to those for whom Spanish was the sole means of expression, Manuel Arbó was the only act in town.

Best remembered (when remembered at all) by the current generation of "pop" film scholars as Martín, the asylum attendant in George Melford's *Drácula*, Arbó enjoyed a prolific film career, spanning some six decades. (The Heinink/Dickson revised edition of Florentino Hernandez Girbál's invaluable *Los que pasaron por Hollywood* has the Spaniard's debut in *Barcelona y sus misterios* in 1915 and his final film, *Vestida de novia*, in 1966.) Per an interview conducted by Hernandez Girbál with Arbó in 1935 (and cited in *Los que pasaron por Hollywood*), *Eran trece* was the most memorable of the eighteen films the actor made within the first year and a half of his arrival in Hollywood. Ironically, when showered with praise for his Chinese detective by the effusive Hernandez Girbál, Arbó demurred and indicated that he had a "tremendous horror" of being typecast, of being considered as incapable of doing anything other than Chinamen. Considering that — prior to *Eran trece*— the actor had only one other Chinese characterization under his belt (Charlie Yong in *Oriente es Occidente*, the Spanish version of Universal's *East Is West* [1930]), such fears are hard to understand.

When first glimpsed on screen, Arbó's detective is nestled amid a roomful of Oriental paraphernalia and, snug in his cap and chung-sam, wields microscope and magnifying glass in true scientific detective fashion. (The existence of this cozy vignette is no guarantee of a sister scene in the Oland/McFadden original. As is evidenced by a comparison of George Melford's and Tod Browning's versions of *Dracula*, costumes and appointments could be changed dramatically without affecting either blocking or continuity. In fact, in the English-language-version dialogue continuity at UCLA, it appears that the entire encounter between Chan and Duff takes place in Chan's office at police headquarters. There is no phone call received by Chan at home.) This is easily the most telling glimpse we have of Chan "with his shoes off" throughout the entire series' run, and the notion that the detective is wont to take his work home with him — plus the obvious warmth with which Duff had shared the family photograph with Inspector Gardner — makes Chan's impassioned decision to hunt down Duff's would-be assassin all the more credible.

To followers of B movies, the most familiar name in the cast would be that of Martín Garralaga (who plays John Ross and Jim Maynard). Like fellow Spaniards Andrés de Segurola and Fortunio Bonanova (and Maltese actor Joseph Calleia), Garralaga started out in the opera, but once he was introduced to the world of filmmaking by Latin bandleader Xavier Cugat, he never turned back. Quite versatile, the actor could portray anything from beaming but brainless playboys (an early specialty) to cold-blooded murderers. That versatility led to dozens of features and continued to pay off handsomely when television called and he appeared in episodes of *Death Valley Days*, *Zorro*, *Sugarfoot*, *My Little Margie*, *Cheyenne*, and numerous other shows. Before his death in June 1981, Martín Garralaga chalked up quite a few film credits, including Republic's *Spy Smasher* and *Casablanca* (both 1942), *The Feathered Serpent* (with Roland Winters as Chan, 1948), *The Unknown Terror* (1957), *Whatever Happened to Aunt Alice?* (1969), and the immortal *Bela Lugosi Meets a Brooklyn Gorilla* (1952). (Hamilton McFadden's John Ross and Jim Everhard were played by the redoubtable C. Henry Gordon, who just about always was the mystery killer unless he was the one flashing a buzzer at the outset of the movie. Lest anyone gripe about too much of a good thing, Gordon wasn't the murderer in *The Black Camel*; the honor there went to Dwight Frye, whose homicidal butler was one of the last significant roles in which that actor got to stand erect, wear a tie, and speak in complete sentences.)

In a brief sequence missing from Hollywood's *Charlie Chan Carries On*, Charlie (Manual Arbó) relaxes at home in all his Chinese finery.

Juan Torena had the distinction of appearing in the first Spanish-language features produced in Hollywood (*Sombras habañeras* and *Sombras de gloria*, both 1929), and he was around at the end of the era, too. Sufficiently fluent in English to appear in many domestic releases (like *Meet Nero Wolfe* [1936] and *Flight to Nowhere* [1939]), the handsome actor occasionally picked up two checks for the English *and* Spanish versions of the same film (most famously, *The Devil on Horseback* [1936]). Torena's Dick Kennaway is a likable chap who credibly survives a spell as nursemaid to a grumpy, secretive old man and who emerges with his dignity intact, the girl on his arm, and smelling like a rose — no mean feat during an era when being the juvenile typically meant being pigheaded or irrelevant. (In the Oland rendition, John Garrick, a Brit noted for playing smooth operators, impersonated *Mark* Kennaway.)

Ana María Custodio — with Torena, billed on the title card — had a short-term contract with Fox. *Eran trece* was followed by her last film in Hollywood, *Mi último amor*, the Hispanic take on *Their Mad Moment*, another notch in Hamilton McFadden's gun belt. Not a great beauty (she pales besides the bubbly and bonita Blanca de Castejón), Custodio doesn't appear to be firing on all cylinders as Elen Potter; not once does she break a thespic sweat or rise above relying on stock gestures and by-the-book mannerisms. Nor does one sense much chemistry between Elen and Dick; their pairing up at the final curtain can be written off to the inevitability of early '30s movie conventions. Returning to Madrid late in 1931, Custodio's career in the Spanish cinema was put on hold for years due to the Spanish civil war. (The lovely Marguerite Churchill had Custodio's part in the domestic release, and, if her performances in similar stuff— Universal's *Dracula's Daughter*, for example, or Warners' *Walking Dead* [both 1936] — are any indication, the American walks off with the prize, gloved hands down.)

Rafael Calvo also had a six-month ticket at Fox, and it's a shame that the studio didn't see fit to extend it. His Inspector Duff is one of the most true-to-life studies in a group which reflects the tendency even the *American* Chan pictures had to reduce most of the dramatic circle to little more than types or caricatures. One is left with the feeling that, had he not been shot down in medias res, Duff would have nailed Ross/Maynard on his own. (With *Eran trece*'s late introduction of Charlie — the Chinese sleuth doesn't toy with his microscope until *41 minutes* into the 79-minute picture — the soon-to-be-traditional loss of a few extraneous cast members is attributed to Duff's sluggish investigation. This is patently unfair; the evolving formula would always include the winnowing of the featured players, even when Charlie blew into sight moments after the opening credits.) Calvo also returned to Spain soon after the Biggers mystery, and Fox's loss became Spanish (and Italian) cinema's gain. (*Carries On* was the last American feature for Briton Peter Gawthorne, whom Leslie Halliwell described as a "splendidly pompous-looking British stage actor." That may be so, and Gawthorne did do scads of English films and did tread the boards in London's West End until his death in 1962, but I'll still take Rafael Calvo, thank you.)

Sharing the longevity enjoyed by most of his male *trece* colleagues, José Nieto parlayed his linguistic skills into a film career which lasted almost fifty-five years and ran the gamut from obscure Spanish silents to mainstream classics (*A Farewell to Arms*, 1957) to bona fide, megabuck blockbusters (*Doctor Zhivago*, 1965). Nieto's Capitán Kin is so obviously a bottom-shelf rotter that — hallway lurking and torn jacket pocket or not — there's no way he could ever turn out to be more than an apprentice gigolo or a parasite. (Still, even sight unseen, the nod has to go to George Brent in *Carries On*.)

The aforementioned Raúl Roulien and Blanca de Castejón make an interesting pair. His Damon Runyonesque Max Minchin — cranky and impatient, with vestiges of comic menace — is the most interesting of the travelers, and, for all my groaning about its superfluity, his last reel talent show (only three minutes in length) remains novel and amusing. Señorita de Castejón's Peggy Minchin is likewise *Guys and Dolls* material, but the pert little actress — who would headline her later Hollywood/Hispanic features — is adept at avoiding the shrillness indulged in by the normal run of English-speaking ex-molls-turned-respectable wives. (As mentioned earlier, the Warren Hymer-Max Minchin is probably akin to the Warren Hymer-whomever, and if Marjorie White as Sadie Minchin is anything like her Rita Ballou in *The Black Camel*, then she can't shine Blanca de Castejón's shoes.)

None of Earl Derr Biggers's stories were great shakes as mysteries, and, save for the Chan series and the quirky *Seven Keys to Baldpate*, the rest of the prolific ex-journalist's scribblings have vanished like *Charlie Chan Carries On*. Basically a hack (an education at Harvard was not a guarantee of exemplary writing skills or good taste), Biggers may not have intended to create an immortal figure in his Chinese detective, but he was quick to jump on the bandwagon when *House without a Key* (1925) took off. Readers familiar with his six novels may have been surprised to discover that the affable sleuth of the movies was several generations removed from the Chan of the books, who (per Robin W. Winks[1]) "often casts a chilling shadow over his ratiocinations." Picture goers familiar with the first five Warner Oland features may not have been surprised to discover that *Charlie Chan's Chance*, *Charlie Chan's Greatest Case*, and *Charlie Chan's Courage* were simply remakes of the detective's first three filmed adventures, massaged to accommodate the ever more popular Oland. Earl Derr Biggers died in 1933, just as Chan was turning into a cash cow.

Charlie Chan Carries On was itself remade as *Charlie Chan's Murder Cruise* (1940), massaged this time around to accommodate Sidney Toler. Carrying nowhere near the shaky "A" status of its lost predecessor, the picture enjoys Montague Shaw as Inspector Duff, Lionel Atwill as the tour-spinning Doctor Suderman (originally Lofton), and old Merciless Ming himself — Charles Middleton — as the camera-toting Mr. Walters. Considerably less fun is the ever-petulant Robert Lowery, whose proscribed lovey-dovey relationship with Marjorie Weaver has to be the most far-fetched thing in the picture.

Nearly a quarter century after his Charlie Chan feature, Manual Arbó played the Frankenstein monster in a parody triptych made in Spain. How much closer to *Eran trece* can you get than *Tres eran tres*?

With the exception of *The Black Camel*, all of the early Oland episodes have scurried into cracks in the framework of time. Although *Eran trece* doesn't allow us to witness firsthand the birth and infancy of the greatest of all Chans (embodied by Warner Oland), it remains a significant and enjoyable picture in its own right, and its having survived the intervening decades allows us a glimpse at that initial episode, as (per the Apostle Paul) through a glass darkly. It is also another example of the engaging world of foreign "sister" productions that, sirenlike, lures commentators and critics (as well as film buffs with an eye for history or intrigue) onto the shoals of creative cinema from an era long gone.

Notes

1. "Sinister Orientals" in *Murder Ink*, ed. Otto Penzler. Workman Publishing Company, New York, 1977, p. 493.

THE MONKEY'S PAW

RKO Radio Pictures— December 28, 1932 (preview); January 13, 1933 (general release)— 58 minutes

Cast: C. Aubrey Smith as Sergeant Major Tom Morris; Ivan Simpson as John White; Louise Carter as Mrs. Jenny White; Bramwell Fletcher as Herbert White; Betty Lawford as Rose Hartigan; Winter Hall as Mr. Hartigan; Herbert Bunston as Samson; Nena Quartero as Nura; J. M. Kerrigan as Corporal O'Leary; LeRoy Mason as Afghan; Nigel de Brulier as Hindu fakir (in prologue); Lal Chand Mehra as Nura's Hindu lover; Gordon Jones as Soldier; Nick Shaid as Hindu fakir; Sidney Bracey as Pensioner; John George as Hindu; Harry Strang, Angus Darrock, Harold Hughes as sergeants; George Edwards as juggler

Credits: *Director*: Wesley Ruggles; *executive producer*: Merion C. Cooper; *executive in charge of production*: David O. Selznick; *assistant director*: Doran Cox; *director of the prologue*: Ernest B. Schoedsack; *screenplay*: Graham John; based on the short story "The Monkey's Paw," by William Wymark Jacobs in his *Lady of the Barge* (New York, 1902) and the play of the same name by Louis N. Parker (New York, January 30, 1922); *director of photography*: Leo Tover; *camera operator*: Harry Wild; *assistant camera operators*: Joe Biroc, Harold Wellman, Jimmie Daly; *additional photography*: Edward Cronjager ASC, Jack MacKenzie ASC, J. O. Taylor ASC, Harold Wellman ASC; *gaffer*: J. Almond; *art director*: Carroll Clark; *set decoration*: Thomas Little, G. Rossi; *photographic effects*: Lloyd Knechtel ASC, Vernon L. Walker ASC, Linwood Dunn ASC; *effects technicians*: Harry Redmond Jr., Marcel Delgado, Orville Goldner; *film editor*: Charles L. Kimball; *music director*: Max Steiner; *music and effects recording*: Murray Spivack; *sound recording*: Hugh McDowell Jr.; *makeup*: Sam Kaufman, Mae Mark, Paul Stanhope; *still photographer*: Oliver Sigurdson

Synopsis: While a blizzard screams eerily outside, Sergeant Major Tom Harris (C. Aubrey Smith)—a stalwart, one-armed retired British soldier—is telling tales about India to his crony, John White (Ivan Simpson), and John's wife, Jenny (Louise Carter). They listen nervously, with a sort of dark delight, for they have long suspected that most of Tom's yarns take shocking liberties with the truth.

At last, Tom holds them in the palm of his hand with a curious yarn about a monkey's paw a Hindu fakir had given him. Anyone holding this paw and making three wishes will have all three come true, but they will come true in such a way that the wisher will wish he had never made the wishes.

As Tom had come in from the icy night outside, old John White pours many a glass of hot grog for him. After a few drinks, Tom takes the very monkey's paw out of his pocket and shows it to John and Jenny. It exercises a powerful fascination upon John. A little scared, but also a little tipsy, so that he becomes bold, John—usually shy and insignificant—steals the paw from Tom's overcoat pocket as the latter is leaving.

John insists to Jenny that he stole the paw for a lark and that he really doesn't believe in silly superstitions. He insists likewise to his son, Herbert (Bramwell Fletcher), when the latter jokes with him about the paw before leaving for the electric company where he is employed on the night shift.

Secretly, John White makes the first of three wishes. He is hoping if a man wishes for something that can do no one evil, the wish cannot be fraught with ghostly consequences. John's wish is that he receive 200 pounds ($1,000) in order to buy a little home for his son and prospective daughter-in-law, Rose (Betty Lawford). He makes the wish after his wife has gone to bed.

The next morning a man knocks on their front door. He is Mr. Samson (Herbert Bunston), a lawyer from the electric company. He tells them that their son, Herbert, was killed during the night, while in the midst of telling fellow workers a story about a monkey's paw. He had laughed so hard that he lost his balance and had become caught in machinery that mangled him beyond recognition.

The lawyer attempts to console them in their bereavement, and, on leaving, hands John White a bit apologetically the company's check for 200 pounds — insurance compensation for an employee killed while on the job.

After the heartbreaking funeral, John's wife and poor Rose, their lost boy's fiancée, reproach him. Why had he made the wish after Tom Morris had warned him of the consequences? It is a pitiful situation. Timid, gentle John White has never meant anyone harm in his whole life.

Suddenly, however, Mrs. White is seized with an inspiration. Where is the monkey's paw? She finds it. She wishes for her son to rise from the dead and live again. No sooner is the wish made than Herbert's old-time gentle rap is heard on the front door. John White is terrified. He fears that if his son returns, looking mangled, it might drive his wife insane. He remembers that there is still a third wish left. While he fumbles around, looking for the monkey's paw, the knocking at the front door becomes more insistent. His wife has found that the bolt is stuck. As she tries hard to open the door — and the knocking has become a loud banging — John White finds the monkey's paw and wishes his son back in his grave and at peace!

The knocking ceases. Mrs. White opens the door. No one is there.

Then John White wakes up. It has all been a bad dream. His son Herbert comes in — to announce that he has been made a foreman at work and will now have enough income to marry Rose.

If that seems to be a quite lengthy list of credits for a 58-minute film that reportedly ended up featuring only the sparsest of supernatural special effects, it must be understood that *The Monkey's Paw* was essentially two separate elements conjoined at the hip. There had been no preproduction plan for a prologue set in India; the prologue was concocted after the main body of the picture had been shot, edited, and polished, and the RKO brass discovered that the final cut was only a shade over a half hour in length. What was in essence a three-reeler had thus far cost the studio nearly $120,000.

The preprologue *Paw* was to have begun with Alan Mowbray sitting by the fire, regaling Ivan Simpson and Louise Carter with the mystical artifact's sordid history. This rather straightforward narrative sequence was to have been spiced up by some optical work that would meld the superimposed face of the most menacing-looking monkey the production staff could find with the flickering fireplace, its attendant smoke, and the like. As anyone familiar with Jacobs's original may remember, the tale's power lay in the assault of the circumstances on the reader's imagination: Mrs. White's scrambling madly to undo the door locks while unholy noises are heard from the outside is all the more powerful for there being nothing there once the door has been flung open. The camera trickery augmenting Mowbray's storytelling, stop-motion choreography of the paw itself (fabricated by Marcel Delgado and animated by Orville Goldner) and a flashback illustrating the magical paw's origins were to be the purely cinematic facets of an authentically British presentation of horror conveyed via suggestion and suspense.

Alan Mowbray's face had been familiar to moviegoers since the early '20s, but his clipped English tones had been audible to those same folks only since the coming of sound. Still, Mowbray had been in well over three dozen features prior to being signed for *The Monkey's Paw*, so he was bringing an established presence to the story. For reasons that are still not perfectly clear — the studio claimed illness on the actor's part — Mowbray was replaced by crusty old C. Aubrey Smith a day into shooting. Smith was head of Hollywood's "British colony," and he was — to the average American, at any rate — more English than any half dozen other "colonists" rolled into one: Few Americans would dispute that the white and woolly Briton and the popular image of the British raj seemed to go hand in hand.

Executive producer Merion C. Cooper had plundered the colony not only for Mowbray (and Smith), but also for Ivan Simpson, Bramwell Fletcher, Herbert Bunston, and Betty Lawford (reportedly Peter's cousin). The only non-Brit among the principal cast was Iowan Louise Carter, who had been playing somebody's mother from the first moment she stepped before a camera, which moment was recorded in 1924's *Truth about Women*. All save Lawford (with only *Paw* and *The Return of Sherlock Holmes* [1929] to her credit) and Carter (*Paw* and 1935's *Mystery of Edwin Drood*) would end up as lower-shelf genre favorites by the end of their careers, but all — including the ladies — were the crucial dramatis personae for the planned shoot of *The Monkey's Paw*.

When the shoot came in at the running time it did (director Wesley Ruggles had shot Graham John's scenario in its entirety; did no one with a practiced eye not anticipate the footage shortfall?), the guano hit the fan and John was sent back to the typewriter for more pages. A solution was reached in the form of a prologue, set among the exotic reaches of India and including a bit of explosive action (supposedly occurring in the Khyber Pass) tossed in as a sop to anyone who might otherwise be unmoved. Nick Shaid ("a genuine Arab," boasts the caption on the original studio still I have from the film), who had been hired to impersonate a Hindu fakir, and New York dancer Nena Quartero — playing the role of "Nura," a native hottie who sought love (but found only disillusionment and death) with the help of the monkey's paw — happily saw their roles expanded in direct proportion to the picture's lengthened running time. Nigel de Brulier — another Brit — and Irishman J. M. Kerrigan were added to the cast, and the Khyber Pass action sequence (filmed near the ever-popular Bronson Caverns) was added to explain Smith's missing limb.

Some six weeks would pass between Ruggles's original ending and the filming of Graham John's new material. The new footage — some 70 scenes worth — virtually doubled the length of the thirty minute anomaly that had given Selznick apoplexy, but the prologue's leading directly into Aubrey Smith's fireside narration necessitated the removal of much of the original flashback sequence, which was now dramatically redundant. Merion Cooper brought in his partner, Ernest B. Schoedsack, to direct the additions, and Schoedsack in turn brought in Jack McKenzie to map out the camera work. All sorts of process shots were added — Mario Larrinaga's talent at glass paintings helped expand the breadth and depth of RKO's standing sets without breaking the budget — and Quartero was now directed to expire at a pace onscreen.

(It's unclear why Wesley Ruggles wasn't tapped to direct the new sequences. He was free to do so, being between pictures [*I'm No Angel* had wrapped at the end of September, while *Bolero* didn't start production until November] the week the new footage and retakes were to be filmed. Selznick may have held Ruggles responsible for the high cost and unacceptable length of the product to that point, but again, shouldn't either Cooper or Pandro S. Berman, his associate producer, have recognized the screenplay's deficiencies from the start? As for Leo Tover's being replaced, the move was probably made due to Schoedsack's familiarity with McKenzie's work, rather than any ill feeling being directed toward Tover. In any event, at the time of the new shoot, Tover was working on *College Rhythm* over at Paramount.)

Genuine Arab Shaid brought exotica, Nena Quartero added erotica, and the prologue added much-needed running time. For all that, the newly reworked *Monkey's Paw* was still a pig in a poke, as it now unreeled at a very awkward fifty-eight minutes. Now basically a $150,000 film, *The Monkey's Paw*— the product of two directors, a half dozen cinematographers, any number of effects technicians, and a jury-rigged, episodic screenplay that drew its extended opening from thin air and its "all a dream" ending from the dreariest of cinematic conventions — presented its parent studio with a serious marketing problem. If it provided the studio with anything, though, it was an excuse to get rid of Wesley Ruggles.

The Monkey's Paw was the last feature Ruggles (1889–1972) directed at RKO Radio. The brother of comedian Charlie Ruggles, Wesley broke into the industry in 1914 and had been one of the original Keystone Kops. Actor eventually metamorphosed into director, and the director so grew in experience and capability (and the estimation of then studio chief and executive producer William LeBaron) that *Cimarron*— RKO's grandest production of 1931— was assigned to him. When LeBaron moved to Paramount, though, it was only a matter of time before circumstances (and David O. Selznick) forced Ruggles (and Leo Tover) to do likewise. Even had *The Monkey's Paw* come in on schedule, under budget, at optimum length, and with superlative notices, the picture — which (per the *AFI Catalog*) ended up costing slightly more than one-tenth of *Cimarron*— would have been the handwriting on the wall for Wesley Ruggles.

Top-billed C. Aubrey Smith was then in the midst of a five-year run that saw him trundle onto a soundstage (usually at MGM) in a different role roughly every seven and a half weeks. This may have been nowhere near the record, of course, but considering the venerable Briton started his Hollywood film career in 1931 (at the age of sixty-eight), the man's vigor was remarkable. Nor did it take long for his popularity — based to no little extent upon his curmudgeonly charisma — to soar. Smith was easily the biggest name and most familiar face in *The Monkey's Paw*, and RKO's move to replace Alan Mowbray with him was a fortuitous coup. No one counted on any of the picture's other principal players to draw flies.

Smith couldn't save *The Monkey's Paw* all by himself, though; there were just too many setbacks to be overcome. Not only did the picture boast no big names,

Shaid flourishes the monkey's paw, as Nena Quartero flashes some thigh. Both *Paw* and thigh have gone missing these many years.

but it also had no real love interest, either: Nura and her honey (played by renowned screen scorcher Lal Chand Mehra, who — in real life — was India's official attaché to the Olympic Games) are part of the exposition; Herbert and his honey (Lawford) are British — need I say more? Even with that marvelously creative prologue, the film was too short to sell on its own or to top a double bill as the "A" attraction. W. W. Jacobs's enormously popular story had been in print continually since 1902, and there had already been two film versions — with the more recent (1923) having been released by Selznick's *father* — that had enjoyed successful runs in the United States. Unfortunately, the earlier pictures had been silents, and their English-language title cards gave no hint of the linguistic difficulties that a British cast, speaking British English (including slang and topical allusions) culled by a British scenarist, could foist on an unsuspecting movie audience in (say) Teaneck, New Jersey.

> While Jacob's [*sic*] story has been somewhat embellished, the main eerie situations remain, and are presented in a tense and effective manner... Characterisation is very good indeed.... The supporting cast is strong in every department.
> [*Picturegoer*, June 17, 1933]

In the old days, British families had to turn to delusional tales spun by officers from the Raj for a decent evening's entertainment. Here, C. Aubrey Smith is dishing it out, and (*left to right*) Ivan Simpson, Bramwell Fletcher, and Louise Carter are taking it in. Nena Quartero's thighs may be found in opposite diagonal corners.

> Resourceful direction, faithful characterizations, convincing settings, dramatic portrayal. Excellent general entertainment with possible exception of squeamish patrons.
> [*Cinema Booking Guide Supplement*, April 1933]

Both of the preceding notices were taken from English publications. *Harrison's Reports*, whose reviewer obviously attended a press screening held before the preview, noted ominously that the company had not yet arranged a release date. Clocking the picture at fifty-six minutes, the reporter concluded that

> This picture has been produced well, but it is too morbid for entertainment purposes. Although the horror part of the picture is shown at the end to have been a dream, the terrible feeling that it leaves in one is not erased... In addition, the atmosphere of mourning and sorrow because of the death of the son is extremely depressing.
> [November 26, 1932]

(For all my kidding about "British presentations of horror based on suggestion and suspense," please note that *Harrison's Reports* found *The Monkey's Paw* more affecting than it had Universal's horrific heavy guns—*Murders in the Rue Morgue, The*

Old Dark House, and *The Mummy*—that had sparked in preview before the RKO film.)

Variety covered the picture (now tagged at fifty-five minutes) some six months later, after it had played *for one day* on a double bill at Loew's Theatre in New York City. Reviewer "Chic" had his finger on the *Paw*'s fading pulse, and his diagnosis wasn't good:

> Too late to ride along with the goose-pimple cycle of last year and too morbid to be regarded with great favor in its own right.... There is a banal "it was a dream" tag that spoils the effect for the appreciative without squaring for the less intelligent. *Paw* is not a picture for the general audience and too labored for the art theatres. It seems to fit nowhere in particular, but may have some "B" success.
>
> [June 6, 1933]

The film did well enough in England to encourage the Brits to have yet *another* go at the property some years later, and Mexico's Calderón Studios gave Jacobs's classic tale some Hispanic flavoring in 1961. To date, the only truly successful American screen adaptation of the tale was by Matt Groenig and his cohorts, for a Halloween *Treehouse of Horror* episode of *The Simpsons*. As for the 1933 Ruggles/Schoedsack mutation, it exists in fragmentary form only (and try to find *that*), its negative having disappeared years ago.

Jacobs's short story was a natural for broadcast during the heyday of radio (the BBC adapted the tale at least twice for its *Appointment with Fear* series), and there have been several television presentations both here and abroad, as well. (Even *Buffy, the Vampire Slayer*, had an episode that borrowed heavily from the tale: Marti Noxon's season-five teleplay, *Monkey's Paw*.) As for other versions that had seen theatrical release, let me suggest the following:

The Monkey's Paw—Magnet Films (UK)—February 1915—2800 feet

Director: Sidney Northcote
With John Lawson as John White

The Monkey's Paw—Artistic Films (UK)—February 1923—5,700 feet

Director: Manning Haynes; *producer*: George Redman; *screenplay*: Lydia Hayward; *cinematographer*: Frank Grainger
With Moore Marriott as John White; Marie Ault as Mrs. White; Charles Ashton as Herbert White; Johnny Butt as Sgt. Tom Morris; Tom Coventry as the engine driver; with A. B. Imeson, George Wynn

The Monkey's Paw—Kay Films (UK)—June 1948—64 minutes

Director: Norman Lee; *producer*: Ernest G. Roy; *screenplay*: Norman Lee, Barbara Toy; *cinematographer*: Bryan Langley; *musical director*: Stanley Black

With Milton Rosmer as Mr. Trelawne; Megs Jenkins as Mrs. Trelawne; Joan Seton as Dorothy Lang; Norman Shelley as Monoghan; Michael Martin as Harvey Kelly; Eric Micklewood as Tom Trelawne; Brenda as Hogan Beryl; Mackenzie Ward as Noel Lang; Alfie Bass as Manager; Hay Petrie as Grimshaw

Espiritismo (Spiritism) — Calderón (Mexico) — 1961 — 85 minutes

Director: Benito Alazraki; *producer*: Guillermo Calderón Stell; *screenplay*: Rafael Travesi, Guillermo Calderón Stell; *cinematographer*: Enrique Wallace; *musical director*: Antonio Díaz Conde

With José Luis Jiménez, Nora Veryán, Beatriz Aguirre, Carmel González, Antonio Bravo

TRICK FOR TRICK

Fox Film Corporation — April 21, 1933 — 66/69 minutes
Cast: Ralph Morgan as Azrah; Victor Jory as La Tour; Sally Blane as Constance Russell; Tom Dugan as Albert Young; Luis Alberni as Metzger; Edward Van Sloan as Mr. Russell; Clifford Jones as David Adams; James Burtis as Sergeant Lombard; Adrian Morris as Boldy; Willard Robertson as Dr. Frank Fitzgerald; Herbert Bunston as Professor King; Dorothy Appelby as Maisie Henry; Booth Howard as Jed Dobson; Jimmy Leong as Chinaman; John George as Dwarf
Credits: *director*: Hamilton McFadden; *assistant director*: George Blair; *screenplay*: Howard J. Green; *contract writers*: Bert Hanlon, Ben Ryan; based on the play *Trick for Trick*, by Vivian Cosby, Shirley Warde, Harry Wagstaff Gribble, Fulton Oursler; *cinematography*: L. W. O'Connell; *technical effects*: William Cameron Menzies; *art director*: Duncan Cramer; *film editor*: Robert Bischoff; *wardrobe*: William Lambert; *musical director*: Samuel Kaylin; *sound recording*: A. W. Protzman

Synopsis: Detective Jed Dobson (Boothe Howard) visits the home of master magician Azrah (Ralph Morgan) as part of his ongoing investigation into the mysterious death of Azrah's erstwhile assistant, Evelyn Maxwell, who had been pulled from the river some six weeks earlier. Dobson goes way back with Azrah — the two men have known and liked each other since the magician's days as a performer at Coney Island — so he's not surprised to find the magus holding a séance, attended by a Mr. Russell (Edward Van Sloan) and his daughter, Constance (Sally Blane).

It devolves that Constance's skeptical fiancé, David Adams (Clifford Jones), had tried to force his way into the house, only to be turned away by Azrah's right-hand man, Albert Young (Tom Dugan); David has meanwhile gained entrance through a window. Confronting Azrah, he accuses him of Evelyn's death and claims that the cancelled checks he has — written by Azrah to Evelyn — somehow support this theory. Within moments, David has been stopped in his tracks by a wall of fire (whipped up by Metzger [Luis Alberni], Azrah's eccentric, scientific sidekick) and manhandled by Albert, who has started the fracas expressly in order to get his hands on those checks.

In walks La Tour (Victor Jory), a rival magician, with whom Evelyn had worked before joining Azrah's act. When Azrah offers to stage a séance that evening in order to gain information from Evelyn's shade, La Tour insists that Azrah work under the rigid conditions that he (La Tour) and psychic expert Professor King (Herbert Bunston) will impose. As the séance is being readied, La Tour has his two henchmen make off with Constance; while the rest of the party is off rescuing Constance, he plans to bribe Albert to sabotage Azrah's performance. The plan goes for naught: The henchmen — a Chinaman (James Leong) and a dwarf (John George) — prove to be inept (they get Constance no farther than the front lawn), and Azrah, having overheard La Tour's attempt at bribery, sends Albert off to Washington to deliver an envelope.

Before the séance gets under way, Azrah informs Dobson that someone in the room is armed. A search uncovers the fact that everybody in the place is packing heat. The guns are collected, La Tour has Azrah securely bound and gagged in his chair, and the lights are lowered. Almost immediately, the lights flash on and off; when they are raised, La Tour is found bound and gagged — and dead. Stabbed through the heart!— in Azrah's place. It is determined that the murder weapon is a penknife that belongs to Evelyn Maxwell's father, who is there in their midst, disguised as Professor King. Receiving Dobson's permission, Azrah continues with the séance.

With the help of his assistant, Maisie Henry (Dorothy Appleby), some of Metzger's ingenious electrical equipment, and recordings of conversations Evelyn Maxwell had before her death, Azrah creates the illusion that the dead girl is there in the room with them. "Evelyn" recounts how La Tour, having gotten her pregnant, discharged her and abandoned her; the distraught young woman could not bring herself to go home and reveal everything to her parents. Her father confesses to having killed La Tour inadvertently, for — having thought that Azrah was responsible for Evelyn's death — he had sought to stab Azrah in the darkened room. He is arrested.

Azrah then explains that La Tour's sending the cancelled checks (written out of charity to Evelyn) to David instead of returning them to Azrah indicated that La Tour had killed Evelyn and was trying to frame his rival. David apologizes for having jumped to conclusions, and Azrah recommends that the young man pay more attention to Constance in the future.

Trick for Trick, the legitimate theatrical production, opened at New York's Sam Harris Theatre on February 18, 1932, barely two weeks after its trio of playwrights had received their copyright notice. (Azrah was Canadian James Rennie — most famously Dorothy Gish's husband for some years— who found practicing the sleight-of-hand skills required for the part more rewarding than learning his sides, which he reportedly regarded as being somewhat underwritten.) Unlike *The Spider*, this magical melodrama didn't have legs and closed after sixty-nine performances. The Fox Film Corporation, which had bought the rights to the play prior to its opening, viewed this as a mixed blessing. On the one hand, it rendered moot the studio's contractual agreement not to release the filmed version before October 15, 1932. On the other hand, the melodrama's quick demise indicated that some substantial overhauls had to be made on the screenplay if the picture was to avoid a similar fate. Contract writers Ben Ryan and Bert Hanlon were assigned to work with scenarist Howard J. Green on the project.

Also hired — to tinker directly on Cosby, Warde and Gribble's original text — was Fulton Oursler: author, playwright, and magic aficionado. (The *AFI Catalog, 1931–1940*, maintains that Oursler was one of the *four* writers responsible for the play, *Trick for Trick*, but I've been unable to find any collaboration for this statement.) It was stipulated that Oursler, who occasionally wielded a wand himself (as "Sandalwood the Magician"), would receive no screen credit for his contributions to the scenario's source material.

With Edmund Lowe doubtless a trifle tired of séances, hypnotic gestures, and bug-eyed yogis, the role of the leading prestidigitator fell to Ralph Morgan, older brother of Frank (who had a wizard of some note in *his* professional future). Morgan had almost played Lowe's brother-in-law (Robert Regent, the inventor of the much-coveted death ray) in *Chandu the Magician* the previous year but was replaced at the last minute by Henry B. Walthall. Ralph had joined the industry during the century's mid-teens, although he certainly didn't get into films for the money: He and Professor Marvel both were heirs to the Angostura Bitters fortune. In the early '30s, the size, frequency, and variety of his film roles increased, and he soon was reckoned as one of Hollywood's most versatile character men. One of his meatiest roles may have been Czar Nicholas in the Barrymore-engorged *Rasputin and the Empress* (1932), but the riskiest part he ever played was that of first president of the upstart Screen Actors Guild the following year.

Morgan's métier was usually villainy, so his benevolent turn in *Trick for Trick* was as much of a departure from the rapidly congealing norm as had been the naïve and guileless Nicholas. His Azrah is the kind of magician every magic-crazy young boy wants to be: living in a castle replete with sliding panels and trapdoors (and a pulsating, art-deco, pseudoscientific laboratory) and appointed with scads of colorful, inexplicable artifacts; attended by faithful retainers and eccentric helpers; possessed of the total sum of magical knowledge respected, admired and genuinely liked by everyone, everywhere, save for the heavy and his brace of henchmen. *The New York Times* advised that "As Azrah, Mr. Morgan is omniscient, omnipotent and omnipresent," and William Cameron Menzies was the power behind that power.

As was the case with *The Spider*, *Trick for Trick*'s plotline is simplicity itself: Someone killed Evelyn Maxwell, and Azrah proves it was La Tour. Everything else is smoke and mirrors. With the film's dramatic foundation downright skeletal, director Hamilton McFadden was compelled to resort to magic tricks and appurtenances to create the illusion that there was more to the story than met the eye. Menzies thrived on this kind of thing, of course, and the sight of a guest being relieved of his coat and hat by disembodied spirits, or of a carpet that takes to rolling unwanted guests out the door (and then to skedaddling back into the house) smacks of both the sort of optical wizardry particular to the movies and the "black arts" stage technique so well know to Fulton Oursler. As the film unreels, any tendencies toward magical monotony are avoided via intermittent displays of illusion (that wall of fire, the shade of Evelyn Maxwell, the moment the entire floor ups and disappears) and sleight of hand (when Azrah insists on producing a series of lighted cigarettes from thin air). As Margaret Tazelaar of the *New York Herald Tribune* reported:

> The high lighting effects produce much of the suspense and strangeness, and the camera angles help the illusion. The plot is merely a series of incidents leading up to the séance at midnight when a murder is committed. It has not been unfolded with any too much clarity, although the constant interruptions for magic will make those who dote on being fooled, forgive all.
>
> [June 12, 1933]

The picture isn't five minutes old when Jed Dobson espies Azrah working mediumistic wonders for John Russell, and every Universal horror fan in the audience whispers, "Edward Van Sloan." (More of the same a couple of reels later, when the

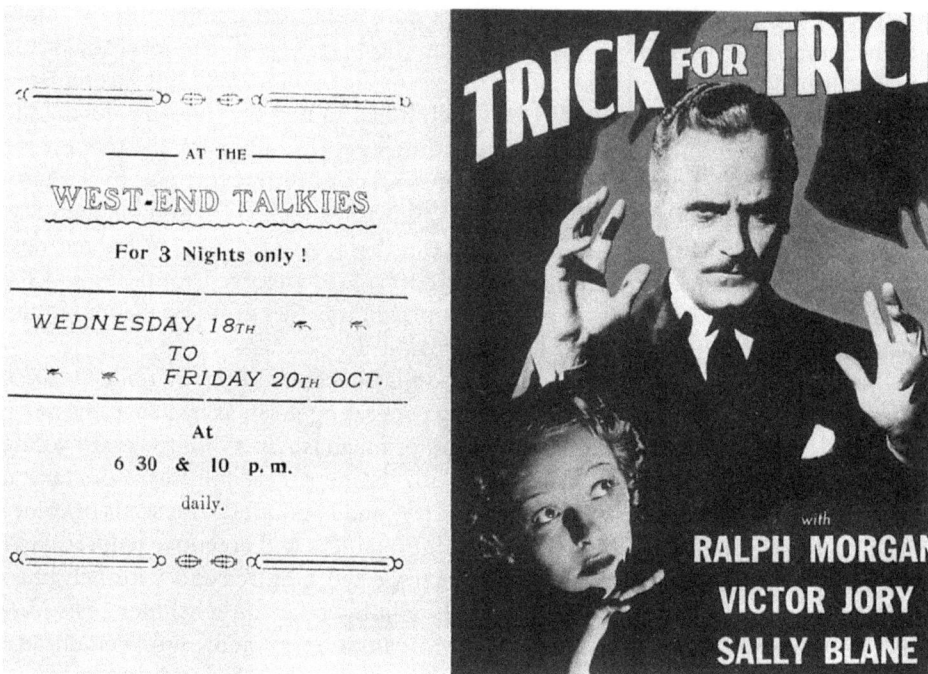

Ralph Morgan, Sally Blane, and lots of hands: the cover of the remarkably bland herald.

door opens and in blows Herbert Bunston.) It's a bit odd seeing Van Sloan — who had been in the driver's seat in *Dracula* and *The Mummy* and on the running board in *Frankenstein* — sitting back, soaking up someone else's wisdom and hope for a change, but the old boy's only there at all to establish Ralph Morgan's innate, near-supernatural beneficence and to get Sally Blane onto the screen. Blane, a near-dead ringer for her more popular sister, Loretta Young, is at once a more genial and outgoing ingénue than the sum of the trio of distressed damsels in the three classic horror films just mentioned. Not so her boyfriend, David Adams (Clifford Jones), who's definitely kith to the angry and whiney and ultimately useless juveniles impersonated by John Boles in *Frankenstein* and David Manners in *Dracula*. Jones is the worst thing about *Trick for Trick*, and even at the end of the picture — when the script demands that his dyspeptic "hero" do a behavioral 180 as proof that the heroine *had* seen something good in him — he's the least kindred spirit in the castle.

Things perk up momentarily when Victor Jory and his entourage strut in. Jory had only had a handful of pictures under his belt at this point, but his La Tour the Not-So-Great already drips with the kind of smarmy nastiness the actor could convey effortlessly when the screenplay warranted it. (*Very* occasionally a film would posit Jory on the side of the angels, but even his heroes came tinged with menace. I first encountered Victor Jory when I was a kid, watching *The Adventures of Tom Sawyer* (1938) on TV. Only Karloff's Monster frightened me more than did Jory's Injun Joe.) *Trick for Trick*'s screenplay, unfortunately, had already stacked the deck so far in Azrah's favor that, by the time he and his oddball lieutenants arrive to get things hopping, the audience views La Tour as nothing more than a minor speed bump in the

Atmosphere, à la Menzies. Soaking it all up are (*left to right*) Edward Van Sloan, Sally Blane, Victor Jory, Willard Robertson, a harness bull, Luis Alberni, Ralph Morgan, and Dorothy Appelby.

race to the exit music. La Tour's every sinister move is parried with ease, and, when the lights are raised and La Tour is sitting there, wearing Azrah's ropes and Professor King's pocket knife, you can't help but feel sorry for him. It takes some heady postmortem revelations on Azrah's part to restore any significant degree of viewer loathing for La Tour, and that just doesn't seem cricket.

La Tour's entourage—consisting as it does of a "Chinaman," a dwarf, and Professor King, the psychic expert—is more colorful than the hapless heavy, but the first two are little more than walking magician's props, gaudy and eye catching. The Chinaman is James B. Leong, born in Shanghai in 1889 and destined to become one of the more familiar Oriental bit players in the early talkie era. The first credit of his I've been able to locate is for *Purple Dawn* (1923), in which he played a character named Quan Foo. The fact that his character had a name was fairly unusual for the time, but the rest of the situation—the "Chinese" leading roles being played by Bessie Love and Edward Piel, for example—was depressingly pro forma. Leong's appearances in many '30s and '40s serials and potboilers went uncredited, and, like so many other "friendly" Orientals, he was frequently hired to impersonate a Japanese during the war years. Over time, Leong ran the gamut of cinematic Chinese stereotypes, and his nameless henchman in *Trick for Trick* doesn't stray off the path.

Ditto with the "dwarf." John George, the Syrian immigrant who played dozens of hunchbacks, dwarfs, or hunchbacked dwarfs opposite everyone from the Man of a Thousand Faces to the Rat Pack, was technically too tall to qualify as either a midget or a dwarf. George debuted as Ali Bara in *Black Orchids* (1917), an early offering by Rex Ingram. As they had for so many European expatriates, title cards obviated the need for proficiency in English, and by the time sound had firmly established itself, George was as adept at American as everybody else. Together with Angelo Rossitto, George had a near lock on his particular niche in the horror and science-fiction field from the mid-'20s on. He did his (mostly uncredited) thing with Lon Chaney in both *The Road to Mandalay* (1926) and *The Unknown* (1927); Conrad Veidt (*The Man Who Laughs*, 1928); Bela Lugosi (*Island of Lost Souls*, 1933; *The Black Cat*, 1934); and Boris Karloff (*Bride of Frankenstein* and *The Black Room*, both 1935). He graced a couple of Charlie Chan adventures (*... in Egypt*, 1935; *... in the City of Darkness*, 1939), appeared in the added footage of *The Monkey's Paw* and, yes, he was in *Chandu the Magician*, too. He even stooged for Henry Brandon's Barnaby, while menacing Laurel and Hardy in *Babes in Toyland* (1934). Here, his dwarf does the usual stuff—slinking around, getting underfoot, being swatted at—without adding anything other than another askew angle in a milieu that's already swimming with them.

Anyhow, James Leong's Chinaman has to do the talking for both henchmen, as John George's dwarf is deaf and dumb. On screen, following the discovery that La Tour has not survived the séance, Leong's character responds in staccato Chinese to Jed Dobson's exasperated questions, and Dobson (and, presumably, the audience) regards this as little more than gibberish. In the picture's dialogue continuity script, however, we learn that the Chinaman has been answering Dobson's questions to the letter. As the print I viewed had no subtitles of any kind, I'm not sure who would have gotten the joke, aside from any Chinese Americans who happened to be sitting in the theater.

It turns out that Professor King is really Mr. Maxwell and that complicated gentleman is Herbert Bunston, and Mr. Bunston, naturally, is forever Dr. Seward: long suffering, slightly confused and not terribly capable. As the last-reel explanatory glimpse of Mr. Maxwell's motivation and personality reveals that he, too, is long suffering, slightly confused and not terribly capable, might we not then argue that Bunston was obviously in some danger of being typecast? The Surrey-born actor had entered films only a few years prior to *Trick for Trick*—as Lord Elton, he mooned over Norma Shearer in 1929's *The Last of Mrs. Cheyney*—but he had been treading the British boards since 1897. Bunston had worked with Ralph Morgan on *Charlie Chan's Chance* (1932) and would venture back into genre territory with *The Monkey's Paw* and *The Moonstone* (1934). Here, his character's fortuitously plunging his dirk into the wrong magician in order to skewer the murderer of Evelyn Maxwell isn't *too* much of a stretch—especially considering the nonstop visual madness that abounds in this picture—although King/Maxwell's wrongheaded proclivities push the ineptitude level of virtually everyone in the picture (save for Azrah) beyond credibility.

There's not much in *Trick for Trick* that *is* credible, but the picture doesn't really suffer for it. You're left with the same mild sense of disorientation that you have at the end of a magic show, rather than the sort of satisfaction that might come from seeing a really splendid film, but there's nothing wrong with the occasional change of pace, is there? The picture does seem to have been fooled with—I still can't figure out what the opening footage of a dredger on a storm-tossed pier has to do with anything—but I've been unable to come up with any information on pre- or postrelease edits. The kidnapping of Constance is another puzzlement; it doesn't seem to go anywhere, story-wise, other than to illustrate, once again, how no one in the joint can do anything right, except for Azrah.

Critic "Rush" put his finger on the catch-as-catch-can flavor of the film when he complained in his *Variety* review that the

> Original idea probably was a murder mystery tale woven into a background of stage magicians, depending for novelty upon certain inside slants of legerdemain. The notion has its possibilities, but in the finished picture that technique has become... overlaid with forced comedy, foggy character and bad exposition of plot.... There are 15 characters listed in the cast, and they play ring-around-a-rosy with the plot and each other until the spectator gives it all up and declines to be carried along by the progress of crime solution.
> [June 13, 1933]

As per the formula of the times, there is a surfeit of comic relief (Luis Alberni, Tom Dugan and Clifford Jones do their thing alternatively and in tandem) without there also being appreciable tension from which such relief is needed. *The New York World-Telegram* failed to see the humor in the situation:

> Acting on the theory that it still continues to be difficult to deal in mystery farces on the screen and make them funny, the adaptor, Howard Green, and the director, Hamilton McFadden, have made the effort to burlesque the plot. Only about half of it comes off.
> [June 12, 1933]

Most of the folks interested in films such as *Trick for Trick* are familiar with McFadden's connection with the earliest of the Warner Oland/Charlie Chan films at Fox. Sadly, of the three features McFadden had directed, only *The Black Camel* (1931) is extant; *Charlie Chan Carries On* and *Charlie Chan's Greatest Case* (1933) have vanished. Still, the meticulous composition on display in both *Camel* and *Trick* is evidence that the man was a director of no little technical ability and imagination and that one ought to mourn the missing Chans for his contributions, as well as those of Warner Oland.

The Spider and *Trick for Trick* were essentially cut from the same cloth, yet one ought not therefore conclude that to see the one is to see the pair. Both pictures are set in the fantasy world of stage magicians, who, although subject as citizens to the penal code, are seen to be something of a law unto themselves. In both pictures, a climactic séance — conducted by the heroic conjurer, with the resigned permission of the ineffective police — succeeds in unmasking the mystery killer. There are lots of other comparable elements as well, but these are shared by the pictures, not only with each other, but also — by virtue of '30s cinematic conventions — with just about every other mystery melodrama produced during that decade. For all that, the films aren't merely carbon copies; rather, they complement each other. Seeing them both is like watching while David Copperfield and Lance Burton each takes his turn in performing the "classics" of stage magic in his own, inimitable style.

I've never known of a print of *Trick for Trick* outside of the collections of the Museum of Modern Art (MOMA), so getting to see Hamilton McFadden's and William Cameron Menzies's handiwork may be quite a challenge. Nonetheless, appointments may be made to have the possibly unique print screened, and the tenacious genre buff may freely choose to pick up the gauntlet that circumstances have thrown down. With its recent move from mid-Manhattan to other locations, however, the *real* trick may be to find MOMA.

DELUGE

Admiral/K.B.S. Productions, Inc.—August 18, 1933—68/70 minutes Distributed by RKO Radio Pictures—Gen. Release: September 15, 1933

Cast: Peggy Shannon as Claire Arlington; Lois Wilson as Helen Webster; Sidney Blackmer as Martin Webster; Matt Moore as Tom; Fred Kohler as Jephson; Ralf Harolde as Norwood; Edward Van Sloan as Professor Carlysle; Samuel S. Hinds as Chief Forecaster; Lane Chandler as Jack; John Elliott as Preacher; Ronnie Cosby as Ronnie Webster; Philo McCullough as Bellamy; Harry Semels as Gang Member; with Edward Le Saint

Credits: *Director*: Felix E. Feist; *associate producers*: Samuel Bischoff, Burt Kelly, William Saal; *assistant director*: Eric Stacey; *special effects director*: Ned Mann; *screenplay*: John Goodrich, Warren B. Duff; based on the novel *Deluge, A Romance*, by S. Fowler Wright; *photographed by* Norbert Brodine; *camera operator*: Harry Davis; *assistant cameramen*: Bert Eason, Johnny Eckhardt, Carl Guthries; *special effects photography*: William N. Williams; *sets*: Ralph De Lacey; *film editor*: Rose Loewinger; *supervising film editor*: Martin G. Cohn; *assistant editor*: Stanley Kolbert; *music director*: Val Burton; *musical score*: Val Burton, Edward Kilenyi, Will Jason; *sound engineers*: Corson Jowett, Hans Weeren; *recording assistants*: Alf Burton, Martin Jackson, Gilbert Pollack; *chief electricians*: Al Cahen, Don Donaldson; *grip*: Robert Murphy; *props*: Charles Henley; *still photographer*: Roman Freulich

Synopsis: (Note: the storyline of *Deluge* is taken from the Italian-dubbed print, which—at fifty-nine minutes—is the only source currently available. Names and "factual data" quoted in the following synopsis follow the track and subtitles of this print.)

Eminent scientists (such as Professor Carlysle [Edward Van Sloan]) are aghast that atmospheric conditions are steadily worsening to the point that worldwide devastation will be the inevitable result. Still-operative communications systems report a continuous string of natural disasters that is wiping humanity from the face of the planet. The latest news is that North America's west coast has sunk into the Pacific Ocean.

Just outside New York, Martin Webster (Sidney Blackmer) attempts to move his wife Helen (Lois Wilson) and children to the comparative safety of a nearby quarry. Martin returns to the Webster home for food and clothing, but worsening weather conditions lead him to assume that his family has been lost. He heads off to find whatever shelter remains.

New York is decimated by tidal waves. The Empire State Building collapses, the Statue of Liberty is dwarfed by the high seas, and ocean liners are tossed about like toys.

When the all-powerful storm has calmed, Martin is found to be safe on what remains of the mainland, in a spot some forty miles from New York. Claire Arlington (Peggy Shannon), a beautiful young swimmer whose plans to paddle around Manhattan Island were disrupted by the tidal wave, has washed ashore on a nearby island, which is apparently in the control of two unstable men, Norwood (Rolf Harolde) and Jephson [sic] (Fred Kohler). It's not long before Norwood attempts to molest Claire and is strangled by Jepson for his trouble. As the men struggle, Claire swims over to the island where Martin is, but Jepson follows after her in a small boat.

In the interim, Martin has managed to set himself up in a comfortable cabin, alongside a cavern that offers additional security. Finding Claire unconscious on the shoreline, he carries her to his cabin and begins to nurse her back to health. He also quickly learns of Jepson's presence on the shore and follows him. Jepson makes contact with a band of rough-looking men — later identified as the Bellamy gang — whose violent behavior has caused them to be thrown out of a community of survivors some twenty miles away. When the recovered Claire announces she's going to see what's left of the world, Martin advises her of the presence of the men, and she agrees to stay with him for the day.

That community of survivors seems to consist of folks who had fortunately spent their vacation in the mountains, instead of at the beach. Apart from a line of men waiting to get a shave, nearly everyone is pitching in to get civilization back on keel. Tom (Matt Moore), one of the group's leaders, has his eye on Helen Webster, but Helen hasn't given up hope that Martin has survived the end of the world. Meanwhile, Martin and Claire are getting to know each other, when Jepson attacks the couple and carries Claire off to the Bellamy gang.

Coincidentally, Tom and the men from the settlement are even then making plans to destroy the Bellamy gang, as the men have found the remains of one of the settler's daughters, who had (apparently) been raped and murdered by the thugs. That night, Martin stabs Jepson and frees Claire; the two head for Martin's cabin, while the Bellamy gang and the wounded Jepson follow. The next day finds the couple holed up in the cavern and ultimately rescued by the men from the settlement. The Bellamys — and Jepson — are left for dead.

Helen, of course, is thrilled to see Martin alive, but the man is torn between the wife he has and the woman he introduced as his wife to the settlers. The tension between Helen and Claire leads to their arguing; Claire insists she will not give Martin up. Martin, however, is chosen to become the sole leader of the fledgling community, and when he heads into Helen's arms following his acceptance speech, Claire makes for the shore. Stripping down, she swims off, presumably to oblivion.

Over the years, there have been loads of films dealing with widespread destruction caused by natural disaster, chiefly because it's wonderful escapist entertainment to watch from the safety of the movie theater as some hapless victims get a real lathering. The sundry foci of devastation presented courtesy of Irwin Allen's "vision" (*The Poseidon Adventure* [1972], *The Towering Inferno* [1974], and the like) or courtesy of other folks hoping to cash in on Allen's vision (like Mark Robson and his *Earthquake* [1974]), leap immediately to mind. Coming off the brutal, divisive Vietnam era, the country obviously was in need of exposure to mass catastrophe and human tragedy that had a definite end and an upbeat message, and these films were the most memorable examples of several years' worth of violent catharses designed to purge the national bowels.

During the latter half of the 1990s, the movie industry released a new series of pictures centered on incipient, widespread death and destruction, but I'll leave it to political cynics younger than I to discuss the underlying motivation there. Wolfgang Peterson's *Outbreak* (1995), for instance, illustrated that dangers inherent in medical experimentation on animals far exceeded the naïve understandings of Dr. Moreau, and the deadly airborne virus chased down by Dustin Hoffman eerily foreshadowed the Western world's preoccupation with chemical and biological weapons scarcely a decade later. In 1997 *Dante's Peak*, Roger Donaldson's sadly predictable tale of the effect of volcanoes on mountain-based assemblages, restricted the appalling devastation to fairly narrow parameters, but the following year brought *two* exercises in depicting the virtual annihilation of the human race: Michael Bay's *Armageddon* and Mimi Leder's *Deep Impact*. Both films were SPFX delights, both sported colorful, charismatic casts, and neither was worth much thought after one left the theater.

The two-decade-long gap between these two spurts of extensive cataclysms was also peppered by other examples of similar product, as had been the lengthy stretch that preceded Allen's initial junkets in the early '70s. *Deluge* was virtually unique in that pre-Allen belt, however, as it illustrated the obliteration of everyday life and of mundane civilization, rather than the destruction of "lost" worlds, jungle-centric societies, or Atlantis. While it does not depict the total dissolution of the temporal world, and thus is not technically an example of "apocalyptic" cinema — the last-reel dust-up in 1951's *When Worlds Collide* and the evaporation of Tattooine in *Star Wars* (1977) are the only truly apocalyptic images I can conjure up at the moment — it remains one of a handful of pictures made since the dawning of the cinema that deals with worldwide trauma and subsequent activity. To be truthful, I wish that the setup for the deluge had been given in greater detail, that there had been more footage devoted to destruction in foreign climes, and that scenes of the initial moments after the reemergence of the sun had received more attention. Once everyone dries off, the story melts into a frontier town adventure bracketing a lengthy (and not terribly well structured) standoff in the wilderness.

The titular flood goes largely unexplained, as it doesn't really have a lot to do other than set up the rest of the picture, which pretty much revolves around a very sexy Peggy Shannon. None of the scientists monitoring the degrading world weather picture can make heads or tails of anything, although the word *eclipse* is tossed around with such portent that one is grateful that the world obviously has experienced nothing other than eclipse-ettes to this point. (Two of the scientists are played by Edward Van Sloan and Samuel S. Hinds, and if cinematic cerebral heavyweights like those two don't know what's up, look out.) Intercut with scenes of high winds, collapsing structures, cascading waves, and general chaos is a sequence in which the aforementioned Miss Shannon's Claire — supine and alluringly lovely — is gently informed that she'll have to postpone her swim. "Orders from the office," a uniformed hunk explains to her, as her leg is languidly greased. "Oh, well, orders are orders," the sultry swimmer replies, unfazed by — or perhaps oblivious to — the disintegration of the world outside her massage room.

It devolves that what saves Claire from the fate of the millions of other New Yorkers is her (offscreen) decision to swim right *into* the midst of the cataclysm that is strewing the heavy shipping thither and yon with no effort whatsoever. Only the rare person might decide to act thusly. Her rare soulmate, then, is Martin Webster, who decides to forego stowing his family in the cellar of his rather solid mansion and, instead, carries them off to whatever safety may be found aside a large group of boulders, where they are exposed directly to the elements. I raise these observations only to indicate that the willful suspension of disbelief—so radically necessary in order to enjoy fully most genre films—is working overtime here.

The SPFX segments that illustrate the science-fiction aspect of the picture are, by our millennium standards, rudimentary and highly uneven. For moviegoers of the early 1930s, they might have been enormously exciting. The fast-paced sequences consist of topical stock footage, some generally decent rear projection, and miniatures of wildly fluctuating quality (not always undercranked sufficiently), designed by Ned Mann and built at Tiffany Studios. The arrival of the floodwaters into New York Harbor remains (for me) the most realistic moment of the entire destruction sequence, and the miniature set—with the Empire State Building reportedly constructed at a height of twelve feet—is the best the film has to offer. Other shots of collapsing buildings are powerful in their movement while remaining unrealistic in their mien. Again, despite how the destruction scenes may strike the modern viewer, no one in 1933 doubted that's where the money was:

> Thrill of a different, imagination-stirring kind is the backbone of this show. The romance is ordinary; the mechanical effects and excitement engendered by disasters give it the novelty that predestines it as one of the most unusually spectacular films of the year.
> [*Motion Picture Herald*, July 8, 1933]

Quibbling over *Deluge*'s logic or continuity, based solely upon a few screenings of the Italian-language print that's currently available, may strike some as being unfair, but that print's the only act in town as of this writing. It may also be argued that dwelling on discrepancies regarding time in a story where circumstances have diluted time's underlying significance is ... a waste of time. Be that as it may, there's only one major head scratcher of note, so this won't take a minute.

In that uncertain period between picking himself up off the postdeluge beachfront and picking Claire up at the relatively same locale, Martin has apparently tinkered together a cabin, replete with an ever-increasing number of creature comforts. (We are led to assume that he has tinkered the cabin together; the only other explanation is that the clapboard shack has miraculously survived the hellish waters that swept away the Empire State Building.) On the inside cabin wall, Martin has been marking the passing days (via a gratuitous Italian insert: We're looking at *Maggio* and *Giugno* here). While gathering supplies (he has an impressive array of shovels on hand in the adjoining tunnel), washing and ironing his clothing, and performing his meticulous daily ablutions—his hair has lengthened not an inch, and his beard has not grown out past three of the clock—he has had time to cross out two months worth of days.

However, a short while later, while Tom is fidgeting over whether to pop the question to Helen (in that cheerful survivors' community), he reminds her that it's been *one month* since the flood and that Martin is probably no longer alive. Unfortunately for Tom, this recital does not get him so far as first base, as Martin will shortly show up—Claire in tow—and no one will give another thought to

Now *that's* a poster!

how long anyone's been anywhere. The discrepancy does give one pause for thought, though.

The only other eye opener regarding time has nothing to do with continuity, but rather with personal satisfaction. In one beautifully timed sequence, Martin has just confessed to Claire that, back when such things mattered, he was a lawyer. An instant later, Jephson jumps on him and brains him with a stick. Although hardly in the same league with any of the aforementioned special effects, it does key the savvy viewer to the fact that the lumpish Jephson was, in fact, a lover of Shakespeare in general and of *King Henry VI, Part II*, in particular.

And who would have sufficient heart to natter about the casting of Bronson Caverns as Martin's safe haven? I mean, traditions are meant to be celebrated, aren't they?

There aren't too many other highly satisfying moments involving the cast, and this is a weakness of the screenplay. Even Helen Webster's subtly signaling her willingness to share Martin in a ménage à trois with Claire is too limp a tease to follow the eradication of most of mankind. Helen is Lois Wilson, a Pittsburgh schoolteacher who entered films in the mid-1910s (she received credit in 1916's *Dumb Girl of Portici*, while Boris Karloff did not) and who made nearly 150 films before taking up with small-screen soap operas (*The Secret Storm, The Guiding Light*) at the outset of the 1950s. Lois's Helen is the traditional amalgam of *faithful* wife, who just *feels* that her husband is still alive — so take a hike, Tom — and faithful *wife*, who argues spousal ownership from a logical — and not a romantic — plane.

Claire's arguments for not sharing Martin are much more fiery and passionate

If Fred Kohler used that rifle correctly, *Deluge* would be a two-reeler for Sidney Blackmer. Peggy Shannon looks on incredulously.

than Helen's statements, so we can only assume that Claire and Martin have been doing the deed when not actually unconscious or in midflight. Arkansan Peggy Shannon had been a Ziegfeld girl in the mid-'20s and was thought a sufficiently hot number to be tapped to replace Clara Bow—the "It" Girl herself—when Bow had a nervous breakdown prior to filming 1931's *Secret Call*. The recurrent sight of Shannon in a very brief bra and panties is perhaps her most unforgettable contribution to the human side of the screenplay, but she does well enough by her lines that Claire is seen to be more than a mere plot device, meant to epitomize lust in the New Age.

Deluge marked one of the very few times Sidney Blackmer played a lead in a motion picture, and the perennial character man's tepid persona and uninspiring demeanor offer vivid evidence as to why this was so.

Burly old Fred Kohler's one-note Jephson is much more colorful and interesting a character than Sidney Blackmer as Martin, or Matt Moore as Tom, or anybody as anybody else (except Shannon), but this may have as much to do with Kohler's forceful physicality as with the scenario's deficiencies. Kohler had devoted his years prior to *Deluge* to becoming one of moviedom's most popular, brutish Western heavies, and the sight of him — armed with his rifle and clad in the sweatiest of torn longjohns— glowering at Rolf Harolde, snarling at Sidney Blackmer, and salivating over Peggy Shannon must have gone a ways in restoring the audience's cinematic equilibrium following the picture's opening shock sequence.

One might say that this picture marked Felix Feist's getting his director's feet wet, at least as far as feature-length releases were concerned. It's debatable whether even the wiliest of veterans could have kept his audiences entranced with the fragmented nature of the screenplay, let alone a man whose only credit prior to *Deluge* was *Football Footwork*, a Pete Smith short from 1932. "Considering the material, young Felix E. Feist has done rather well technically in spots," observed *Variety*, but the praise translated not into additional offers to direct features. After the RKO pickup hit the screens, Feist went the entire decade without directing another feature film on his own; he did keep busy, however, with additional novelties from Smith and Robert Benchley. Almost every mention of Feist I've read (in conjunction with commentary on *Deluge*) indicates his involvement with the script of 1953's *Donovan's Brain*, and this—plus late-career television work on episodes of *The Outer Limits* (1963) and *Voyage to the Bottom of the Sea* (1964)—round out the genre buff's files on Feist.

Unlike his director, cinematographer Norbert Brodine (aka Brodin) had been active in films since 1919, and among the plums he had shot prior to working at Admiral Productions was Wallace Worsley's *Blind Bargain* (1922) and Frank Lloyd's monumental *Sea Hawk* (1924). Throughout the '30s, Brodine would win renown as a technician of wide range, capable of handling everyone and everything from John Barrymore in *Counsellor at Law* (1933) to Margaret Sullavan in *The Good Fairy* (1935) to Roland Young in *Topper* (1937) to Lon Chaney Jr. in *Of Mice and Men* (1939) and *One Million B.C.* (1940). His work throughout the '40s would remain as varied and impressive, although it appears that he worked less frequently on more prestigious projects than he had during the earlier decade. Together with Harry Davis, Brodine photographed all of the non-SPFX footage in *Deluge*, and I read an opinion that some of Ellsworth Fredericks's late-reel establishing shots in Don Siegel's *Invasion of the Body Snatchers* may have been inspired by the Bronson Caverns sequences in *Deluge*.

Variety's Abel wasn't overly impressed by either the story ("elementary") or the special effects, which, he stated, "unreeled in none too convincing a manner." He did, however, take a moment to praise the picture's dedicated music score, which the slender array of modern commentary has variously attributed to nearly a dozen different composers. Mordaunt Hall (of *The New York Times*) must have cribbed his thoughts from Abel: "The destruction of skyscrapers is never particularly real and the rushing waters seem strangely out of focus at times. The dialogue never rises above the action of the story and the players deserve sympathy" (October 9, 1933).

Richard Watts Jr. played three on a match when he submitted his notice to the *New York Herald Tribune*:

> The collapse of the Manhattan skyline never quite succeeds in scaring you the way it should, but it is well enough depicted to be an entertaining screen stunt. Unfortunately, the story of the survivors is so completely feeble that any possible interest in the picture called *Deluge* is as rapidly and completely destroyed as the photoplay destroys New York.
> [October 10, 1933]

The scenario may have done poorly by the survivors, but Sydney Fowler Wright's source novel devoted nearly 400 pages to detailing their fortunes and travails. Of necessity, a truckload of characters populating the novel went absent in the film, and it was decided that the destruction scenes would spur greater frisson if they encompassed the decimation of New York, as experienced by that city's terrified citizens, rather than—as they were in the book—centered on the British midlands and reflected in the attitudes of domestic farm animals. A change that absolutely had to be made, if the picture was ever to get past the censors and be screened anywhere within Western civilization, involved the novel's coda, wherein Martin ended up with both Helen *and* Claire!

Deluge was Fowler Wright's second novel. His first, *The Amphibians*, which was self-published when its author was fifty years old, was intended to be the first of a trio of books that would detail British life after the flood. (In *Dawn*, the second and only subsequent volume to *Deluge*, Wright ventures back in time: New characters are introduced and the flood is viewed through their eyes.) Science fiction and fantasy novels played only a part in Fowler Wright's varied output; historical fiction, crime stories, and critical writings about World War II also saw publication. Poetry had been his first love, though, and in 1917 he helped found the Empire Poetry League, whose membership quickly came to include Gilbert Keith Chesterton. As I write this, Gus Fowler Wright—the author's grandson and literary executor—is bringing up to speed a comprehensive website devoted to his grandfather's life and writings.

Its fabled destruction footage was about the only thing available from *Deluge* for the longest while. Republic Pictures ended up with the clips, and Ned Mann's flood sequences were incorporated into the studio's 1939 feature, *S.O.S. Tidal Wave*, as well as showing up in serials *Dick Tracy vs. Crime, Inc.* (1941) and *King of the Rocketmen* (1949). (Not long after his work on *Deluge*, Mann headed over to Old Blighty, where he contributed his expertise to such gentle fantasies as *The Ghost Goes West* [1936] and *The Man Who Could Work Miracles* [1937], and the not-so-gentle *Things to Come* [1936].)

Englewood Entertainment's VHS of *Deluge* was made from the 1934 Italian release version—*La Distruzione del Mondo*—a print of which was uncovered in a Rome cinema archive by Forrest J Ackerman back in 1981. Englewood augmented the fifty-nine-minute release with subtitles (some of which are unfortunately marred by typos and misspellings), and the video—issued as part of the Science Fiction Gold Series—is perhaps the most readily available title in this book. Fans of the film who wish to see the full-length, English-language original—unavailable to me as I write this chapter—are advised to approach S. Fowler Wright's heirs via www.sfw.org.

THE VANISHING SHADOW

Universal — January 1934 — 12 chapters — c. 240 minutes

Cast: Onslow Stevens as Stanley Stanfield; Ada Ince as Gloria Grant; James Durkin as Carl Van Dorn; Walter Miller as Wade Barnett; William Desmond as MacDonald; Richard Cramer as Dorgan; Frank Glendon as Cadwell; Sidney Bracey as Denny; Edmund Cobb as Kent; Philo McCullough as Smuggler; Beulah Hutton as Sally; Don Brodie as Pilot; Lee J. Cobb as Construction Foreman; Al Ferguson as Stroud; Monty Montague as Badger; William Steele as Policeman; with Tom London

Credits: *Associate producer*: Henry MacRae; *director*: Louis Friedlander; *story*: Ella O'Neill; *screenplay*: Het Mannheim, Basil Dickey, George Morgan; *art director*: Thomas F. O'Neill; *photography*: Richard Fryer, ASC; *film editors*: Edward Todd, Alvin Todd; *futuristic electrical machinery*: Kenneth Strickfaden

Synopsis:

Chapter One: "Accused of Murder"

Electrical genius Carl Van Dorn (James Durkin) is visited by Stanley Stanfield (Onslow Stevens), also an inventor and the son of the recently deceased publisher of the *Tribune*. Stanfield shares his scientific blueprints with Van Dorn, and the result is a device that renders its wearer invisible, save for his shadow. While Stanfield runs off to the office of stockbroker John Cadwell in order to sell some bonds to finance additional research, Van Dorn experiments with a robot of his own design. En route to Cadwell's office, Stanfield saves a young woman — Gloria Grant (Ada Ince) — from being hit by a fire truck. The grateful young woman allows the young inventor to drop her off at the *Tribune* offices — where she works — and reveals that she is the estranged daughter of Wade Barnett (Walter Miller), the unscrupulous businessman who drove the senior Stanfield to an early death.

It turns out that Cadwell is in cahoots with Barnett, who orders the stockbroker to acquire Stanfield's bonds under any circumstances. Stanfield shows up at the offices moments later; he and Barnett have words, the businessman pulls a gun, and Cadwell is shot in the struggle. Thinking Cadwell dead — and realizing that Barnett will try to frame him for the death — Stanfield escapes back to Van Dorn's laboratory. He is tailed there by Barnett's henchmen, who are led by Dorgan (Richard Cramer). Stanfield disappears by means of the invisible ray, and he agrees to hide out at Van Dorn's secret laboratory at the beach. First calling Gloria, whom he "trusts implicitly" despite a minutes-long acquaintance, Stanfield drives off, followed by the henchmen; Van Dorn leaves a few minutes later in his own car. Hoping to elude his pursuers, Stanfield tries to beat a train to the crossing, but his car is struck by the speeding locomotive.

Chapter Two: "The Destroying Ray"

Stanfield jumps from the car moments before impact but lies stunned on the ground nearby. The carload of villains withdraws to a safe distance, as a motorcycle cop rides up. He and Van Dorn find Stanfield, who leaves with his partner; they manage to lose Barnett's men and arrive safely at the beach laboratory.

Back in the city, Gloria goes to see her father for the first time in ten years, and she learns that Cadwell is still alive. The henchmen follow Gloria home, where they overhear her making an appointment with Stanfield to meet that night. When the young man arrives, he is accompanied by Van Dorn, who is armed with a destroying ray of his own invention. They are beset by Dorgan and the others, who have been lying in wait. As Stanfield dukes it out with one of the men, Van Dorn whips out his destroying ray. Grabbed from behind, he struggles this way and that. The ray sweeps throughout the room and is about to reach the dazed Stanfield and Gloria.

Chapter Three: "The Avalanche"

Stanfield ducks out from under the beam and, grabbing the ray from Van Dorn, holds the villains at bay. When Gloria tries to get past them, however, she is seized, and they all escape, having first disabled Van Dorn's car. Now that he realizes that he is not wanted for murder, Stanfield is all for calling the police, but Van Dorn has other plans.

Gloria has been brought to "The Pines," a large manor house complete with a "prison room"; she is attended to by Sally (Beulah Hutton), a henchwoman. Visiting his daughter, Barnett nearly tricks her into revealing Stanfield's whereabouts; when his ruse fails, he returns to his office in the city. There, he informs Cadwell that he will obtain Stanfield's shares of *Tribune* stock, which will give him control of the newspaper. Using the invisible ray, Stanfield visits Barnett's office, where he learns where Gloria is being held. Thanks to the ray, he helps her escape from The Pines, and the couple drive off, followed by Dorgan and the other men. Thinking a "road closed" sign is merely a ruse to have them stop, they drive through the barricade, and their car is engulfed by falling debris as explosives are detonated by a roadside construction gang.

Chapter Four: "Trapped"

Miraculously, Gloria and Stanfield successfully make their way through the exploding mountainside; their gas tank, however, has been punctured, enabling Dorgan and his men to follow the car's fuel trail. Stanfield gives Gloria the vanishing ray. After disappearing before their eyes, the plucky heroine steals the gang's car, and she and Stanfield head for the laboratory at the beach. Van Dorn is not happy to see Barnett's daughter in his sanctum sanctorum but apologizes to her after he learns of her bravery.

Barnett and Cadwell understand that they must keep Stanfield and *Tribune* city editor MacDonald (William Desmond) from meeting. Van Dorn demonstrates his "electric torch," a heat ray device that can potentially cut a hole in a battleship, to his young allies. The three leave, Gloria to the newspaper in order to arrange that all-important meeting and Stanfield to retrieve his *Tribune* stock. The plan calls for the stock to be stowed in Van Dorn's impenetrable safe, which has been booby-trapped with a chemical ray that burns all the oxygen within the safe, thus killing any intruders.

Gloria shows up minutes after the stocks have been deposited and the safe is rearmed; Barnett's thugs storm in behind her. A fight breaks out, Van Dorn is rendered unconscious, Gloria—who manages to make a call to the police—is temporarily waylaid by a thrown chair, and Stanfield is punched right into the safe. The door slams shut, and the chemical ray begins to do its thing. A siren causes the hoods to flee, while Gloria, very unsteady on her feet, tries desperately to burn a hole in the metal door with the electric torch. It seems, however, that the young woman faints before she can save Stanfield.

Chapter Five: "Hurled from the Sky"

It turns out that Gloria does not faint. Instead, she manages not only to burn that hole in the safe door, but also to stick her hand in and fiddle with the unfamiliar mechanism in order to open the vault. Meanwhile, the villains—managing to shake the cops from their tail—report back to the Barnett Building. Barnett tries vainly once again to convince his daughter to use her influence on Stanfield. A bit later, she returns and waits in her parked car as the invisible Stanfield works his way upstairs to spy on the criminal mastermind. Dorgan has kidnapped MacDonald and is holding him at Frisbee Island—a remote spot, accessible only by airplane—until the stockholders' meeting has ended. Stanfield and Gloria drive out to the airport, pursued once more by a carload of henchmen. Stanfield punches the pilot, and he and Gloria take off. Some extraordinarily lucky pistol shots fired by the men on the ground far below disable the plane. Gloria parachutes safely into the water, but Stanfield and the plane crash full force into the foam.

Chapter Six: "Chain Lightning"

Luckily, while the crash has totaled the plane, Stanfield is none the worse for wear. He and Gloria hang onto the wreckage until they are rescued by a passing speedboat, which deposits them ashore a short distance away. Before long, they are picked up by Van Dorn. In the interim, Barnett has bought time by convincing the assembled *Tribune* stockholders that they cannot hold their meeting without Stanfield or MacDonald, neither of whom is present. After the company departs, the henchmen report Stanfield's and Gloria's apparent demise in the plane crash. Barnett is visibly moved and orders that MacDonald be released on the mainland.

Back at the lab, Gloria wants one more chance to save her dad from himself, so she heads to his office to convince him to mend his ways. (Van Dorn has given Stanfield and Gloria an hour to act and return, otherwise he will take things into his own hands.) Unbeknownst to Barnett, the invisible Stanfield is a witness to the conversation. Unbeknownst to Gloria, while her dad is pretending to see things in a different light, he's tapping out orders in Morse code to his henchmen in the anteroom that Gloria be followed when she leaves. In the hallway, Stanfield lets Gloria in on this, and the two leave the building via the back stairs. They head for the *Tribune* offices and are happy to find MacDonald there. The city editor assures Stanfield of his total support, and, in return, the young inventor demonstrates his vanishing ray.

In the hour in which all of these events have transpired, Van Dorn has rigged up his impenetrable vault with new booby traps. The allotted time to return having expired, Van Dorn packs his destroying ray and heads over to the Barnett Building, where he threatens Barnett with annihilation if Stanfield and Gloria are not produced within five minutes. The young couple, meanwhile, has checked in at the lab. While Stanfield repairs to an adjoining room to divest himself of the vanishing ray, Gloria heads for the vault, only to be caught fast in a pattern of deadly electric arcs.

Chapter Seven: "The Tragic Crash"

In the nick of time, Stanfield runs in from the other room and yanks Gloria to safety. She recovers in a few moments, during which time Van Dorn, who has gone to Barnett's office to square accounts, has been tied up by Dorgan. Stanfield learns of this when he calls Barnett to warn him about Van Dorn. Van Dorn is taken to the prison room at The Pines, a fact the invisible Stanfield discovers while spying in the corrupt businessman's office. When Barnett's secretary, Denny (Sidney Bracey), complains of seeing shadows all over the walls, Barnett calls Dorgan (who now has Van Dorn's destroying ray) and advises him to keep his eyes open.

Gloria arrives at the beach laboratory, where, unwittingly, she drives through the electric gates with Kent (Edmund Cobb), one of Barnett's hired thugs, on her tail. Kent surprises her and Stanfield but is stunned by one of Van Dorn's booby traps when he attempts to get the *Tribune* stock from the safe. Nonetheless, he soon escapes. At The Pines, Stanfield knocks Badger out and then frees Van Dorn, who—donning the vanishing ray mechanism—slips out the front door. Using the electric torch, Stanfield burns his way through the bars on the window in the prison room and soon joins Van Dorn and Gloria in their car. Dorgan and the other men jump into their car, and a high-speed chase ensues. Swerving to avoid an oncoming car, Gloria drives right off the cliff, and the car tumbles over and over, hurling the passengers to their doom.

Chapter Eight: "The Shadow of Death"

Van Dorn is the first to recover his senses and—hearing the thugs approaching—becomes invisible. As Dorgan and his gang capture Stanfield and Gloria, the unseen Van Dorn rescues the pair, and the three head back into town. The destroying ray is once again in the possession of its inventor.

Stanfield confronts Barnett in his offices, and a fight breaks out. Overpowering Barnett and Denny and Cadwell and Kent, Stanfield runs out of the building. Meanwhile, Dorgan and Badger have found a way to enter Van Dorn's laboratory, where they watch—hidden behind a Chinese screen—as within minutes the inventor inadvertently reveals his impenetrable safe, "tests" the vanishing ray (thus demonstrating how to operate it) and repeats aloud the valuable information Stanfield gives him over the phone. Van Dorn is tied up a short time later, and an invisible Dorgan makes for the *Tribune* offices, where Stanfield and MacDonald have just finished signing invaluable proxy documents. When he materializes, he pulls a gun on the startled MacDonald, whom he orders to "Hand over those proxies!"

Chapter Nine: "Blazing Bulkheads"

As MacDonald hands over the stock, Van Dorn—armed with his destroying ray—barrels into the room, knocking Dorgan over. The wily henchman becomes invisible, however, and avoids being rendered lifeless as he escapes. It appears that Barnett finally has all the stock plus both proxies. Just as things begin to look really dim, Van Dorn unveils yet another ray machine at his lab: This one — an "antidote" to the vanishing ray — will paralyze anyone wearing the device.

Barnett, having discovered that MacDonald had palmed "old, worthless" stock off on his chief henchman, has ordered Dorgan back to the lab. He enters, invisibly, but is paralyzed upon materializing. Gloria leaves to make another appeal to her father's innate goodness, while a carload of henchmen storm the lab, beat up Stanfield and Van Dorn (who manages to put in a phone call to the cops during the melee), and leave, with Stanfield their prisoner.

As usual, Gloria gets nowhere with her father, but she does hear a word — "dolphin"— that causes her and the soon-recovered Van Dorn to realize that Stanfield is being held prisoner on a schooner bearing that name. Tied up in the hold where Barnett stores his contraband liquor, Stanfield struggles to free himself as a carelessly tossed cigarette ignites the cargo. As the drunken henchmen above-decks become aware that the ship is on fire, the liquor explodes.

Chapter Ten: "The Iron Death"

Before the schooner is completely destroyed by the flames, Gloria leads Stanfield to the safety of a nearby powerboat, where Van Dorn awaits. Back in the city, Kent tells Barnett that Stanfield perished in the conflagration, and Cadwell advises him that a forged bill of sale would be of much more value than the now-worthless proxies.

At the *Tribune*, MacDonald wants to call in the police, but Gloria wants another go at her father's conscience. Heading back to the Barnett Building, she learns this time around that Stanfield's stock certificates have been stored in the office wall safe. Van Dorn has meantime demonstrated his robot to Stanfield; the inventor admits that, should anything happen to the mechanical man's controls, it would "crash its way through brick walls and crush every obstacle in its path!" Gloria returns and spills the beans about the wall safe. That night, an invisible Stanfield makes his way into the office and retrieves his property with the electric torch.

While this is going on, Dorgan and the others have found that they can enter the beach compound merely by climbing over the wall. They do so and lie in wait for the returning Van Dorn and company. The thugs jump the trio as soon as they enter the lab, but Van Dorn looses the robot on the henchmen, who flee in terror.

Chapter Eleven: "The Juggernaut"

The robot chases the thugs back to the compound wall; they climb over it, and the robot punches a hole through it in order to follow them. As the henchmen scamper into their car, Dorgan fires a shot at the mechanical man, and Van Dorn falls. He rises in a moment, having been only grazed by the bullet, but he appears to be insane. He and the robot wander off.

Stanfield goes to put his stock in the *Tribune* safe, but Gloria is visited by her father. Feigning contrition, Barnett tricks his daughter into summoning Stanfield. Even though he knows it's a trap, Stanfield shows up invisibly, but he's seized upon materializing, and he and Gloria are whisked to The Pines. Van Dorn — cackling maniacally—and the robot also show up at The Pines, and the mechanical man storms right through the assembled thugs, whose barrage of gunshots has no effect on it. Fearing for her father's safety, Gloria runs inside, only to see the robot squeezing the life from Stanfield, whom fate has left—tied to another chair—in the iron man's path.

Chapter Twelve: "Retribution"
For some reason, the robot drops Stanfield before any serious damage is done and turns its attention to Barnett, who is cowering on the floor. The robot then stops dead in its tracks. Barnett and the henchmen leave the prison room with dispatch, but Dorgan is angered when his boss calls him "yellow." Barnett heads back to his offices, and the thugs carefully return to The Pines, where Dorgan overhears Stanfield telling everyone that his stock is in MacDonald's safe. Holding the three at gunpoint, Dorgan has them tied up. He takes the vanishing ray, and—with the electric torch he appropriates from Van Dorn's downtown laboratory—makes for the *Tribune*. There, he knocks MacDonald out, steals the stock and visits Barnett.

Dorgan announces that he has Stanfield and Gloria and that it will take a $50,000 payment from Barnett to ensure his daughter's safety. This news reawakens a bit of decency within Barnett, who promises to have the cash for Dorgan at The Pines by noon the next day. At the appointed time, he shows up with a satchel filled with money, but so do the police, whom Barnett had called the day before. Irate, Dorgan shoots Barnett before a policeman shoots him. Dying, Barnett makes his peace with Gloria.

Soon after, the *Tribune* posts a headline about Stanfield's taking over the newspaper, and he and Gloria—each of whom is wearing a vanishing ray—kiss and disappear from sight simultaneously.

While the feature-length picture represented an outgrowth of the short films with which the cinema industry debuted, the serial was a hybrid of the two. The art form came to consist of weekly two-reel episodes that would—when shorn of repetitious titles and recaps of earlier action—essentially added up to a healthy couple of hours' entertainment. Simplified plot lines that required little in the way of exposition and that were long on action made the serials popular with just about everybody, and few viewers worried overmuch about missing an episode or two. (More than a handful of serials shot the bulk of their expository wads via plus-length [usually three-reel] first chapters; even these could be supplanted by second-chapter introductory scrawls.) It is generally acknowledged that Republic Studios produced the best serials with the greatest regularity, but Mascot, Columbia and Universal—along with a handful of Poverty-Row independents—also made their presence felt in the chapter-play market.

A hefty percentage of sound serials were either Westerns or—like Mascot's enjoyably goofy *Phantom Empire* (1935)—Western-ish. Few genres could withstand near-infinite padding with the resilience of the Oater, and fewer could be shot on a smaller budget. Aviators, military types, government forces, youth gangs, and a wide variety of what were basically cops accounted for an additional chunk of the output, and over the years these were complemented by a wide array of wonder dogs, jungle dwellers and superheroes.

The superheroes nearly always battled supervillains—at least when the rigors of World War II didn't see them squaring off against the Axis powers—and these sagas almost always centered on a blatant science-fiction premise. In his inevitable quest for world domination, the villain might employ such proven crowd pleasers as a device that causes invisibility (albeit within awkward circumstances), a death-ray machine (that lacks but one component to be fully operational), a process (easily reversible) that reduces good, strong men to evil, mindless zombies, and a robot. If he didn't have a robot on hand, a gorilla was an effective stopgap measure, but, with apologies to Rogers and Hammerstein, there is nothing like a robot.

We're not talking zombies here, not even l-a-r-g-e zombies, of the kind so readily crafted by William (Stage) Boyd in Sherman S. Krellberg's *Lost City* (1935). Nor are we considering robotlike suits of armor that encase an all-too-human heavy, à la Don del Oro in *Zorro's Fighting Legion*, a 1939 Western-ish from Republic. We mean robots, and it must be said up front that the serials introduced some of the most distinctive-looking mechanical men ever to hit the screen. There were, for example, those delightfully cheesy, hat-wearing tin men of the aforementioned *Phantom Empire* (although it is said that they were originally fabricated for a musical number in the 1933 feature *Dancing Lady*). And that sleek, impressive fellow in Republic's *Mysterious Dr. Satan* (1940), who was himself a streamlined version of the robots from the studio's earlier (1936) *Undersea Kingdom*. As for the "metalogen man," who shared title space with Crash Corrigan's gorilla suit in Columbia's *Monster and the Ape* (1945), the company would later rework the automaton's head into a helmet that would disguise the titular villain in *Atom Man vs. Superman* (1950). In its own, inimitable, low-budget way, the serial crafted metallic icons that remain as fresh and as instantly recognizable as any of their more intricate and costly relatives from *Metropolis*, *The Day the Earth Stood Still*, and *Forbidden Planet*.

Now, the Universal serials everyone thinks of right off the bat—the *Flash Gordon* trilogy (with Larry "Buster" Crabbe)—have no robots to speak of. They *do* have lion men, hawk men, shark men, clay men, rock men, tree men, ape men, reptiles, tigrons, gockos, orangopoids, and wonderful old Charles Middleton as Ming the Merciless, however, so the absence of automata is scarcely noted. (Appearing in the first *Flash* are some armor-encased foot soldiers who sure look robotlike but who are, apparently, only armor-encased foot soldiers. *Flash Gordon Conquers the Universe*, the last and best appointed of the three, features robotlike "annihilations," but while the concept was nifty—annihilations are humanoid bombs—the execution was poor; the robots are all too clearly stuntmen in metallic sweat suits.) The other Universal serial that jumps immediately to mind—*Buck Rogers* (also with Larry "Buster" Crabbe)—is, the Zuggs apart, virtually creature-less. *The Phantom Creeps*— the studio's 1939 chapter-play starring Bela Lugosi—unveiled in its dyspeptic metal giant what has to be one of the most unforgettable cinematic robots. (Still, a Universal feature film—1941's *Cracked Nuts*—went *Phantom* one better: Its plot hinges on a fake mechanical man which is constructed to resemble the character played by Mischa Auer, complete with hairpiece.)

It devolved to a Universal science fiction chapter-play that *didn't* showcase Larry "Buster" Crabbe or Bela Lugosi—1934's *Vanishing Shadow*—to debut a "genuine" robot onscreen in a sound serial format. (No one less than Harry Houdini had been on the scene when, during the heyday of silent serials, "Q, the Automaton" lumbered menacingly throughout the fifteen episodes of Octagon Films' *Master Mystery* [1919]. Alas, "Q" turned out to be bogus.) Despite this signal honor, however, the robot — readily identifiable to the cognoscenti due to the repeated publication over the years of a handful of stills from the production — does not play a major role in *The Vanishing Shadow*: The quite wonderful "iron man" is but a minor weapon in the familiar arsenal, which includes a device that causes invisibility and a death-ray machine.

William Everson once wrote how lost films almost inevitably disappoint upon being rediscovered due to their inability to live up to inflated reputations based chiefly on hearsay and succulent movie stills. This is essentially true, although I am far from alone in singing the praises of *Mystery of the Wax Museum* or *The Old Dark House*, despite a sheaf of prose by weighty personalities who confessed to being let down — in some cases, almost fatally — by the reemergence of 35mm elements. I've been unable to find major screeds anywhere on the impact or importance or undisputed genius of *The Vanishing Shadow*, and its recent reappearance has (so far) failed either to spark revisionist diatribes or to garner hosannas. It's a fun serial — good without being *very* good — and, for all its lengthy inaccessibility, it's quite familiar: Much of its claptrap and many of its doohickeys have been on display these past sixty years in *The Phantom Creeps*.[1]

The lack of commentary on the chapter-play must be due to its being out of the public eye for so long. In *Days of Thrills and Adventure* (1970), the late serial guru Alan Barbour limited his coverage of *The Vanishing Shadow* to passing remarks, while the serial merited only a photograph and caption in his subsequent *Cliffhanger* (1977). What's less, Jim Harmon and Don Glut omitted any mention whatsoever of *Shadow* in their 1972 *Great Movie Serials*, an otherwise wonderful overview of the art form aimed at popular (i.e., nonexpert) audiences. Over the years, a small handful of stills was published and republished, with the most interesting of the lot depicting the aforementioned robot. With the serial once again open for business, however, we discover that that intriguing mechanical man is on screen for about eight minutes in total; making judgment calls based solely on movie stills has never been a trustworthy practice.

Throughout the film, Onslow Stevens's character is driven to see his father's newspaper, *The Tribune*, expose the machinations of villainous businessman Walter Miller. This is all well and good, but the formulaic action patterns required by serials — the constant back-and-forth struggle between good guys and bad guys to do or stop from doing whatever it is that the plot turns on — are really rather mundane. All Stanfield has to do is call a stockholders' meeting and then — with the help of William Desmond's MacDonald — take over legal control of the paper and continue on with his quest. It begs the question to note that if he picks up the phone and calls around in chapter one, the movie would be over in chapter two. Likewise, if Miller orders Richard Cramer to plug the young do-gooder at that first meeting and then forges his signature to a backdated bill of sale, we would be denied entrée into the fascinating world of vanishing rays, destroying rays, heat rays, paralyzing rays, and so forth. Even my quibbling that the requisite dance deals with stock certificates, proxies, and such — paraphernalia that just aren't as inherently interesting to serial buffs as invisible crusaders and mechanical juggernauts — is halfhearted.

The dramatis personae in serials are normally only an inch or two from cardboard, and the assemblage here is no exception. Who's got time for character development when most of an episode's footage is devoted to cheating on the previous one's ending, doing a step or two of the dance, and setting up the next fall? Then again, who really needs character development when the art form cheerfully settles for character *types*? A hero, a sidekick, a heroine, a brains villain, a few brawn heavies, and a passel of stuntmen (who may well be playing the brawn heavies while doubling for the good guys) are all that's needed to move the plot, such as it is.

Cute-as-a-button Ada Ince does well in the undemanding role of Gloria Grant (née Barnett), but after the umpteenth time the script requires her to give her old man "one more chance," viewers begins to feel around the sofa for a paralyzing ray of their own. Given that Barnett's plans include the destruction of Stanfield's credibility, the ruin of his finances, and the trashing of his future, it's got to be disheartening for the young man to hear Gloria admit, "Stanley, you know I'm interested in you, but I'm interested in father, too." When chapter eleven sees the robot storm into The Pines (where Stanfield sits, trussed securely to a chair), Gloria runs fearlessly through the mansion door, hoping to save her *father*. Earlier, just after Stanfield had been rescued from the exploding liquor ship, Gloria heads over yet again to the Barnett Building to sprinkle pixie dust on the pater. Her invitations to conversion lead (as always) to naught, but she does discover some absolutely crucial news: the whereabouts of Stanfield's stolen *Tribune* stock. As there are still two chapters to unreel before the denouement, she takes the time to go home and shower and change her outfit before spilling the beans to the anxious Stanfield and Van Dorn. I found fewer than a half-dozen film credits for Ince, plus the fact that she first drew breath on June 2, 1913, in Louisville, Kentucky. Whither she went a lifetime later remains a mystery.

Character man James Durkin is rather good as Carl Van Dorn. The Canadian actor, who died approximately the same time *The Vanishing Shadow* ended its twelve-week run, infuses the electrical genius with a simpatico slant that is only hinted at in the scenario, where the loopy inventor is delineated as being forever on the edge. Whether cackling madly after being shot in or at or near the head by the frantic Dorgan or devising lethal booby traps for his impenetrable vault on short notice, Durkin reins in the cartoonish aspects of his character as best as he can. Hey, a good look at Gloria is all it takes to call the crazed Van Dorn down from Bela Lugosi-like heights with the result that, in the twinkling of an eye, the art-deco robot is history. While the scenario didn't provide him (or anyone) with much wiggle room, Durkin's stage experience enabled him to lend a jot of nuance to the characterization. He had appeared (as had Onslow Stevens) in Universal's *Secret of the Blue Room* in 1933, but it's not clear whether the studio had intended the Canadian — whose film debut had been but three years prior to *that*—for inclusion in the hype when it advertised the mystery as "The 10-Star Picture."

Universal had little doubt that Onslow Stevens *was* one of those stars. The son of character actor Housley Stevenson, Stevens had made his debut as secondary lead in the studio's twelve-chapter *Heroes of the West* the year before *Blue Room*, and, apart from his occasionally being lent out to Fox or to William Randolph Hearst's Cosmopolitan Pictures, he and Universal remained faithful partners. The relatively

Ada Ince, holding a gun (or something) and looking determined, rubs shoulders with Onslow Stevens, who's holding a gun and looking determined (or something). (Courtesy of Marty Kelly.)

young contract player (he was thirty when *Heroes* saw the carbon arc) soon graduated from serials (once he got past 1932's *Jungle Mystery*) to features, as he and the studio grew mutually comfortable with each other. Stevens's assignment to 1934's *Vanishing Shadow*, then, was akin to his being poked in the eye with a sharp stick.

In *Counsellor-at-Law*—based upon Elmer Rice's award-winning Broadway play—Stevens had appeared with John Barrymore, Bebe Daniels and Melvyn Douglas, while performing under the direction of up-and-coming Laemmle kith William Wyler. In *Secret of the Blue Room*—an American rendition of the original German silent, based on Erich Philippi's popular novel—he shared screen time with Gloria Stuart, Lionel Atwill and Paul Lukas, and veteran import Kurt Neumann was at the helm. *The Vanishing Shadow*, by contrast, was one of the first (if not *the* first) productions directed by Louis Friedlander[2]; at the age of thirty-three, the New Yorker was not only inexperienced, but was also scarcely older than Stevens himself. The screenplay would be drawn primarily from the prolific scribblings of Basil Dickey, the cornerstone of Universal's chapter-play wing and the author of the one-dimensional scenarios of *Heroes of the West* and *Jungle Mystery* (and virtually every other early sound serial Universal produced). Instead of playing opposite some of the movies' biggest names (even if they were on their way up or, more likely for Universal, on their way down), Stevens would headline the cast (sharing title card billing with the virtually unknown Ada Ince), would have Durkin as his secondary lead, and would receive support from such names as Walter Miller, Eddie Cobb, Monty Montague, and William Desmond: men for whom chapter-plays had always forestalled watering down the whiskey. (In fact, the Irish-born Desmond, about midway through a lengthy career that had commenced in 1915 and that would, by the actor's death in 1949, number close to 200 films, had been widely hailed as "king of the silent serials.")

Stevens raised the very dickens at the thought of *The Vanishing Shadow*, but a contract is a contract. He may have found consolation in the fact that it would be his *last* serial.

As Stanley Stanfield, Stevens is the quintessential serial hero: moral (he's forever preventing Van Dorn from blasting the heavies to kingdom come), tenacious (all that persistent fading-away), and physically fit, which he demonstrates by repeatedly besting two or three guys with his gloved fists.3 His strength is as the strength of ten because his heart is pure. On a purely superficial level, however, Stevens's manly inventor-cum-avenger is ill served by a pencil-line mustache and a light-colored fedora that seems better suited to an organ grinder; the overall effect is not pleasant.

Most old movie buffs will recall Richard (aka Rychard) Cramer as an occasional foe of Mr. Laurel and Mr. Hardy; his Judge Beaumont in the 1932 short *Scram*, for example, disproved once and for all the notion that the forces of goodness couldn't be bone chilling in their own right. A few years later, as "Big" Nick Grainger, he memorably menaced the boys again in 1940's *Saps at Sea*, their last Hal Roach Studios production. Cramer was much more than just another ugly face in Stan and Babe's world, though. Like his *Vanishing Shadow* co-heavies, he showed his mug to obvious advantage in well over 150 films, in a career that stretched from the waning silent days until the beginning of the '50s. What's more, his voice was every bit the equal of his mug; the most innocuous of lines could be twisted by his patented nasal rumble into threats of the first order. When one of his *Vanishing Shadow* gang wonders aloud just what is going on, Drogan intones, "We're waiting for Staaaaaanfield to make up his mind to sign over that valuable stock we've been chasin' around after!" You have to look to Bela Lugosi to find another actor who worked the language in so unique (and unorthodox) a fashion.

Of course, the real stars of *The Vanishing Shadow* are the scientific gizmos that Van Dorn whips up "like a bride whips up an omelet." It's fun to note how some of the items—like the "electric key" that opens the gates to the beach laboratory or the "electric torch" which can burn its way through anything—are sold in K-Mart nowadays; sic transit science fiction. Also amusing is the almost ludicrous ease with which one may learn to operate the gadgets: All it takes for Drogan to master the vanishing ray is a few seconds' glimpse of Van Dorn's *back* through the crack in a Chinese screen. (Let's not get into why there'd even be a Chinese screen in a laboratory in the first place.) For all that, the control panel on the vanishing ray is obfuscation itself when compared to the later, jacket-mounted dashboard of the *King of the Rocketmen*. Implicit in all this is that Van Dorn must have first invented a minuscule, incredibly powerful battery; everything (presumably) is powered by electricity, yet there are no extension cords to be found. Each and every item hums loudly and, well, *electrically* when in operation, although the vanishing ray hums only while its wearer is actively coming or going from sight (the control belt reads "in" and "out"); once the wearer is invisible, there's not a peep to be heard. Go figure.

(The team of Mannheim, Dickey and Morgan [nor ought we forget Miss O'Neill] raises scientific and linguistic hackles early on in the proceedings, and these loopy illogicalities support the narrative for all twelve pulse-pounding episodes. For starters, they have Van Dorn referring to his vision-impeding apparatus first as the "invisible ray," then as the "vanishing ray." Now this "ray"—by almost *any* definition the word connotes some sort of linear projection—is cast by a mechanism that is worn around one's waist; the person who is rendered invisible when bathed in the "ray" is thus positioned *behind* the device that emits it. I gave this some thought and concluded that there must be a lens on the flipside of the belt that focuses the beam right at Stanfield's viscera. [It ought to be clear from this that I have *way* too much time on my hands.]

(A couple of chapters into the serial, the screenwriters change adjectives abruptly, and the ray—qualified early on as "invisible"—is thereafter tagged as "vanishing." This interesting shift in qualifiers most likely resulted from a halfhearted stab at giving some verbal support to the serial's title, which really needed all the help it could get: Stanfield's shadow ends up being the only thing that *doesn't* vanish. The willful suspension of disbelief that indulging in many dramatic exercises requires allows us to ignore the Hardy Boys-level scientific question posed by the narrative: Just how can an object through which light *passes* cast a shadow? Nevertheless, the process induces a little head-scratching.

(Unless the ray *creates* a shadow [rather than merely dealing ineffectually with the shadow that's already there], we have to contend with the issue of the awkward and selective placement of light. The shadow is so frequently seen, negotiating its life-size form along some wall or another, that it becomes as blatant a sign of its owner's presence as would his clothing and hat. [Toward the end of chapter eight, MacDonald forthrightly hails the shadow of the person he believes to be Van Dorn as surely as he would the man himself.] But what light sources are casting this shadow? In scenes where the shadow is in a room with other folks, no one else casts a shadow that *begins* to match *that* one. And while Barnett's secretary, Denny, repeatedly complains of seeing a shadow on the walls, he's not speaking of his own, yet he's sitting plop against the window that's providing all the illumination to the room.

(Sure, the shadow was left visible so that the audience had some way to follow the progress the hero [or the inventor, or the villain, or the skirt] was making in any given scene. Henry MacRae's budget denied him even a fraction of the special effects money that Junior Laemmle had enjoyed for the previous year's plum, *The Invisible Man*, so John P. Fulton's wizardry was supplanted by an obvious conceit. Had the chapter-play been titled almost anything other than *The Vanishing Shadow*, though, none of this complaining would be necessary.)

Van Dorn's stuff may not always be terribly efficient—a gangly periscope used to monitor the electric gate fails miserably to detect villains at an opportune moment—but it is unfailingly eye-catching. Well-crafted design compensates for the occasional shortcoming: The destroying ray, for example, has been accoutered to hang under a gentleman's suit coat. (The destroying ray never really destroys anything other than a few potted plants, but it still sees more action than the villains' rods. *The Vanishing Shadow* is remarkably shy on gunfire. Drogan clips Van Dorn in one scene, and a trio of subordinate heavies unloads about a dozen shots each from their revolvers at the mechanical man in the next. That tightly wound mayhem, plus the fatal shots that wrap up the whole story, are about all she wrote. When it comes to tying folks up, though, the serial rivals the best bondage film that Irving Klaw ever produced.)

The paucity of robot footage, however, is both surprising and deplorable. The "iron man" is allowed to stomp back and forth briefly in Van Dorn's city lab in the first chapter and then is left idling behind the sliding door for the next ten episodes. On the other end of the chapter-play, once Van Dorn recovers his sanity following Stanfield's near-demise in chapter eleven, he immediately shuts the robot down, citing the myriad dangers involved. (Serial superbuff Jim Stringham and I both believe that Stanfield's inexplicable escape from the robot was the result of poor editing and that somehow little Gloria was supposed to have been instrumental in calling off the automaton.) More surprising is the fact that the robot never reappeared in other serials from the period, the way most of the handheld devices did. Van Dorn's lab full of buzzing and whirling gimcracks had, of course, been appropriated from Universal's 1931 blockbuster, *Frankenstein*, and *those* wonderful machines—designed and fabricated by real-life master of electrical malarkey Kenneth Strickfaden—would return to the screen with the frequency of summer lightning.

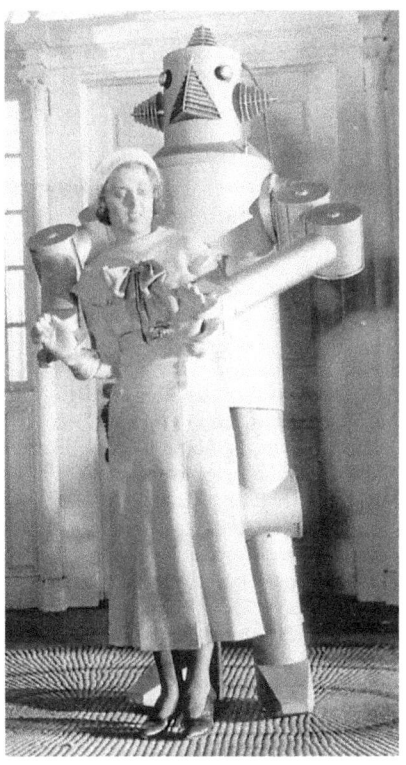

Worry not! This scene does not appear in the serial. Ada Ince never finds herself in anyone's arms. (Courtesy of Jim Stringham.)

Louis Friedlander's direction is as good as can be expected, especially when one considers the man's lack of experience and the stark limitations of the screenplay. The good guys and the bad guys circle each other warily, and there are the formulaic parries and thrusts, but the plot — such as it is — is ultimately driven more by scripted coincidences than by flailing fists. (While any number of serials relied upon serendipity to get their usually underplotted narratives moving, Universal's own *Mummy's Tomb* [1942] is the only genre feature film I can recall where the action unreels as it does solely because the antagonist — Turhan Bey's smarmy Mehemet Bey — is inevitably *in just the right spot* to overhear everyone else's plans.) Friedlander, who would later adopt "Lew Landers" as an alternative nom de cinéma, is listed by some sources as one of the editors (albeit uncredited as such) of *The Vanishing Shadow*. Given the frenetic pacing of his classic Karloff-Lugosi barnstormer *The Raven* the very next year, it's evident that the man's energy was a hallmark of his work from day one.

Despite my myriad grousing and the occasional continuity flub (e.g., a late-chapter recap card tags Van Dorn's beachfront hideaway as his "mountain laboratory"), *The Vanishing Shadow* is a diverting way to spend an afternoon. The *Motion Picture Herald*, a trade-oriented publication that pulled no punches when appraising new releases, hailed *Shadow* as being "worth exhibitor attention for the juvenile trade" (March 31, 1934). Not quite the epic fantasy of a press-book blurb, perhaps, but a zillion times more credible.

Notes

1. Back in the '70s, Universal/16, a Chicago-based 16mm film rental company, had any number of prints of the serial to rent. Following the introduction of videocassette technology, 16mm lost its edge in the home-viewing market, and gradually companies like Universal/16 went under. These rental libraries usually sold off their inventory to film collectors, and *The Vanishing Shadow* subsequently disappeared thus, only to resurface recently.

2. In the chapter on *The Raven* (1935) in my book on Universal Studios' "golden age" horrors (*Of Gods and Monsters*, McFarland, 1998), I wrote how Friedlander was "a veteran director with loads of experience" and that much of his output "had consisted of horse operas and mainstream 'B's'" (p. 235). The research I've done for this book leads me to believe that the sources I consulted with regard to this subject for *OGAM* were wrong. There is evidence that Friedlander *was* a member of the production staff of *The Man Who Laughs* (1927) and that he was probably similarly involved in other of the studio's silent efforts, but I can find no record anywhere of his having directed a film prior to the 1934 serials.

3. Consonance and serial nomenclature frequently went hand in hand like cheddar and cheese, French and fries, and Crash and Corrigan. And not just character names, either, although rhythmic arrangements like Stanley Stanfield, Gloria Grant, Betsy Baxter (GG's counterpart from Mascot's *Phantom Empire*), and Killer Kane (Anthony Warde lugged that one around in Universal's *Buck Rogers*) were fairly commonplace. The chapter-plays themselves were (nearly as often as not) released with titles that fairly tripped off the tongue: the early '30s alone offered such fantastic fare as *Terry of the Times, Battling with Buffalo Bill, The Galloping Ghost, Gordon of Ghost City, Mystery Mountain, Perils of Pauline, The Red Rider*, and *Tailspin Tommy*. All in all, the allure of alliteration played its own pernicious part in trivializing serials for the ticket-buying public.

THE WITCHING HOUR

Paramount Productions, Inc.—27 April 1934—63-64 minutes

Cast: Sir Guy Standing as Judge Martin Prentice; John Halliday as Jack Brookfield; William Frawley as Jury Foreman; Judith Allen as Nancy Brookfield; Tom Brown as Clay Thorne; Olive Tell as Helen Thorne; Richard Carle as Lew Ellinger; Ralf Harolde as Frank Hardmuth; Purnell Pratt as District Attorney; Frank Sheridan as Chief of Police; Gertrude Michael as Margaret Price; Ferdinand Gottschalk as Dr. von Strohn; John Larkin as Clarence; Selmer Jackson as Henry Walthal; Howard Lang as Judge; George Webb as Assistant District Attorney; Guy Usher as Dick Wingate; Robert Littlefield as Ambrose; Ernest Hilliard as First Lawyer; Arthur Stuart Hull as Second Lawyer; George Reed as Train

Credits: *Director:* Henry Hathaway; *producer:* Bayard Veiller; *executive producer:* Emanuel Cohen; *assistant director:* Neil Wheeler; *screenplay:* Anthony Veiller; *cinematography:* Ben Reynolds; *editor:* Jack Dennis; *recording engineer:* Harold Lewis

Synopsis: Back in the Gay Nineties, Clay Thorne (Tom Brown)—son of Philadelphia socialite Helen Thorne (Olive Tell)—is wooing Nancy Brookfield (Judith Allen), daughter of Jack Brookfield (John Halliday), a Kentucky gentleman who frequently acts as "house" to a large group of well-heeled gamblers. Jack occasionally has flashes of second sight, as when (on the very night Clay pops the question to Nancy), he calls an end to the wagering not long before the police pull up to raid the place.

The police are not Jack's only problems, however. Local tough guy and sleazy politico Frank Hardmuth (Ralf Harolde) wants to muscle in on the gambling action at the Brookfield manse and to put the moves on the Brookfield heiress, as well. Jack very pointedly threatens to kill Hardmuth before tossing him out on his ear. Future son-in-law Clay also requires some attention, as the lad blanches at the sight of a cat's-eye ring that Jack has accepted in exchange for cash. Jack unknowingly hypnotizes the young man as he tries to calm his fears, and—it devolves—he also insinuates his murderous subconscious into Clay's receptive mind. When Clay stares at the cat's-eye ring the following day, he is overwhelmed by this implanted urge to see Hardmuth dead, and he kills him. Coming out of the trance, Clay is appalled to find himself accused of murder.

With the case seemingly open and shut, no lawyers offer to step up to the bar in Clay's defense. Desperately, Helen asks her old friend Judge Martin Prentice (Sir Guy Standing), to plead for her son. Prentice, who knows about Jack's preternatural gifts, is retired and thus begs off initially, but after a visit from the specter of Helen's mother, Margaret Price (Gertrude Michael)—with whom Prentice had been in love—he agrees to argue for the young man's innocence.

True to everyone's expectations, the defense is up against it: Even with Jack Brookfield's full cooperation—he admits openly to wishing Hardmuth dead—Prentice's argument that murder can be committed via inadvertent thought transference is met with laughter. It takes a bravura act of courtroom dramatics—Jack hypnotizes the jury foreman into shooting the district attorney (albeit the gun proffered had been loaded with blanks)—to win an acquittal for young Clay.

Where to start?

The Witching Hour's most obvious departure from the formulaic tale of weak-willed victims and insidious, arm-waving mesmerists is its very carefully positing of the fact that the fellow who pulls the trigger has been hypnotized unintentionally by the nicest guy in the movie. Granted, Jack Brookfield may be technically breaking the law by offering a safe (and meticulously accoutered) haven to any local gentry willing to have a go against the odds, but his is an honest establishment. So upright is the man that he refuses to gamble, as his preternatural mental prowess would take the element of chance out of the gaming.

Inadvertence and integrity, then, are the rails on which the narrative chugs from casino to courtroom, and the scenario consistently underscores both. The unfortunate downside to all of this carefully established background is that the murder itself—seen once and for an instant within the framework of a flashback—appears to be of secondary importance to all the surrounding exposition. If the director and scenarist conspired to downplay the more sensationalist elements of telepathy and hypnotism, then they shouldn't have also denuded the murder of its fascinating detail. Some ticket buyers will put up with hypnotic folderol in the course of enjoying a nice, juicy murder, and vice versa, but there's not much of an audience for thrillers in which both components have been dried out and filleted before presentation.

Someone with a greater eye for symbolism than I might well maintain that Jack's laying a haymaker on Hardmuth is a visual metaphor for his fight against dishonor, and I'd go along with that. He puts up with Hardmuth's snarling over territorial rights ("I'm the boss in this town," boasts the little weasel) but lowers the boom when Nancy's name—and, by extension, Nancy's *good* name—enters the picture. (The younger Brookfield is noodling "Those Endearing Young Charms" on the Steinway as Clay strides in to ask her to change that name, and there's never for a moment any thought that those young charms were headed elsewhere.) The scenario thus paints a portrait of an ethical gentleman, a loving and protective parent, and—the unfortunate business of the murder apart—a no-nonsense, caring friend.

Early on in the proceedings, it appears that Jack is merely a passive receptacle for other people's thoughts. "The thought is stronger in your mind than any other thought," he explains to Lew Ellinger, while unerringly naming cards that Lew has cut to at random, "and I get it! It explains why I don't gamble." It's this aspect of his extrasensory perception that he speaks of when he broaches the subject with Judge Prentice, who takes the discussion a step further: "Thoughts are dangerous things, and a man like you, Mr. Brookfield, should guard his thoughts very carefully." Thus, Jack has capabilities of which even he is unaware, and he discovers them only after young Clay has accurately discharged a firearm in the direction of Hardmuth. Brookfield's unconscious mind can tap into the unconscious minds of others! (Not for nothing are the strains of "Beautiful Dreamer" heard under the opening and closing credits.)

In the last reel Jack is systematically tapping into the unconscious mind of the smirking jury foreman (William Frawley). (Judge Prentice's arguments had hitherto been met with derisive chuckles from the jury, which couldn't refrain from snickering even when the district attorney was rightfully dressed down for playing dirty pool with an expert witness for the defense.) Jack purposefully mesmerizes the foreman, who picks up a revolver and fires it point blank at the D.A. In the twinkling of an eye, Clay has been exonerated, the women are breathing more easily, and Judge Prentice is headed home to his slippers and fireplace.

Nice ending, of course, even if it doesn't actually prove anything other than Jack Brookfield could (if he wanted to) manipulate the thoughts and feelings of the local legal branch as easily as he had (inadvertently or no) those of his prospective son-in-law. Let's let it go at that, shall we?

The picture could have used a bit more action to offset all the chatter about telepathy; that solid right to the chin and the brace of gunshots do what they can, but the picture remains dialogue heavy. A few special effects would have done wonders to enliven the action, but the scenario denies Jack any opportunity to demonstrate the more visually oriented aspects of his preternatural gifts. Jack's sudden awareness of the impending police raid could easily have survived a momentary pique of the key lighting or an unobtrusive violin tremolo, if only to clue the audience that something untoward was happening. The bit about impressing Lew Ellinger by naming the ten of spades is cute, but could there be any psychic experiment less purely cinematic than a card trick? And the only time the furniture rises from the floor is when the servants cart off and hide the gambling paraphernalia. It might be argued that the film's subtle handling of the preternatural element does give one pause for thought — and thinking has never hurt anyone yet — but even in the nouvelle talkie years, movie-goers wanted something visual to complement all the gabbing they were hearing.

Despite the lack of flashy optical effects, the picture is well photographed and atmospherically lit. Even the sundry talking head exchanges reflect the sort of creativity and care that was seldom accorded "B" films like *The Witching Hour*. Director Henry Hathaway — who was a child actor before becoming a property man and then an assistant director — had been sitting behind the camera for only two years prior to this assignment. Given that Paramount had tossed nothing but low-budget Westerns his way up to this point, Hathaway was already showing a capable hand and a keen eye. Working closely with cinematographer Ben Reynolds, he gave Anthony Veiller's screenplay a highly contrasted, black-and-white palette on which to unfold. The moodiest vignettes in Hathaway's later *House on Ninety-Second Street* can trace their roots back here.

I'm still not sure what the title refers to, and I watched the film intently several times. Nothing particularly dastardly, amazing, or even notable happens at midnight (the "witching hour"), and even the reasonably atmospheric still I've chosen as an illustration of the film's temporal parameters seems loath to cooperate in this regard. I've also plunged into Thomas's novelization of his play and come up empty from that source, as well.

The cast is not bad, save for Tom Brown, who is merely all right when pitching woo at Judith Allen, but seven shades of ghastly when emoting about the cat's-eye ring. Clay's high-pitched aversion to that particular type of jewelry must be endured if Jack is to twist the boy's mind around his little finger, but couldn't Brown have been directed to depict raw terror via some thespic technique other than nasal whining? Brown was one of the decade's much utilized lower-shelf juveniles, but I'm familiar with his work only here and in Universal's interesting *Man Who Cried Wolf* (1938), where, once again, he's accused of shooting the guy the picture's elder protagonist wanted dead. He's better in *Wolf* than he is here, but that's not saying much. Fans of classic television will doubtless remember Tom as Paul Ray (in *Rocky Jones, Space Ranger*, 1954), Lieutenant Rovacs (*Mr. Lucky*, 1959), and Ed O'Connor (on *Gunsmoke*, from 1968 to 1972). Tom was also on *General Hospital* for a number of years, but I don't yet consider soap operas part of "classic TV."

Whether by accident or design, as Judge Martin Prentice, the British-born Sir Guy Standing has not a jot of an English accent, while John Halliday — who haled from Brooklyn — sounds as if he had been reared by Charles Dickens. No complaint here; merely an observation. William Frawley's nameless jury foreman is etched in the same kind of burly crankiness as were virtually all of his movie roles, and I'm not complaining about that, either. My introduction to Frawley was via *I Love Lucy*, and his Fred Mertz — whom I still dearly love — was merely any and all of his big-screen grouches, mellowed a tad and given a cadre of equally larger-than-life personalities with whom to work. Judith Allen is pretty, Olive Tell is competent, and Gertrude Michael (as the shade of Margaret Price) is charming, but none of the women really has much to do.

A minor point: Both the 1916 and 1921 screenplays retained the playwright's explanation that Clay's family was "cursed" with a fear of cat's-eyes and while this mention may not have kept the *audience's* eyes from rolling, it helped explain the juvenile's otherwise peculiar behavior. The 1934 version, which eschewed any reference to familial kookiness, thus proffered a Clay who may very well be several cards short of a full house. When coupled with the actor's propensity to channel all of his dramatic excesses through his nasal passages, this omission did nothing to limn the juvenile flatteringly.

At present, Henry Hathaway's *Witching Hour* is available only via the "gray" video market.

The 1934 incarnation of *The Witching Hour* was the third adaptation of Augustus Thomas's eponymous stage work to hit the screen within eighteen years. The play, a Shubert Brothers' production, enjoyed a decent run (some 212 performances) following its premiere in November 1907 at New York's Hackett Theatre. Thomas, a prolific writer — he penned more than twenty plays (many of which opened on the Great White Way) in as many years— went on to script, produce, and direct a handful of films himself. While *The Witching Hour* was the most oft-filmed of Thomas's output, *The Copperhead* (1918) was without doubt his magnum opus, if only for providing Lionel Barrymore with the most popular of his stage roles. (Nonetheless, New York drama critic Burns Mantle did tag *The Witching Hour* as one of the "best plays of the decade.")

The 1916 version saw Anthony P. Kelly (whose professional high-water mark would be his massaging E. W. Hornung's efforts into John Barrymore's *Raffles, the Amateur Cracksman*, the following year) rework Thomas's original *Hour* into a manageable scenario for the Frohman Amusement Corporation. (Some of the very few

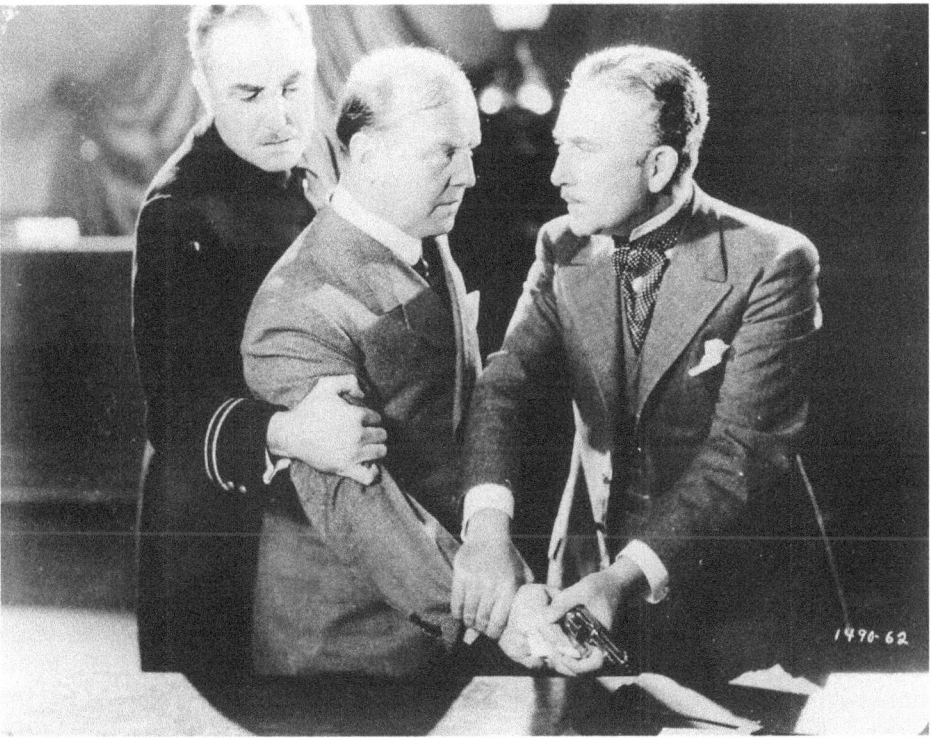

Top: Judith Allen and Tom Brown are amazed to discover that the "witching hour" is 2:00 AM!
Bottom: It's all Jack Brookfield (John Halliday) can do to keep the jury foreman (William Frawley) from shooting the district attorney. No, the D.A. is not played by Vivian Vance.

latter-day mentions of this picture indicate that its source play was based on the novel *Caleb Powers*. The *AFI Film Catalog* states pointblank that "No evidence of that novel's existence has been discovered," and I've been unable to locate any reference whatsoever either here or in Europe in the course of a year's research.) George Irving directed the picture (he would direct the Great Profile in *Raffles*, as well) which was shot at the corporation's Flushing (New York) studios and which opened at seven reels in Manhattan on December 10, 1916. The film was released locally by Frohman and nationally via the State Rights system, and that may help explain why the picture disappeared somewhere along the way.

Frohman had initially wanted John Mason — who had created the role of Jack Brookfield in the Broadway production — to headline its cast. The part went instead to fifty-three-year-old C. Aubrey Smith, who was even then (with this, his fourth picture) en route to becoming one of the most beloved — and the crustiest — of Hollywood's famed British colony. Freeman Barnes was the only one of the Broadway cast to be held over for the screen version; the rest of the cast came from the company's roster of contract players.

Praised for its faithfulness to its legitimate predecessor, 1916's *Witching Hour* is sufficiently different from the sound version to warrant a brief plot recap:

> The Jack Brookfield herein gambles heavily, while using those telepathic powers of his to unfair advantage. Jack's niece, Viola, is being pursued by Clay Whipple, son of Helen Whipple, a widow with whom Jack was once (and is now again) enamored. The Whipples suffer from a family phobia regarding cat's eyes, and Clay kills Tom Denning when Denning taunts him with a cat's-eye stickpin. Unfortunately for Clay, District Attorney Hardmuth is his romantic rival for Viola's hand, as well as having (corrupt) political aspirations to the governor's mansion.
>
> Via inadvertent mental imagery, Jack shows Hardmuth the means of assassinating the current governor, and the district attorney hires Raynor, a degenerate gambler, to do the deed. In the courtroom, Jack uses his psychic abilities to cause Raynor to confess. Hardmuth's complicity in the assassination conspiracy causes the case against Clay to be thrown out. Clay and Viola are united, as are Helen Whipple and Jack, once Jack has promised to quit gambling.

Judge Prentice, who served as a secondary catalyst in the available 1934 version, didn't have much to do in the 1916 original, if the scant plot recap is any indication. As if to restore whatever balance had been lost by the broadening of that role, however, the sound version omits altogether the second violent death — the assassination of the governor — that would lead to the legal abnegation of Clay's culpability in the first.

Although contemporary reviews seem to suggest that the Frohman thriller hadn't set the world on fire, the property was remade by Famous Players–Lasky five years later. Elliott Dexter played Jack Brookfield in the Paramount release, and Judge Prentice — who is at least mentioned by name in extant film record — was played by Winter Hall. For aficionados such as us, the most recognizable name to be found in the cast scroll may be that of A. Edward Sutherland (as Clay). "Eddie" Sutherland would ultimately foreswear acting, of course, and go on to direct some of the kinkiest thrillers — think of *Secrets of the French Police* and *Murders in the Zoo* — to come out of Hollywood during the early '30s. Moviegoers preferring classic comedians to macabre murderers may recall that Sutherland also was at the helm of *International House* (1933), *Mississippi* (1935), and *Poppy* (1936), among others, with Bill Fields; *The Flying Deuces* (1939) with Laurel and Hardy; and Abbott and Costello's first screen appearance, *One Night in the Tropics* (1940).

Julia Crawford Ivers penned the scenario for the 1921 release, whose storyline appears to hover midway between the flanking versions. Within the framework of all that cat's-eye craziness, Clay again kills Tom Denning—who, this time around, is governor elect—and is shortly thereafter convicted and sentenced to hang. Jack convinces Judge Prentice that the boy deserves a retrial while exposing the prosecuting attorney's involvement in the murder. The attorney tries to shoot Jack, but Jack's mental powers thwart the attempt. Clay is acquitted in that second trial, and he and Viola appear to have found happiness at last.

Although unavailable to the general public, a preserved print of the 1921 *Witching Hour* may be found in the collections of the Library of Congress. Jon Mirsalis— renowned film historian, composer of silent film scores, and world-class accompanist —viewed the picture at the 1986 Minneapolis Cinecon (the film's last public showing) and recalls it being "very spooky with lots of wonderful visual touches." Visual delights aside, interest in the film may well be due to its being one of the few surviving pictures directed by William Desmond Taylor.

The Witching Hour—Frohman Amusement Corporation— December 10, 1916—7 reels

Cast: C. Aubrey Smith as Jack Brookfield; Marie Shotwell as Helen Whipple; Robert Conness as Frank Hardmuth; Jack Sherrill as Clay Whipple; Freeman Barnes as Tom Denning; Lewis Sealy as Judge George Prentice; William Eville as Lou Ellinger; Robert Ayerton as the Judge; Helen Arnold as Viola Campbell; Etta De Groff as Mrs. Campbell

Credits: *presented by:* William Sherrill; *director:* George Irving; *scenario:* Anthony P. Kelly; *cinematographer:* William A. Reinhart

The Witching Hour—Famous Players–Lasky—April 10, 1921—7 reels

Cast: Elliott Dexter as Jack Brookfield; Winter Hall as Judge Prentice; Ruth Renick as Viola Campbell; Robert Cain as Frank Hardmuth; Edward Sutherland as Clay Whipple; Mary Alden as Helen Whipple; Fred Turner as Lew Ellinger; Genevieve Blinn as Mrs. Campbell; Charles West as Tom Denning; L. M. Wells as Judge Henderson; Clarence Geldert as Colonel Bailey; Jim Blackwell as Harvey

Credits: *presented by* Jesse Lasky; *director:* William Desmond Taylor; *scenario:* Julia Crawford Ivers; *cinematography:* James Van Trees; *assistant director:* Frank O'Connor

DOUBLE DOOR

Paramount Productions, Inc.—May 4, 1934—75 minutes

Cast: Evelyn Venable as Anne Darrow; Mary Morris as Victoria Van Brett; Anne Revere as Caroline Van Brett, her sister; Kent Taylor as Rip Van Brett, her half brother; Sir Guy Standing as Mortimer Neff; Colin Tapley as Dr. John Lucas; Virginia Howell as Avery; Halliwell Hobbes as Mr. Chase; Frank Dawson as Telson; Helen Shipman as Louise; Leonard Carey as William; Ralph Remley as Lambert; Burr Caruth as Reverend Dr. Loring

Credits: *Director:* Charles Vidor; *producer:* E. Lloyd Sheldon; *assistant director:* Russell Matthews; *screenplay:* Gladys Lehman, Jack Cunningham; based on the play *Double Door*, by Elizabeth A. McFadden; suggested by Hermine Klepac; *photography:* Harry Fischbeck; *camera operator:* Fred Mayer; *assistant cameraman:* Neal Beckner; *art directors:* Hans Dreier, Robert Odell; *editor:* James Smith; *sound:* Phil G. Wisdom; *still photographer:* Sherman Clark

Synopsis: In New York (c. 1910), young Rip Van Brett (Kent Taylor) is set to marry beautiful nurse Anne Darrow (Evelyn Venable), who has lovingly seen him through some rough sledding, health-wise. Rip's older half-sister Victoria (Mary Morris) is against the marriage, as she is adamant in her regard for Darrow as a gold digger. In rapid succession, Victoria purloins the family pearls that Rip was going to present to his bride, scissors him out of the will, and then has him appointed custodian of the family fortune—which, of course, he can manage but cannot touch—thus ensuring that he'll have no time for romance.

What's more, Victoria threatens to imprison her sister Caroline (Anne Revere) in the secret room where their father had been found dead, unless Caroline also treats "that woman" abominably. Caroline, whose own youthful romances had been forever squelched by Victoria, accedes to her sister's demands, at least for the moment. After months of being virtually alone and unwelcome in the house, Anne confers with Dr. John Lucas (Colin Tapley), a young man she had thought to marry before meeting Rip. Acting on John's advice, Anne arranges to invite her own guests to the Van Brett house. This seems to backfire when Victoria accuses Anne of being unfaithful with John, and Anne is forced to admit to Rip that she had met with John sans chaperone—but innocently—earlier that same day.

Despite the circumstantial evidence, Rip gets his back up and announces his plans to take Anne away from the wretched house, even if it means losing whatever money he might have inherited. That night, however, Victoria lures Anne into the secret room with promises of restoring to her the pearls that had "gone missing" and then shuts the soundproof door behind the terrified woman. Telling Caroline that the muffled screams she heard were the result of a dream—and threatening her with commitment to a mental institution—Victoria deals with witness problems. Later, she tells Rip that Anne had eloped with John and that it is time to dismiss the servants and close the house up for the rest of the season.

When John turns up empty handed the next morning, Rip grows suspicious, and Caroline reveals the secret vault after the dog yaps incessantly at the wall. Rip forces Victoria to open the door; Anne, who had swooned, is extracted and revived. Not to be outdone, Victoria tries to maneuver Caroline into the vault. She is foiled by the family lawyer, Mortimer Kneff (Sir Guy Standing), who then threatens to have her imprisoned unless she reinstates Rip in the will. Caroline walks out with Rip and Ann and, when Neff leaves, Victoria enters the safe to retrieve the pearls. The door shuts and locks behind her.

Based on "the play that made Broadway gasp," Paramount's 1934 rarity *Double Door* is one of the earliest melds of domineering mother figure, cavernous mansion, and ominous secret chamber to hit the sound screen. Mary Morris's Victoria Van Brett is at once less shrill and more understated than had been Eva Moore's Rebecca Femm (matriarch of James Whale's definitive *Old Dark House*), but she isn't — as was her predecessor — merely one attraction in a certifiably lunatic sideshow. Unlike Femm, Van Brett cleaves closer to "normal" behavior, but "normal," of course, is a relative term, and it's the bizarre relationships among relatives that serve as the foundation for both Elizabeth A. McFadden's eponymous drama and Charles Vidor's film adaptation.

The source play, in which Mary Morris and Anne Revere created the roles they played in the feature film, had closed only weeks before Gladys Lehman and Jack Cunningham delivered their scenario to producer E. Lloyd Sheldon. The crème of New York Society had *not* supported the play, as it was reputedly based on the misadventures of the Wendel family, moneyed eccentrics whose Fifth Avenue manse was the site of more than one scandal that (briefly) involved the police, but never the newspapers. Despite decent enough reviews, H. C. Potter and George Haight's production of *Double Door* closed after 143 performances.

Now this sort of thing might lead one to ask why a major studio would choose to film an adaptation of a play that didn't last a half season on Broadway. Some thoughts on that one: First, *Double Door* doesn't come near to holding the record. That same year, Universal would opt to film *The Man Who Reclaimed His Head*—a pacifist potboiler starring Claude Rains, Lionel Atwill, and Joan Bennett—despite the fact that the "legitimate" original had closed within a month of opening on the Great White Way. The play lost all kinds of money, and recent research by this writer has demonstrated that the film never quite edged into the black, either. Revenue aside, the picture has developed something of a cult following over the intervening decades. This has provided no consolation whatsoever to Universal in any of its myriad incarnations, and *Man Who Reclaimed His Head* still has not seen any sort of authorized entry into the home viewing market.

Moreover, properties with small casts, unit sets, and timeless appeal (the thought of watching the moneyed set get its comeuppance is the very *stuff* of tragedy) have a virtual lock on profitability. Pictures made for a dime will always earn a buck; it's the pictures made for a buck that you have to watch.

I'm not alone in feeling that *Double Door* has the *feel* of a Universal picture. Maybe not the kind of "feel" that one gets from *Frankenstein* or *Dracula*, but the ticket buyer who had reveled in the sort of frisson the studio had achieved with the aforementioned *Old Dark House* (1932) or *Secret of the Blue Room* (1933) would have felt very much at home meandering through the Van Brett mansion. It may well be that Paramount felt the same way, for the film's press-book copy shows how the studio's publicity staff wasted no time in comparing Morris with Universal's "Titans of Terror":

> Miss Morris has the advantage of Lugosi and Karloff in that she does not resort to make-up to achieve her frightful characterizations. She plays them straight, without histrionics, her voice well modulated and cultured, her face calmly beautiful. Yet she can make an audience shudder with one lift of her fine hands, or a flashing look from her deep-set eyes.

This was Morris's first and *only* film, although she had a lengthy theatrical career, appearing in such O'Neill warhorses as *Beyond the Horizon*, *Desire under the Elms*, and *The Great God Brown*, so the plural posited by the press-book scribes is a mite unclear. She did merit the greater part of the publicity campaign, though, and perhaps that comparison with Karloff and Lugosi was apropos: Like the signature roles of those hardy souls, her Victoria Van Brett is every inch a monster. It's difficult to determine for whom she has the most contempt: her business associates, her servants, or her family. She has browbeaten her sister, has all but emasculated (psychologically) her half-brother, and has demeaned and alienated her future sister-in-law. She has no allies, only victims, so there is no one to gasp or mourn when the double door closes behind her at the end.

The Motion Picture Production Code had been introduced by censorship czar Will Hays back in 1930, and the Catholic church's Legion of Decency was founded the year *Double Door* hit the screens. Thus confronted by two sets of all-seeing, ever-disapproving eyes, the scenario purposefully left vague the question as to whether Victoria Van Brett's being locked in the chamber was an accident or an action that was tantamount to suicide. Suicide was never an acceptable means to an end, although it was allowable if the victim had been portrayed as being in the throes of madness (cf. Claude Rains's John Jasper in *Mystery of Edwin Drood*, 1935), or it was a noble gesture, resulting in a much greater good (see Margaret Irving as the duchess in *The Outcasts of Poker Flat*, 1937). Of course, inasmuch as both of these films were based upon classic works by immortal authors (although Dickens had died with *Drood* unfinished), there was a certain literary integrity that could be cited in allowing the exceptions to the code.

Wouldn't the words "Welcome to my house. Come freely. Go safely, and leave something of the happiness you bring," spoken by Bram Stoker's Dracula to Jonathan Harker, be a fitting caption here? Marry Morris as Victoria Van Brett.

On the whole, Morris's Victoria Van Brett is so blatantly villainous that, were the film a murder mystery or gentleman-detective outing rather than a melodrama, the canny viewer would recognize that the miserable recluse was being set up to be done in. With this clearly not the case, she is, in the words of *New York Herald Tribune* film critic Lucius Beebe, "a spinster of malevolent forcefulness who has dedicated her life to defending the resources and integrities of the Van Brett family."[1] As she views virtually all of the other principal cast members as being real threats to that integrity, her Machiavellian behavior is consistent and ubiquitous. Nonstop villainy, unbroken by even a hint of levity, irony, or grandeur, can become monotonous and even run the risk of becoming ludicrous. Morris's scheming witch thus suffers in any comparison to Boris's or Bela's horrors, whose evil is always tempered by crazed jocularity, personal suffering, or (especially with Bela) operatic flamboyance. Victoria ought to spew her venom with panache, not restraint, if she aspires to such heady company, and although she is inexorably remorseless in her schemes, these suffer from uniformity in technique and understatement in execution. Despite the fading opulence of her Fifth Avenue mansion and the aura of dissolution and decay and despite even the double door itself, Victoria Van Brett's unrelenting drive to bend others to her will results, not in an unforgettable portrait of wickedness incarnate, but in what Hannah Arendt called "the banality of evil." This, coupled with the fact that most of the current crop of horror fans has been weaned on gore, pyrotechnics and computer-generated images (CGI), virtually guarantees that Van Brett (and *Double Door*) will disappoint if and when acquaintances are made.

Reviewer "Kauf" offered his assessment of the cast for the May 8, 1934 issue of *Variety*:

> Mary Morris, who did the main part in the stage version, also does it on the screen. She's a capable and schooled performer but constantly underlines her performance so much that she's not believable except in a few moments. What acting honors there are go to Evelyn Venable as the outside girl. Anne Revere as the younger spinster sister, Kent Taylor as the boy and Colin Tapley as the friendly physician all over-act.

Double Door marked Evelyn Venable's fourth feature film, and every one of those saw the personable young woman sharing screen time with Kent Taylor. The Ohio-born youngster (she was barely twenty when *Cradle Song* premiered in 1933) had basically gotten her start due to the friendship that had sprung up between her father and noted stage thespian, Walter Hampden, and — prior to her entering films — had attained a measure of renown playing Roxanne to Hamden's Cyrano and Ophelia to his Hamlet. Genre fans remember her best for Paramount's *Death Takes a Holiday* (1934), comedy buffs think *Mrs. Wiggs of the Cabbage Patch* (a Paramount misfire from that same year, with W. C. Fields and ZaSu Pitts), and she was the voice of the Blue Fairy to the delight of almost everyone in Walt Disney's *Pinocchio* (1940). Following a ten-year career that saw her involved in two dozen films, Venable returned to the stage — her first love — and spent decades at UCLA, where she taught classical languages and reintroduced Sophocles et al. to the university drama department. Evelyn Venable died at the age of eighty in 1993.

Her *Double Door* honey stayed active in Hollywood some thirty years longer than Miss Venable and showed his handsome map in nearly 100 *more* features. He

Bracketing the juveniles are Mary Morris (left) and Anne Revere (right) from the original Broadway production, *Double Door* (Photofest).

had left his native Iowa (as Louis Weiss) in 1931 and succeeded in finding some work as an extra. Changing his name to the decidedly more marquee-friendly Kent Taylor, he slowly moved from bottom-of-the-crawl to featured roles, before graduating to full-blown, stock hero parts by the middle of the decade. Taylor was never less than a serviceable, lower-shelf leading man throughout the course of his lengthy career, but it doesn't appear that he was ever given the opportunity to be anything more. Searching his film credits for undeniable "A" pictures results more in starting arguments than in finding gold, and most genre buffs might recognize his name only for his participation in a batch of low-budget horror and science fiction movies made while he was entering his senior years. I dimly recall his playing Boston Blackie on early '50s TV and genuinely mourn the loss of his Duncan MacLain in Universal's "lost" Crime Club entry *The Last Express* (1938). But, at least until the script requires him to display some testosterone late in the proceedings, his Rip Van Brett in *Double Door* is not his finest hour.

Along with Mary Morris, Anne Revere made her screen debut recreating her stage role in *Double Door*. Unlike Morris, Revere continued on in films (and its near relative, television) for some thirty-five years, although it's been suggested that her being descended from American Revolutionary War figure Paul Revere remained the actress's greatest claim to fame.*

> The tendency at the Paramount [Theater] yesterday was to take Victoria Van Brett too lightly. From the safety of balcony seats, audiences could afford to taunt the old lady as she crept around the second floor with her plots to drive her half-brother's wife out of the house. But there was an end of flippancy when Victoria, with lighted candle and enigmatic smile, lured the trusting girl into the secret chamber.
> [A.D.S., *The New York Times*, May 5, 1934]

Finding watchable video copies of *Double Door* is quite a challenge, but — as there's no way Paramount (or Universal, or whoever owns Universal or the rights to this old Paramount "meller" [melodrama] nowadays) will ever see its way to releasing a director's cut on DVD — it's a challenge that one ought to embrace. Although the picture may have been criticized for its excessive underlying gloom even in the earliest days of its initial release, it had — and still has— its shuddery moments. Unlike Universal's *Secret of the Blue Room*, which was remade *twice* within ten years (and which was itself an anglicized sound reworking of a silent German original), *Double Door* never enjoyed an updating or a more modern reinterpretation, nor has its eponymous legitimate source received any professional restaging worthy of published critical comment. However, McFadden's play was adapted and small-screened on the *Kraft Television Theatre* on May 7, 1947. Elinor Wilson smiled enigmatically in that one.

---

*Still, she attained genre immortality as the scheming spiritualist who drives Boris Karloff's character over the edge in Columbia's memorable *The Devil Commands* (1941).

BLACK MOON

Columbia Pictures Corp. — June 15, 1934 — 68/69 minutes

Cast: Jack Holt as Stephen Lane; Fay Wray as Gail; Dorothy Burgess as Juanita Lane; Cora Sue Collins as Nancy Lane; Arnold Korff as Doctor Perez; Clarence as Muse Lunch; Eleanor Wesselhoeft as Anna; Madame Sul-Te-Wan as Ruva; Lawrence Criner as Kala; Lumsden Hare as Macklin; Henry Kolker as Doctor; Theresa Harris as Sacrificed Girl; Fred Walton as Butler; Billy McClain, Charles Moore, Robert Frazier, Ada Penn, Anna Lee Johnson as House Servants; Lillian West as Maid; Lillian Smith as Nurse; Edna Franklin as Mother of Sacrificed Girl; William H. Dunn as Langa; Grace Chapman as Welfare Worker; Edna Tichenor as stand-in for Dorothy Burgess; Kay Konrad as stand-in for Fay Wray; William Lally as stand-in for Jack Holt; Lee McNally as double for Dorothy Burgess

Credits: *Director:* Roy William Neill; *associate producer:* Everett Riskin; *assistant director:* Robert Margolis; *screenplay:* Wells Root; based on the novel *Black Moon* by Clements Ripley; *photographed by* Joseph August; *camera operator:* Dave Ragin; *assistant cameraops:* Marcel Grand, Jack Andersen; *film editor:* Richard Cahoon; *dance director:* Max Sheck; *sound engineer:* Edward Bernds; *technical advisor:* Don Taylor; *grip:* Eddie Blaisdell; *props:* Stanley Dunn; *still photographer:* Irving Lippman

Synopsis: Businessman Stephen Lane (Jack Holt) has never understood why his wife, Juanita (Dorothy Burgess), prefers to sit on the bedroom floor, thumping on a drum, instead of socializing more with him and their daughter, Nancy (Cora Sue Collins). A psychiatrist diagnoses her as being neurotic, and her insistence on returning to Saint Christopher, the island where she was born and raised, is making Stephen crazy. Juanita's uncle, Dr. Perez (Arnold Korff), sends his overseer, Macklin (Lumsden Hare), to try to dissuade the young woman from returning home, but before he can spill the beans to Stephen, the overseer is slain by a native of the island, who has accompanied Macklin to civilization. Thus, against his better judgment—and without that crucial information from Macklin—Stephen allows his wife and daughter to go to Saint Christopher. He insists, however, that his secretary, Gail (Fay Wray), go along for the little girl's sake.

Once again on the island, Juanita soon grows distant from her uncle and her child, while becoming more and more involved in the native voodoo rituals. Ruva (Madame Sul-Te-Wan), the native woman who had reared Juanita, begins to take an interest in Nancy. Worried, Gail radios Stephen, imploring him to come to Saint Christopher. After the message is sent, the radio operator is found hanged. Not long after, Anna (Eleanor Wesselhoeft), Nancy's nursemaid, is also murdered.

Stephen is brought to Saint Christopher by Lunch (Clarence Muse), a black American from Georgia who is enamored with a local girl. Stephen discovers that Juanita has become actively involved in the natives' voodoo practices. He is led by Lunch to a voodoo ceremony, in which Juanita acts as the high priestess in what is obviously to be a human sacrifice—of the very girl whom Lunch loves. Stephen shoots the high priest, hoping to prevent the sacrifice, but the girl is murdered nonetheless after Stephen and Lunch flee the scene. Dr. Perez is hopeful that the high priest's having been killed will put an end to all the savagery, but it turns out that Stephen merely wounded the man, and the natives are up in arms.

Together with Lunch, the white population of Saint Christopher holes up in an armed tower on the edge of the Perez plantation. They succeed in holding off the enraged locals, but Juanita betrays her family and leads some of the natives to a separate entrance to the tower via a secret door in the manor house. The little band is smoked out of the fortified room, although Perez escapes to his yacht in the confusion. The master plan calls for Perez to be killed — his death will transfer ownership of the island to Juanita — and for Stephen and Gail to be sacrificed ritually.

Lunch and Perez help them escape, however, and the natives now call for Juanita to sacrifice Nancy in place of the white couple. For the first time, Juanita is torn between her breeding and her blood, but she prepares to kill her child, nonetheless. Stephen, who has followed her into the jungle, shoots her before she can injure the girl. He and the others flee Saint Christopher on Lunch's boat. Dr. Perez chooses to stay on, as the natives' sundry thirsts seem to have been slaked once again.

Black Moon offers absolutely zilch in terms of the sort of supernatural hoo-hah that one has come to associate with films dealing with voodoo. Shot only a couple of years after the Halperin brothers introduced the term "zombie" into the parlance of B-movie aficionados, *Moon* made no effort to establish ties with any tales of the walking undead. True, a pin-infested effigy does have a brief cameo, and toxic substances are surreptitiously introduced into the beverages of unsuspecting characters, but these elements are either shrugged off incredulously or surmounted with ease and a smattering of medical savvy. The underlying force that draws Juanita back to Saint Christopher — where it then brings out the very worst in her — is occasionally aired, but never satisfactorily explained.

Were the film structured differently, such a lack of exposition might be acceptable; indeed, it might even be requisite. When shoehorned into place among the bits and pieces we do have, however, it's just not enough to lead even the most willing viewer down the road to catharsis and value for the dollar. The basic problem with *Black Moon* is the character of Juanita Stone.

She's not the heroine, you see; Wray's Gail fills that bill — predictable and formulaic though it may be — quite nicely. Nor is she the protagonist; that's Holt's Stephen. Nor — and this is where it gets sticky — is she the antagonist. She may be an antisocial malcontent who cannot find happiness in the company of her supposed peers. Or a thirties-version feminist, looking for fulfillment away from the traditional yokes of husband and child. ("I can't stand it here any longer," she moans, in a whiney diatribe that addresses either option. "I'm only half alive!") Or, she might very well be the weak-willed dupe of a carefully concocted conspiracy. No matter which she *is*, she is *not* the force that rises up to frustrate all that is good and spearhead the advancement of evil. *That* force, as outlined by a basically narrow and racist screenplay, is the population of Saint Christopher. And I don't mean the five white folks, either.

It's those blacks, you see; two thousand of them on that little island are up to no good. Dr. Perez (the decidedly non-Hispanic Arnold Korff) endeavors to explain to Steven how the blacks have tried to "wipe out" his family settlement "six times in the last 100 years!" It's been a while since the locals have made a go at it, so—what with Juanita coming home and all—it seems like a good idea to try to massacre everyone again. You understand that if the doctor is dispatched, the island will belong to the lovely Juanita, who will then, one would assume, free the populace from whatever it is they need to fight against with appreciable regularity.

And there are the drums. When the natives aren't pounding away at them from every corner of the island, Juanita's thumping on a play-it-at-home version while sitting fetchingly on her bedroom floor. The woman hears drums all the time, even when there aren't any drums. This can mean only one of two things: either the drums are so pervasive a presence in her life that she must forswear her cosmopolitan, small-drum existence in order to get back to where there are some really *big* drums, or she's skipping some notes on that great sheet music of life. Never in the picture do we learn whether the drums convey a specific message, induce a soporific state, or incite one to action. "The natives are restless," intones Dr. Perez (to the intense satisfaction of the genre viewer), who establishes somewhat later that one need only worry when the drums *stop*. This can't mean that some poor native must go on and on, drumming incessantly, during the fifteen-year periods that separate the regularly scheduled rebellions, can it?

Human sacrifice is discussed and enacted without the screenplay's slightest attempt at making it relevant to the proceedings. Its playing a requisite part in voodoo rituals is established, but to what end? No gods are invoked, no maledictions are launched, no discernible results are evinced (apart from a sudden drop in the census figures). Just prior to the denouement, Juanita warns Stephen, "Tonight my people demand blood for blood. If it were my own blood—my child's—I would give it." It's unclear whether her people want what's usually referred to as "Old Testament justice"—a life-for-life trade-off for the natives who were unfortunately slain while they were trying to murder the white folks—or merely that, as the moon is high, it's sacrifice time, once again. Human sacrifice and drums are trotted out because these two items are listed in the standard voodoo catalogue, and one ought not to attempt a voodoo picture without them.

Again, there is neither any mention of zombies, nor the slightest reference to life after death. No one (save for Juanita, or the possibly drugged victims at the sacrifices) ever appears to be within spitting distance of a trance. Nowhere is there any evidence of voodoo's supposedly lethal "power of suggestion"; coming upon one of those dolls, prickled with pins, and a slew of other bizarre items that ought to make him stand up and take notice, Stephen is unmoved: "Hummmph!" he snorts. "More black magic."

The upshot of all this is that voodoo in *Black Moon* is presented less as a supernatural agency or religion than as an insidious means of effecting a banal and ignoble end: the unseating of the legal owners and the "restoration" of the island to native governance. There's a "high priest," but a faceless substitute effortlessly takes his place when Stephen wings him with his revolver. While not quite a MacGuffin, the voodoo coloration is an ultimately expendable element whose absence would leave a more mundane—if admittedly unsettling—account of a young woman's efforts at seizing untimely control of property that would sooner or later revert to her anyhow. The story might as readily have been set in Myrtle Beach, where Juanita — motivated by avarice and extreme social consciousness— plotted to remove Perez from his position as chair of the board of the family corporation with the help of an equally shallow and driven country club set. As the sundry voodoo components are very much present, though, they slant the picture in an awkward and unacceptable direction.

Point to consider: How predictable, treacherous, and inept *are* these Saint Christopher blacks if they haven't been able — in six attempts, over a hundred years— to do away with a mere carload of exploitative overseers? Inasmuch as everyone appears to be, if not happy, at least *tolerant* of the conditions on the island for fifteen years or so at a crack, what sets them off with depressing regularity? Voodoo? Are there no elders who, having participated in a few unsuccessful uprisings during their lifetimes, mightn't suggest some other way of dealing with "the man?"

In recounting how things have become deplorable, Dr. Perez confesses that he was "careless" after the uprising that claimed Juanita's parents' lives in having allowed Ruva to take care of the orphaned girl. Now, it's not clear whether Juanita shares in Perez's *stupid* gene the way she shares his pigmentation, but the resulting picture is not pretty. We see Uncle Doctor as being (all things considered) really little better than an idiot; I mean, wouldn't *you* offset the numerical odds with a few dozen white hired hands-cum-mercenaries, given the goings-on over the last 100 years? We note that the natives *also* have rifles. We understand that they're bound (by those hereto totally ineffectual voodoo rituals) to bang the drums until they decide to stop and only then to attack. If even a mouth breather like Dr. Perez can spot this as S.O.P., how are we to assess the aggregate intelligence of those thousands of black dissidents? They might just as well *be* "monkey chasers," as Lunch describes them. That wholesale dismissal, however, is racist.

Furthermore, is Juanita's presence crucial to the success of the natives' latest revolt? I mean, they don't seem to have been terribly successful to date without her. Is she the Great White Hope? She appears to be the only new element in the traditional native-uprising formula: Beat those drums, sacrifice a few folks, then make for the compound and get shot. She *does* know about the secret door to the tower, and she *does* introduce the latest in smoking-them-out technology, and she *is* next in line for the deed to the island when Dr. Perez is rendered defunct. If the unfolding narrative is meant to suggest that only with the help of a white woman — who has been systematically infused over the course of her thirty-odd years with (for want of a better phrase) the "collective malevolence" of a century's worth of angry black people — can all of the island's native citizens hope to overthrow the yoke of repression? Well, that's racist, too. Either way you slice it, the indigenous population of Saint Christopher is portrayed as being inherently evil and profoundly incompetent, and it takes a white presence to bring things to fruition.

Such racism as is depicted in the scenario was par for the course in 1934, and it would be grossly unfair to hold this mid-'30s melodrama accountable to standards that the intervening decades of peaceful protest, violent confrontation, and ongoing legislation are still revising. Given Hollywood's *Sitz im Leben* back then, though, rare was the black actor who could find employment as anything other than a slave, servant, naysayer, criminal, comic relief, or halfwit. The male stereotypes ran the gamut

Dorothy Burgess never looked so good, not in the entire 69 minutes of *Black Moon* (Photofest).

from the shiftless, no-account, childishly superstitious dullards who moved at glacial speed while mumbling variations on "Lawdy, Lawdy, I's a comin" (à la Stepin Fetchit) to the bug-eyed, no-account, razor-wielding conmen, prone to spontaneous comic outbursts ("Feets! Don't fail me now!") and acres of malapropisms (Mantan Moreland, sans pareil). In there somewhere was a run of Uncle Toms, Harlem slicksters, near-imbecilic brutes, and other, maliciously skewed offshoots. The female characters offered to black actresses ranged from Mother Earth-ish slave mammies to coquettish near-whites, looking to cross the line; from slaves, maids, and occasional girlfriends of Mr. Moreland and his kith, to "dusky Delilahs" (and downright whores), looking for nothing more than cheap liquor and some "sugar." *Black Moon* eschews the more clownish or benevolent takes on the individual—"Mammy" Ruva is a scorpion—and instead offers its take on an entire black *society*, which (it has been carefully shown) is built on deceit, betrayal, self-delusion, and murder.

Surprisingly, offsetting the picture's (and the era's) underlying racial malaise is Clarence Muse's portrayal of Lunch McClaren, an American black—late of Georgia—who is adventurous, articulate, and very quick to distance himself from the locals on Saint Christopher. He can be humorous without being foolish, and his conversations with Jack Holt's character are man to man, not white man to black man; their relationship remains refreshingly condescension free. Lunch is more at ease among the whites on the island as, with the exception of the native girl with whom he professes to be in love, he mistrusts the "monkey chasers," whom he also holds in contempt.

This raises another, equally interesting point: Purposefully or not, the screenplay subtly contrasts the American black man with the Caribbean black man. The former is in every way more independent and responsible and less easily led than his island counterpart. It may be argued that Lunch's associating with the white population of Saint Christopher ultimately allows him to escape with his life, while the natives who toil for Perez and his family (like that unfortunate radio operator) are slain for their presumption and treachery. This American black man joins forces with American whites he has just met, and together they see the horror through to the end. In contrast, the native black man who accompanies Macklin to New York—and who, presumably, has known the overseer all his life—kills him dispassionately. With the scenario offering no evidence that the native was entranced to commit the murder, we may well infer that, so far as the "island blacks" are concerned, murder is the nature of the beast.

It's clear that Lunch McClaren hardly personifies Hollywood's paean to the black American male, as the qualities Lunch exhibits in the film were noticeably absent in those insignificant and demeaning roles offered to the era's black actors. The easy relationship that Lunch enjoys with Stephen Lane is much more the exception than the rule, cinematically, and the likelihood that the plot wrinkle glanced harmlessly off the psyches of moviegoers south of the Mason-Dixon Line is nil. Still, the screenplay's wishful thinking goes out of its way to pit black against black, and the bottom line may have been ideological: America, the land of freedom and opportunity vs. Saint Christopher, the site of unending violence, named for the patron saint of lost causes.

Despite the fact that his lengthy screen career (nearly 150 films, basically spanning a half-century) consisted mainly of tertiary roles (innumerable are his porters), Clarence Muse remains one of the most widely respected black actors in the cinema. In addition to alternating leads in "all colored" movies with his mainstream Hollywood work, he held a doctorate in jurisprudence and was a serious student of the theater. (Check out his observations on the "Viennese style" of acting as found in America in Robert Cremer's *Lugosi: The Man behind the Cape*.) When not on screen, he might pen a story or fabricate a screenplay, serve as technical advisor, or compose songs and incidental musical themes. At least once, he was hired as dance director. Per the credits of Bobby Breen's 1939 *Way Down South*, Muse did virtually everything except direct and paint the garage. Honored as one of the first inductees into the Black Filmmakers' Hall of Fame, Clarence Muse died, a day shy of his ninetieth birthday, in 1979. (Stepin Fetchit likewise was voted into the BFHF, but it's tougher for today's younger fans of older films to assess his work, as the au courant, politically correct crowd has excised lots of Fetchit footage from existing prints.)

As for the others, Dorothy Burgess does a nice job as Juanita, although she really doesn't have much of an opportunity to let loose dramatically until the final scenes, in which she's torn between her bonds to the natives and her love for her daughter. Jack Holt does the best he can to make Stephen Lane less of a typical, straight-as-an-arrow Jack Holt hero and more of a multilayered protagonist, and he's not bad; the sundry moments he spends with little Cora Sue Collins are touching and, more importantly, believable. Fay Wray is gorgeous as the stock secretary-in-love-with-her-boss and, given that it's obvious from the get-go that Dorothy Burgess's affections will end up being tragically misplaced, one merely waits for the inevitable denouement when she and Holt are romantically intertangled. Arnold Korff makes Perez look like an idiot, but that's the screenplay's fault, not his. When he suggests, time and again, that the solution to whatever crisis is at hand is for everyone to "get some sleep," you have to wonder how he's lasted this long. As Ruva, Madame Sul-Te-Wan (born Nellie Conley; she was Dorothy Dandridge's grandmother) is properly sullen looking, which quality may pass for menace and mystery.

Black Moon was based on Clement Ripley's novel of the same name, which had been published only the year before. Columbia snapped up the rights, a screenplay was demanded of Wells Root, and Roy William Neill's derriere was assigned the director's chair. The first films that leap to mind when Neill's name is brought up are the Universal Sherlock Holmes features, of course, as he directed every one of the Rathbone/Bruce gems except for the first in the series, *Sherlock Holmes and the Voice of Terror*; he produced most of them, as well. The Holmes' films came at the tail end of Neill's lengthy career, however — he died in London in December 1946 — which began with his first (and last) performance as an actor, in Thomas H. Ince's *Corner in Colleens* (1916). Neither terribly happy in front of the camera nor — per a review I was able to track down — terribly good at it, O'Neill assumed directorial command (with Ince's blessing) of *The Girl Glory* (1917) and never looked back from there. Among the more than 100 features he directed are a handful of obscure mid-'30s thrillers that are recalled with joy by genre aficionados (when they are recalled at all), like *The Menace* (1932), *The Circus Queen Murder* (1933), and *The Ninth Guest* (1934). Neill was also responsible for helping Boris Karloff magnificently enact the double role of Anton and Gregor (arguably a *triple* role) in the splendid 1935 Columbia horror offering, *The Black Room*.

Much of the impact of *Black Moon* is due to Neill's vision, but there are several instances in which circumstances conspired to undercut both the drama and the atmosphere. Neill's cinematographer was Joseph August. Behind the camera since 1912 and the man who photographed many of William S. Hart's classic early Westerns, August had already been recognized for his abilities in such silents as *Dante's Inferno* (1924), *Tumbleweeds* (1925), and *The Beloved Rogue* (1926). For whatever reason — budgetary or scheduling limitations seem the most likely — August elected to shoot the *Black Moon* voodoo rituals day for night, and this profoundly weakens the mood of the picture. The attempted effect is a complete failure, and the shots of the daytime plantation exterior (most of which were shot inside the studio) are, if anything, *darker* than the sacrificial sequences, supposedly held in the light of the moon. As one need only cast an eye at August's wonderful work in *The Informer* (1935), *The Hunchback of Notre Dame* (1939), or the exquisite *Portrait of Jennie* (1948)—or even several of the moody *interiors* in *Black Moon*—to appreciate the scope of the man's artistic palette, these glaring visual disappointments lead to no little head scratching.

Variety tossed some bouquets to Roy William Neill and the cast but stated that the scenario possessed "dubious elements." Reviewer "Shan" suggested that "If some prolog action had been offered to indicate how the voodoo fascination had been inculcated perhaps the picture would screen to better reaction," and I agree wholeheartedly. Regular moviegoers had begun to connect the tropics with human sacrifice courtesy of films like *Trader Horn* (1931), *Tarzan, the Ape Man* (1932), and *King Kong* (1933), but their only other cinematic avenue of exposure to voodoo had been the Halperin brothers' *White Zombie* (1932), where the more insidiously supernatural treatment of the topic may have been associated with the presence of Bela Lugosi. There weren't too many folks who walked in on *Black Moon* carrying any significant background on voodoo with them, and the picture, starting abruptly with a dreamy-eyed Juanita beating her drum, does nothing to pave the way for what follows.

Shan's critique also tiptoes around the film's racial sensitivities, as he notes, "There may be innumerable spots where the picture of a married white woman dancing in the heathen religious rites will not prove attractive."

Very little has been written about *Black Moon* since the film's release, and it devolved to Turner Classic Movies to finally screen the picture several years back, after a decades-long absence from public view. (In issue #194 of *Starlog* magazine, even Fay Wray admitted that she had almost erased the picture from her consciousness; she does not so much as mention it in her 1989 autobiography, *On the Other Hand*.) In issue #43 of *Scarlet Street* magazine, Ken Hanke maintains *I Walked with a Zombie* owes the picture "an undeniable debt." "It looks very much like *Zombie* director Jacques Tourneur saw this film before embarking on his own," offers Hanke, "and if he absorbs its strengths, he also managed to avoid its central weaknesses." A careful reading of their works reveals that neither Edmund G. Bansak (*Fearing the Dark: The Val Lewton Career*), nor Chris Fujiwara (*Jacques Tourneur: The Cinema of Nightfall*) shares that opinion, but the then-obscurity of *Black Moon* may have mitigated against its being considered by either of these worthy gentlemen.

Black Moon is thus a competent thriller with inherent plot absurdities that are somewhat balanced by decent performances.

Like *The Witching Hour*, it may be found in the gray market.

LE GOLEM

A. B. Barrandov Film — February 19, 1936 — 100/95/91/83 minutes
Cast: Harry Baur as Rudolph II; Roger Karl as Chancellor Lang; Charles Dorat as Rabbi Jacob; Ferdinand Hart as the Golem; Roger Duchesne as De Trignac, an antiques dealer; Aimos as Toussaint, his servant; Gaston Jacquet as Friederich, prefect of police; Jany Holt as Rachel; Tania Doll as Madame Benoit; Germaine Aussey as Countess Strada; Marcel Dalio as Jew; Julien Carette as Jester; with Robert Ozanne, Stanislas Neumann, Karel Schleikert, Walter Schorsch, Antonin Jirsa, Jan Cerny, Alfred Basyr, Frantisek Mlejnek, Frantisek Jerhot, Charles Goldblatt
Credits: *Producer:* Charles Philip; *director:* Julien Duvivier; *production manager:* Josef Stein; *script:* André-Paul Antoine and Julien Duvivier; based on the famous Prague legend and the eponymous novel by Gustav Meyrink; *dialogue:* André-Paul Antoine; *sets:* André Andrejew and Stepán Kopecky; *cameraops:* Jan Stallich and Václav Vich; *music:* Josef Kumok; *sound recording:* Bedrich Polednik; *editing:* Jirí Slavicek; *studio:* Studios A/B Prague Barrandov; *sound tape recording:* Tobis-Klangfilm
Czech release title: *Golem*
Aka: *The Legend of Prague*

Synopsis: Julien Duvivier's *Le Golem* picks up some years after Paul Wegener's story leaves off.

The Jews of the Prague ghetto are not only once again oppressed, but also in danger of starving, and the talk turns to reactivating Rabbi Löw's Golem, which has been stowed in the synagogue attic for safekeeping. Rabbi Jacob (Charles Dorat)—Löw's chosen successor—urges patience, averring that they'll receive a sign when the time is right to bring the man of clay back to life. Jacob's young wife, Rachel (Jany Holt), has faith in her husband's pronouncements, but she, too, is growing weary of oppression.

Everyone, it seems, is subject to the lunatic whims of Emperor Rudolph II (Harry Baur), whose obsession with the occult had led him to underwrite a vast "laboratory" populated by cock-eyed inventors, alchemists and wizards. Rudolph is mindful of the growing unrest among the Jews, and his abject terror that the Golem will prowl once again allows his mistress, the Countess Strada (Germaine Aussey), and his chancellor, Lang (Roger Karl)—himself a lapsed Jew—to keep the emperor in check and off balance.

During a food riot in the town square, the countess is rescued from harm by antique dealer-cum-flimflam artist, De Trignac (Roger Duchesne), and his manservant, Toussaint (Aimos). The Frenchman is hurt in the melee, but he is found by Rachel, who brings him back to her house, where she tends his wounds. While he remains infatuated with the countess, De Trignac is now indebted to the rabbi's wife.

For reasons of state, Rudolph allows himself to become engaged to his cousin, Isabel of Spain. This infuriates the countess, who charms De Trignac into stealing the Golem from the synagogue attic and secreting it in an unused passage in the massive palace. Should push ever come to shove, the statue will give Strada the leverage she needs to dispose of the threat of Isabel.

Friedrich (Gaston Jacquet), the prefect of police, informs the chancellor and the terrified emperor that the statue has now vanished. Lang orders Rabbi Jacob to the palace, and an imperial edict threatens with imminent hanging any Jews found guilty of complicity in the disappearance of the Golem. Rachel appeals to De Trignac for help, and the antiques purveyor convinces Rudolph to accept what is reputed to be Charlemagne's sword in return for Jacob's release. As the rabbi returns to the ghetto, Rudolph wanders through the cavernous reaches of his palace and comes upon the Golem, nestled amidst a pile of ancient chairs and candlesticks. When his request for a gesture of camaraderie goes unheeded by the inert statue, the emperor flails away frantically with his sword; in his madness, he skewers one of the soldiers who has come running in response to his fearful cries.

The Golem is chained to the walls of an underground dungeon, and Rudolph orders that the Jewish leaders—including Jacob—likewise be imprisoned until they can be executed. Jacob had earlier whispered to Rachel that "When the beast roars, the Golem will awake" and had revealed to her the mighty word of life that would empower the giant man of clay. As the palace fills with revelers to honor Rudolph, Rachel starts at the roaring of the hungry lions in the adjoining cells. Remembering her husband's message, she carves the Hebrew characters for *emet*—"truth"—on the clay-man's forehead and watches, transfixed, as the light of life comes into his eyes.

The Golem snaps his chains and begins his inexorable ascent from the dungeons, collapsing the palace's massive walls as he does so. Panic ensues as the lions follow the behemoth through the corridors. Those courtiers who are neither trampled in the mad rush to escape nor pummeled by the Golem are attacked by the ravening beasts. Friedrich's head is crushed beneath a hefty clay foot, and Karl is hurled from a palace window to his death. With his soldiers powerless to stop the mystical juggernaut, Rudolph takes the low road and abdicates. As the troops of Mathias, Rudolph's benevolent brother, approach Prague, Jacob erases the first Hebrew character from the Golem's forehead—leaving the Hebrew word *met*, or "death"—and the creature disintegrates in the midst of the jubilant populace.

In 1915 Woodrow Wilson was in the White House, Europe was at war, and Prague was one of the most important literary capitals in the world. Such native proponents of esoterica as Rainer Maria Rilke, Franz Werfel and Franz Kafka impressed the intelligentsia, but it was a local legend, rather than the local talent, that roused the common folk. Austrian Gustav Meyrink had penned *The Golem*, a romanticized reshuffling of the tale of a Hebraic juggernaut that had haunted the Czech environs for centuries, and the novel struck a chord that resonated deep within the national spirit.

According to the legend, sixteenth-century Rabbi Judah Löw ben Bezuzel—a denizen of Prague's Jewish ghetto—had created from clay a being to protect the "Chosen People" from the excesses of their anti-Semitic neighbors. (Also making the rounds were tales of the misadventures of *another* dabbler in clay, a Rabbi Eliahu Baal Shem of Chelm, but Löw-level literary celebrity continued to elude him.) The *Sefer Yetzira* (*Book of Creation*)—the oldest extant Talmudic text on cosmology and the occult properties of numbers—listed formulae that had been associated by medieval German Hassidic Jews with the creature called *golem*, a term that literally meant "incomplete being." With the *Yetzira* thus the source of Rabbi Löw's white magic—and that word *golem* traceable to the original Hebrew of Psalm 139—there was both Talmudic and biblical justification for the name given to the otherwise unholy savior of Prague.

Meyrink's *Golem* was a sensation. Even as war raged about them, students of Jewish folklore and seekers after fine literature seized on the novel as an artistic mitzvah. Several years later, in fact, Yiddish dramatist Leivick Halpern fashioned a powerful play from the collected material, and the *Habima*—an internationally renowned Hebrew theater company from Bialystok (in Russian Poland)—adopted the work as one of its signature pieces. (R'Moshe Chayim Ephraim Bloch also wrote his own version of the goings-on in medieval Prague shortly after Meyrink. *Der Prager Golem, von seiner Geburt bis zu seinem Tod* [aka *The Golem: Legends of the Ghetto of Prague*] was begun while Bloch was serving as chaplain to Jewish prisoners of war and was completed not long after the war had ended. Bloch's Rabbi Löw not only created a golem, but also went so far as to name him "Joseph.")

Despite the far-flung influence of his masterpiece, however, the Viennese author had been beaten to the punch by a novice film actor from East Prussia. While on location for Apex/Bioscop's *Der Student von Prag* in 1913, Paul Wegener had likewise become familiar with the legend and had spearheaded an hour-long cinematic adaptation of it a year before Meyrink's novel saw the light of day. Granted, *Der Golem* (1914) chronicled the clay behemoth's misadventures in the early twentieth century rather than some 300 years earlier, but the novelty of the theme and its imaginative presentation contributed to making the film a winner. (As was *Der Student von Prag*; film historian Henri Langlois went so far as to call the pair of Wegener epics "the sources of Germany's national film art.")

Anyhow, the Great War raged on, and, in 1917, Wegener once again directed himself in what has come to be regarded as the genre's first sequel, Bioscop's *Der Golem und die Tänzerin* (*The Golem and the Dancer*). (Sharing the behind-the-camera honors with Wegener was Rochus Gliese, who also designed the production; in the 1914 original, Henrik Galeen had codirected.) This time around, however, Wegener portrayed an actor who donned the makeup to facilitate seducing a dancer upon whom he had cast his eye. The titular Tänzerin was played by Wegener's real-life spouse, Lyda Salmonova, who had performed the heroinely duties in the original feature, as well. It has recently been reported that a well-worn, somewhat deteriorated nitrate print of *Der Golem und die Tänzerin* nestles in the private collection of an anonymous, albeit well-heeled, European film collector; this claim cannot be verified. Apart from the briefest of clips, the 1914 original remains lost.

In 1920, Wegener was back in the saddle. *Der Golem, wie er in die Welt kam* (*The Golem, How He Came into the World*), truer to the legend that the burly actor had found so entrancing, made an impressive impact when released in a nearly devastated Europe and a newly giddy America. Caught up in a thrust into Gothic expressionism and bolstered by the monetary backing of investors desperate to help reverse the ravaged economy (and by monies freed up by a cessation of hostilities), the staff at UFA (Universum Film AG) pulled out all stops in recreating medieval Prague and thus restoring the awesome Man of Clay to his traditional haunts. Designing those haunts was the great German architect Hans Poelzig — the creator of the *Grosses Schauspielhaus* in Berlin — who had been approached by Wegener just after the war. As related by Eisner, Poelzig's wife, Marlene (a sculptress of no little repute) fashioned models from her husband's sketches, and these served as the blueprints for the sets. In all, a total of fifty-four buildings — some life-size, some miniatures, some fabricated in graduated perspective — were caressed by Karl Freund's lenses in the course of the filming.

Poelzig's medieval city was all pointed towers, turrets, and architectural cones, and its Jewish inhabitants — as delineated by Wegener and his old partner and coscenarist, Henrik Galeen — were nearly to a person lean and lanky and accoutered with wild hair, striated beards, and what have come to be popularly known as "witches' hats." The Wegener Golem — rounded of edge and nearly as wide as it was tall — thus stood out from its Jewish allies and their surroundings. Although he was a product of faith, desperation, and the *Kabbala*, the Golem was — like Moses — doomed ever to be a stranger in a strange land. *Der Golem, wie er en die Welt kam* ends with a small girl saving the beleaguered city via an act of childish curiosity: Her slender fingers pluck the medallion (and its contents, a scrap of paper inscribed with this account's empowering word — *Aemer*) from the gargoyle's chest. Saved yet again by unconventional means, the townspeople rejoice and — per the story — go on to cleaning up the remnants of the city after packing the Golem off into storage.

Much has been made of Wegener's Golem helping to fuel the creative fires of James Whale's *Frankenstein*, and the comparisons and contrasts of the parallel monster and child scenes — uncomprehending engines of destruction sidetracked by the innocent insouciance of a child; the inadvertent death of the one by the other — are apparent even to the most casual of viewers. A great deal of effort has likewise been expended in attempts at establishing more than casual, spiritual ties between the two grotesques, as if to nail down some sort of creative cause and effect between a medieval Eastern European legend and the creative unconsciousness of an earthy — but still rather provincial — Romantic Age English female writer. Studies in speculative psychology can be fun, but, short of finding something along the lines of a lost diary entry in which Mary Shelley gushes enthusiastically over a recently heard tale of beleaguered European Jews and their handmade deus ex machina, one is left with the short list of the seven basic plot lines and the admonition from the first book of Ecclesiastes that, after all, there is nothing new under the sun.

Le Golem was a sequel to, and not a remake of, *Der Golem, wie er in die Welt kam*, and while actor Ferdinand Hart's Clay Man doesn't spend a fraction of the time Wegener's did stomping around the city, he also plays a role in the power struggle that is radically different from the one his Germanic predecessor played. Much of the early footage in the 1920 film was devoted to the myth of the Golem, to the cabalistic processes needed to articulate and activate the ponderous statue, and to the gradual acclimation that takes place between the Jewish townspeople and their magical ace-in-the-hole. Löw's creature is clearly a supernatural force, and the studied contrast between the mundane tasks he is first given to perform and the unbridled power he later displays occupies the bulk of the running time.

From the later film's opening moments, Duvivier's Golem is a given — although the statue is inaccessible, its whereabouts and its prowess are well known — and everyone from the emperor to the lowliest street urchin is frantic to learn if and when Jacob is going to push the mystical button and launch again his instrument of vengeance. No one mulls over the creature's preternatural essence or muses about its occult origin; its quasi-religious grounding may have been crucial to the process of its creation, but, apparently, it has long since been ignored or forgotten. For Duvivier's Jews, the Golem is merely a violent tool to be empowered as the need arises. In fact, in stark contrast with Otto Gebühr's regally idle Emperor Luhois in Wegener's 1920 classic, it is Harry Baur's Emperor Rudolph who is consumed with magic, alchemy, and the unholy sciences here.

Then, too, this Golem is more a concretized symbol of the drive to overcome repression and inequity than Wegener's had been. Designed and shot during a period in which Europe was still affected by the Depression and in which the burgeoning anti-Semitism of the nouveau Nazi party was evident to those who had eyes to see, *Le Golem* proffered a solution to persecution and intolerance which was grounded in a mythos as mystical — and, therefore, as wildly romanticized — as the Niebelungen, yet was, when realized, banal and — worse — temporary. As delineated by the script, Hart's behemoth is the type of messiah the Jewish zealots were still awaiting even as Christ was crucified: a figure of irresistible physical force who would offer a quick fix to the Chosen People's chronic problems. As if reflecting this "secularization," the cabalistic dimensions which had powerfully spiced the last of Wegener's silent features are, save for the encrypting and effacing of this version of the *emet*, absent here; this Golem is essentially drawn along the lines of the cavalry arriving in the nick of time. (Apart from the underlying theme itself, the only real nod to the supernatural on the part of the Jews is the eerily atmospheric prayer meeting in which the ethereal presence of Rabbi Löw momentarily possesses one of the ghetto elders.)

Pierre Leprohon (in his *Julien Duvivier* in *Anthologie du Cinéma*) notes dispassionately that the director "adapted the theme so as to make, not a machine turning against its inventor, but a force which delivers an oppressed people." This departure distanced the film both from Wegener's classic silent and from the sundry other mid-'20s and early-'30s thrillers (epitomized by the aforementioned *Frankenstein*) in which the monster's mutiny had become the inevitable formulaic hinge. Duvivier's insistence on inserting this prolabor social commentary ("Revolt is the right of slaves!") was doubtless a brazen and inflammatory move at the time, but nowadays it is of dramatic superfluity and, if anything, further dilutes the character's weakly wrought quasi-religious dimension.

Despite its having been shot in Czechoslovakia's A. B. Barrandov Studios (and being registered under its Czech title, *Golem*), *Le Golem* was released only in French. Reportedly budgeted between two and three hundred thousand dollars, the film originally unreeled (in late 1935) at 100 minutes. At its Paris opening (on February 19, 1936), five minutes had been excised in an effort to tighten what some critics had regarded as its "overly leisurely" pace. When the film appeared with subtitles at New York City's *Fifty-Fifth Street Playhouse* in March of 1937, it ran some 91 minutes (both editing and titles were the work of the playhouse's managing director, Martin J. Lewis, and its publicity director, Herman G. Weinberg), and this was the version that prompted *The New York Times*' Frank Nugent to observe:

> "The Golem" is a handsome production by any standards except the literary. It needed something beyond huge sets, vivid costumery and rich photography to disguise the inadequacy of its plot and [Harry] Baur's performance becomes a magnificent cloak for a naked and spindling script.
>
> [March 22, 1937]

The film opened in Britain later in 1937, having been titled locally and trimmed to 83 minutes; a reissue the following year saw the film renamed *The Legend of Prague*, cut to an astonishing 70 minutes and saddled with English dialogue read by English actors in (per the *BFI Monthly Film Bulletin* critic) "monotonous and 'over-refeened' voices." Remarkably, the print currently available on video seems to derive from the "New York" version with its Lewis and Weinberg subtitles, which was then augmented with footage from the Parisian release. (There are thus several uncomfortably long stretches in which something of possible import is discussed and no translation is forthcoming.) In a welcome departure from the usual deplorable state of affairs, we are thus possessed of a print that is as close to the director's cut as one could possibly hope.

That having been said, we ought to note the preponderance of commentary on the film's deliberate pace and irrelevant padding, which has transcended the years. It is rare to find unanimity among critics, and *Le Golem* could have been pulled this way and that had the clay behemoth sought to follow the sundry opinions of the paid reviewers concerning the latter half of the picture. Nonetheless, those critical voices were as one in finding the first couple of reels slow and hesitant. Duvivier, it was felt, had eschewed a true "vision" of the theme by succumbing to the allure of "visuals," in the form of jaw-dropping sets and acres of costumes and props. Almost to a person, the same reviewers mourned the director's reducing the titular character to the status of one of those props, focusing more on romantic liaisons than on the relationship between the natural and the preternatural and on telling his story via a series of precariously interrelated episodes rather than as a cohesive unit. (Interestingly, contemporary British critics, having only a severely cut print with which to work, still noted that the film suffered from "a serious lack of continuity" and that Duvivier "left many loose ends to his story.")

"One immediately realizes the shortcomings of a film which taints a potent and beautiful legend," wrote Raymond Chirat in *Julien Duvivier* (*Premier Plan*, 1969),

> by introducing a number of scenes of flirtation and light comedy, especially when badly depicted by certain actors who appear poorly disguised and embarrassed in their wigs and doublets. One musically grandiloquent night has certain passages which, in silence, would be poignant [pp. 94–95].

The night of which Chirat writes sees the climactic razing of the palace, and those with an ear for music—the same folks who had praised the authentic Hebrew chants used in the opening synagogue scenes—went on to complain that the droning themes that Josef Kumok had composed to accompany the sequence were hackneyed and grew "quickly tiresome."

If the legend had been (to use Chirat's word) "tainted" by scenes of flirtation and light comedy, it was positively tarred by scenes that saw the Clay Man being used as a pawn in a lover's quarrel. In his two serious features, Wegener had depicted the giant threatening a ghastly retribution if made to perform tasks unworthy of his essence and quest and raging against humanity out of unrequited love. Duvivier has the Countess Strada steal and hide the Golem — much as a jealous woman might purloin and conceal a compromising letter — to give her leverage concerning Rudolph's supposed marriage of state to the Spanish princess. Later, catching the emperor drunkenly pawing a brace of lovely courtiers, Strada locks him in his chamber, refusing in her pique to warn him that the Golem — like an outraged husband — is en route to the bedroom to exact a terrible revenge. Whereas Wegener the storyteller had made his audiences aware that the legend itself warned of the peril of trivializing the Golem, Duvivier the storyteller introduces subplots which make the creature nothing more than a clumsy plot device, like an errant love note or the sword of Charlemagne.

Granted, a picture concerned with the delivery of an entire subjugated people ought to be on a scale in keeping with the scope of its theme. Still, extant documentation doesn't indicate whether Duvivier had purposefully endeavored to award his treatment of the Golem saga a magnitude which he may have felt it deserved, but the hefty budget allowed art directors Andre Andrejew and Stepán Kopecky to construct not only another spired ancient city (in partial forced perspective), but also a series of truly cavernous interiors which — when taken together — elicit the image of a palace of indescribable size and proportion. Andrejew had earlier won notoriety for his sets in 1931's bizarre *Die Dreigroschenoper* (*The Three-Penny Opera*), and *Le Golem* producer Frank Kassler virtually gave the designer carte blanche to recreate both the royal palace and Prague's famed synagogue. While one can thus quibble little with the bulk or appearance of either edifice, the synagogue's vast "attic" expanse, as well as the impressive spaciousness of Jacob's and Rachel's adjacent living quarters, leave little doubt that this sound rendition was meant to leave its silent forebear in its epic dust.

For all this decorative onscreen excess, modern critics have waxed most favorably over two vignettes whose power lay in their intimate nature rather than in any display of volume or mass. *The Forum Cinema*'s Arthur Vesselo has found that

> *The Golem* has one terrific moment — transcending all the attempts at lavish spectacle — which few films can have equaled: the moment when Rachel, in the abyss of despair, suddenly sees the figure of the Golem before her eyes, hears the roar of the lion reverberating in her ears, and knows that the Rabbi's prophecy, of which she had given up all hope, is to be fulfilled not only in spirit but to the very letter.

In the July 1979 issue of the *BFI Monthly Film Bulletin* (later reworked into Phil Hardy's *Encyclopedia of Horror Movies*), Tom Milne saw the picture's defining moment rather as

> one brilliant sequence in which, goaded by his uncontrollable terror, Rudolf sets off alone on a nocturnal odyssey through shadowy corridors and echoing halls, intent on destroying the Golem, but instead coming face to face with his nightmare, shyly confiding his terrible loneliness to

Emperor Rudolph II and his brain trust. Harry Baur (seated, center) gives the most powerful performance in *Le Golem*.

someone who will at least listen: "You should understand that, like me you're half-man and half-spectre. Just make a small sign, and I'll know you're my friend."

Both contemporary and modern criticism peg Harry Baur as *Le Golem*'s shining star, and the celebrated French actor *is* the only one of the principals to consistently draw the viewer to himself and away from the production's occasionally intrusive enormity. Baur had honed his craft on the stage before making his debut in *David Golder* (1930), an early talkie for which Duvivier had penned the screenplay, and would go on to appear in a half-dozen more Duvivier efforts before his death — hastened by torture at the hands of the Nazis— in 1943. In 1938 the affable and eccentric Baur — hailed as "classic French cinema's greatest character actor" by Lenny Borger, resident film historian at *Sight and Sound* magazine — would join the ranks of Germany's and America's finest character men when, along with Conrad Veidt and Lionel Barrymore, he would number his eponymous *Rasputin* among his most memorable screen performances.

As Rudolph II, Baur is the glue which holds the episodic *Golem* together, and while even he is a tad reticent in the opening reels, he quickly asserts himself with a command which no one — certainly not the padded and scowling Ferdinand Hart — can even approximate for the rest of the running time. Like Britain's Tom Milne, Raymond Chirat also considers the picture's most sublime moment to be the actor's:

> As to the acting, Harry Baur's extraordinary creation carries the drama and the film on his shoulders alone. His whispers, his trembling gestures, both his herky-jerky and his fluid movement, the extremes of his mimic ability taken to their farthest limits—a dazzling lesson by a great comedian to whom one is in debt. The best sequence, where Rudolph addresses the immobile Golem: only several words, yet it is quite ... Shakespearean [p. 95].

Variety's "Kauf" seconded the motion in his review following the New York opening. Taking the gist of Chirat's sentiment a couple of steps further, the critic found Baur's impersonation of the terrified emperor to be

> among the top acting jobs of all time, his scene with the clay statue (before it is imbued with life) being one which will live forever in the memories of those who see it.
>   [March 24, 1937]

Although most were also Duvivier "regulars," none of the rest of the cast is in Baur's league. Still, Roger Karl is quite good as Chancellor Lang, a corrupt official of true Machiavellian proportions. We are informed that Lang is an "ex-Jew," yet nothing further is made of this, and, ultimately, the revelation adds nothing to either Karl's portrayal or the story itself. Born Roger Trouve in 1882, Karl could boast that his screen debut was courtesy of *les frères* Lumiere. He appeared in the brothers' silent novelties for a while before making something of a name for himself—that name being Roger Karl—as a legitimate actor with the Sarah Bernhardt company. Karl went on to renown as a painter, musician and writer; per his obituary in the June 13, 1984, *Variety*, he had had a four-volume work, "Diary of a Man from Nowhere," published shortly before his one-hundredth birthday. The Jacques-of-all-trades died in Paris at age 102.

Germaine Aussey's Strada is quite the most attractive of the distaff characters, but even her profound misuse of the Golem doesn't elevate her scheming much above the norm for suspicious lovers in melodramatic circumstances. Aussey was only twenty-four years old when Duvivier hired her on as the tempestuous countess, and her film career would last but six years more. In 1942, the lovely Parisienne married circus entrepreneur John Ringling North and promptly called it quits, movie-wise.

Jany Holt does a nice job as Rachel, and her big moment—rightfully praised by Vesselo and others—allows the actress to emerge from the intense, but mousy, persona she had enacted to that point. Charles Dorat's Rabbi Jacob, on the other hand, is soft spoken and piously ineffectual to the point of being irritating; Pauline Kael's description of the Christ figure from her review of Pasolini's *Gospel According to Saint Matthew* fits Dorat like a glove: His Jacob is a loathsome, prissy young man. Neither Roger Duchesne (as De Trignac, the antiques dealer) nor Aimos (as Toussaint, his comic relief sidekick) does a bad job; it's just—as was mentioned before—neither character really has much place in a story such as this one. Gaston Jacquet plays Police Prefect Friedrich as a basically decent sort—still, we're never quite sure why his allegiance to Countess Strada takes precedence over his loyalty to the emperor—and his being crushed underfoot by the Golem is a strong vignette, weakened only somewhat by the obviously rubber constitution of his head.

We might choose either to consider Ferdinand Hart's Golem purely on his own merits or to compare him to Wegener's icon; in either instance, the French actor's characterization suffers. There's no denying that, in Tom Milne's words, Hart looks like "a well-fed wrestler in a rubber suit with a permanent scowl on his deeply-tanned face [who] comes on more like a refugee from a Bond film than a legendary object of terror." As the makeup and costume had been designed with no input from the actor, and as Duvivier and Antoine had meticulously delineated and restricted the narrow parameters of Golem activity, Hart (like Baur, an émigré from the stage) was left with little to do except go through some basic and repetitious motions. His best moments really belonged more to cinematographers Vaclav Vich and Jan Stallich, for it was they who managed the simple but telling lighting effects that denoted the arrival and departure of life in the Golem's otherwise inexpressive eyes.

Hart handles the requisite scenes of destruction as well as can be expected, and the collapse of yard-thick walls and the toppling of the city gates are completely credible and downright impressive. Having Hart clad in what appears to be a sweat suit and a cape precluded the need for extensive body makeup, although it does present the image of Rabbi Löw's having sculpted this massive body — and then having either dressed it or commanded it to dress itself — and this is both kinky and screwily illogical. When the Aemer is defaced by Jacob and the Golem disintegrates, a jump cut allows the substitution of a mounted photograph of Hart's head and shoulders to take the heat; as the background apparently also disintegrates, the effect is not terribly convincing. Presaging all those last-reel effects displays in countless Dracula movies, nothing remains of the Golem save for his clothing.

With Wegener as much the auteur of his Golem epics as the impersonator, it is useless to compare the thespic weight he and Hart brought to their roles. From *Der Golem, wie er in die Welt kam*, we can see how the screenplay was a series of canny dramatic peaks and valleys; how there was a unification of theme and how the persona of the Golem was the undeniable focal point, even amid the business of Florian, Miriam, and their torrid, if goofy, affair; how the clay man could vary in both expression and reaction to the circumstances at hand (potent to this day is the memorable shot of Wegener clenching his teeth and widening his eyes in bestial fury); and how he represented the unmanageable fury of the supernatural, which could breach all barriers and withstand all onslaughts save for the innocence of a child. Hart, in his turn, was pointed in the desired direction, directed to push this and pull that, and advised never to let the glower slip from his face. For all the acting that was required by the role, Le Golem might just as well have been played by a golem.

In his tribute to Duvivier (in *Le Figaro littéraire*, November 6, 1967), Jean Renoir eulogized the eclectic director as a "great technician," a "rigorist," and "a poet."

> His films are never mere expositions of a subject; he lures us into a
> world at once realistic and unreal. This world is never just the product of
> his imagination; it also derives from his acute capacity for observation.
> His characters are real, yet they are also fantastic.

Duvivier was one of France's "big five of the golden '30s," along with Marcel Carné, René Clair, Jacques Feyder, and, of course, Renoir. The Lille-born director and frequent screenwriter gradually developed his own stylistic patterns through work

You know, if you *clearly* mark the entrances, stuff like this never happens. Ferdinand Hart.

abroad, including *L'Ouragan sur la montagne* (*The Hurricane on the Mountain*, 1922), his first collaborative effort (here, with the Germans and Swiss). Throughout the course of the next forty-five years, a succession of some sixty adventure sagas (*Le mystère de la Tour Eiffel*, 1928), detective stories (*Pépé le Moko*, 1937), religious dramas (*Golgotha*, 1935), literary adaptations (*Maria Chapdelaine*, 1934), studies of the human spirit (*Le petit monde de Don Camillo* [*The Little World of Don Camillo*, 1952]), comedies (*Allo Berlin, ici Paris* [*Hello Berlin, Paris Here*, 1932]) and compilation features (*Tales of Manhattan*, 1942) sprang from his pen or followed his vision, and marked Duvivier as an artisan impossible to pigeonhole.

Nestled among such diverse Duvivier treasures are several offerings of interest to horror aficionados. One of the earliest of the genre compilations, Universal's *Flesh and Fantasy* (1943) was a chilling follow-up to the already cited *Tales of Manhattan*, which had also drawn upon the wide appeal of Charles Boyer for a good measure of its success. Germane to the picture's profitability, too, was its element of poetry; parapsychology and nuance supplanted the studio's normal mélange of overt horrors. The first segment (well played by Betty Field, Edgar Barrier, and Robert Cummings) drew on Ellis St. Joseph's story about the relationship between inner truth and beauty; it wrought an intensely dramatic reversal to the year's *other* notable unmasking scene, which had capped Arthur Lubin's *Phantom of the Opera*. The second episode — intentionally Val Lewton-ish in its subtleties — pitted seer Thomas Mitchell against attorney Edward G. Robinson, and the result — adapted from Oscar Wilde's "Lord Arthur Saville's Crime" by St. Joseph, studio scenarist Samuel Hoffenstein, and Ernest Pascal — was easily the most chilling of the three. The third vignette, taken from a story by Laslo Vadnai (who had collaborated on Universal's 1940 kitsch classic, *Seven Sinners*), wound up heavy on Charles Boyer and dreams of Barbara Stanwyck, and a shade light on the macabre, but led the ticket buyers back into the daylight with a neat mix of catharsis and continental charm. As much the product of Hollywood savvy as of Gallic finesse, *Flesh and Fantasy* was the most marketable of Duvivier's thrillers. Boyer and a armful of Hollywood's British colony guaranteed worldwide distribution, and the picture, which never floated too far from the clearly delineated banks which lined the mainstream, delivered the gelt as well as the goods.

The Universal picture was made during Duvivier's second sojourn to the United States. Earlier — in 1938 — he had been invited by MGM to work some magic to equal his acclaimed *Pépé le Moko* within the environs of southern California, and *The Great Waltz* (née *The Life of Johann Strauss*) had filled the bill. Albeit aided by both an assistant director and a second-unit man (and with Victor Fleming supervising retakes and Josef von Sternberg directing a handful of scenes without onscreen credit), Duvivier was the visionary of record, and MGM was more than happy with his handiwork. As 1939 dawned and the American cinema rejoiced in what would prove to be a yearlong heyday, Duvivier returned to France and two disparate projects.

The first, *La fin de jour* (*The End of a Day*), was another of his ego builders, a sentimental comedy which he had cowritten as well as directed. The second was *La charrette fantôme* (*The Phantom Carriage*), a sound remake of Victor Sjöström's *Körkarlen* (aka *The Phantom Chariot, Thy Soul Shall Bear Witness, The Stroke of Midnight*; anywhere from 1919 to 1921, depending upon whom one consults). With his original version, the Swedish auteur would go Duvivier one better, not only by scripting and directing his tale of drunkenness and the personification of Death, but by topping the cast list, as well. Selma Lagerlöf's source novel would prove resilient enough to weather two remakes (including countryman Arne Mattsson's in 1958), although Duvivier's turn, while knee deep in transparent entities, concerned itself more with the maudlin potential of tubercular seamstresses and soup kitchens and so proved the least purely cinematic of the three treatments.

And, of course, the Frenchman's *first* shot at a horror theme (apart from an unreleased two-reeler — *Le logis de l'horreur* [*The House of the Horror*] — in 1922) had revisited a subject that had first seen the light of a carbon arc during the silent days: *The Golem*.

We might well return to *The New York Times'* Frank Nugent to cap this discussion. Like the majority of his confrères, Nugent rejoiced in Harry Baur's Rudolph and deplored having to sit through almost everything else that preceded the last reel chaos.

> As the cringing, blustering, fear-crazed and sadistic tyrant, he turns in a portrayal that matches even his superlatively fine work in *Crime and Punishment* and *Les Miserables*. But Rudolph cannot always fill the screen, and when he is absent one cannot avoid the realization that Andre-Paul Antoine's script has been attenuated almost beyond endurance.
>
> [March 22, 1937]

Nugent's comments bring us full circle to an admission that whereas the strength of Wegener's *Der Golem* had been its faithful adherence to the legend's occult elements, the potent Wegener presence and the frightening and fascinating progeny of such a mix, Duvivier's interpretation had bypassed the aura of the supernatural for more mundane *affaires du coeur* and had, for all intents and purposes, made the Golem a tertiary (and wholly unnecessary) character. Rudolph's distress over the incipient invasion by Mathias might just as well have fueled his paranoia, much as Shakespeare's Richard III kept close and anxious watch on Henry Tudor's movements across the English Channel. The arrival of his brother's troops and the simultaneous uprising of his own dissatisfied subjects would have brought the emperor's mounting hysteria to a head; Rudolph would have been no less deposed, nor the citizenry any less satisfied.

In such a scenario, an implacable instrument of Jewish vengeance would be moot, and therein lay the problem: Duvivier and Antoine's script *is* just such a scenario.

THE SCARAB MURDER CASE

British and Dominions Film Corporation/Paramount British — Trade shown: November 27, 1936 — 68 minutes — General release: May 24, 1937 aka *The Scarlet Murder Mystery*

Cast: Kathleen Kelly as Angela Hargreaves; Wally Patch as Inspector Moor; Wilfred Hyde-White as Philo Vance; Henri de Vries as Dr. Bliss; John Robinson as Donald Scarlett; Wallace Geoffrey (Jeffries) as Salveter; Stella Moya as Meryt Amen; Grahame Cheswright as Makeham; Rustum Medora as Hani; Shaun Desmond as Detective

Credits: *Director:* Michael Hankinson; *producer:* Anthony Havelock-Allen; *screenplay:* Selwyn Jepson; based on the eponymous novel by S. S. Van Dine; *assistant director:* C. B. Digby-Best; *cinematography:* Claude Friese-Greene

Synopsis: While Philo Vance (Wilfred Hyde-White), the eminent American private detective, is on vacation in England, he disappoints his secretary, Angela Hargreaves (Kathleen Kelly) — who has detective leanings herself — because he does no "sleuthing." Vance's friend Scotland Yard's Assistant Commissioner Makeham (Grahame Cheswright) calls on the American, only to be summoned to the Bliss Egyptological [*sic*] Museum. It turns out that Mr. Kyle, a wealthy philanthropist, has been murdered — apparently with a heavy statue of Sakhmet, the goddess of vengeance. Makeham invites Vance to accompany him, and Angela insists on going, too. Kyle, who was guardian to the elderly Dr. Bliss's young Egyptian wife, Meryt Amen (Stella Moya), and uncle to his assistant, Salveter (Wallace Geoffrey), had financed the doctor's expeditions but was beginning to find them too expensive.

In charge of the preliminary investigations at the museum is Inspector Moor (Wally Patch). Moor finds several clues — including Dr. Bliss's scarab tiepin (discovered *under* the body) — that point to the doctor's guilt. The inspector is all for arresting Bliss (Henri de Vries) at once, although he was found asleep in his study (having apparently drunk some drugged coffee) and swears that he did not see Kyle. Thinking quickly, Vance shows how it was not necessary for the murderer to be present. He finds a stub of pencil on top of the cabinet on which Sakhmet stood and demonstrates how the statue was tilted forward by the pencil; when these items were arranged just so with a nearby curtain ring, the pulling of the curtain would bring the heavy statue down on the victim's head.

Finding Angela constantly in his way, Vance pretends to suspect Donald Scarlett (John Robinson), Bliss's secretary, and sends Angela to keep an eye on him. Vance persuades the police to release Bliss, even though he tries to slip out of the country. That night the doctor reports an attempt on his life: Someone has thrown an Egyptian dagger at his bed. All evidence points to Salveter, who is in love with Bliss's wife. Salveter admits to writing a letter to Meryt in hieroglyphics but attempts to explain it away as merely an exercise in his ongoing Egyptian studies. Scarlett, who has confronted Angela and is now working with her, finds the letter to be more than Egypt oriented and questions Salveter about it. Salveter declares that it is not his letter, but a forgery.

As Scarlett is telephoning to tell Angela this, he is attacked. Vance, Angela, Makeham and Moor rush to the museum and rescue the young man from suffocating in a sarcophagus. Vance then admits that he knew all the time that Bliss was guilty, but he had arranged clues with such diabolical cunning to point to Salveter that no jury would have convicted him; even now they don't have a clear case against him. Vance lets Hani (Rustum Medora), the doctor's Egyptian servant, overhear the conversation, and Hani—who resents the desecration of his country's ancient tombs—arranges for Sakhmet to claim another victim: the guilty Dr. Bliss.

Once again, Vance sees justice done, but he loses his secretary, as Angela and Scarlett decide to make theirs a life partnership.

> Adapted from one of S. S. Van Dine's popular Philo Vance detective novels, this picture makes the fundamental mistake of permitting action to play second fiddle to dialogue. For the first half an hour or so it holds and interests, because the story certainly has ingenuity, but after that the incessant talk becomes tedious and takes the edge off intended thrills. The acting, however, is pretty good, and this, together with title values, should get the film over in other than first-run halls.
>
> Acting—W. Hyde-White acts with disarming smoothness as Philo Vance, Henri de Vries is sound as Dr. Bliss, and Stella Moya, Grahame Cheswright and Rustum Medora are adequate as the major suspects. Wally Patch amuses as a Cockney inspector, and Kathleen Kelly and John Robertson make the most of the love interest.
>
> Production—The snag in this picture is the director's inability to get a move on. The deductions and twists are fashioned by an ingenious pen, but the very fact that they are described verbally rather than acted in the general sense limits the entertainment's punch. The unexpected happens, but only with a casualness that leaves one cold. The staging is very unpretentious—it is restricted to a few interiors.
>
> Points of Appeal—Title and author values, sound acting, and British qualification.
>
> [*Kinematograph Weekly* December 3, 1936, p. 27]

Paramount had seldom stumbled onto so happy a professional marriage as the joining of William Powell with Philo Vance. The studio had taken something of a chance casting the handsome actor as the debonair sleuth, as Powell had built his career to date on the bedrock of black-hearted villainy. (Less risky had been the casting of perennial heavy Warner Oland as Sax Rohmer's evil Mandarin, Fu Manchu.) Powell went on to play the sleuth three times while the decade was changing hands (*The Canary Murder Case, The Greene Murder Case* [both 1929], and *The Benson Murder Case* [1930])—four times, if his brief in-character cameo in *Paramount on Parade* (1930) is considered—and Paramount was anxious for more of the same. Author S. S. Van Dine (the nom de plume of Willard Huntington Wright, a pseudointellectual who swallowed his contempt for detective fiction when he proved unable to make a living via autocratic criticism and a facility for artistic minutiae) had prepared these three novels as a unit and had found in Scribner's[1] — and then in Paramount — the perfect milieu in which to make some easy, and desperately needed, cash.

Scribner's had no difficulties to speak of, but an early fly in Paramount's ointment had been *The Jazz Singer*, or — more properly — the combination of Louise Brooks and the advent of the sound era. *The Canary Murder Case*, already in the can, saw its release postponed while most scenes were reshot using the new talkie technology. The studio was anxious to promote the picture as the first all-talking detective film, and reassembling the cast — all of whom had gone on to other studios or assignments — was a troublesome enough endeavor. The fact that Brooks, an enigmatic actress whose striking beauty would enthrall American picture-goers for years to come, had immigrated to Germany proved to be the coup de grace. For the actress, hopping the pond was not a bad move: *Die Büchse der Pandora* and a remake of *Das Tagebuch einer Verlorenen*, both 1929 and both under the direction of Georg Wilhelm Pabst, would bring her immortality. When Brooks proved unwilling to junket back across the Atlantic for sound retakes, however, Paramount was forced to resort to some woefully rudimentary dubbing, employing an actress whose voice, in the opinion of many of the critics — if not of the majority of avid ticket buyers — could not even *begin* to jibe with the "Canary's" full-lipped sensuality.

This disparity, plus a change of the directorial reins (Frank Tuttle was brought in to replace Malcolm St. Clair early on in the shooting of the "sound version"), made Wright/Van Dine uneasy. Both Tuttle and the man he replaced had made their mark in silent films, but St. Clair's name — at this point, at any rate — was associated with "quality" pictures. Tuttle, on the other hand, was considered by many to be a journeyman director of unremarkable films, and it was felt that his remaining on to direct the studio's adaptations of *Greene* and *Benson* was due more to his gumption than to any obvious affinity he displayed for Philo Vance. Even Van Dine, a cinematic babe in the woods, couldn't fail to see that *Greene* (which, like *Canary*, was released in both silent and sound formats) suffered from a s-l-o-w pace that had not afflicted its predecessor.

With all of its theaters wired for sound by the change of the decade, Paramount saw no need to release silent prints of its third Vance feature. (The order of Scribner's publications had been *Benson*, *Canary* and then *Greene*; the transition from silence to sound and the need to metamorphose Van Dine's cerebral novels into visually oriented motion pictures dictated a change in the sequence of production and release.) Instead, *The Benson Murder Case* sired *El cuerpo del delito*, an all-Spanish-language production aimed at audiences south of the border. As would happen the following year with Universal's *Dracula/Drácula*, *El cuerpo* was shot at night on the same sets the American cast used during the day. Featured among the Hispanic cast were Barry Norton, who would play "Juan" Harker in the later vampire epic, and Carlos Villarías — el Conde Drácula himself — as John F. X. Markham. (An afterthought: There is no record that Wright/Van Dine — revealed to be a bigot of the first order by his biographer, John Loughery — had any problem with Hispanics dropping their hard-earned dinero to see a film in which he had a financial interest.[2])

While Paramount was busy transforming the rather academic format of the novels it had purchased into viable scenarios (William Powell's Philo Vance would prove in every way to be less cold, haughty and opinionated than Van Dine's), *The Bishop*

Murder Case—planned as the first volume in a *second* Vance "trilogy"—was published, snapped up (by MGM), and hustled in front of the cameras. Making things more than a trifle awkward for the competition, MGM unveiled *The Bishop Murder Case*—a full-fledged, no-baloney talkie—in theaters during the few months that separated *Greene* from *Benson*. Audiences growing used to thinking "Powell" when they thought "Vance" now had to contend with the presence of Basil Rathbone. (And even Rathbone, a splendid character man never regarded primarily for his ability to project great warmth, made Vance less of an obnoxious know-it-all than did the source novel.) Powell's reemergence in the role a couple of months later would shift the balance back toward Paramount, and the studio, determined not to be caught napping again, pounced on the next Vance novel before it was published. This would be Van Dine's fifth, *The Scarab Murder Case*. Trade announcements began to circulate and, had events been allowed to take their normal course, the in-house accountants would soon begin to project earnings against expenses. But the problems had started.

One problem was that Powell's contract with Paramount—along with those of other such luminaries as Maurice Chevalier, Clive Brook, Nancy Carroll, Kay Francis and the Marx Brothers—expired during fiscal 1932–1933, and it was feared that much of the cinematic appeal of Van Dine's brilliant if quirky detective was grounded in the charismatic actor. (Rathbone's reading of the role had encouraged no sequels.) When Powell headed over to MGM, he assumed the mantle of Dashiell Hammett's Nick Charles, and the subsequent, wildly popular *Thin Man* series all but left Philo Vance at the gate.

More tellingly, while en route to MGM and the role with which he *would* be associated for life, Powell had paid a call at Warners. There—under the able direction of Michael Curtiz—he had headlined a pip of a Vance picture that is still regarded as superior to either Paramount or MGM's rudimentary and overlong early talkies. If Powell's walking out had proven painful for Paramount, the studio's watching helplessly as Warners' opening credits bragged "William Powell returns as Philo Vance in *The Kennel Murder Case*" had to be devastating. That the whole craziness transpired on the coattails of the Great Depression ... it was as if a frustrated bettor at the track had torn up his winning ticket and tossed the pieces into the wind. *The Kennel Murder Case* was a great hit and made a ton of money, but Powell—who was soon to find in Nick Charles and Myrna Loy *two* matches made in heaven—bid adieu to Philo Vance nonetheless.

Problem number two was that audiences hadn't taken to *The Benson Murder Case* as they had the two earlier mysteries. When *Variety* sniffed that "The public reaction is against the school of you-know-who," Paramount put on hold any immediate plans for more cinematic adventures of you-know-who. Exacerbating the situation was the fact that Wright/Van Dine was beginning to run out of steam, so far as Philo Vance was concerned. While *The Scarab Murder Case* had sold enough copies to keep casual readers supplied and Charles Scribner's Sons happy, it was the first of Van Dine's Vance epics to be critiqued by "house" reviewers, and even they began to cluck worriedly over elements in the novel—Vance's frequent apostrophes, Van Dine's ubiquitous footnotes—that had been accepted without comment in the earlier volumes. The author's opulent lifestyle demanded that the erudite detective from Thirty-Eighth Street make an appearance once or twice a year, and MGM and Warners were

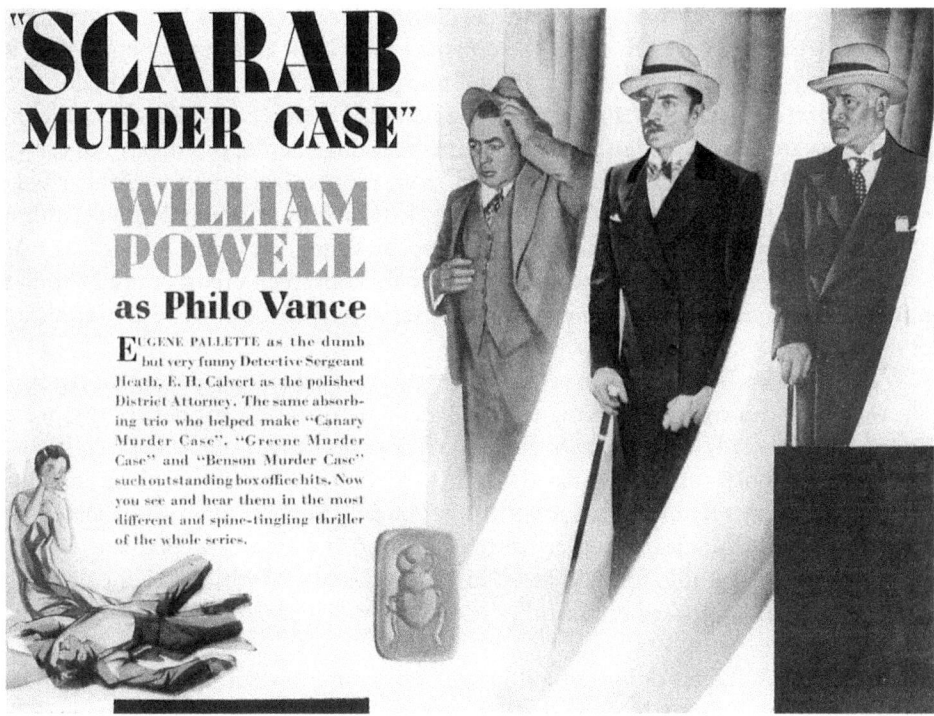

Now, this is the sort of thing Paramount had in mind for *Scarab* before the guano hit the fan.

quick to rework the increasingly pedestrian novels into increasingly ordinary motion pictures. Following Powell's triumph in *The Kennel Murder Case* in 1933, the Vance films began a bumpy, downward spiral that left them, in the end, little better than adequately accoutered programmers; the novels themselves had begun to fail following *Kennel*'s publication earlier that same year.

In itself, this trend mightn't have changed Paramount's mind about laying another Van Dine mystery in the national lap. What the cash-strapped company needed, though, was a hit — a succession of hits, actually — and it was felt that marshalling ever-decreasing resources on a property that was flashing clay feet both on the printed page and on the screen would be a major mistake. Besides, apart from seeing that the rights to his Vance novels seemingly went every which way all at once, Van Dine had demonstrated zilch in terms of loyalty to Paramount by peddling a dozen short stories to Warner Brothers for the express purpose of having them massaged into a series of two-reelers. Thus, during the 1931–1932 Vance movie "blackout," Vitaphone's *S.S. Van Dine Mystery Series* — starring John (Perry White) Hamilton and Donald Meek — kept Van Dine's name in the public eye in a regular, if somewhat diluted, fashion. What's more, in early '33, Warners had also released a non-Vance detective feature (*Girl Missing*) to rather routine reviews and average box office. The bottom line was that — again — by the time *The Kennel Murder Case* was out there cleaning up, no one who was anyone associated either Philo Vance or S. S. Van Dine with Paramount.

For the next few years, one could count on either MGM or Warners to unveil an annual Vance adventure. Still, with the cinema's premier Philo Vance impersonator now well on his way to being the cinema's only Nick Charles impersonator, it was anybody's guess as to who would be Philo the next time around. Initially, one could at least be assured of a reasonably big name: Warren (Perry Mason) William, Paul Lukas and Edmund Lowe all took turns wearing the dapper dick's homburg. When, in 1937, after Paramount emerged from reorganization and halfheartedly reworked *The Greene Murder Case* (the rights to which the studio still owned) into *Night of Mystery*, it expected audiences to accept as Vance one Grant Richards, a reasonably good-looking nobody whose only previous onscreen credit could be found midway down the scrawl in *Hopalong Cassidy Returns* (1936). But we're getting ahead of ourselves.

Back in March 1933, on the verge of bankruptcy, Paramount-Publix (as the studio was then known) was looking to move a couple of dozen properties that were no longer financially feasible, and that description fit *The Scarab Murder Case* to a tee. It seemed only natural to offer the rights to Warner Brothers as, since September of 1931, every reel of film in America that bore S. S. Van Dine's name also bore Jack Warner's. It's unclear whether Paramount's terms were unacceptable to Warners or whether that studio found it more advantageous to deal with Van Dine directly; either way, Warners passed on *Scarab*—as did MGM—and there were no other takers.

Paramount-Publix duly went off into receivership. Restructuring took a while, but the Paramount Pictures (Inc.) that emerged once the doors were reopened in 1935 was hale and hearty and headed by Adolf Zukor, the new chairman of the board. As the company reorganization had involved British money, Paramount was now legally obligated to produce a certain number of films in Britain, and it was decided that *The Scarab Murder Case* would serve nicely as "British Paramount's" premier effort. While the feature would have the distinction of being the first to be shot at the new Pinewood Studios, however, it was budgeted as an unambitious little "B," which was quite a departure from the production status the "Hollywood Paramount" features had enjoyed a few years earlier. This mattered little, as there was never any intention to export the film across the Atlantic or, indeed, out of the United Kingdom. *Scarab* thus fell victim to a (literally) insular distribution scheme that virtually ensured that the film — once "disappeared"— would never be rediscovered in foreign climes.

Naturally (apart from the Dutch Henri De Vries), the principal cast was British. With no need to pander to overseas markets, the company saved money by hiring entertainers who had local followings, like Stella Moya (first and foremost, a cabaret singer) or Kathleen Kelly, for whom *Scarab* was the midpoint of a brief career consisting entirely of undistinguished British programmers. Or character man Wally Patch, who would spend some forty years in the business and make over 175 feature films (including a couple of beauts: G. W. Pabst's *Don Quixote*, starring the incomparable Chaliapin, and Lothar Mendes's classic, *The Man Who Could Work Miracles*; he could also be found in Gaumont's *High Treason*) without leaving the United Kingdom but once.

In this milieu, there is little wonder that the role of Philo Vance was entrusted to thirty-three-year-old Wilfred Hyde-White (aka Wilfrid Hyde White, aka Hyde

White), an alumnus of the prestigious Royal Academy of Dramatic Arts and a relative novice, cinematically. Admittedly, Hyde-White had already shown his face in such fare as *Night Mail* (1935) and *Rembrandt* (1936), although while his face made the latter film, his name did not; his presence therein went uncredited onscreen. (In a letter to the editor of *Scarlet Street* magazine, producer Richard Gordon recounted how, when he was casting *The Cat and the Canary*, he had met Hyde-White. "He referred to *Rembrandt* as his first film and when I cautiously mentioned *The Scarab Murder Case*, which was produced the same year, he looked at me and said, 'You're a dangerous man, Mr. Gordon'" [no. 19; Summer 1995; p. 4]).

While the actor would attain a degree of international renown in his later years—his signature role of Colonel Pickering, in the 1964 production of Lerner and Lowe's *My Fair Lady*, fell into his lap during his sixtieth year—as leading man of *The Scarab Murder Case* he had to content himself with third billing, behind the aforementioned Kelly and Patch. If a small dose of self-effacement enabled him to deal with the billing, a large measure of dramatic license ensured that Hyde-White's clipped British tones would be no more out of place in Philo's mouth than had Lukas's Eastern European accent. For all that, his being cast as the frequently insufferable New York detective may have worked seriously against both the film's box-office potential and the likelihood of a reissue. While British movie goers went to the flickers often and enthusiastically, they did not normally see the same picture more than once, and thus it may have been foolhardy to entrust a still-popular screen character to an essentially unknown

This is how things turned out for the first release of "British Paramount."

actor. If, as film historian William K. Everson averred, Hyde-White was at the time "without the comedic polish that came to him in later years," the actor may well have inherited the role only because he was British and came cheap.[3]

Without the film, of course, it's unfair to stick too many pins in the leading man's performance, and there's virtually nothing else to go on. Thus, *The Scarab Murder Case* may well be the most obscure film in this book. Queries sent out to five European archives came back empty, and requests mailed to the major photograph repositories within the United States produced no results. (Oddly enough, there is a seemingly endless supply of reprints of the picture's four-page press book out there, and we have that to thank for one of the unexciting illustrations that accompanies these remarks.) Apart from a scant and rather poorly written notice, even the British Film Institute has nothing in its myriad collections. For whatever reason, the picture does not seem to have been reviewed by *any* British newspaper that maintains an archive. Thus, we have to let this discussion lapse here.

Notes

1. Wright had first approached Horace Liveright with the Vance manuscripts. As the original publisher of "The Modern Library," Liveright had brought the works of E. E. Cummings, William Faulkner, Sherwood Anderson, Theodore Dreiser, and other literary heavyweights (in whose company Willard Wright longed to be considered) to the American public in affordable editions. A true entrepreneur, Liveright also dabbled in the performing arts: He had brought Hamilton Deane's stage dramas *Dracula* and *Frankenstein* to Broadway and had commissioned playwright and journalist John Balderston to "Americanize" the former. In the transfer of the two properties from stage to screen, however, both his own overbearing personality and studio politicking left Liveright in the cold; none of the revenue windfall from Universal's productions devolved onto him. As for "Van Dine," Liveright chose to pass and was once again denied a share in the subsequent bonanza.

2. *Alias S.S. Van Dine: The Man Who Created Philo Vance*. Charles Scribner's Sons, New York, 1992.

3. William K. Everson. *The Detective in Film*. Secaucus, NJ: Citadel Press, 1972, p. 88.

SH! THE OCTOPUS

Warner Brothers-First National — December 11, 1937 — 54 minutes
Cast: Hugh Herbert as Kelly; Allen Jenkins as Dempsey; Marcia Ralston as Vesta Vernoff; John Eldredge as Paul Morgan; George Rosener as Captain Hook; Brandon Tynan as Captain Cobb; Eric Stanley as David Dahl Harriman; Margaret Irving as Polly Crane; Elspeth Dudgeon as Nanny; Lew Harvey, Henry Otho, Frank Hagney, Ed Biby as Sinister Plotters; Mary Doyle as Nurse
Credits: *Executive producers:* Jack L. Warner, Hal B. Wallis; *associate Producer:* Bryan Foy; *director:* William McGann; *assistant director:* Arthur Lueker; photographed by Arthur Todd ASC; *dialogue director:* Hugh Cummings; *screenplay:* George Bricker; based on the play *Sh! The Octopus* by Ralph Spence; *art director:* Max Parker; *film editor:* Clarence Kolster; *gowns:* N'Was McKenzie; *sound:* Francis J. Scheid

Synopsis: In the midst of a howling storm, marine artist Paul Morgan (John Eldredge) is admitted to the abandoned lighthouse he intends to use as a studio by Captain Cobb (Brandon Tynan), and the two men are quickly joined by Captain Hook (George Rosener), the erstwhile light tender. Although the structure has supposedly gone unused for years, the tallow on a candle is still soft and warm. After Morgan finds a wallet that Hook identifies as the property of inventor David Dahl Harriman, a "rich fool from the city," the old salts leave the artist alone to his surroundings and his thoughts.

Nearby, detectives Dempsey (Allen Jenkins) and Kelly (Hugh Herbert) read of the recent appointment of Police Commissioner Clancy and his promise to capture master criminal "The Octopus," for whom a $50,000 reward has been offered. Visions of big bucks dancing in their eyes — Kelly's wife is presently at the maternity hospital — the men meet up with Vesta Vernoff (Marcia Ralston), a young woman certain that she has just seen the corpse of her stepfather in the old lighthouse. She explains that her stepfather had invented a radium ray of such enormous power that The Octopus would murder for it.

Back at the lighthouse, Morgan espies a corpse, dangling by its feet from the cupola; he does *not* see two tentacles that have slithered noiselessly from a secret panel behind him. The tentacles withdraw at the sound of a knock at the door, and Morgan steps back into the shadows as Kelly, Dempsey and Vesta Vernoff (hereafter, VV) enter. They, too, spot the hanging cadaver, and VV states that she had followed her father to the spooky old building after she and Nanny had found a handwritten note on his bedroom floor: "Be there at ten. Bring it with you. Don't fail." — "signed" by a drawing of an octopus.

Tentacles commence to wave in the shadows, and the detectives drag Morgan out from his hiding place. VV shouts out "Paul!" and rushes into his arms, but she is rebuffed by the artist, who claims never to have seen her in his life. Moments later, out of earshot of the policemen, the young couple exchange some furtive words. Another knock at the door sees Hook back inside, an unconscious woman in his arms. Apparently VV is acquainted with Hook, too; more surreptitious dialogue ensues as the waterlogged damsel gradually revives. She declines to identify herself, hinting only that she had been "boatwrecked." A secret panel slides open, revealing a staircase to the cupola. Before anyone can take to the stairs, tentacles pull the lamp cord from its socket, and the room is plunged into darkness. When the lights are restored, Hook is nowhere to be seen, and a ringing bell calls the cops back to the door. This time, it is *Nanny* looking to come in out of the rain!

Another secret door pops open, and a body rolls out: It is Captain Cobb, who had been slugged by someone (or some*thing*) as he sought to return with a note for VV. The note is terse: "Wallet marked DDH inside pocket," and, in a trice, everyone is rifling *Cobb's* pockets. Dempsey then confiscates all the wallets in the room, and the cops head for the cupola to release the body. Once it has crashed onto the floor below, the corpse is found to be a dummy, accoutered with ketchup for blood. The dicks frisk the dummy for its wallet (and, yes, it has one), but Morgan—packing *two* pistols—covers them while VV retrieves all those wallets. VV is fingering the wallet marked DDH when a gruff voice cries out, "Don't open that! You'll blow us all off the island!"

The voice belongs to Captain Hook, whose sudden reappearance passes without remark. A mournful foghorn bears more bad news. "The foghorn!" screams Captain Cobb. "It always blows when The Octopus comes in his submarine!" The mystery woman spots a pair of tentacles snaking in through an inside door. She screams, and the appendages pull the door shut. Another tentacle intrudes (from the outside!) and the front door slams. More tentacles appear on the other side of the lighthouse; they, too, do their work and the terrified occupants are securely locked in. Then, from the roof, issues gas.

Morgan has Dempsey pull *another* secret door open, and everybody heads for the basement, except Captain Hook. Sliding the bolt on the trapdoor, he guffaws, only to be seized from behind by at least four tentacles—which have emerged from yet another panel—and pulled, kicking and cussing, back into the wall. Down below, Morgan, VV, et al. find themselves in an extensive cave and proceed to investigate. The mystery woman, who has identified herself as Polly Crane, lets out a shriek before discovering that what appeared to be a second dangling corpse was merely a diver's suit and helmet.

Polly wanders off as Morgan and Vesta watch (through a hole in the cave floor) an octopus cling to an underwater crag. The two whisper conspiratorially together, and the scene is repeated within moments, except that Polly takes VV's place. At this juncture, Kelly and Dempsey flash *their* guns and demand all those wallets back. An investigation of the cave basement reveals a wooden door where, previously, there had been none. Breaking down the door, the cops fall 15 feet to the floor of the lighthouse subbasement, which must be at least 20 feet below water level. Returning to the group, Dempsey dresses Kelly in the diving suit, instructs him to "explore for a way out," and pushes him into the sea through the hole in the floor.

In a flash, the octopus attacks the plucky cop, who fights for his life. Amid all the excitement, a groan is heard behind one of the walls. Dempsey fires off a few rounds, the lights go out, the women scream, and when order is restored, it's found that Captain Cobb and VV have disappeared from the cave. Remembering the struggling Kelly, the two men pull him back through the hole via his safety line. When the diving helmet is removed, however, the man inside is not Kelly, but Hook! Kelly is still wrestling the cephalopod ("Hey, Dempsey!" and the trademark "woo-woo" are heard from below), which deposits the saturated policeman back on the cave floor.

Suddenly, dissonant chimes sound, and a voice rings out: "Quiet, you fools! That music will be your funeral march when you hear it again! Ha ha ha ha!" Morgan steps up and reveals himself to be Farrell, a federal officer. Hook also produces a badge, while claiming to be Everson, of the "Intelligence Department." (Dempsey: "Another cop, huh?" Hook: "That's right. I've been working on this case for nine years." Kelly: "Any clues?") A loud knock, and *everybody* pulls a gun. It's Polly, who opens the trapdoor from above. She and Morgan swap a few more private phrases as the men climb up the stairs. Kelly is directed to stay behind so as to investigate further.

Upstairs, Dempsey works at convincing all the forces of justice to work as a team and to split the reward. Polly confesses to being a representative of the Peace League, which is after Harriman's death ray. The reward's looking more meager, what with a four-way split—when Cobb reveals himself to be none other than "Green, of the International Police." Forgotten by all, Kelly sits wearily below, not noticing that a section of the rough-hewn wall behind him has opened. Enter Nanny.

> NANNY: "I'm a harmless old woman. Help me. I'm in fear of my life."
> KELLY: "Nothing to worry about while Kelly is on the job."
> UNKNOWN MALE VOICE: "That's what *you* think!"

Nanny sells Kelly a load of hay about the deed to her "little farm" being lost somewhere in the pile of papers Kelly is now carrying. Finding what she was looking for in the wallet marked DDH, the old woman shrieks and points to the underground entrance to the sea: "It's a submarine! The Octopus! Here!" That's all Kelly has to hear; he's up the stairs in a flash and fires a warning shot into the cupola.

Everyone comes running out, just in time to see the tower light flash and to hear those eerie chimes again. "The Octopus music," cries Kelly. "He said he'd play our funeral march!" Nanny shrieks and points again. Casually climbing the steps leading up from the basement is a tall man, wearing a hat and trenchcoat, but as dry as a bone. The stranger claims to be Clancy, the new police commissioner, but VV, flashing *her* pistol, cries out "Father!" It's not Clancy, but David Dahl Harriman. Before the confusion can begin to get serious, a huge tentacle slithers into the room and grabs Hook. Despite there being enough guns at hand to arm a militia, no one takes a shot at the tentacle. Nanny begins to laugh hysterically.

"You're The Octopus!" yells Morgan, as Nanny metamorphoses into a ghastly old witch, replete with mottled skin, discolored teeth and warts. "I have a pair of arms for each of you," she cackles, "arms that will strangle." Stupefied, nobody thinks to point any pistols at the sea hag, and she yanks her own gun out, covering the crowd. She waves the men back toward the wall, which slides silently upward behind them. Madly weaving tentacles encircle Morgan, Cobb, and Harriman, and pull the three into the closing wall.

With a tap of her pistol, the villainess opens two more secret doors. "On that switchboard, my fools, are hundreds of switches. One of them will open the doors of this place and give you freedom; another, if you pull it, will blow this lighthouse to bits!" Strangely enough, two tentacles reach up from the floor trap and pull The Octopus to her apparent doom. Better late than never (but always late), the two cops fire a fusillade into the gaping trapdoor and slam the trap shut. The four remaining adventurers run into the secret room, where they begin, *gingerly*, to throw switches. The third time is the charm. With a loud report—like yet another gunshot—the lighthouse explodes into a million pieces!

A fade, a cut, and the supine Kelly is being given oxygen. Surrounded by familiar faces, he finds himself in the maternity hospital. "You fainted," explains Captain Hook. "You're a father!" Cobb, Morgan and Hook are physicians (the latter's gleaming hook is seen to be a stethoscope earpiece), while VV and Polly are nurses. And what of The Octopus? "You silly boy. I'm your mother-in-law."

Dear God! Not that hoary "It was all a dream!" thing again! Uh-huh. Years before *Dallas* (or was it *Dynasty*?) took the venerable concept to its most incredulous extreme (and Bob Newhart, to its most clever), *Sh! The Octopus* gave it its most vigorous workout. The overdone and unappreciated plot twist had been an achingly familiar out during the silent years; more than one speechless Dr. Jekyll became Mr. Hyde only while asleep. The disappointment of having all that fantasy turn out to be fanciful was matched only by the disturbing tendency of some early horror films to explain away supernatural events by rational means.

Sh! The Octopus has to take the heat for its dream denouement, but, happily, its ending is not the usual, feeble cop-out, but a satisfying and logical wrap to what's gone on earlier. The dream stuff doesn't hurt a bit when one recalls the numerous hints sprinkled throughout the film that *these* circumstances and *these* events could not possibly be happening in real time, real space, and real life. Although it's not apparent until the end, the picture is absolutely forthright in its unfolding, as if to defy the audience not to conclude that the screwy and impossible goings-on could be anything but someone's crazed hallucination.

A quick look at the impossibilities only underlines the picture's honesty. The excellent miniature of the lighthouse establishes its isolation—it's situated on the tiniest of "islands," and long shots reveal no land within sight—and its desolation: It has been inoperative and abandoned for quite some time. The fact that it is, of course, a dark and stormy night, reinforces the idea that any approach to the beacon is nigh impossible. Yet, despite gale-force winds, torrential rain, and monstrously high seas, folks arrive at the lighthouse as regularly and casually as shoppers at a supermarket. They walk in after a knock at the door, leave with a wave of their hand, and return from the damnedest places or for the most peculiar of reasons. Captain Cobb turns up—rather, he rolls dramatically out of a wall—having initially set out to make the life-threatening trip back to the lighthouse just to hand over a note about the contents of *his own* pockets!

Lights go on, lights go off, women scream, guns are fired—*lots* of guns are fired. Throughout the picture, pistols materialize and vanish with astounding regularity; what's more, they are flashed, confiscated, bent *and* straightened out instantaneously, and multiply like rabbits in a warren. Never have so many people packed so many rods in one film. Chuck Jones and his pals at Termite Terrace would have been hard pressed to keep up with the sheer number of gats that turn up in this, one of Warners' few "live action cartoons." For all that, as the Octopus is cackling away at her most maniacal in the penultimate moments of the last reel, no one uses any of the available firepower to capture her or save themselves, although everyone is flourishing at least one pistol each!

Apart from Kelly and Dempsey (and *maybe* Vesta Vernoff), none of the characters are who they originally claimed to be. Where else but in a married cop's nightmare would all the participants turn out to be cops, save for the villain of the piece, and she, of course, is his mother-in-law? The nonstop production of badges and credentials might very well have been snatched from the script of some unmade sequel to *The Great Piggy Bank Robbery.*

The intrigue leads to lots of confusion, but where would a dream be without confusion? Each of these characters knows at least one of the others—lots of bewildering asides establish this pattern—but no pair knows any other pair. Only Vesta knows more than one of the others, and that includes Morgan (who's really Farrell), Nanny, and her stepfather, who strolls up from the basement and claims to be the police commissioner. Of course, as he's just been sworn in, he's not known to either of the two city cops, either, but, given the fact that the cops are Hugh Herbert and Allen Jenkins, not much can be deduced from *that.*

At first, Morgan denies knowing Vesta, and he doesn't let on he knows Polly. Polly, who fudges accounts of how she got to the island, identifies herself late in the picture as a member of the "Peace League" (shades of *High Treason*), which wants the death ray for itself. Cantankerous Captain Hook (who's really Everson from Intelligence) has been working on this "case" for nine years! And Captain Cobb (unmasked as Martin Green of the International Police) is saved by Nanny from being gunned down by Vesta, who is irate at Cobb's betrayal of her stepfather. This sort of madness can only be part of a feverish dream, right? (I'll pass on its also being S.O.P. for daytime TV soap operas.)

Then there's the lighthouse, a marvel of construction. Built atop a minute, rocky crag, it boasts not only a basement, but a subbasement, as well. Not a surface in the joint doesn't house a secret panel, and one has to wonder that the structure hasn't collapsed for want of a supporting wall. Not only do these doors slide open to reveal poured concrete staircases and phosphorescent eyes (the apertures come in all shapes and sizes), they also swivel and pivot to permit the unencumbered flow of unconscious seamen, convenience of movement to varying numbers of tentacles, right of passage to the titular heavy, and access to closeted master control boards. Doors appear from nowhere, only to lead nowhere. There is a gaping hole in the floor of the basement, which looks *down* into the bottom of the bay, and a walled pool (into and from which helmeted divers pour) *above* the basement floor. Only in a dream (or an Ed Wood movie) can a room exist above water level and still allow people to move sideways into the water.

And those perplexing questions... Whose is the male voice that cries out warnings and hurls imprecations from the empty air? Whence comes the eerie and off-key signature theme music of the Octopus? If a suited-up Captain Hook is fired from the torpedo tube of a submarine, how does his severed air hose and safety line end

Hugh Herbert, Marcia Ralston, and Allen Jenkins stand entranced in the shadow of the Octopus.

up in the cave, instead of Kelly's? Why would anyone go to the trouble of hanging a dummy from the lighthouse tower? Or of placing an inverted bottle of ketchup in its suit pocket? Or of providing the dummy with a wallet?

Regarding the Octopus, herself, while it must have been a radical departure to have the supervillain of the piece turn out to be a (sort of) female, was this done solely to make the mother-in-law joke at the end a bit stronger? If Nanny has been prancing around their lighthouse with the rest of the cast, who fired Hook from the submarine? Are there henchpersons? To whom do those ubiquitous tentacles belong? Is there a band of highly trained cephalopods who have sworn fealty to their mistress and who hope for a hand (as it were) in the coming new world order? If that is the case, how to explain the Benedict Arnold of octopi who does in the boss just before the big boom?

Nope, there ought to be no complaint about the dream ending coming as a surprise (or a disappointment); they told us as much all along, didn't they?

For a quickie "B" offering, the lighting and photography are top notch. Arthur Todd manages to find every ominous niche in the basic but excellent sets, and several of the shots—particularly that of the dummy/corpse, hanging from the cupola— are outstanding. Apart from the necessarily flat illumination used in the scene where an octopus is seen flailing away on the underwater rock, the lighting scheme demonstrates various degrees of blackness, with nary a shade or shadow overlooked. The only false note struck is a scene in which one candle lights up the entire cave. Since the camera stares dispassionately as an obvious bank of lights comes up behind the hero and his little candle, one can only presume that the blatant fraud committed here was meant to be noticed.

There's a lot of music in *Sh! The Octopus*, and most of it is quite good; all of it is uncredited. Swelling music frequently serves as counterpoint to the extinguishing of lights, and—together with an array of screams, gunshots, and miscellaneous storm noise—keeps the action fully accompanied. This is no mean feat, as *Sh! The Octopus* is, of course, a Warner Brothers movie, designed and directed to unreel at a rat-a-tat pace. Scarcely a minute goes by without the introduction of a new character, the disappearance of an old one, a suspicious bit of dialogue, a brace of shrieks, or a volley of gunfire. If one were at all serious about keeping track of the goings-on, one would need at least eight legs and a mind like a steel trap.

Director William McGann made a respectable enough career out of second features, many of which leaned toward the West and most of which were shot on the Warners' back lot. Exhibiting a real knack for keeping the characters and the plot line in an ongoing hysterical state, McGann could probably have been used to great effect in some of the more somnolent space operas of the early sixties. He moved from directing to doing special effects photography in the mid-'40s, however, and he was the "genius of the lamp" behind the crawling hand that haunted Peter Lorre in 1946's *Beast with Five Fingers*. Thus, *Sh! The Octopus* remains his only "real" genre credit, although he did crank out entries in a number of mystery series, such as the tepid (but fast-moving) Perry Mason thriller *The Case of the Black Cat* (1936). McGann retired from the industry in the early fifties and died in 1977.

The film was a mélange of elements taken from plays written by Ralph Spence and by Ralph Murphy and Donald Gallagher. The task of picking and choosing plot details and then of blending the resultant comedy mystery was left to George Bricker, a prolific screenwriter who specialized in comedies and mysteries and who had a hand in just about everything from PRC's ghastly *Gas House Kids* to PRC's nasty *Brute Man* (via Universal, also 1946). Pretty much notorious as a hack with a tin ear when it came to authentic dialogue, he copped the credit for a number of mid-'40s misfires, like *Pillow of Death* and *She-Wolf of London*. Firmly entrenched in the lower end of the double bill, Bricker freelanced for much of his three-decade career, collecting credits and paychecks from majors and minors alike.

Interestingly, no credit for makeup or special effects is given in the film itself. Presumably art director Max Parker had more than just a say in the design of the slippery lighthouse, but whether he was the guiding light for the basically well-done tentacle manipulation is anybody's guess. Elspeth Dudgeon's on-camera transformation from Nanny to Sea Hag was done with colored filters, a technique perfected by Rouben Mamoulian in his *Dr. Jekyll and Mr. Hyde* (1931), and most likely director McGann, anticipating by several years his switch to a more magical facet of filmmaking, had a hand in this. Inasmuch as Perc Westmore, patriarch of the Westmore makeup dynasty, was working on and off at Warner Brothers at the time (it was he who received credit for Lionel Atwell's classic map in the studio's 1933 *Mystery of the Wax Museum*), he may also have been responsible for the design and execution of the relatively simple (but effective) job done on Dudgeon.

Dudgeon's "cross-dressing" role as centenarian Sir Roderick Femm in James Whale's *Old Dark House* marked both the actress's cinematic debut and apex. Movies and Dudgeon apparently hit it off, though, as she showed up in some of the decade's bigger hits, including *Camille* (1936) and *Pride and Prejudice* (1940). Genre-wise, Wilkie Collins's *Moonstone* (1934) and a role in support of Charles Laughton in 1944's *Canterville Ghost* pretty much complete the list. Still, there are quite a few film historians who maintain that the old gypsy who bitches about the whereabouts of the salt in *Bride of Frankenstein* (1935) is Dudgeon, in another Whale-induced, albeit unbilled, bit.

Dudgeon does an admirable job as Nanny: She coddles the vacuous Vesta, disposes of numerous guns, and puts the disturbed heroine down for a nap as if she were Mother Love, having done it all her life. Later, pleading for Kelly's help in finding the deed to her small farm allows Dudgeon the chance to spoof the traditional old women's roles (set-upon mother, set-upon grandmother, set-upon elderly spinster) etched in stone by silent movie convention. Her unmasking scene gives her the opportunity both to put the lie to the helpless old lady shtick and to chew the secret-paneled scenery. All in all, a bravura performance by the venerable actress, who died in 1955.

John Eldredge spent his well-over-thirty-years in films switching hats constantly. Never a strong enough personality to inspire confidence as an action hero (even the sight of Paul Morgan behind *two* guns leaves room for doubt), his turns as secondary heavies, cowards and slouches were more satisfying, but still not totally credible. One always got the feeling that Eldredge's characters needed lots of help to make their point.

The actor almost always conveyed an air of lethargy, whether called upon to render support in comedies (*The First Traveling Saleslady*, 1956), Westerns (Alan Ladd's first: *Whispering Smith*, 1949), or G-man epics (*Persons in Hiding*, 1939). Skipping from studio to studio as readily as he moved among genres, he ambled through a few entertaining Universal spookers (*Horror Island*, *The Black Cat*—both 1941, and *The Mad Doctor of Market Street*, 1942) en route to equal or lesser things. Eldredge's big horror and science fiction credit has to be his role as Police Chief Collins in the excellent *I Married a Monster from Outer Space* (1958). At least in *IMAMFOS* his character (possessed by an alien) was *supposed* to act calm and unconcerned.

Captain Hook (Brandon Tynan) wishes that he had to contend with only the *shadow* of the Octopus.

For every movie buff who knows Allen Jenkins by name, there are a hundred who recognize him on sight. Born Alfred McGonegal in 1900, Jenkins perfected the slightly crude but good-hearted Joe who could function with equipoise on either side of a badge. The actor was quite at home with comedy but could, if required, bare his teeth or shed a tear with the best of them. One of his finest straight roles was in the truly classic RKO programmer *Five Came Back* (1939), in which he enjoyed a moving death scene.

Jenkins handles Dempsey the Detective as one of his typically loutish lawmen: loud, grating, ineffably honest, totally sincere, and just this side of hopelessly incompetent. Playing off Hugh Herbert may not have offered the actor the chemistry that a similar part—playing one of the dizzy dicks opposite Frank McHugh in RKO's excellent *Tomorrow at Seven* (1933) did—but that is much more due to George Bricker's meticulously planned lunacy than it is to shortcomings on the part of either *Octopus* comic. For all his faults, Dempsey remains a likeable man, and concern for his safety (and for Kelly's) is one of the reasons that the film's dream ending works.

Eccentric comedian Hugh Herbert is *very* much an acquired taste; I happen to enjoy his antics. Master of befuddlement and king of nonsensical chatter, Herbert "woo-wooed" his way through well over a hundred films, either as top comic or second banana, supporting everyone from W. C. Fields (*Million Dollar Legs*, 1932) to Wheeler and Woolsey (*Diplomaniacs*, 1933) to Buster Keaton (*The Villain Still Pur-*

sued Her, 1940) to Olsen and Johnson (*Hellzapoppin*, 1941) to Arthur Lake and Penny Singleton in their popular Blondie series.

Herbert was relatively long in the tooth when, at forty-one years of age, he made his film debut in 1928's *Caught in the Fog*. From that point until his death in 1952, the comedian ran himself ragged, woo-wooing endlessly for movie and radio audiences. Most proud of his Snout, the tinker, in Warners' 1935 *Midsummer Night's Dream*, Herbert turned up everywhere, including the comedy-mystery genre. Universal's *The Black Cat* (1941) reunited him with *Sh! The Octopus*'s sleepy-eyed costar, John Eldredge, but the mix of sputters and spooks didn't sit comfortably with viewers, most of whom found the unshaven Bela Lugosi to be the funniest thing in the film.

As the ineffably good-natured Kelly, Herbert does his thing and does it well. Quieter (all things being relative) than Dempsey, Kelly delivers under-the-breath comments that, while only occasionally genuinely funny, seem to be the kind of eye-opening remarks that one would probably make, if only one had sufficient nerve. Dempsey to VV: "Did your stepfather usually hang around in this lighthouse?" Kelly (to himself): "He certainly is hanging out a lot around here now."

The rest of the cast does all right, with Margaret Irving's wiseacre stealing any leftover honors from the two old salts. Irving had started off as an ingénue in the waning days of silent film and had matured into a semidowager type by the close of the thirties. In 1936, her Lilli Rochelle had caused Boris Karloff's tormented Gravelle to go even further off the deep end in *Charlie Chan at the Opera*, her only other genre credit. George Rosener and Brandon Tynan are both okay as the captains, but Tynan gets the nod for at least attempting to draw a distinction between his Captain Cobb and his international policeman, Green. Rosener plays his "dual" role on one note: sour; maybe spending nine years in disguise on one case is enough to make any man forget his true personality.

Sh! The Octopus is an awful lot of fun for the right-minded viewer, but admittedly there are legions of folks who believe the picture is just plain awful. Still, I think that it's a shame the film isn't better known. It's been years since it was on television and, as fewer and fewer black-and-white programmers make it onto the small screen, it may never reappear. (As with most of the titles in this book, it may devolve to Turner Classic Movies to save this one from vanishing [albeit with perpetual care] into the recesses of a dispassionate film archive.)

It's odd that the 1937 release, which had virtually all of what was left of the horror field to itself, should have disappeared so completely. This peculiar circumstance, like so many of the other elements in *Sh! The Octopus*, can be viewed two ways: Either its release during the horror drought somehow worked against its being noticed as a genre effort, or Warner Brothers' typical lack of enthusiasm for second-feature publicity campaigns failed to light the requisite fire under anybody. This latter assessment is probably closer to the truth. With any hoopla whatsoever, the film — whatever its objective merits — would have stood out from its more respectable neighbors like a yodeler at choir practice. As the film had just barely made feature length, however — it runs a few seconds *under* fifty-four minutes — there would have been little point in investing any kind of real money in a picture which under no circumstances could stand on its own. (Copyright records list a *sixty*-minute running time, and while I can't for the life of me imagine what could be missing, there is the little matter of the quartet of "sinister plotters" listed in the cast scrawl who are nowhere to be found in the feature itself.)

An extremely minor bottom-of-the-bill offering, *Sh!* doesn't claim to have anywhere near a lock on innovation, but it offers a wry and ballsy variation on the haunted house, colorful mystery villain theme that had packed 'em in since nickelodeon days. With a new wrinkle on the "clutching hand" formula, frenetic pacing, madcap characters, and plot exposition that flirts openly with the lunatic fringe, the movie actively encourages head scratching and second guessing from its initial Sturm to its final Drang.

APPENDIX: *THE MYSTERY OF DR. FU MANCHU*— EPISODE 10: *THE FIERY HAND*

While almost all *The Mystery of Dr. Fu Manchu* two-reelers exist today, they have been virtually inaccessible until quite recently. October 2003 saw the British Film Institute playing host to a series of public showings of the Lyons Fu Manchu series, as well as other picturesque — and, in many ways, remarkable — short films Stoll (and other studios) foisted on appreciative audiences in the 1920s.

Unfortunately for me, I had crossed the Pond several years earlier, when — saddled with plans for this book and hopes of screening what very may well have been the only chapters still in Christendom — I hightailed it over to the BFI. There I was informed that there were viewable materials on only three chapters: *The Fiery Hand*, *The Queen of Hearts*, and *The Miracle*, and that a fourth title — *The Shrine of the Seven Lamps*— had only just deteriorated to the point of being non-projectable. The mother lode of newly-found Fu footage (say *that* three times fast!) hadn't yet been struck, and so far as I (or anyone at the Stephen Street headquarters) knew, the 35mm reels laying on the nitrate screening room floor were all that was left of the fabulous old adventure series.

Thankfully, I was dead wrong. The Coleby/Lyons Fu Manchu shorts are once again available to researchers and to film mavens whose schedules may coincide with possible future showings of the series in and around London. For those whose circumstances may not afford them the opportunity to junket to England for the express purpose of being tickled by these short films, here — culled from notes taken during a struggle with a brittle nitrate print and a quarrelsome movieola — is a scene-by-scene account of *The Fiery Hand*, episode 10 of *The Mystery of Dr. Fu Manchu*.

Reel one
 Title:
 All trace of that malignant genius, Dr. Fu Manchu, had vanished, until Inspector Weymouth called one morning to see Nayland Smith.

 Interior. Nayland Smith's parlor:
 Smith (Fred Paul) and Petrie (Humberston Wright) are seated, smoking pipes. Weymouth (Frank Wilson) stands before them.

Title (Smith):
"What gives you the impression that what happened at The Gables is connected with Fu Manchu?"

Title (Weymouth):
"Because two mysterious deaths have occurred there quite recently. Two tenants have died at The Gables. They were not poisoned or bitten by venomous insects; They just died of fear — STARK FEAR!"

Smith and Petrie glance at each other.

Title (Weymouth):
"The house is now unoccupied and has the reputation of being haunted."

Title (Smith):
"All right, Weymouth. I'll investigate the matter and communicate with you later."

Weymouth leaves.

Fade to a title in an Oriental style font:
Somewhere in London...

Interior. Fu Manchu (Harry Agar Lyons) is seated at a desk, writing in a journal or diary. The mandarin wears a skullcap and an ornate chung-sam. (All interiors connected with Fu Manchu's lair are tinted amber.)

Title:
Two days elapse.

Interior. Back in Smith and Pertrie's digs. As Petrie is writing, the door opens, and a gentleman wearing a patently false beard enters. Petrie reacts, but the stranger is Nayland Smith, in another of his canny disguises.

Title (Smith):
"It's all right, Petrie. I've leased The Gables in the name of Professor Maxton."

Smith opens a suitcase he is carrying; it appears to be filled with old clothing.

Title (Smith):
"In case you care to visit the house, Petrie, I have brought these things. My tenancy commences tonight."

Petrie is bewildered.

Title (Petrie):
"But, Smith. What possible reason can there be for disguise?"

Title (Smith):
"Every reason. I did not entirely trust the house agent."

Cut to Title:
The Gables

Interior. Rear of taxi. Both Smith and Petrie are in disguise. They exit the cab and approach The Gables.

Title:
Nothing now but a couple of studios, until one comes to The Heath…

Exterior. Smith and Petrie walking toward The Heath, the main House. En route, they stop. (All nighttime exteriors tinted green.)

Title (Smith):
"Whilst at The Gables, we must assume false names. You are Professor Pierce!"

Interior. The two enter the house and move around downstairs a bit before going upstairs to the first floor. (Print changes to amber tint as they enter upstairs room.) There's a table, set with a decanter, siphon and glasses. Smith pours a drink.

Title (Smith):
"Now, Pierce, a whiskey and soda before we look 'round."

Petrie accepts the glass, but a noise startles him; he spills his drink all over himself.

Title (Smith):
"The ghost wastes no time! This is not new to me! I spent an hour here last night and heard the same sounds."

Petrie does not appear to be calmed much by this pronouncement, but he manages to finish his drink. Smith moves over to the fireplace, where he turns and begins to speak LOUDLY. (This is conveyed by all capital letters in the title.)

Title (Smith):
"My dear Pierce, do you hear the tinkling of bells?"

Smith runs back and whispers the following in Petrie's ear.

Title (Smith):
"Keep it up, Petrie. Someone is listening!"

Petrie then yells (all caps again):

Title (Petrie):
"I heard it distinctly, Maxton!"

Smith moves into an adjoining hallway; the tint changes to green. He runs up the stairs, into a bedroom. (In the interim, Petrie moves cautiously about the amber-tinted room.) Using his torch, Smith examines the floor by the walls. He finds about a half-dozen mousetraps, in each of which is a mouse.

Downstairs, Petrie reacts with horror as the door to the amber-tinted room opens slowly, by itself. A moment later, the door *closes* slowly, by itself, and a cut brings us back upstairs. Smith rejoins Petrie on the lower floor, and the two don their hats, move into the foyer, and prepare to leave. There is a spontaneous puff of smoke in the fireplace behind them. Smith runs out of frame; Petrie stands there, terrified. Smith runs back onto the screen. Petrie quails as he sees the transparent form of an arm—bearing a knife—coming toward him. Both men take off, and run into the back yard.

Cut to:
Interior, amber-tint: Fu Manchu is mixing a sinister-looking concoction.

Cut to Title:
Nayland Smith explains the mystery of The Gables.

Interior. Smith and Petrie's digs: The men are removing their disguises.

Title (Petrie):
"I think the only decent thing you can do is explain that terrible ordeal."

Title (Smith):
"Certainly, Petrie. Mice! Strapped onto their bodies were little bells which caused the tinkling we heard."

Petrie looks on, a bit at sea, as Smith opens a valise.

Title (Smith):
"In my first visit to the Gables, I bored holes in the wainscoting, and before each, I set one of these traps."

Petrie manages inadvertently to free all the mice.

Title (Smith):
"The mice were admitted into the wall cavities from some cellar underneath, Petrie. Almost childish, is it not? But it proves to me that Dr. Fu Manchu has a hiding place under The Gables."

Petrie reacts.
(End of reel one.)

Reel Two
Interior. As before.

Title: *To the door comes Aziz, Karamenah's brother.*

(The exterior, as indicated above, is bathed in a green tint; the interior, in amber.) Petrie brings Aziz (Pat Royale) inside.

Title (Smith):
"This is a trap, Petrie!"

Title (Aziz):
"No, sir. It's no trap. I've only come to try and find my sister. Help me find my sister!"

Flashback.

Exterior. A desert oasis. A slave trader enters, with Karamenah (Joan Clarkson) and Aziz in tow. Fu Manchu, who is dressed in traditional Arab raiment, leers lustfully at the lovely young woman. He buys the young siblings with a bag of coins. The slave trader runs off; Karamenah and Aziz are immediately surrounded by everyone else in sight and dragged offscreen.

Back to present.

Title (Aziz):
"That is how my sister came into the power of the Hakim, Fu Manchu!"

Nayland Smith glances out the window.

Title (Smith):
"Sergeant Carter has just arrived. He and Aziz can remain here until our return."

Carter enters, as Smith and Petrie leave.

Title: *The Studio.*

The Studio is an enormous mansion, which — an awning apart — bears not a little similarity to the manor house at The Gables. Smith and Petrie, again in disguise, wander about the property before entering the building. Inside is Karamenah; she signals the men to be silent. Smith flourishes a revolver.

Title (Karamenah):
"For God's sake! Go back! I have risked my life to come here tonight! He knows, and is ready!"

Smith and Petrie head for a pair of curtains, as Karamenah cries out.

Title (Karamenah):
"I tell you, it is death to go behind those curtains!"

Smith throws Karamenah to the floor. He and Petrie stomp up the steps, rush behind the curtains despite the warning, and immediately find themselves caught in a cage. The cage is really an elevator, which descends into a dungeon-like room, appointed throughout with Chinese artifacts.

A group of dacoits come out to drag the prisoners from the cage. Smith draws his revolver and fires wildly at least a dozen times. The dacoits scatter; no one is hit. Smith and Petrie proceed into the dungeon proper, as Fu Manchu strikes a gong. Six turbaned thugs rush out to seize the two men. More shots are fired; again, no one is hit. The men are tied up securely.

Upstairs, Karamenah appears to be searching for something. Back in the dungeon, Smith is chained to the floor; Petrie is tied in a chair. Fu Manchu gloats.

Title (Fu Manchu) (All of Fu Manchu's dialogue titles are printed in an ersatz-Oriental script.):
"Mr. Nayland Smith! Doctor Petrie! Here in these vaults, I have waited patiently for you both. My trap was ready, always ready."

Petrie espies a sword, hanging not far from the spot where he sits. Fu Manchu follows the doctor's eyes.

Title (Fu Manchu):
"Even if you had the dexterity of a Mexican knife-thrower, you would be unable to reach me, dear Dr. Petrie. The weapon near your hand, Doctor, is known as "The Friend's Sword."

The men regard each other.

Title (Fu Manchu):
"Always Mr. Nayland Smith's friend, you shall remain so 'til the end. I have arranged for this."

Fu Manchu strikes the gong again, and the turbaned dacoits run in, carrying stacks of cages.

Title (Smith):
"Oh, my God! It's the 'Sixth Gate!'"

Fu Manchu smiles.

Title (Fu Manchu):
"I see you recognize this... errr... happy little invention, Mr. Smith, which we call in China the 'Six Gates of Joyful Wisdom.'"

The dacoits position the stack of cages over Smith's chest. Petrie looks on, apprehensively.

Title (Fu Manchu):
"Credit Mr. Nayland Smith with great courage, but I predict you shall use the "Friend's Sword," Doctor, not later than when I shall raise the third gate."

Another dacoit appears. He hands a basket-like cage to Fu Manchu.

Title (Fu Manchu):
"Cantonese rats, Doctor Petrie: the most ravenous in the world. These I shall place in the first compartment, called the "Gate of Joyous Hope.""

Smith struggles in his chains.

Title (Smith):
"The sword, Petrie! Spare me the humiliation of asking mercy from that fiend!"

Petrie strains to reach the sword. Fu Manchu drops to his knees in order to place the rats into the compartment.

Title (Fu Manchu):
"It may interest you to know, Mr. Smith, that the second compartment is called the 'Gate of Mirthful Doubt.'"

Petrie gets the sword and positions it over Nayland Smith's throat.

Title (Fu Manchu):
"The raising of the first gate is always a crucial moment, Mr. Smith."

Entering suddenly from stage left is Karamenah, waving a revolver. She shoots Fu Manchu in the face. Amid general chaos, she releases Petrie, and the two of them then set out to release Smith. Fu Manchu grabs his face and collapses to the floor.

Title: *From out the Valley of Death...*

Interior. Smith and Petrie's flat: Smith is smoking a pipe. Karamenah and Aziz hug each other and fawn a bit on Dr. Petrie.

Title (Smith):
"What have you done with the body of Dr. Fu Manchu?"

Weymouth gestures, helplessly.

Title (Weymouth):
"We haven't been able to get it. That end of the vault collapsed two minutes after we hauled you out."

Finis

If *The Fiery Hand* is a typical episode of *The Mystery of Dr. Fu Manchu*, a few remarks are in order. Apart from Harry Agar Lyons—who, as Rohmer's Mandarin, doesn't so much act as pose—the efforts of the rest of the cast are little better than competent. Fred Paul's Nayland Smith is straightforward to the point of being one-dimensional, while Humberston Wright's Petrie mugs constantly and furiously; his antics in the haunted house are right out of Hal Roach or Mack Sennett. Joan Clarkson is a pretty and resolute Karamenah, but Pat Royale (Aziz) must have been a charter member in the Ghastly Child Actors' Guild, along with Baby Jane Quigley and Donnie Dunagan.

The sets are serviceable without being memorable, and, unfortunately, that includes Fu's underground dungeon, a locale that should have been the highlight of the picture. A bit more attention to lighting in the flashback scene in Arabia might have given the flats greater dimension, but nothing short of a complete overhaul by the art director would have lessened the scene's cheap and artificial look. One of the contemporary trade reviewers noted that the production values of the Fu Manchu films appeared to be appreciably lower than those of the earlier Holmes series, and the modest sets and appointments on display in *The Fiery Hand* do nothing to argue the question.

Because there are splices in the BFI print that was available for viewing, I have no way of knowing whether any serious footage is missing from *The Fiery Hand*. There don't appear to be any gaps in the narrative, but Aziz's appearance is a tad abrupt, and the two first-reel inserts of Fu Manchu seem somewhat pointless. Nonetheless, director A. E. Coleby (who also helped adapt the story for the screen) succeeded in transferring the "Boy's Own" flavor of the stories to screen, and therein may lie the reason for the happy union of Fu Manchu, Stoll Pictures, and black ink: the appeal to the British working class.

INDEX

Numbers in **bold** indicate photographs.

Aaron's Rod 23
Abbott and Costello 171
Abraham Lincoln 49
Ace of Cads 46
Ackerman, Forrest J 1, 2, 150
Adler, Luther 59
The Adventure of the Torture Cage 17, 28–29
Adventures of Sherlock Holmes (series of Stoll shorts) 10–11, 14
The Adventures of Superman (television program) 54
The Adventures of Tom Sawyer 138
Aimos 194
Alberni, Luis **139**, 141
Alexander (Hermann) 109
Alexander, J. Grubb 70
Allen, Irwin 144, 145
Allen, Judith 167, 168, **169**
Allo Berlin, ici Paris (*Hello Berlin, Paris Here*) 196
Alvarado, Don 59
American Movie Classics 6
The Amphibians (novel) 150
Anderson, Sherwood 206*n*
Andrejew, Andre 192
Antoine, André-Paul 195, 198
Appelby, Dorothy **139**
Arbó, Manuel 122–123, **126**
Arbuckle, Roscoe 35
Armageddon 145
Arsene Lupin 35
Arthur, Johnny 35
Arvidson, Linda 48
Astor, Mary 52
Atom Man vs. Superman (serial) 157
Atwill, Lionel 126, 160, 173, 214
August, Joseph 184–185
Aussey, Germaine 194
The Avenging Conscience 35

Babes in Toyland 140
Bacon, Lloyd 76–77, 79
Balcon, Michael 98
Balderston, John 206*n*

Barabbas (novel) 41, 42
Barcelona y sus misterios 123
Barnes, Freeman 170
Barrier, Edgar 197
Barrymore, John 52, 68, 69, 75, 77, 84, 85, 86, 87, 89, 149, 160, 168
Barrymore, Lionel 35, 84–85, 86–87, 91, 168, 193
The Bat 4, 77
The Bat Whispers 53
Baur, Harry 190, 191, **193**–194, 195, 198
Bay, Michael 145
The Beast with Five Fingers 213
Beck, Calvin 1, 2
Beery, Wallace 51
Behind That Curtain 84, 85, 116
Bela Lugosi Meets a Brooklyn Gorilla 124
The Bells 85
Belmore, Lionel 87
The Beloved Rogue 53, 68, 184
Bennett, Barbara 31
Bennett, Constance 31
Bennett, Joan 31, 173
Bennett, Richard 31
The Benson Murder Case 200, 201, 202
The Benson Murder Case (novel) 201
Berkeley, Busby 77
Berman, Pandro S. 130
Bey, Turhan 163
Beyond the Horizon (drama) 174
Biggers, Earl Derr 2, 67, 70, 116, 117, 120, 125–126
Birth of a Nation 34
The Bishop Murder Case 202
The Bishop Murder Case (novel) 201–202
The Black Camel 72, 117, 120, 122, 123, 124, 125, 126, 140
The Black Cat (1934) 140
The Black Cat (1941) 214, 216
Black Dragons 75
Black Moon 6, 178–**182**, 183–185
Black Orchids 139

Black Oxen 33
The Black Room 140, 184
Blackmer, Sidney **148**
Blackstone, Harry 109
Blade am Satans Bog (*Leaves from Satan's Book*) 42
Blane, Sally **138**, **139**
A Blind Bargain 77, 149
Boggs, Francis 71
Bolero 130
Boles, John 138
Bonanova, Fortunio 123
Borden, Olive 60, **61**, 63, **65**
Bosworth, Hobart 71–72
Bow, Clara 148
Boyd, William (stage) 157
Boyer, Charles 197
Brandon, Henry 140
Breen, Bobby 183
Brendel, El 111
Brent, George 125
Brentano, Lowell 108, 109, 112
Bretherton, Howard 53–54
Brewster's Millions 44
Bricker, George 103, 213–214, 215
Bride of Frankenstein 140, 214
Brittain, Leslie 13
Brodine, Norbert (aka Brodin) 149
Brook, Clive 202
Brooks, A.M. 16
Brooks, Louise 201
Brown, Tom 167, 168, **169**
Browning, Tod 7, 58, 123
Bruce, Nigel 184
The Brute Man 213
Die Büchse der Pandora (*Pandora's Box*) 201
Buck Rogers (serial) 157
Buffy, the Vampire Slayer (television program) 133
Bunston, Herbert 129, 138, 140
Burgess, Dorothy **182**, 184
Burns, Edmund 72
Burroughs, Edgar Rice 75
Burton, Lance 141
Busch, Mae 60

227

Das Cabinet des Dr. Caligari 85
The Café L'Egypte 27
Caleb Powers (novel) 170
The Call of Siva 14, **16**, 20
Calleia, Joseph 123
Calvo, Rafael 125
Camille 214
The Canary Murder Case 200, 201
The Canary Murder Case (novel) 201
The Canterville Ghost 214
Capra, Frank 78
Captain Blood 53
Carné, Marcel 195
Carroll, Nancy 202
Carter, Louise 128, 129, **132**
Casablanca 7, 124
The Case of the Black Cat 213
The Cat and the Canary (1927) 69, 70
The Cat and the Canary (1979) 205
The Cat Creeps 74
Caught in the Fog 216
Ceballos, Larry 77
Chaliapin, Feodor 204
Chandu the Magician 4, 35, 111, 137, 140
Chaney, Lon 5, 7, 10, 33, 35, 51, 58, 62, 63, 69, 77, 79
Chaney, Lon, Jr. 149
Chaplin, Charlie 76
Charlie Chan at the Opera 216
Charlie Chan at the Wax Museum 54
Charlie Chan Carries On 2–3, 72, 116, 117, 120, 121, 122, 123, 125, 126, 140
Charlie Chan in Egypt 140
Charlie Chan in Paris 121
Charlie Chan in the City of Darkness 140
Charlie Chan's Chance 72, 126, 140
Charlie Chan's Courage 126
Charlie Chan's Greatest Case 72, 126, 140
Charlie Chan's Murder Cruise 126
La Charrette fantôme (*The Phantom Carriage*) 197
Chesterton, Gilbert Keith 150
Cheswright, Grahame 200
Chevalier, Maurice 202
Cheyenne (television program) 123
China Clipper 34
Chinatown Nights 17, 29
The Chinese Parrot 2, 66–**68**, **69**–72, 90, 116
Christensen, Benjamin 7, 77
Churchill, Marguerite 124

Cimarron 130
The Circus Queen Murder 184
Clair, René 195
Clarkson, Joan 13, 15, **22**, 223, 226
The Clue of the Pigtail 14, 19–20
Cobb, Eddie 161
Coleby, A.E. 3, 11, 12, 14, 41, 219, 226
College Rhythm 130
Collins, Cora Sue 184
Collins, Walter 103
Collins, Wilkie 214
Conan Doyle, Arthur 10, 11, 14, 41, 75
Connelly, Campbell 104
Conners, Barry 109, 120, 121
Conscience 40
Conte, Richard 112
Conti, Albert **68**
Copperfield, David 141
The Copperhead (drama) 168
Cooper, D.P. 13
Cooper, Gladys 41
Cooper, Merion C. 129, 130
Corelli, Marie 40–42, 46, 49
Corner in Colleens 184
The Corpse Vanishes 75
Corrigan, Ray "Crash" 157
Cortez, Ricardo 42, 45, 46–47, 53
Costello, Dolores 51
Costello, Helene 51–52, **53, 55**
Costello, Maurice 51
The Coughing Horror 27
Counsellor at Law 149, 160
Courtenay, William 108
Cox, Jack 101
Crabbe, Larry "Buster" 157
Cracked Nuts 157
Cradle Song 175
Cragmire Tower 27
Cramer, Richard (aka Rychard) 52, 158, 161
Cricks, R.H. 12
Crime and Punishment 198
The Cry of the Nighthawk 22–23
Cuerpo del delito, El 201
Cugat, Xavier 123
Cummings, E.E. 206n
Cummings, Robert 197
Cunningham, Jack 173
Curtiz, Michael 202
Custodio, Ana María 124

Dallas (television program) 210
Dancing Lady 157
Dandridge, Dorothy 184
Daniels, Bebe 160
Dante's Inferno 184
Dante's Peak 145
Daudet, Alphonse 11

David Copperfield 35
David Golder 193
Davis, Harry 149
Davis, Phil 111
Dawn (novel) 150
The Day the Earth Stood Still 157
Dead Men Tell 54
Deane, Hamilton 206n
Death Takes a Holiday 175
Death Valley Days (television program) 123
de Brulier, Nigel 69, 129
de Castejón, Blanca 121, 124, 125
Deep Impact 145
Deep Purple 108
Delgado, Marcel 129
Del Ruth, Roy 77
Deluge 7, 143–**147**, **148**–150
Deluge (novel) 150
Deluxe Annie 31
De Mille, Cecil B. 42, 77
Dempster, Carol 42, 46, 47–48
The Denishawn Dancers 48
De Putti, Lya 42
The Derby Winner 17
de Segurola, Andrés 123
Desire Under the Elms (drama) 174
Desmond, William 158, 160
La Destruzione del Mondo see *Deluge*
The Devil and Daniel Webster 78
The Devil Commands 177
The Devil Doctor (novel) 13
The Devil Doll 35
The Devil on Horseback 124
Devil's Advocate 47
de Vries, Henri 200, 204
Dexter, Elliot 170
Dick Tracy vs. Crime, Inc. (serial) 150
Dickens, Charles 11, 174
Dickey, Basil 160
Dieterle, William 78
Diplomaniacs 215
Disney, Walt 175
Do Detectives Think? 52
Doctor Faustus (drama) 40
Doctor Jekyll and Mr. Hyde (1931) 214
Dr. Sin Fang (feature) 17, 29
Dr. Sin Fang Dramas 11, 17, 28–29
Doctor X 107
Doctor Zhivago 125
Don Juan 52
Don Quixote 204
Donaldson, Roger 145
Donovan's Brain 149
The Doomed Regiment (short story) 93n
Dorat, Charles 194

Index

Double Door 172–177
Double Door (drama) 173, **176**
Douglas, Melvyn 160
The Dove 4
Dracula 71, 72, 107, 108, 123, 138, 173, 201
Dracula (drama) 206*n*
Drácula 120, 123, 201
Dracula's Daughter 124
Dreamers (drama) 96
Die Dreigroschenoper (*The Threepenny Opera*) 192
The Dreiserodore 206*n*
Duchesne, Roger 194
Dudgeon, Elspeth 214
Dugan, Tom 141
du Maurier, George 11
The Dumb Girl of Portici 147
Dunagan, Donnie 226
Duncan, Lee 51, 55
Dupont, E.A. 43
Durkin, James 159, 160
Duval, Shelly 60
Duvivier, Julien 6, 186, 189–190, 191–192, 193, 194, 195, 196–197, 198
Dynasty (television program) 210

Earthquake 144
The Easiest Way 68
East Lynne 17
East Is West 123
Eldredge, John 214, 216
Elvey, Maurice 7, 10–11, 12, 14, 41, 101
Emerald, Nell 17, 18
Engholm, Harry 42
Eran trece 2–3, 72, 113–**119**, 120–**124**, 125–126
Espiritismo (*Spiritism*) 133
The Eye of Siva (drama) 13

Fagin 11
Fairbanks, Douglas 4, 69
The Faker 77
Falk, Lee 111
The False Faces 35
A Farewell to Arms 125
The Fatal Warning (serial) 52
Fauchois, René 59
Faulkner, William 206*n*
Faust 40
Faust (literature) 40
Faust and Marguerite 40
Faust and Mephistopheles 40
Fawcett, L'Estrange 101
Fazenda, Louise 77
The Feathered Serpent 124
Feed 'Em and Weep 35
Feist, Felix E. 148–149
Fetchit, Stepin 182, 184

Feyder, Jacques 195
Field, Betty 197
Fields, W.C. 171, 175, 215
The Fiery Hand 23–24, 219–226
La Fin de jour (*The End of a Day*) 197
Finkel, Samri (see: Fulton Oursler)
The First Traveling Saleslady 214
Fishbeck, Harry 43
Five Came Back 215
Flash Gordon (serial) 157
Flash Gordon Conquers the Universe (serial) 157
Fleming, Claude **92**
Fleming, Victor 197
Flesh and Fantasy 197
Fletcher, Bramwell 129, **132**
Flight to Nowhere 124
Floradora (Broadway musical) 77
The Flying Deuces 171
Flying Down to Rio 121
Football Footwork 149
Footlight Parade 77
Forbidden Planet 157
Forty-Second Street 77
Fowler, Gene 86
Fowler Wright, Sydney 149–150
Fox, William 5
Francis, Kay 202
Frankenstein 7, 85, 120, 138, 163, 173, 189, 190
Frankenstein (drama) 206*n*
Frawley, William 167, 168, **169**
Fredericks, Ellsworth 149
Frenguelli, Anthony 17
Friedlander, Lewis 160–161, 163, 164*n*
Froggy's Little Brother 12
Frye, Dwight 124
Fulton, John P. 162
The Fungi Cellars 21
The Further Adventures of Sherlock Holmes 11
The Further Mysteries of Dr. Fu Manchu 12, 15, 16, 26–28

Galeen, Henrik 188, 189
Gallagher, Donald 213
Garon, Pauline 92
Garralaga, Martín 120, 123–124
Garrick, John 124
Gas House Kids 213
Gates, Harvey 75
Gawthorne, Peter 125
Gebühr, Otto 190
General Crack 77
General Hospital (television program) 168
The Gentle Monster 54
George, John 139–140

The Ghost Goes West 150
Ghost Parade (novel) 91
Gilbert, John 83, 87, 118
Gill, Basil 102, 103
The Girl Glory 184
Girl Missing 203
Girl Who Stayed at Home 48
Gish, Dorothy 136
Gliese, Rochus 188
The Glory of Love 51; see also *While Paris Sleeps*
God's Good Man 41
Goethe, Johann Wolfgang von 40
The Golden Pomegranates 27–28
Goldner, Orville 129
Der Golem 188
Le Golem 6, 186–**193**, 194–**196**, 197–198
The Golem (novel) 187, 188
Der Golem und die Tänzerin 188
Der Golem, wie er in die Welt kam 188, 195, 198
Golgotha 196
The Good Fairy 149
Gordon, C. Henry 124
The Gospel According to Saint Matthew 194
Goudal, Jetta 92
Gray, Anne 17
The Great Gay Road 12
The Great God Brown (drama) 174
The Great Piggy Bank Robbery 210
The Great Prince Shan 12
The Great Train Robbery 40
The Great Waltz 197
Greeley, Horace 107
Green, Howard J. 136, 140
The Green Ghost (short story) 86
The Green Ghost (novel) 91
The Green Ghost 91; see also *Le Spectre Vert*
The Green Mist 27
The Greene Murder Case 200, 201, 202, 204
The Greene Murder Case (novel) 201
Grey, C.G. 98
Greywater Park 28
Gribble, Harry Wagstaff 136
Griffith, D.W. 6, 34, 35, 42–43, 44, 46, 48–49
Grit 84
Groenig, Matt 133
Grot, Anton 107
The Guiding Light (television program) 147
Gunsmoke (television program) 168

Haight, George 173
Hall, Charles D. 69
Hall, Winter 170
Halliday, John 108, 168, **169**
Halperin brothers 179, 185
Halpern, Leivick 188
Hamilton, John 203
Hammett, Dashiell 202
Hampden, Walter 175
Hanlon, Bert 136
Harolde, Rolf 148
Harris, Robert 75
Hart, Ferdinand 189, 193, 195, **196**
Hart, William S. 184
Hathaway, Henry 167, 168
Hats Off 7
Hayakawa, Sessue 12
Hays, Will 174
Heale, Patrick K. 17, 103
Hearst, William Randolph 159
Hecht, Ben 86, 87, 89, 90, 93*n*
Hellzapoppin 216
Herbert, Hugh **212**, 215–216
Heroes of the West (serial) 159, 160
Heyward, Leyland 86
High Treason 7, 94–**97**, 98–**102**, 103–104, 204, 210
High Treason (drama) 98
Hindle Wakes 101
Hindle Wakes (drama) 84
Hinds, Samuel S. 145
His Majesty, the American 84
Hitchcock, Alfred 98
Hitchcock, Raymond 59, 60
Hobbs, Robert 17
Hoffenstein, Samuel 197
Hoffman, Dustin 145
Holmes, Stuart 35
Holt, Jack 179, 184
Holt, Jany 194
Hopalong Cassidy Returns 204
Hope Chest 48
Holy Orders (novel) 41
Hood, Darla 35
Hornung, E.W. 168
Horror Island 214
Houdini, Harry 157
Houghton, Stanley 101
The Hound of the Baskervilles 11
The House of Horror 75, 77
The House on 92nd Street 167
The House Without a Key (novel) 125
The House Without a Key (serial) 67, 116
Howard, David 122
Hume, Benita **102**, 103
The Hunchback of Notre Dame (1923) 33

The Hunchback of Notre Dame (1939) 185
Hyde-White, Wilfred 2, 200, 204–205
Hymer, Warren 121, 125

I Love Lucy (television program) 168
I Married a Monster from Outer Space 214
I Walked with a Zombie 185
I'm No Angel 130
In a Lotus Garden 11
Ince, Ada 159, **160**, **163**
Ince, Thomas H. 184
The Informer 185
Ingram, Rex 139
Innocent 41
The Insidious Dr. Fu Manchu (novel) 9
International House 171
Intolerance 48
Invaders from Mars 4
Invasion of the Body Snatchers 149
Invisibility 31
The Invisible Man 5, 32, 162
Irving, George 170
Irving, Margaret 174, 216
Is Zat So? 59
Island of Lost Souls 140
Isn't Life Wonderful? 48
It's a Wonderful Life 78
Ivers, Judith Crawford 171

Jacobs, W.W. 131
Jacquet, Gaston 194
Jamison, Bud 76
The Jazz Singer 122, 201
Jeans, Ursula 96, 104*n*
Jenkins, Allen **212**, 215
Jennings, DeWitt 53
John, Graham 129
Johnson, Tor 53
Jolson, Al 122
Jones, Chuck 210
Jones, Clifford 138, 141
Jory, Victor 138, **139**
Journey's End (drama) 97
Jungle Mystery (serial) 160
Just Imagine 111

Karamenah 28
Karl, Roger 194
Karloff, Boris 11, 52, 77, 84–85, 86, 87, 89, 90, 91–92, 117, 138, 140, 147, 163, 174, 175, 177, 184, 216
Kassler, Frank 192
Keaton, Buster 35, 90, 215
Kelly, Anthony P. 168
Kelly, Kathleen 200, 204, 205
Kennedy, Edgar 72

The Kennel Murder Case 202, 203
Kerrigan, J.M. 129
Keystone Kops 130
King Kong 75, 185
The King of Kings 77
King of the Kongo (serial) 77, 84, 85
King of the Rocketmen (serial) 150, 161
Kingston, Jerome 75
Klaw, Irving 163
Klein, Philip 109, 120, 121
Kline, Ben 72
The Knocking on the Door 21–22
Kohler, Fred **148**
Kopecky, Stepán 192
Korff, Arnold 179, 184
Körkarlen (*The Phantom Chariot*) 197
Kotsonaros, George 52–**53**, 56
Kraft Television Theatre 177
Krauss, Werner 85
Krellberg, Sherman S. 157
Kubrick, Stanley 96
Kuwa, George 90

Ladd, Alan 214
Laemmle, Carl 67, 68, 69, 70
Laemmle, Carl, Jr. 162
Laemmle, Rosabelle 85–86
Lagerlöf, Selma 197
Lake, Alice **32**, 33, 35
Lake, Arthur 216
Landers, Lew *see* Friedlander, Lewis
Lang, Fritz 98
La Rocque, Rod 42, 46
Larrinaga, Mario 130
Lasky, Jesse 43
The Last Adventures of Sherlock Holmes 11
The Last Express 177
The Last of Mrs. Cheyney 140
The Last Warning 70, 71
Laughton, Charles 214
Laurel and Hardy 7, 52, 118, 140, 161, 171
Lawford, Betty 129
Lea Lyon 69
LeBaron, William 130
Leder, Mimi 145
The Legend of Prague see *Le Golem*
Lehman, Gladys 173
Leni, Paul 2, 4, 68, 69–71, 72, 90, 116
Leong, James B. 139, 140
Lerner, Jacques 59, 60, **61**, 63
Lerner and Lowe 205
Leroy, Mervyn 77

Index

Levy, Louis 101, 104
Lewis, Martin J. 190, 191
The Life of Johann Strauss see *The Great Waltz*
The Light on the Wall 28
Lightning Warrior 51
Liveright, Horace 206n
The Living Death 28
Lloyd, Frank 149
Logan, Jacqueline 77, **78**
Le Logis de l'horreur (The House of Horror) 197
Lombard, Carole 78
London After Midnight 7, 35, 51
The Lone Defender 51
Long, Walter 52
López Rubio, José 121
Lord Arthur Saville's Crime (literature) 197
Lorre, Peter 213
The Lost City (serial) 157
Love, Bessie 139
Löw, Rabbi Judah 187–188, 189, 190
Lowe, Edmund 59, **108**, **110**, 111, 136, 204
Lowery, Robert 126
Lubin, Arthur 197
Lugosi, Bela 18, 35, 75, 107, 111, 121, 122, 140, 157, 161, 163, 174, 175, 185
Luguet, André 92
Lukas, Paul 160, 204, 205
Luke, Keye 116, 121
Lyons, Harry Agar 11, 12, 13, 14–15, **16–17**, 18, **22**, 25, 219, 220, 226

MacDonald, J. Farrell 59
MacRae, Henry 162
The Mad Doctor of Market Street 214
The Mad Genius 75, 107
Madame Sul-Te-Wan 184
The Maltese Falcon 53
Mamoulian, Rouben 214
The Man from Hell's River 51
The Man Who Could Work Miracles 150, 204
The Man Who Cried Wolf 168
The Man Who Laughs 62, 70, 140, 164n
The Man Who Reclaimed His Head 173
The Man with the Limp 24
The Man with the Miracle Mind (short story) 108
Mandrake the Magician 111
Mann, Ned 146, 150
Manners, David 138
Le Manoir de Diable 40
A Man's Past 69

Maria Chapdelaine 196
Marlowe, Christopher 40
Marsh, Oliver 35–36
Marx Brothers 202
Mason, John 170
The Master Christian (novel) 42
The Master Mystery (serial) 158
Matieson, Otto (aka Mattiesen) 53
Mattsson, Arne 197
May, Joe 43
Mayer, Edwin Justus 86, 87, 91
Mazzei, Anthony 100
McCormack, Frank 31
McFadden, Elizabeth 173, 177
McFadden, Hamilton 116, 117, 121, 122, 123, 124, 137, 141
McGann, William 213, 214
McGill, Barney 75
McHugh, Frank 215
McKenna, Kenneth 4, 111
McKenzie, Jack 130
Medora, Rustum 200
Meek, Donald 203
Meet Nero Wolfe 124
Mehra, Lal Chand 131
Melford, George 69, 123
Méliès, Georges 3–4, 32, 33, 36, 40
The Menace 184
Mendes, Lothar 204
Menjou, Adolphe 42, 43–46, **47**
Menzies, William Cameron 3–4, 107–108, 111, 137, 141
Mercia the Flower Girl 18
Merivale, Philip 59
Mervyn, Anthony 96
Metropolis 98, 99, 100, 157
Meyrink, Gustav 187, 188
Mi último amor (My Last Love) 124
Michael, Gertrude 168
Middleton, Charles 126, 156
The Midnight Cruise 112
The Midnight Summons 27
A Midsummer Night's Dream 2 1 6
Miljan, John 78–79, **88**, 89
Miller, Walter 158, 161
Million Dollar Legs 215
Milton, John 40
The Miracle 20–21, 219
Les Misérables 198
Mississippi 171
Mr. Lucky (television program) 168
Mr. Wu (1919) 10
Mr. Wu (1927) 10
Mitchell, Thomas 197
A Modern Thelma 41
The Monkey Talks 5, 57–**61**, 62–**65**

Monkey's Paw 133; see also *Buffy, the Vampire Slayer*
The Monkey's Paw (1915) 133
The Monkey's Paw (1923) 133
The Monkey's Paw (1933) 6, 127–**131**, **132**–134, 140
The Monkey's Paw (1948) 133–134
The Monster 35, 36, 75
The Monster (drama) 31
The Monster and the Ape (serial) 54, 157
Montague, Monty 161
The Moonstone 140, 214
Moore, Carlyle 31, 33
Moore, Eva 173
Moore, Matt 148
Moorhead, Natalie **92**
Moran, Lois **110**
Moreland, Mantan 182
Moreno, Antonio 107, 120
Morgan, Frank 137
Morgan, Ralph 136–137, **138**, **139**, 140
Morosco, Walter 54
Morris, Mary 173, **174**, **176**, 177
Morrison, James 31, **32**
Mowbray, Alan 128–129, 130
Moya, Stella 200, 204
Mrs. Wiggs of the Cabbage Patch 175
The Mummy 132–133, 138
The Mummy's Tomb 163
The Murder of Delicia (novel) 41
Murders in the Rue Morgue 62, 132
Murders in the Zoo 170
Murnau, F.W. 43
Murphy, Ralph 213
Murton, Walter H. 13
Muse, Clarence 183–184
My Fair Lady 205
My Little Margie (television program) 123
Le Mystère de la Tour Eiffel 196
Mysterious Dr. Satan (serial) 156
The Mysterious Mr. Wong 18
The Mystery of Bangalore 70
The Mystery of Dr. Fu Manchu 3, 9–26, 219, 226
The Mystery of Edwin Drood 129, 174
The Mystery of Fu Manchu (novel) 9, 13
The Mystery of the Wax Museum 53, 107, 158, 214

The Naulahka 107
Negri, Pola 118
Neill, Roy William 184, 185
Neumann, Kurt 160
Newhart, Bob 210

Nieto, José 125
Night Flight 35
Night Mail 205
Night of Mystery 204
The Ninth Guest 184
Nixon, Marian 71, 72
Nixon, Marni 103
Normand, Mabel 77
North, John Ringling 194
Norton, Barry 201
Norwood, Eille 10, 11
Noxon, Marti 133

O'Donohue, J.T. 59
Of Mice and Men 149
Oland, Warner 2, 11, 14, 16, 67, 72, 77, 116, 117, **119**, 120, 121, 122, 123, 124, 125, 126, 140, 200
The Old Dark House 133, 158, 173, 214
Olsen and Johnson 216
One Increasing Purpose 59
One Million B.C. 149
One Night in the Tropics 171
O'Neill, Eugene 174
Oppenheim, E. Phillips 10
Oriente es Occidente (East Is West) 123
Osbourne, Vivienne 78
Oswald, Richard 43
Our Gang 35
L'Ouragan sur la monatgne (The Hurricane on the Mountain) 196
Oursler, Fulton 108, 109, 112, 136, 137
Oursler, Grace 109
Outbreak 145
The Outcasts of Poker Flat 174
The Outer Limits (television program) 149

Pabst, Georg Wilhelm 201, 204
Pacino, Al 47
Paradise Lost (literature) 40
Paramount on Parade 200
Park, E.L. 85, 117
Parker, Max 214
Pascal, Ernest 197
Patch, Wally 200, 204, 205
Patience 70
Paul, Fred 11, 12, 13, 15, 16, 17, 219, 226
Pemberton-Billing, Noel 96, 97–98, 99, 103
Pépé le Moko 196, 197
Persons in Hiding 214
Peterson, Wolfgang 145
Le Petit monde de Don Camillo (The Little World of Don Camillo) 196

Petrie and Lewis 107
The Phantom Creeps (serial) 157, 158
The Phantom Empire (serial) 156, 157
The Phantom of Crestwood 78
The Phantom of Paris 35
The Phantom of the Opera (1925) 64, 79
Phantom of the Opera (1943) 197
Piccadilly 72
Piel, Edward 139
Pierce, Jack P. 60
Pillow of Death 213
Pinocchio 175
Pitts, ZaSu 175
Plaisetty, René 10
Poe, Edgar Allan 35
Poelzig, Hans 189
Poelzig, Marla 189
Poppy 171
Porter, Edwin S. 40
Portrait of Jennie 185
The Poseidon Adventure 144
Potter, H.C. 173
Powell, William 200, 201, 202, 203
Der Prager Golem (literature) 187
Price of Happiness 46
Pride and Prejudice 214
Prince Cuckoo 70
Prinz Kuckuck see Prince Cuckoo
Public Hero #1 52
Puritan Passions 33
Purple Dawn 139
Purviance, Edna 76

Quartero, Nena 129, 130, **131**, **132**
The Queen of Hearts 24–25, 219
Quigley, Baby Jane 226

Raffles, the Amateur Cracksman 168, 170
Rains, Claude 5, 12, 98, 173, 174
Rains, Fred 12
Ralston, Marcia **212**
Rasputin (1938) 193
Rasputin and the Empress 137
Rathbone, Basil 41, 184, 202
Das Rätsel von Bangalor see The Mystery of Bangalore
Raucourt, Jules 92
The Raven (1915) 35
The Raven (1935) 163, 164n
Reeves, Keanu 47
Reinhardt, Max 70
Rembrandt 205
Renavent, Georges 92
Rennie, James 136
Renoir, Jean 195

The Return of Sherlock Holmes 129
The Return of the Terror 54
Revere, Anne 173, 175, **176**, 177
Reynolds, Ben 167
Rice, Elmer 160
Richards, Grant 204
Riffraff 52
Rigby, L.G. 59
Rilke, Rainer Maria 187
Rin Tin Tin 5, 51, 54, **55**, 56
Ripley, Clement 184
Roach, Hal 226
The Road to Mandalay 35, 69, 140
Robertson, John 200
Robertson, Willard **139**
Robinson, Edward G. 197
Robson, Mark 144
Rocky Jones, Space Ranger (television program) 168
Rogers and Hammerstein 156
The Rogue Song 74
Rohmer, Sax 9–10, 11, 12, 13, 14, 16, 17, 18
A Romance of Two Worlds (novel) 41
Rosener, George 216
Ross, Phil 13
Rossitto, Angelo 140
Rough Waters 51
Roulien, Raúl 120, 121, 125
Royale, Pat 14, **22**, 223, 226
Ruggles, Charlie 130
Ruggles, Wesley 129, 130, 133
Ryan, Ben 136

The Sable Lorcha 67
The Sacred Order 26
St. Clair, Malcolm 201
St. Denis, Ruth 48
St. Joseph, Ellis 197
Saintsbury, H.A. 96, 104n
Salmonova, Lydia 188
Samuelson, G.B. 41, 42, 96
San Francisco 35
Sappho 11
Saps at Sea 161
Satans Sorger (literature) 42
Saville, Victor 101
The Scarab Murder Case 2, 199–**203**, 204, **205**–206
The Scarab Murder Case (novel) 202
Scaramouche 53
The Scarred Face 28
The Scented Envelopes 14, 18–19
Schatten (Warning Shadows) 33
Schoedsack, Ernest B. 129–130, 133
Scram 161
The Sea Beast 69

The Sea Hawk 149
Sebastian, Dorothy 87, 89, 92
The Secret Call 148
The Secret of Lourdes (novel) 91
Secret of the Blue Room 159, 160, 173, 177
Secret of the Chateau 53
The Secret Storm (television program) 147
Secrets of the French Police 170
Selznick, David O. 129, 130
Sen Yan's Devotion 12
Sennett, Mack 77, 226
Serving a Summons 12
Seven Days in May 35
Seven Footprints to Satan 7, 53, 69, 75
Seven Keys to Baldpate 125
Seven Sinners 197
Sh! The Octopus 6, 103, 207–**212**, 213–**215**, 216–217
Shaid, Nick 129, **131**
Shannon, Peggy 145, **148**
Shaw, Montague 126
Shawn, Ted 48
She-Wolf of London 213
Shearer, Norma 140
Sheldon, E. Lloyd 173
Shelley, Mary 189
Shem, Rabbi Eliahu 187
Sherlock Holmes (1922) 84
Sherlock Holmes (1932) 90
Sherlock Holmes (series of Stoll shorts) see *Adventures of Sherlock Holmes*
Sherlock Holmes (series of Universal features) 184
Sherlock Holmes and the Voice of Terror 184
Sherriff, R.C. 97
Shirley, Dorinea 15
The Shrine of the Seven Lamps 26, 219
The Si-Fan Mysteries (novel) 13
The Sign of Four 11
The Silver Buddha 25
Simpson, Ivan 128, 129, **132**
The Simpsons (television program) 6, 133
Singing in the Rain 118
Singleton, Penny 216
Sjöström, Victor 197
Smashing Through 101
Smith, C. Aubrey 129, 130, **132**, 170
Smith, George Albert 40
Smith, Pete 149
Smith, Thorne 84
Sojin, Kamiyama **68**, **69**, 71, 72, 88, 90, 91, **92**, 116
Sombras de gloria 124

Sombras habañeras 124
Somerville, Robert 9
The Sorrows of Satan (novel) 40–41
The Sorrows of Satan (1917) 41–42, 49
The Sorrows of Satan (1926) 6, 38–**44**, 45–46, 47–49
S.O.S. Tidal Wave 150
Le Spectre Vert 91–92
Spence, Ralph 103, 213
The Spider (drama) 108, 136
The Spider (1931) 4, 105–**108**, 109, **110**–112, 137
The Spider (1945) 112
Spy Smasher (serial) 124
S.S. Van Dine Mystery Series 203
Standing, Sir Guy 168
Stanwyck, Barbara 197
Star Wars 145
Stark Mad 5, 35, 73–**76**, 77–**78**, 79
Steamboat Bill, Jr. 90
Sternberg, Josef von 197
Stevens, Onslow 158, 159–**160**
Stevenson, Housley 159
Stewart, Jimmy 78
Stoll, Sir Oswald 10, 12, 13
Stoll Picture Productions 9, 10, 11, 12–13, 16, 18, 41, 219, 226
Strickfaden, Kenneth 162
Strong, Percy 101
Stuart, Gloria 160
Der Student von Prag 188
Suedo, Julie 14
Sugarfoot (television program) 123
Sullavan, Margaret 149
The Sultan's Power 71
Sunset Boulevard 78
Supernatural 78
Surrender 69
Sutherland, A. Edward "Eddie" 170–171
Svengali (1931) 75, 107
Swanson, Gloria 55

Das Tagebuch einer Verlorenen (*Diary of a Lost Girl*) 201
A Tale of Two Cities 35
Tales of Manhattan 196, 197
Talmadge, Norma 31
Tapley, Colin 175
Tarzan, the Ape Man 185
Taylor, Kent 175–177
Taylor, William Desmond 171
The Teeth of the Tiger 108
Tell, Olive 168
The Temptations of Satan 40
Tense Moments with Great Authors 11
Termite Terrace 210

The Terror 75, 77, 79
The Test 55
Thalberg, Irving 85–86
Their Mad Moment 124
Thelma (novel) 41
The Thief of Bagdad 4, 64, 69, 71
The Thin Man (MGM series) 202
Things to Come 150
Thomas, Augustus 168
Thomas, Jameson **102**, 103
Thrilling Stories from the Strand Magazine 12, 16
Thurston, Howard 109
The Toddlma 31
Toler, Sidney 54, 116, 126
Tollaire, August 59, 60
Tomorrow at Seven 215
Topper 149
Torena, Juan 124
Torrence, Ernest 90, **92**
Tourneur, Jacques 185
Tourneur, Maurice 51
Tover, Leo 130
The Towering Inferno 144
Trader Horn 185
The Trap 54
Treehouse of Horror 6, 133
Tres eran tres **126**
Trick for Trick 3, 4, 6, 135–**138**, 139–142
Trick for Trick (drama) 136
Trilby (British, 1922) 11
Trilby (1923) 33
The Truth About Women 129
Tumbleweeds 184
Turner, Florence 71, 72
Turner, Ted 6
Turner Classic Movies 6, 216
Tuttle, Frank 33, 201
2001: A Space Odyssey 96
Tynan, Brandon **215**, 216

Under the Tide 17, 29
Undersea Kingdom (serial) 157
The Underworld (drama) 31
Unger, Gladys 59
The Unholy Night 6, 79, 80–**88**, 89–**92**, 93
The Unholy Three (1930) 79
The Unknown 140
The Unknown Purple 4, 5, 30–**32**, 33–**34**, 35–**37**, 79
The Unknown Purple (drama) 31
The Unknown Terror 124

Vadnai, Laslo 197
The Valley of Fear 96
Vance, Vivian 169
Van Dine, S.S. 2, 200–201, 202–203, 204, 206n

The Vanishing Men (proposed screenplay) 31
The Vanishing Shadow (serial) 5, 151–**160**, 161–**163**, 164
Van Sloan, Edward 31, 137–138, **139**, 145
Veidt, Conrad 3, 62, 68, 69, 70, 72, 140, 193
Veillers, Anthony 167
Vélez, Lupe 120
Venable, Evelyn 175
Vernal, Marcel 4
Vestida de novia (*Bridal Dress*) 123
Vibart, Henri 103
Vidor, Charles 173
Vidor, King 122
Vilches, Ernesto 122
The Villain Still Pursued Her 215
Villarías, Carlos 201
Voyage to the Bottom of the Sea (television program) 149

Das Wachsfigurenkabinett 2, 4, 68, 70
Wagner, Sidney 122
The Walking Dead 124
Wallace, Edgar 10
Walsh, Raoul 5, 64, 108
Walthall, Henry B. 33–34, 79, 137
Ward, Arthur Henry *see* Rohmer, Sax
Warde, Shirley 136
Warner, H.B. 77–**78**
Warner, Jack 51, 59, 204
Wax-Works see *Das Wachsfigurenkabinett*

Way Down South 183
We Faw Down 52
Weaver, Marjorie 126
Wegener, Paul 186, 188–189, 190, 192, 195, 198
Weinberg, Herman G. 190, 191
Wells, H.G. 10
The WereWolf of London 75
Werfel, Franz 187
West, Roland 4, 31, 32, 33, 35–36, 77
The West Case 14, 19
Westmore, Perc 214
Whale, James 5, 85, 96–97, 173, 189, 214
Whatever Happened to Aunt Alice? 124
Wheeler and Woolsey 215
When Worlds Collide 145
While London Sleeps 5, 50–56
While Paris Sleeps 33, 51
While the City Sleeps 51
The Whispering Shadow (serial) 35
Whispering Smith 214
White, Marjorie 125
White Zombie 185
Wilbur, Crane 31
Wilcox, Hebert 12
Wilde, Oscar 197
Wiles, Gordon 4
Willard, John 69
William, Warren 204
Wilson, Elinor 177
Wilson, Frank 12, 13, 219
Wilson, Lois 147
Wilson, Woodrow 187
Winters, Roland 116, 124

Winton, Jane 59, 60
The Witching Hour (drama) 168
The Witching Hour (1916) 168, 170, 171
The Witching Hour (1921) 168, 170–171
The Witching Hour (1934) 5, 165–**169**, 170–171, 185
The Wizard 52
A Woman's Honor 31
Wong, Anna May 72
Wong Howe, James 4, 107, 111
Wood, Ed 210
Wormwood (novel) 41
Worsley, Wallace 149
Wray, Fay 179, 184, 185
Wright, H. Humberston 13, 15, **22**, **102**, 103, 219, 226
Wright, Willard Huntington (see: S.S. Van Dine)
Wyler, William 160

The Yellow Claw 10
The Yellow Claw (novel) 9
Young, Loretta 138
Young, Noah 52
Young, Roland 84, 87, 89, 91, **92**, 149

Ziegfeld, Florenz 77
The Zone of Death 28
Zorro (aka *The Adventures of Zorro*; television program) 123
Zorro's Fighting Legion (serial) 157
Zukor, Adolph 42, 204

www.ingramcontent.com/pod-product-compliance
Ingram Content Group UK Ltd.
Pitfield, Milton Keynes, MK11 3LW, UK
UKHW050534150426
5217IPUK00026B/1930